D1436182

THE MIND OF ST PAUL

THE MIND OF
ST PAUL

BY
WILLIAM BARCLAY

COLLINS
ST JAMES'S PLACE, LONDON
1958

© WILLIAM BARCLAY, 1958
PRINTED IN GREAT BRITAIN BY
COLLINS CLEAR-TYPE PRESS : LONDON AND GLASGOW

CONTENTS

PREFACE

These chapters originally appeared as a series of weekly articles in the pages of *The British Weekly*. I have to thank the previous editor of that paper, Rev. Shaun Herron, for giving me the opportunity to write them in the first place, and the present editor, Rev. Denis Duncan, for now giving me permission to republish them in book form. To the original series I have added two chapters, one on Sin and the other on the Church in the thinking of Paul.

These chapters do not in any way claim to be an exhaustive and complete Theology of Paul. I have simply gone direct to the Pauline letters to find out what Paul said and thought on certain great subjects. Their aim will be fulfilled, if they send people back to the reading of Paul's letters themselves.

WILLIAM BARCLAY

Trinity College,
Glasgow,
February, 1958

I

THE MAN OF TWO WORLDS—
THE WORLD OF THE JEW

CHRISTIANITY began with one tremendous problem. Clearly the message of Christianity was meant for all men. It was because God so loved the world that He sent His Son (*John* 3: 16). It was Jesus' confidence that, if He was lifted up, He would draw all men unto Him (*John* 12: 32). The Church regarded it as her commission that she must go and teach all nations (*Matthew* 28: 19). It was clear that Christianity had a message for all the world, and that unless that message was delivered, the Church would fail in her God-given duty.

But the fact remained that Christianity was cradled in Judaism; and, humanly speaking, no message which was meant for all the world could ever have had a more unfortunate cradle. The Jews were involved in a double hatred—the world hated them and they hated the world.

No nation was ever more bitterly hated than the Jews. Cicero called the Jewish religion "a barbarous superstition" (Cicero, *Pro Flacco* 28); Tacitus called the Jewish nation "the vilest of people" (Tacitus, *Histories* 5: 8).

Anti-semitism is no new thing; it flourished in the ancient world.

No nation ever hated other nations as the Jews did. It is true that some few Jews held that the Jews were meant to be a light to the Gentiles to lead them to God; but for the most part the Jews were convinced that the fact that they were the chosen nation involved what to them was the equal and the opposite fact that all other nations were rejected nations. At their worst they could say: " The Gentiles were created by God to be fuel for the fires of hell." " The best of the serpents crush; the best of the Gentiles kill." It was even forbidden to give a Gentile mother help in her hour of direst need, because to do so would only have been to bring another Gentile into the world.

The Gentiles were acutely conscious of this hatred. Tacitus believed that if a Gentile became a proselyte to Judaism, the first thing he was taught was to despise the gods, to repudiate his nationality, and to hold worthless his parents, children and friends (Tacitus, *Histories* 5: 5). Juvenal declared that if a Jew was asked the way to anywhere by anyone, he would refuse all information except to a fellow-Jew, and if anyone was looking for a well, he would refuse to direct him to it, unless he was circumcised (Juvenal, *Satires* 14: 103, 104).

In Alexandria the story was current that the Jews had taken a deliberate oath never to show kindness to any Gentile, and it was even said that the Jewish religious ceremonies began with the yearly sacrifice of a Gentile

(Josephus, *Against Apion*, 2, 8, 10). The friends of Antiochus Sidetes urged him to exterminate the Jews because " alone of all nations they refuse all fellowship and intercourse with other nations and suppose all men to be enemies " (Diodorus Siculus 31: 1, 1). Josephus quotes the charge of a certain Lysimachus that Moses charged the Jews to show goodwill to no man, never to give good but always evil counsel to others, and to overturn and destroy whatever altars and temples of the gods they might encounter. Apion himself affirmed that the Jews swore by the God of heaven and earth and sea never to show good will to a man of another nation, and especially never to do so to the Greeks (Josephus, *Against Apion*, 1: 34; 2: 10).

The problem which faced Christianity was acute. It had a message for all men; and yet in the eyes of the world it was a Jewish thing, and the Jews were the most bitterly hated and hating people in the ancient world.

Clearly one thing was necessary—a man who could somehow form a bridge between the Jewish and the Greek worlds. Obviously such a man would be hard to find; such a man would be unique; and yet, in the providence of God, the hour produced the man—and that man was Paul.

In his life of Scott, Lockhart quotes a saying of an old countryman about the way in which the lines of life had fallen for Paul, and, in his *Life and Letters of Paul*, David Smith took the saying as the very text for the life of Paul: " He was makin' himsell a' the time; but he didna ken maybe what he was about till years had passed." Life had been moulding Paul to be the bridge between the Jews and the Greeks, to be the unique channel through whom Christianity went out to all the world.

First of all, let us look at Paul the Jew. To the end of his life Paul was proudly, stubbornly, unalterably a Jew. When he wrote to the Corinthians in answer to the charges of his detractors, he took his stand on his Jewish lineage: " Are they Hebrews? So am I. Are they Israelites? So am I. Are they the seed of Abraham? So am I " (2 *Corinthians* 11: 22). The three words he uses all have their own meaning. A *Hebrew* was a Jew who could still speak Hebrew in contradistinction to the Jews of the Dispersion who had forgotten their native language for the Greek of their adopted countries. An *Israelite* was specifically a member of the covenant nation. To be *of the seed of Abraham* was to have absolute racial purity. Paul's claim was that there was nowhere in the world a purer Jew than he.

He made the same claim when he wrote to his friends at Philippi: "If any other man thinketh that he hath whereof he might trust in the flesh, I more; circumcised the eighth day; of the stock of Israel; of the tribe of Benjamin, an Hebrew of the Hebrews; as touching the law, a Pharisee; concerning zeal, persecuting the Church; touching the righteousness which is in the law, blameless " (*Philippians* 3: 4-6). When he wrote to the Church at Rome, he made the proud statement: "I also am an Israelite, of the seed of Abraham, of the tribe of Benjamin " (*Romans* 11: 1).

Again and again Paul's Jewishness comes out. When he was writing to Gentiles, the ancient Israelites are our fathers (1 *Corinthians* 10: 1). Even writing to the Church at Rome, Abraham is our father (*Romans* 4: 1), as is also Isaac (*Romans* 9: 10). To Paul, the Church is the Israel of God (*Galatians* 6: 16). No passage in all Paul's letters throbs with a greater intensity of feeling than the passage in *Romans* where Paul cries out that he himself would gladly consent to be accursed if he might only bring to belief his kinsmen after the flesh (*Romans* 9: 3). Paul's speeches in *Acts* paint the same picture as his letters do. It is Paul's claim to the military commander in Jerusalem: " I am a man which am a Jew of Tarsus, a city in Cilicia " (*Acts* 21: 39). The next day, when he is under examination, it is his opening statement: " I am verily a man which am a Jew, born in Tarsus, a city in Cilicia, yet brought up in this city at the feet of Gamaliel, and taught according to the perfect manner of the law of the fathers " (*Acts* 22: 3). When he is on trial, it is his claim: " I have lived in all good conscience before God until this day . . . I am a Pharisee, the son of a Pharisee " (*Acts* 23: 1, 6).

Paul did not doubt that God had set so much of Himself in His world that all men had had the chance to know Him and were inexcusable if they remained in ignorance (*Romans* 1: 19, 20); but even when he has proved that the Law cannot save men, and even when he has insisted that the Gentiles have a law within their hearts, he can still cry out: " What advantage then hath the Jew? or what profit is there of circumcision? " And then he can answer: " Much every way; chiefly, because unto them were committed the oracles of God " (*Romans* 3: 1, 2).

Again and again there breathes through the thought of Paul his pride and joy in the privilege of being a Jew, one of the chosen people of God. Paul was the apostle to the Gentiles, but it would be totally to misunderstand him to think that he was ever hostile to the Jews. As Deissmann finely points out: " Paul shows nothing of the renegade's hatred." It often happens that when a man becomes a renegade, a convert, a pervert—call him what you will—he becomes bitter against that which he has left. It is true that Paul had broken once and for all with Judaism, but at heart he was still a Jew who would gladly have laid down his life to bring fellow-Jews into the same faith as he himself had so gloriously discovered. Deissmann points out how this Jewishness of Paul comes out again and again in the everyday words and actions of Paul's life.

When Paul is dating things, it is in terms of Jewish dates and festivals that he always thinks. He writes to the Corinthians that he will stay at Ephesus until Pentecost (1 *Corinthians* 16: 8). In the narrative of the voyage to Rome, it is said that " sailing was now dangerous because the fast was now already past " (*Acts* 27: 9). The fast in question was the Day of Atonement (*Leviticus* 23: 27-29) which fell in September, and in the ancient world sailing was considered unsafe between the months of September and March. The points of time from which Paul took all his dates were the great Jewish festivals and feasts.

Paul did not himself abandon the ancestral laws and

customs of his own people; in many things he was still a devout Jew. Timothy's father was a Greek but his mother was a Jewess, and so we find Paul taking and circumcising Timothy in order that Timothy might be able to work amongst the Jews (*Acts* 16: 3). The Nazirite vow was a vow which a devout Jew would take when he wished to express special gratitude to God. We find Paul himself taking that vow; we find that he had " shorn his head at Cenchrea; for he had a vow " (*Acts* 18: 18). When Paul arrived in Jerusalem, we find him undertaking to be responsible for the expenses of certain men who were engaged in carrying out the Nazarite vow in order that he might make it clear that he was no destructive renegade from the Jewish faith (*Acts* 21: 17-26).

Paul never forgot his Jewish origin; he never turned his back on the faith of his fathers; to Paul it was natural to say: " Unto the Jews I became as a Jew " (1 *Corinthians* 9: 20).

But it was not only in his words and actions that Paul's essential Jewishness came out; it was equally clear in his thoughts. Paul was a man of one book, and that book was the Old Testament. But there was this difference—when Paul quoted the Old Testament normally his quotations were not taken directly from the Hebrew; they were taken from the Septuagint, the Greek translation of the Old Testament, which Jews all over the world used.

Paul was brought up in a Greek city; all the wealth of Greek literature lay open to him; yet at the most he only quotes a heathen writer twice. In *Acts* 17: 28 he

quotes the phrase: "We are also his offspring," from
Aratus, a Greek poet, and in *Titus* 1: 12, the condemnation
of the Cretans, "The Cretans are always liars, evil beasts,
slow bellies," is from a poet called Epimenides. Although
all the wealth of Greek literature lay open before him,
Paul's book was the Old Testament. Possibly it was not
all he knew, but certainly it was all he needed.

When Paul uses the Old Testament, he uses it as a Jew
would use it. Again and again he introduces an Old Testament quotation with the phrase: "It is written." That
was the normal Greek legal phrase for a law or an agreement or a condition that was unalterable and inviolable.
Paul's view of scripture as the voice of God was a Jewish
view.

When Paul uses the Old Testament, he often allegorises
it as a Jewish Rabbi would. For instance he takes the law
of *Deuteronomy* 25: 4 which says that the ox must not
be muzzled when it is treading out the corn as an allegory
of the fact that the Christian apostle and preacher must
receive the material support of the Christian Church (1
Corinthians 9: 9). In *Galatians* 4: 22-31 he works out a
long allegory of the old and new covenants based on the
story of Sarah and Hagar. In 1 *Corinthians* 10: 4, he uses
the rock from which the Israelites received water in the
desert as an allegory of Jesus Christ. When Paul used scripture in that kind of way, he was using it an a way that
any Jew would recognise, appreciate and understand.

Not only did Paul know the Old Testament as a devout
Jew might know it; he was also a trained Rabbi and he

knew the Old Testament as a Rabbi knew it. He knew not only the Old Testament; he also knew the special traditions of the Rabbis. He says in *Galatians* 3: 19 that the Law was given through angels (cp. *Acts* 7: 53; *Hebrews* 2: 2). In the Old Testament itself there is no mention of angels in regard to the Law; in the old story, the Law was given direct by God to Moses. But as the years went on the sheer distance between God and man began to be stressed. Men began to be fascinated by what is called the transcendence of God. They began to hold that God could never have had first-hand dealings with any man, not even with Moses, and that He must necessarily have used angels as His intermediaries; and so the Rabbinic tradition arose that the Law came to men from God by the mediation of angels. Paul knew that tradition and used it for his purposes.

Galatians 3: 17 says that the Law was given 430 years after Abraham. That again is a Rabbinic addition to the Old Testament story. In 1 *Corinthians* 10: 4 Paul speaks of " the rock that followed them." According to the traditions of the Rabbis the rock from which the children of Israel received water in their wilderness journeyings actually followed them throughout their journeyings ever after. That is a miracle story which is not part of the Old Testament narrative. It was one of the Rabbinic traditions and Paul knew it and used it.

If ever there was a Jew who was steeped in Judaism, that Jew was Paul. Let us before we leave the Jewish side of Paul look again at the claims he had to be the Jew *par excellence*. We have already cited his own list of

Jewish qualifications as he gives it in *Philippians* 3: 4-6. He was circumcised on the eighth day; that is to say, he bore in the body the badge and the mark that he was one of the chosen people, marked out by God as His own. He was of the race of Israel; that is to say, he was a member of the nation who stood in a covenant relationship with God, a relationship in which no other people stood. He was of the tribe of Benjamin. This is a claim which Paul reiterates in *Romans* 11: 1. What is the point of this claim? The tribe of Benjamin had a unique place in the history of Israel. It was from Benjamin that the first king of Israel had come, for Saul was a Benjamite (1 *Samuel* 9: 1). When the tragic split of the kingdom came, Benjamin and Judah were the only two tribes who had stood true to Rehoboam (1 *Kings* 12: 21). Benjamin was the only one of the patriarchs who had actually been born in the land of promise. When Israel went into battle, it was the tribe of Benjamin which held the post of honour. The battle-cry of Israel was: "After thee, O Benjamin" (*Judges* 5: 12; *Hosea* 5: 8).

In lineage Paul was not only an Israelite; he was of the aristocracy of Israel. He was a Hebrew of the Hebrews; that is to say, Paul was not one of these Jews of the Dispersion who, in a foreign land, had forgotten their own tongue; he was a Jew who still remembered and knew the language of his fathers.

He was a Pharisee; that is to say, he was not only a devout Jew; he was more—he was one of "The Separated Ones" who had foresworn all normal activities in order

18

to dedicate life to the keeping of the Law, and he had kept it with such meticulous care that in the keeping of it he was blameless.

No one could say that Paul had abandoned Judaism because he did not understand it, or did not fully realise what it was. No one could say that Paul had been driven from Judaism because he had only experienced a truncated or imperfect version of it. No one could say that Paul was opposed to the principles of Jewish religion because he had misunderstood them or knew them only from the outside. Paul knew Judaism at its best and at its highest; he knew it from the inside; he had gone through all the experiences, both of height and of depth, that it could bring to any man. Paul was the man ideally fitted to understand Christianity with all its Jewish background, and to bring Christianity to the Jews. There was one half of the world to which Paul was, by his whole training and upbringing, the ideal missionary.

But there was another half of the world, the great Greek world which lay far beyond the confines of Palestine and the boundaries of Judaism. To the Jews it was easy for Paul to become as a Jew, for he was a Jew. He must now go on to see how he could also become a Greek to the Greeks. We must now go on to see the other background of this Paul who was so uniquely a man of two worlds.

II

THE MAN OF TWO WORLDS—
THE WORLD OF THE GREEK

WE HAVE seen the essential Jewishness of Paul; and we must now turn to the other side of the picture. If there was one thing of which Paul was certain it was that his unique privilege was to be the apostle to the Gentiles.

After Paul's conversion on the Damascus Road, word from God came to the astonished Ananias that Paul was coming to seek his help. Not unnaturally Ananias tended to regard the one-time arch-persecutor of the Church with a certain suspicion; but the voice of God came to him: " He is a chosen vessel unto me, to bear my name before the Gentiles " (*Acts* 9: 15). From that time forward Paul never lost an opportunity of insisting upon his apostleship to the Gentiles. In his first recorded sermon, at Antioch in Pisidia, when the Jews rejected the offer of the gospel, it is the claim of Paul and Barnabas: " The Lord hath commanded us, saying, I have set thee to be a light of the Gentiles " (*Acts* 13: 47). When the Jews of the Synagogue of Corinth showed themselves violently opposed to the Christian message, Paul's answer was:

" From henceforth I will go unto the Gentiles " (*Acts* 18: 6). In his defence before the infuriated mob at Jerusalem, Paul recalls how God's voice had come to him after the stoning of Stephen: " Depart: for I will send thee far hence unto the Gentiles " (*Acts* 22: 21). In his speech before King Agrippa, it is Paul's claim that God had definitely commissioned him to preach to the Gentiles (*Acts* 26: 17, 23).

Again and again in his letters Paul discloses this same special consciousness of being uniquely the messenger of Christ to the Gentile world. He longs to come to Rome that he may have some fruit there, as he has had among other Gentiles (*Romans* 1: 13). In the same letter he takes to himself the title of the apostle to the Gentiles, and calls himself the minister of Jesus Christ to the Gentiles (*Romans* 11: 13; 15: 16). In *Galatians* he says that the very purpose for which Christ was revealed in him was that he might preach Him among the Gentiles (*Galatians* 1: 16). And the same letter gives us a picture of a kind of agreement by which Peter went to the Jews and Paul to the Gentiles (*Galatians* 2: 1-10). In the letter to the Ephesians Paul writes of himself as the prisoner of Christ for you Gentiles, and speaks of the grace that was given to him to preach to the Gentiles (*Ephesians* 3: 1, 8). In the *Pastoral Epistles* Paul is described as a teacher of the Gentiles (1 *Timothy* 2: 7; 2 *Timothy* 1: 11).

If ever a man was conscious of a destiny, that man was Paul, and the destiny was to bring the message of the good news to the Gentiles world.

What special qualifications had Paul for this task? How did it come about that this member of the Jewish racial and intellectual aristocracy could be specially fitted to take Christianity to the Gentiles?

First of all, Paul was a citizen of Tarsus, and in that citizenship he took no small pride. When the military commander in Jerusalem was about to treat him like a common revolutionary, Paul stopped him with the imperious statement: " I am a man which am a Jew of Tarsus, . . . a citizen of no mean city " (*Acts* 21: 39). When he addressed the hostile mob, he began by giving his credentials: " I am verily a man which am a Jew, born in Tarsus, a city in Cilicia." (*Acts* 22: 3.)

Tarsus was indeed no mean city. It was a city as far back as 860 B.C., for Shalmaneser of Assyria listed it among his conquests. Rather more than five hundred years later Tarsus saw Alexander the Great bathe in the icy waters of the River Cydnus, and catch a chill which nearly caused his death. Three hundred years later still, Tarsus was the dazzled spectator of one of Cleopatra's most famous exploits. Mark Antony was in Tarsus preparing for war against the distant Parthians on the far eastern borders of the Roman Republic. He suspected Cleopatra of plotting against him with his opponent Cassius, and he summoned her to appear before him. She appeared—in her own good time, and in her own flamboyant way.

Plutarch tells the story: " She received several letters both from Antony and his friends to summon her, but she took no account of these orders; but at last, as if in mockery of them, she came sailing up the River Cydnus in a barge with gilded stern and outstretched sails of purple, while oars of silver beat time to the music of flutes and fifes and harps. She herself lay all along under a canopy of gold, dressed as Venus in a picture, and beautiful young boys, like painted Cupids, stood on each side to fan her. Her maids were dressed like sea nymphs and graces, some steering at the rudder, some working at the ropes. The perfumes diffused themselves from the vessel to the shore which was covered with multitudes . . . The market-place was quite emptied and Antony at last was left alone sitting upon the tribunal, while word went through all the multitude that Venus was come to feast with Bacchus for the common good of Asia."

Shalmaneser, Alexander the Great, Antony and Cleopatra —truly Tarsus had seen the drama of history.

Tarsus was in the province of Cilicia, and it was one of the great centres at which the trade of the Mediterranean and of the hinterland of Asia Minor converged. It was specially famous for the manufacture of goats' hair felt, out of which tent-cloth, hangings, blankets, clothing, belts and saddles were made—and one of its greatest sons was a tent-maker.

Its greatness in trade was its own notable achievement. It lay on the River Cydnus. Two hundred feet wide, the river swept through the centre of the city. It lay ten miles inland from the mouth of the river. Half-way between Tarsus and the sea the river broadened out into a lake called Lake Rhegma. It was to that lake that Cleopatra

came. The engineering skill and the commercial ambition
of the Tarsians had lined three sides of that lake with
harbours, docks and arsenals, and the ships of the Mediterranean sailed fully laden into, and out of, that harbour.
In days when piracy was rampant the possession of a
harbour in such a sheltered and easily defended position
was a most priceless advantage.

But the Tarsians had performed an even greater feat
than that. Thirty miles inland from Tarsus the huge Taurus
range reared its bulk and its height; and there were few
or no roads across it. But opening down into Tarsus there
were the world famous Cilician Gates. There was a part
of the range where a little stream came through a gorge
which was little more than a cleft in the rock. Sometime
in the dim and distant past, so long ago that the date was
not even known, men from Tarsus had chiselled out of the
rock of that narrow gorge, a carriage road beside the little
river, and by that road the rich trade of the hinterland of Cappadocia and Galatia descended into Tarsus.
Truly the Tarsians had succeeded in making their city
great.

But not only was Tarsus a great commercial city; it
was also a university town. Perhaps the university of
Tarsus was not so academically distinguished as the
universities of some of the older cities. But in one thing
Tarsus surpassed them all, even Athens and Alexandria.
It was a well-known fact that the enthusiasm for learning
was greater in Tarsus than in any other city in the world.
It never needed to import scholars; it had more than

enough of her own. In fact, one of the most famous exports of Tarsus was scholars. Its young men went out to fill the chairs in other universities.

In particular, Tarsus was famous for philosophers, and especially for philosophers of the Stoic school. Strabo names five famous Stoics who were born in Tarsus— Antipater, Archedemus, Nestor, Athenodorus Cordylion (who was the friend and adviser of Augustus himself) and Athenodorus, the son of Sandon. In the nearby town of Soli, Chrysippus and Aratus, two of the greatest of all the Stoics, were born.

So much did Tarsus love and respect and admire learning that there was a time when Athenodorus and his fellow-philosophers not only taught their students but also governed the city. And in regard to government Tarsus was fortunate; either by luck or by good guidance it had always chosen the right side in the civil wars, and it had been rewarded with the status of a *civitas libera,* a free city, self-governing and independent.

Such was the place where Paul was born and brought up. It was a city so cosmopolitan that none could walk the streets without coming into contact with the ends of the earth. It was a city with such a history that none could live in it without some sense of greatness. It was a city with such a desire for knowledge, such a respect for scholarship, and such an intellectual ferment of thought that no thinking young man could entirely escape the contagion of the thronging ideas which crowded the air.

If a man was destined to be a missionary to the world

at large, there was no better place in all the east for him to grow to manhood than in Tarsus. But Paul had an even more valuable qualification to be the apostle of the Gentiles, for he was a Roman citizen.

When Paul and Silas were thrown into gaol in Philippi and scourged without trial, the declaration, on the next day, of Paul's Roman citizenship brought from the local magistrates a terrified and abject apology (*Acts* 16: 37-39). In Jerusalem the Roman military commander was compelled to arrest Paul to prevent a riot. They were about to bind Paul and to examine him under the lash, but Paul's declaration of his Roman citizenship halted the whole proceedings on the instant (*Acts* 22: 24-30). When Paul was a prisoner at Cæsarea and, when he felt that any just trial was an impossibility, he made his appeal to Cæsar, and, because he was a Roman citizen, none could deny his request (*Acts* 25: 9-12).

Roman citizenship was no empty honour, and no formal dignity. The Roman law was clear; a Roman citizen could not be bound and could not be scourged; a Roman citizen could not be crucified. "It is a breach of the law for a Roman citizen to be bound; it is a crime for him to be beaten," said Cicero. If a man claimed Roman citizenship, no matter where he was, to the ends of the earth, the might and majesty of Rome was behind him. "How often," said Cicero, "has this exclamation, 'I am a Roman citizen,' brought aid and safety even among barbarians in the remotest parts of the earth!"

Paul was proud of his Roman citizenship. In Philippi

he insisted on a public apology from the local magistrates before he would even consent to emerge from the prison into which they had wrongly thrown him (*Acts* 16: 37). When the military commander at Jerusalem commented that he himself had bought the citizenship at a great price, Paul proudly answered: " I was free born " (*Acts* 22: 28).

Not only was Paul proud of his citizenship; he was proud of the Roman Empire. When he wrote to the Christians at Rome, he bade them be subject to the powers that be, for these powers had been given their authority by God (*Romans* 13: 1-5). In the *Pastoral Epistles* the duty of praying for the Emperor is laid upon the Church (1 *Timothy* 2: 1-3). 2 *Thessalonians* 2: 6, 7 is a rather puzzling passage. In that passage the thought is that in this world there is a power which is restraining the swelling insolence of evil; and to Paul that power was Rome.

In the ancient world the Roman citizenship was an accolade of honour and a safe-conduct to the ends of the earth. Paul possessed that citizenship, and he was proud of it. It will be interesting to surmise how Paul's family received that citizenship.

There were two kinds of Roman citizenship. There was that which conferred *commercium*, trading rights, and that which conferred not only *commercium*, but also *connubium*, marriage rights. And it is clear that it was full citizenship which Paul enjoyed.

We may begin with certain things which we may regard as facts. Paul was born in Tarsus (*Acts* 22: 3); and Paul's father, like Paul himself, was a Pharisee (*Acts*

23: 6). It is in the last degree unlikely that a man who was a Pharisee would willingly live out of the land of Palestine. We cannot think that at some time Paul's father had emigrated to Cilicia in search of fame and fortune; a Pharisee would never willingly have lived away from the sacred soil of the Holy land; it must have been some stern necessity which brought him there.

Further, Roman citizenship could be acquired in several ways. It could be purchased, although not everyone would be accepted as a suitable purchaser. It was by purchase that the Roman military commander in Jerusalem had acquired his citizenship (*Acts* 22: 28). It is quite certain that no Pharisee would ever go out of his way to purchase Roman citizenship. It was not that the Pharisees were hostile to Rome; they were in fact willing to live under any government which would allow them to live in accordance with the Law; but a Pharisee would have been totally uninterested in becoming a Roman citizen.

The citizenship could be granted to chosen people for distinguished services to the Roman state, especially in time of crisis and of need. It was given to Roman soldiers when they had completed twenty-four years' service. It is hardly likely that the citizenship came to Paul's family in either of these ways.

Sometimes, in reward for some act of fidelity or as a special mark of favour, the citizenship was given to the whole population of certain towns or areas—and it may well be that it was in this way that Paul's family first received the citizenship. Let us see if we can trace any way in which that might have happened.

Jerome passes on to us a tradition regarding Paul's family. He gives it in two forms. " Paul was of the tribe of Benjamin, and from a town in Judæa called Gischala. When this town was captured by the Romans, he migrated with his parents to Tarsus in Cilicia, and by them he was sent to Jerusalem for the study of the law, and was there trained by Gamaliel, a most learned man."

The second form is: " We have received a story like this. They say that the parents of the apostle Paul came from the district of Gischala in Judæa, and that, when the whole province was laid waste by the hand of Rome, and when the Jews were dispersed throughout the world, they were transferred to Tarsus, a city in Cilicia, and that Paul, who was at that time a mere lad, accompanied his parents."

Wherever Jerome got that story, it cannot be true. We have Paul's own word for it that he was born in Tarsus and not in Gischala. Gischala was in Galilee; it was the last city to capitulate in the last terrible days when the Romans finally broke the Jews, but that was in A.D. 67. True, there was savage fighting near Gischala in 4 B.C. in the troubles that followed the death of Herod. But, no matter how we try to explain it, Jerome's story does not seem to fit the facts.

David Smith felt that Paul's citizenship might be explained in this way. In 63 B.C. Pompey invaded and captured Jerusalem. At that time he carried thousands of

Jews back to Rome as slaves. In due time these Jews
settled down in Rome and prospered. They ultimately
came to possess a part of the city as their own; and when in
4 B.C. a Jewish embassy came to Rome, it was greeted by
no fewer than 8,000 Jews who were resident in Rome.
Many of these Jews became citizens. Julius Cæsar, for
instance, had been specially kind to the Jews, and as
Suetonius the historian tells us, when Julius Cæsar died,
"a throng of foreigners went about lamenting each after
the fashion of his country, above all the Jews." It might
be that Paul's father or grandfather had been among those
carried off to Rome, had acquired the citizenship, and later
come to Tarsus.

There is still another suggestion. About the year
175 B.C. great changes happened in Tarsus. At that time
Antiochus Epiphanes refounded and reorganised the city.
In the reorganisation citizenship was thrown open to the
Jews, for they were useful and often wealthy citizens, and
many Jewish families either migrated or were transported
to Tarsus at that time. It is by far the most likely thing
that Paul's ancestors came to Tarsus then. That move would
make them citizens of Tarsus, but not yet of Rome.
Thereafter, there were times when Tarsus had the closest
possible connection with Rome. In 64 B.C. it was the
headquarters of Pompey, the great Roman general who
purged the seas of pirates and the roads of brigands and
who brought peace to Asia Minor. No doubt many
received the citizenship under him. In 47 B.C. Julius Cæsar
came to Tarsus on his eastern campaigns, and so enthusiastic

were the Tarsians in his support that they changed the name of their city to Juliopolis, although the new name did not last. Certainly many Tarsians would have received the citizenship then. In 42 B.C. Mark Antony had his head-quarters in Tarsus; and again the citizenship would have been conferred on many, although Mark Antony, who needed money, would be more likely to sell the citizenship than to gift it. Finally in 31 B.C. Augustus conferred many benefits on Tarsus in gratitude for her fidelity to his cause. It may well have been at one of these times that Paul's family first received the citizenship.

Here indeed we have something of significance. If it be true—and as it may well be true—that behind Paul there lay generations of family residence in Tarsus, then Paul grew up in an atmosphere in which he was as familiar with Greek and Roman thought as he was with the Jewish thought of his own nation.

In order that Christianity might go out to all the world a unique person was necessary—and Paul was that person. Here uniquely was the man of two worlds, the man who was Jewish to the last fibre of his being, but also the man who knew the Romans and the Greeks as few Jews knew them. Here indeed was the man prepared by God to be the bridge between two worlds, and to be the bridge by which the Gentiles might come to God.

III

PAUL'S THINKING ABOUT GOD

WE HAVE seen the background out of which Paul grew. Now we go on to look at his actual thought and teaching, and we begin with Paul's thinking about God.

Every Jewish Synagogue service began, and still begins, with the recital of the Shema, and the great basic sentence of the Shema is: "Hear, O Israel: the Lord our God is one Lord" (*Deuteronomy* 6: 4). In that sentence there is laid down an uncompromising monotheism. In a world which believed in many gods the Jews believed in one God, and that for Paul, too, is the beginning of his thinking about God.

He writes to his people at Corinth: "There is none other God but one . . . To us there is but one God" (1 *Corinthians* 8: 4, 6). The belief in the one true God may be said to be the foundation stone of all Paul's thinking.

But there is another great dominant thought in all Paul's teaching. This God who is the one God is also God the Father. There is not one single letter that he ever wrote in which Paul does not call God *Father* (1 *Thessalonians* 1:

1; 2 *Thessalonians* 1: 2; *Galatians* 1: 3; 1 *Corinthians* 1:
3; 2 *Corinthians* 1: 2; *Romans* 1: 7; *Ephesians* 1: 2;
Colossians 1: 2; *Philippians* 1: 2; *Philemon* 3).

Now these two great foundation beliefs of Paul complete
and complement each other. If Paul were to say that there
is one God, and leave it at that, the might and majesty
and power of the lonely God would be secured and safe-
guarded. If Paul were to say that God is Father, the
benevolence and the love and the goodwill of God would
be stressed. The first statement, the statement of what we
might call God's onlyness, assures us of God's power, but
says nothing of any interest He may have in men. The
second statement assures us of God's kindliness, but gives
us no guarantee that the kindliness may not be frustrated
and hindered. But when the two ideas are put together, we
get the full, rounded idea of God, as a God whose power is
always motivated by His love, and whose love is always
backed by His power. So Paul sums it up: "To us there
is but one God, the Father" (1 *Corinthians* 8: 6); and in
that single phrase he gives us the Christian assurance of a
God whose power will never be used except in love, and
a God whose loving purposes because of his power can
never be frustrated.

To Paul, this God and Father was also Creator. "All
things," he said, "are of God" (1 *Corinthians* 11: 12).
"Of Him and through Him and to Him are all things"
(*Romans* 11: 36). With this idea of God the Creator,
Paul joins the idea of the Son as God's instrument, and
agent in creation, just as John was later to do in an even

fuller way. Paul speaks of " one Lord Jesus by whom are all things " (1 *Corinthians* 8: 6). He speaks of God who created all things by Jesus Christ (*Ephesians* 3: 9). " By Him," he says, " all things were created " (*Colossians* 1: 16). This is the doctrine which John states so definitely in the prologue to his gospel when he says: " All things were made by Him and without Him was not anything made that was made " (*John* 1: 3).

It may seem strange to us that Paul makes so much of God as creator, and of the Son's part in the work of creation. But he did so in answer to an increasing tendency of thought in the ancient world. This tendency was later to become known by the name Gnosticism, and since much of the New Testament is written against a background of Gnosticism, and is written to counteract Gnostic tendencies, it is as well to see here at the beginning what Gnosticism was.

Gnosticism was an attempt to solve the problem of sin and suffering in this world. The Gnostics believed that spirit is essentially good, and that matter is essentially evil. They further believed that the creation of the world was out of matter which already existed, and that this matter was essentially flawed. If we may put it so, the whole trouble about the world is that it is made and fashioned out of faulty material. The stuff of which the world is formed is evil. The Gnostic went on to say that, since God is pure spirit and altogether good, he could not possibly Himself have touched and handled and fashioned this flawed matter. So, in order to touch matter, God put out a series of emanations, or æons, as they called them. Each succeeding emanation was a little farther away from God, until at the end of this long line and series there was an emanation so distant from God that it could touch and handle matter. It was this emanation which actually created the world.

The Gnostics went further. As the emanations grew farther and farther from God, they knew less and less about God. At some part in the series, an emanation is arrived at who is entirely ignorant of God. Then still lower down in the series the emanations become not only ignorant of but actively hostile to God. And so in the end the Gnostics came to believe that the world was created by a creator God who was ignorant of and hostile to the true God.

The final step in Gnostic thought was to hold that this ignorant, hostile, creating God was to be identified with the God of the Old Testament; and the real God, who was pure spirit and remote from the work of creation, was to be identified with the true God, the God whom Jesus came to make known to men.

This line of thought became increasingly common in the ancient world. The ancient world was haunted by the thought of the evil matter. That is why so many of the New Testament writers stress the fact that God is Creator, and that God's instrument in creation is not some distant, ignorant, hostile æon, but His Son and His Word. The Gnostic believed that we live in an evil world; the Christian believes that God made all things and made them well.

But Paul also believed that God's act of creation was also an act of self-revelation. To put it in a modern way,

Paul believed that God put so much of Himself into the world that by studying the world men ought to be able to arrive at God. That is the meaning of the famous passage in *Romans* 1: 19-21. " For the invisible things of Him from the creation of the world are clearly seen, being understood by the things that are made, even His eternal power and godhead; so that they are without excuse." It was Paul's belief that God's act of creation was an act of self-revelation; that this world was the garment of the living God; that if men had the eyes to see and the heart to understand they could see God everywhere in the world which He made.

A great artist tells that it was his father who taught him to see and to love beauty. His father used to take him out in the evening time, and the father and son would lie in the long grass beside the wood. They would watch the rabbits play, and the birds swoop by, and the corn field rippling like the waves of the sea beneath the wind. One evening there was a sunset of surpassing majesty and splendour, and at the sight of it his father stood up, removed his cap and looked at the splendour of the dying sun, and said: " My son, it is God." Paul would have wished every man to see and to make that act of instinctive reverence.

Paul believed that God's interest in the world did not end with the work of creation. He believed that God was still the sustaining God, whose work of creation was still going on. He saw that continued activity of God in the processes of the natural world. "Neither is he that planteth anything," he said, " neither he that watereth; but God that giveth the increase " (1 *Corinthians* 3: 7). Paul had discovered the truth that must continually be rediscovered. Man can do many things. He can change things, and alter them, and modify them, and rearrange them. But he cannot create them. Man controls many forces, but man does not control the force of life, and he cannot make a living thing. Creation is the prerogative of God; the secret of life is with God. Paul never thought of a God, who, as it were, wound things up and set them going, and then left them to themselves. He thought of a God always and continually active and at work in the universe which He had made. Creation and providence both belong to God.

So far we have been seeing God as it were in world affairs. Now we must go on to see how Paul thought of God, not only as active in the world, but active in his own life.

Paul saw God's hand in his own spiritual pilgrimage. He saw his life as something planned and designed by God. He speaks of God " who separated me from my mother's womb " (*Galatians* 1: 15). He speaks of God " separating him unto the gospel " (*Romans* 1: 1). Paul thought of himself as a man set apart by God for a special purpose even before he was born. He sees his apostleship not as something to which he attained, not as something to which he was called by men, but as something which came to him by plan and design of God. " Paul, an apostle of Jesus Christ," he says, " by the will of God " (2 *Corinthians* 1: 1). Even more fully he sets it out at the beginning of Galatians: " Paul, an apostle, not of men, neither by man, but by Jesus Christ and God the Father" (*Galatians* 1: 1). Paul saw God, not only in the great lines of world creation and world history but also in his own life. Paul would have agreed with the man who said that every man is a dream of God.

Paul went even farther than that. He did not see God only in the great events and the crucial moments on which his life had hinged. He saw God in the life of everyday. When he writes to the Corinthians he tells them: "I will come to you shortly, if the Lord will" (1 *Corinthians* 4: 19). When he writes to the Roman Church he tells that he prays, "If by any means now at length I might have a prosperous journey, by the will of God, to come unto you" (*Romans* 1: 10). To Paul the God who created the world was never too busy to be bothered with his own life.

Another way of putting this would be to say that to Paul God was a supplying God. This God, who created men, and who directed their lives, did not leave men to carry out His commandments unaided and to go upon His tasks unassisted. With the need came the power; with the task came the ability to do it. "Not that we are sufficient of ourselves," said Paul, "but our sufficiency is of God" (2 *Corinthians* 3: 5).

In the midst of his troubles, when life was an almost intolerable burden, he heard God say: "My grace is sufficient for you; for my strength is made perfect in weakness" (2 *Corinthians* 12: 9). Even when he was in prison in Rome he writes to his friends in Philippi; "My God shall supply all your needs " (*Philippians* 4: 9). John Buchan described an atheist as a man who has no invisible means of support. To Paul a Christian was a man who had the continual support of God.

The relationship between God and Jesus is something to which we shall have again and again to return. But at the moment we must note that God was behind every single act of the life of Jesus.

God was behind the Incarnation. God was behind the coming of Jesus into the world. His coming into the world was not, as it were, something which the Son suggested. It is God who is the prime mover and who is behind it all. So Paul speaks of God sending His Son in the likeness of sinful flesh (*Romans* 8: 3). He says that " when the fulness of time was come God sent forth His Son " (*Galatians* 4: 4). To Paul, in the fullest sense of the term, the coming of Jesus into the world was an act of God.

God was behind the Cross. The Cross was not an independent act of Jesus. The Cross was not solely the result of the fury and the sin of men. The Cross was an event within the plan and the purpose of God. " Jesus," says Paul, " who was delivered for our offences " (*Romans* 4: 25). " Jesus," says Paul, " who gave Himself for our sins, according to the will of God " (*Galatians* 1: 4). " He that spared not His own Son," says Paul, " but delivered Him up for us all " (*Romans* 8: 32). It is none other than God who is behind the coming of Jesus into the world, and the sacrifice of the life of Jesus upon the Cross.

God was behind the Resurrection. Here indeed is one of

the most familiar thoughts of Paul, a thought to be found in every epistle. In *Galatians* 1: 1 Paul speaks of "Jesus Christ, and God the Father, who raised Him from the dead." In *Romans* 4: 24 he speaks of "Him that raised up Jesus our Lord from the dead." God is behind both our quickening from sin and its death and the raising of Jesus from the death of the Cross. "God hath quickened us together with Christ," he writes (*Ephesians* 2: 5). "You," he writes, "being dead in your sins hath He quickened with Him" (*Colossians* 2: 13). The Resurrection was to Paul, not so much an achievement of Jesus, as an act of God.

For Paul, God was behind the Incarnation, the Cross and the Resurrection. Here is something which we shall have to recall to our minds again and again. There is a way of presenting the gospel which comes perilously near to blasphemy, a way in which Paul's gospel especially is wrongly presented. Sometimes the gospel is presented as if there was a contrast between a stern and angry God and a gentle and loving Christ, as if there was a contrast between a God who was the judge of the souls of men and a Christ who was the lover of the souls of men, a contrast between a God who wished to condemn and a Christ who wished to save. Sometimes the gospel is presented in such a way that it sounds as if Jesus Christ had done something to change the attitude of God, as if He had changed God's wrath to love, as if He had persuaded God's uplifted hand not to strike the contemplated blow. Nothing could be farther from the truth, and nothing could be a graver distortion of the gospel of Paul. As John saw so clearly, it was because God so loved the world that He sent His Son into the world (*John* 3 : 16). As Paul saw so vividly, it was God who was behind the whole process of redemption. It is God's love, God's desire to save which dominates the whole scene. The initiative is the initiative of God. Behind every act of Jesus is God. Jesus to Paul was not the pacifier of the wrath of God; He was the bringer of the love of God. And now we must go on to study that divine initiative in fuller detail.

IV

THE DIVINE INITIATIVE

SIMONE WEIL has said: " One might lay down as a postulate: All conceptions of God which are incompatible with a movement of pure charity are false. All other conceptions of Him, in varying degree are true." There is a way of presenting Paul's gospel which is incompatible with the pure charity of God. Sometimes Paul's gospel is preached in such a way that God and Jesus Christ are set over against each other and contrasted with each other. The love and the grace and the mercy of Jesus Christ are set over against the wrath and the austerity and the judgment of God. The implication is that through something that Jesus did the attitude of God to men was changed, that God was persuaded and pacified by Jesus Christ into changing His condemnation into forgiveness.

The more we study of Paul's own writings, the more we see that any such conception is the reverse of the truth as Paul saw it. If one thing is clear, it is that, to Paul, the whole initiative of the process of salvation lies with God.

The will behind the whole process of salvation is the will of God. Paul writes to the Corinthians, " He who stablishes us with you in Christ, and hath anointed us, is God " (2 *Corinthians* 1: 21). He speaks to the Thessalonians of " the will of God in Christ Jesus " (1 *Thessalonians* 5: 18). He writes to the Galatians of " Jesus who gave Himself for our sins, according to the will of God " (*Galatians* 1: 4).

So far from God's attitude being changed by anything that Jesus did, it was precisely God's attitude to men that Jesus expressed. So far from God's purpose being deflected by anything that Jesus did, it was precisely the purpose of God that Jesus came to fulfil. Salvation did not come to men in opposition to the will of God; it came because it was the will of God.

It was the love of God which was behind the whole process of salvation. Paul writes to the Thessalonians that " our Lord Jesus Christ Himself, and God, even our Father, who has loved us, and has given us everlasting consolation" (2 *Thessalonians* 2: 16). It was His love that God commended to us in the death of Christ (*Romans* 5: 8). It is the goodness of God which leads men to repentance (*Romans* 2: 4). It is from the love of God that nothing can separate us (*Romans* 8: 39). It is by God's mercies that Paul appeals to men (*Romans* 12: 1). He writes to the Ephesians of God " who is rich in mercy, because of the great love wherewith He loved us " (*Ephesians* 2: 4). It is the Father Himself who has made us " fit to be partakers of the inheritance of the saints in light " (*Colossians* 1: 12). Jesus Christ came to tell men, not that God hates sinners, but that He loves them. Is is the simple fact that no one ever wrote with such lyrical splendour of the love of God as Paul did.

43

Even to suggest that Paul contrasted the love of Christ and the wrath of God is to make a travesty of his gospel.

It is God who is behind the initiative of reconciliation. In that great passage in 2 *Corinthians* 5: 18-20 three times in as many verses the initiative in reconciliation is referred to God. It is God who has reconciled us to Himself in Jesus Christ. God was in Christ reconciling the world unto Himself. And the final appeal is: " Be ye reconciled to God."

In *Romans* 5: 10 it is we who are reconciled to God. In *Colossians* 1: 20 it is God, who is making peace by the blood of the Cross, and reconciling all things unto Himself. In all Paul's writings God is never spoken of as being reconciled to man, for the simple reason that any such reconciliation is totally unnecessary. Always the one thing necessary is that man should be reconciled to God. The responsibility for the breach between man and God lies, not with God, but with man. It was man's attitude to God which needed to be changed. God's attitude to man always was and always must be patient love, unwearied forgiveness, and undefeatable seeking.

Paul can speak quite indiscriminately about the Gospel of Jesus Christ and the Gospel of God. The very essence of Paul's preaching was good news about God brought to men by Jesus Christ. He tells the Thessalonians that " we were bold in our God to speak unto you the gospel of God " (1 *Thessalonians* 2: 2). He tells them that he preached to them the gospel of God (1 *Thessalonians* 2: 8, 9). Yet in the very same letter he can speak of Timothy our fellow-

44

labourer in the gospel of Christ (1 *Thessalonians* 3: 2). He speaks of himself as being separated unto the gospel of God (*Romans* 1: 1). Jesus did not come to introduce to the world a new-made gospel as a substitute for news of the wrath of God. It was precisely good news about the love of God that Jesus came to bring.

Whenever Paul speaks about the grace of God, his habit is to associate God and Jesus Christ in this matter of grace. Nothing could be further from the thought of Paul than to think that all the grace was of Jesus and all the stern justice was of God. The grace which Jesus brings to men is nothing other than the grace of God. It is that very grace of God which was in Jesus Christ. When he writes to the Thessalonians, he speaks of " the grace of our God and the Lord Jesus Christ " (2 *Thessalonians* 1: 12). He greets the Galatians with " grace and peace from God the Father and from our Lord Jesus Christ " (*Galatians* 1: 3). He speaks to the Corinthians of " the grace of God which is given you by Jesus Christ " (1 *Corinthians* 1: 4).

The grace behind the whole process of salvation is the grace of God. Jesus neither discovered nor created grace; He brought to men the already existing grace of God.

It was God who sent Jesus Christ into this world. It is not that Jesus, as it were, said: " I will take the initiative and will go into the world and make my sacrifice and lay down my life, if perchance it may pacify my Father's anger and free men from the wrath to come." If we may put it so, it was that God laid upon Jesus the task of providing the way to salvation, which was already His only aim.

Paul tells the Galatians that God sent His Son in the fulness of time (*Galatians* 4: 4). He tells the Corinthians that it is God who made Jesus Christ to be sin for the sake of men (2 *Corinthians* 5: 21). Jesus is the unspeakable gift of God (2 *Corinthians* 9: 15). The gift of eternal life is the gift of God (*Romans* 6: 23). God sent His Son into the world in flesh which was exactly like our own (*Romans* 8: 3). It is Paul's supreme proof of the lengths to which the love of God will go that God who spared not His own Son will surely go to any lengths in his love and care for men (*Romans* 8: 32). The fact that Jesus came into the world at all is due to nothing else than the seeking love of God.

It has so often happened that a distorted version of Paul's gospel has been preached and taught to men, and the disastrous result of that distortion has been that men have so often had a division in their minds between God and Jesus. They have come to look on God as a person to be feared and Jesus as a person to be loved. They have felt at home with Jesus, but strange and uncomfortable and scared of God. They have looked on Jesus as their defence and rescuer from the wrath of God. So deeply is that ingrained into the minds of some people in their younger days that they never wholly grow out of it. They feel that Jesus is indeed their friend, but they are haunted rather than helped by the very thought of God.

In John we come upon that immortal sentence: " He that hath seen me hath seen the Father " (*John* 14: 9). The tragedy is that to so many people God is the opposite of Jesus; but the whole teaching of the New Testament, and above all the teaching of Paul, is that when we look on the seeking love, the unwearied forgiveness, the infinite compassion, the yearning gentleness of Jesus, we are looking at the heart of God, fully displayed as nowhere else in all the world.

Jesus did not come to save men against the will of God; He came to bring men the good news that God wanted nothing so much as that men should come home to Himself in contrite love and trust.

THE CALL OF GOD

WE HAVE seen how Paul believed with his whole heart that God was behind the whole process of salvation. The initiative in salvation is a divine initiative, the initiative of God.

But to Paul the matter was even more personal than that. If we say that it is the will of God that is behind the whole process of salvation, and if we leave it at that, we might feel that the whole purpose of God was a kind of generalised purpose aiming at the salvation of mankind. But Paul was sure that the purpose of God was not a generalised but an individualised purpose, that God's purpose was not so much the salvation of mankind, but the salvation of each individual man. As Augustine put it in the famous sentence with which Paul would have wholeheartedly agreed: "God loves each one of us as if there was only one of us to love." For that reason Paul makes a great deal of the call of God.

The call of God is not simply a wide, general call to all mankind; it is God's personal summons and invitation to each individual man. God does not only purpose the salvation of all mankind, he has " His own secret stairway into every heart." He invites each man individually to respond to Him.

The idea of the call of God runs through all Paul's letters; and it is of the greatest interest and the greatest significance to see to what Paul believed God is calling men.

Paul believed that God is calling men to salvation. He writes to the Thessalonians that God is calling them, not to wrath, but to obtain salvation (1 *Thessalonians* 5: 9). God has from the beginning chosen them to salvation (2 *Thessalonians* 2: 13). It is God's aim to rescue men from the hopeless situation in which they find themselves, and to liberate them from the chains in which they have involved themselves.

The ancient world felt pessimistically that it had lost the moral battle. " Men," said Epictetus, " were sorely conscious of their weakness in necessary things." " Men love their vices and hate them at the same time," said Seneca. "It is not only that we have acted amiss," he said. " We shall do so to the end." Persius, the Roman poet, wrote despairingly: " Let the guilty see virtue and pine that they have lost her for ever." He spoke about " filthy Natta benumbed by vice." " When a man," said Epictetus, " is hardened like a stone, how can any argument deal with him ?" Seneca declared that what men needed above all was " a hand let down to lift them up." The ancient world was deeply conscious that it was inextricably entangled and enmeshed in sin. It felt helpless in this world, and under certain judgment in the next. In such a situation God called men to accept the deliverance, the rescue, the redemption, the salvation that He was offering men through Jesus Christ

Paul believed that God was calling men to holiness. He tells the Thessalonians that God calls them to a holy life (1 *Thessalonians* 4: 7). The root meaning of the word holy (*hagios*) is *different*. To be holy is to be different; it is to have a different standard, a different peace and beauty from the stained, frustrated, defeated life of the world. God calls men to a life in which there has opened out the possibility of a new victory over sin and a new loveliness and beauty.

Paul believed that God was calling men to peace. He tells the Corinthians that they are called, not to bondage, but to peace (1 *Corinthians* 7: 15). Wherein lay this peace? The ancient world could never get beyond a belief in the blind tyranny, the utter indifference of the sheer capriciousness of the gods. Man was what Homer long ago had called the *paignion theōn*, the plaything of the gods. How could man know peace if he forever trembled at the thought of the eternal judge? How could he know peace if he believed that he lived in a world which did not care? How could he know peace if he felt that he was caught up in a blind fate and an iron determinism which would crush the life out of him? How could he know peace if he felt that he was the helpless plaything of the immortal gods? But peace comes when a man realises that the sum total of things is under the direction of one whose name is Father and whose heart is love. The call of God is a summons to men to find the peace of realising that the world is their Father's house.

Paul believed that God's call was a call to grace. He tells the Galatians that God calls them to the grace of Christ (*Galatians* 1: 6). The basic meaning of grace is something which is freely and undeservedly given in the sheer generosity of God. Grace is something which a man could never deserve and never earn, but which is given to him in the outgoing love of God.

Here indeed was something new. Until this time men had seen God in terms of law. God had laid down certain laws. The dilemma was that these laws must be kept, but could never be kept. They were both obligatory and impossible. Man was for ever in default. But now in Christ God calls to men to realise that they cannot earn, but can only accept in wonder, His rescuing and redeeming love. The minute a man realises that, the tension of life is gone.

Paul believed that God's call was a call to fellowship with Christ. He tells the Corinthians that God has called them into the fellowship of Jesus Christ (1 *Corinthians* 1: 9). The supreme horror of life is loneliness; and the supreme value of life is friendship.

In one of the Socratic dialogues a simple soul who had been admitted to that great fellowship which gathered around Socrates, was asked to name the boon in life for which he was most grateful. His answer was: "That being such as I am, I have the friends I have." The call of

God is to share the greatest friendship in the world, the friendship of Jesus Christ.

Paul believed that the call of God was a call to share the Kingdom and the glory of His Son. He tells the Thessalonians that God has called them to His Kingdom and His glory (1 *Thessalonians* 2: 12). The invitation of God is the invitation to share in the present power and the future triumph of Jesus Christ. Even in days of persecution, even in days when the world seems to be winning, it is the man who has accepted the invitation of God who is ultimately on the winning side.

Paul believed that that call of God was a call which had been sounding out from all eternity. He writes to the Ephesians that they were chosen before the foundation of the world (*Ephesians* 1: 4). Sometimes the Cross is depicted as if it were a kind of emergency measure of God, as if He had tried the Cross when all other things had failed. It is the belief of Paul that through all eternity God has been loving His men; that through all eternity man's sin has been breaking His heart; that through all eternity God's love has been sacrificing and suffering and seeking for men.

It is as if the Cross was a window opening for one moment of time upon the eternal suffering love of the heart of God. In one of Ibsen's plays there is a passage like this about Christ: "Where is he now? Has he been at work elsewhere since that happened at Golgotha? . . . Where is he now? What if that at Golgotha, near Jerusalem, was but a wayside matter, a thing done, as it were, in the passing? What if he goes on and on, and suffers and dies and conquers again and again from world to world? " That may be a startling way to put the matter. But the fact remains that the Cross is the sign and symbol in a moment of time of the sacrificing love which has been in the heart of God from the foundation of the world.

Paul believed that the call of God came to men supremely in Christ. He writes to the Roman Christians that they are among those who are called by Jesus Christ (*Romans* 1: 6). All through the ages God has been sending His call to men, by the voice of conscience, by the experiences of life, by the voices of the prophets, by the events of history. These things men might be too blind to see, and too dull to appreciate, but in Jesus Christ there comes the supreme call, so plain that none can fail to hear it.

Paul believed that God's call came by the preaching of the gospel. He writes to the Thessalonians that God had called them by the gospel which he had preached (2 *Thessalonians* 2: 14). Two things emerge from that. First, the call was the call of the *gospel*. The call was not the call of a threat; it was the call of good news. It was not the summons to avoid damnation; it was the invitation to accept love.

Second, it came to men by preaching. Men must be confronted with the call and the invitation of God. It is the task of every Christian, it is the task of the Church, and it is supremely the task of the preacher to bring to men who have never heard it, or who refuse to listen to it, the call of God.

VI

PAUL'S THINKING
ABOUT JESUS CHRIST

WHEN WE try to find out what Paul thought and believed about Jesus Christ, we must begin by remembering two things. First, Paul was not a systematic theologian. Paul was not in the least like a man sitting in a library or in a study carefully and logically compiling a system of theology. First and foremost Paul argued from experience. When he talks about Jesus, he is not offering us something which is the fruit of thought and deduction and study and the careful balancing of one theory against another theory and one philosophy against another philosophy. He is continually saying: " This is what happened to me. This is what I have experienced. This is what Jesus did for me. This I know to be true."

It is quite true that it may be a quite unfair distinction to make. But it is true to say that Paul's interest was not in theology, but in religion. He was never concerned to draw up and work out a system which would be fully satisfactory to the mind and intellect: he was concerned to tell men of an experience-based faith, by which they might live. When Paul speaks of Jesus, he is simply setting down his own experience of his risen Lord.

Second, we must remember that there was nothing static about Paul's belief. Paul was for ever faced with the ever moving and changing stream of human experience. He was for ever involved in changing situations. He had to meet one error after another; he had to match himself with one set of thinkers after another; he had to deal with one heresy after another. He was living in days when the Church was still in a ferment, days long before the time when the Church had settled down to an institutional orthodoxy. And to meet each changing situation and problem he had to draw new truth and new treasures out of what he himself called the unsearchable riches of Christ. He was ever discovering new greatnesses and new adequacies in Christ. No matter how long Paul had lived he would never have arrived at a static religion.

It is said that a certain famous lady was asked what quality she regarded as most necessary for a person to possess in order that he might excel in life. She answered in one word: " Adaptability." In the highest possible sense, and not in any time-serving sense, Paul's theology was an adaptable theology. It was always deepening and developing and widening to meet the new situations which the life of the growing Church brought to him. That is why it is not possible to make a neat pattern of Paul's thinking about Jesus, for as the years went on Jesus became ever more wonderful to Paul.

We must begin somewhere, and we begin with that which is most basic. With the exception of 2 *Thessalonians* and *Philemon*, there is not one single letter in which Paul does not refer to Jesus as the Son of God. In every other letter, either by direct statement or by unmistakable implication, we meet that conception which for Paul was the starting point of all things.

And it is to be noted that again and again this statement that Jesus is the Son of God occurs at the very beginning of Paul's letters as if by it he struck what was for him the keynote of the Christian gospel (cp. 1 *Thessalonians* 1: 10; *Galatians* 1: 16; 2: 20; 4: 4; 1 *Corinthians* 1: 9; 2 *Corinthians* 1: 19; 1: 3; *Romans* 1: 3; 1: 9; 8: 32; *Ephesians* 1: 3; *Colossians* 1: 3). First and foremost Paul believed and insisted that Jesus stood in a unique relationship with God.

And yet there is something else to be set beside that. Never at any time did Paul identify Jesus Christ and God. He never equated Jesus Christ and God. He may and does equate the love and the gospel and the grace and the work of Jesus Christ and of God, but never does he as we might put it, personally identify Jesus and God.

Nowhere does Paul reach greater heights in his conception of Jesus than in the letter to the Colossians, where he goes the length of saying that Jesus is the fulness of the godhead bodily (*Colossians* 2: 9) yet even in that letter he has the picture of Jesus at the right hand of God (*Colossians* 3: 1). We have no wish to take a phrase like that with a crude literalism, yet it remains true that no one could even use it unless he had a clear distinction in his mind between Jesus Christ and God.

Paul goes even further than that. There is a sense for Paul in which Jesus is subordinate to God. He writes to the Corinthians: " But I would have you know, that the head of every man is Christ . . . and the head of Christ is God " (1 *Corinthians* 11: 3). In his picture of the end of things, he writes to the Corinthians: " And when all things shall be subdued unto Him, then shall the Son also be subject unto Him, that put all things under Him, that God may be all in all " (1 *Corinthians* 15: 28). And on the same lines is that great cry of triumph in 1 *Corinthians* 3: 22, 23: " All (things) are yours; and ye are Christ's; and Christ is God's."

No one ever had a higher conception of Jesus Christ than Paul had, and yet it is still true to say that for Paul nothing was ever allowed to detract from the lonely supremacy of God. The work of the Son is ever done in obedience to the Father. Behind every event, action and word in the life of Jesus stands God.

It is here we come to one of the most difficult doctrines in all theology, the pre-existence of the Son. We usually consider that doctrine a characteristic of the thought of John. But it is in Paul too. We get a glimpse of that belief in the strange old story which Paul uses in 1 *Corinthians* 10: 4. The Rabbis had a legend that the rock from which the Israelites drank in the desert followed them for ever after in their wanderings and was to them a continual source of refreshment. Paul refers to that legend and uses

it; and then he adds the comment: " That rock was Christ."
Whatever else he means, he means that the spiritual re-
freshing power of the Son goes back to the days of Israel
in the desert.

In *Ephesians* 3: 11 he speaks of " the eternal purpose
which God purposed in Jesus Christ." That is to say,
before time and the world began, the work of Christ was
in the mind, the plan, the purpose of God. In *Colossians*
1: 15 Paul speaks of Jesus Christ as the image of the
invisible God, and the first-born of every creature. Certainly in Paul's mind was this conception which we call
the pre-existence of the Son.

How can we explain that doctrine to ourselves in such
a way that it will really mean something? No one can
fully explain it or understand it, but there are two ways
in which we can think of it.

First, there is a very simple way. At its simplest this
doctrine means that God was always like Jesus. It means
that God was not once stern and hard and austere and
severe, a God of judgment and of wrath, and then that He
suddenly became gentle and gracious and loving towards
men. It means that before time began God was like Jesus.
It means that in Jesus we see God as God always was, and
is, and ever shall be.

Second, there is a more complicated way in which we
can try to explain this. God is Father, Son and Holy Spirit.
That is the doctrine of the Trinity. Now we connect God
the Father with the life-giving work of creation; we connect God the Son with the saving work of redemption;

we connect God the Spirit with the illuminating work of revelation. But we must strenuously avoid one mistake. We are very apt to think of this as a kind of series in time. We are apt to think of God first as Creator, then second and afterwards as Redeemer, then still later, as Enlightener and Illuminer. We are apt to think of God creating the world, and then, when the world went wrong, setting out to redeem the world, and then still later, when Jesus had left the earth sending the illumination of the Holy Spirit. But what the doctrine of the Trinity says is that God is always, from before time, through time, and when time shall end, Creator, Redeemer, Sustainer and Enlightener. Through all eternity God creates and is still creating; through all eternity God redeems and is redeeming; through all eternity God sustains and enlightens and is still sustaining and enlightening.

To speak of the pre-existence of the Son is to say that God did not begin to redeem men when Jesus Christ came into this world, but that throughout all ages the redeeming power and the sacrificial work of God had been at work. To speak of the pre-existence of the Son means that the love which was demonstrated on Calvary is an eternal movement of the heart of God to men.

VII

THE INCARNATION

THE central fact of Christianity is that in Jesus Christ God came into this world, that in Jesus Christ God took the life of man upon Himself. This is the doctrine we call the Incarnation, for the word *Incarnation* literally means *the becoming flesh*. How that could happen men are still trying to explain, and throughout the ages, they have worked out their theories. The method we may never know; the fact we most certainly and blessedly do know. Paul saw the Incarnation from two sides.

Paul saw the Incarnation from the side of God, the Father. To Paul the Incarnation was in the most literal sense an act of God. God sent His Son in flesh like the flesh of any man (*Romans* 8 : 3). It is the love of God which is in Jesus Christ our Lord (*Romans* 8 : 39). It was God who was in Christ reconciling the world unto Himself (2 *Corinthians* 5 : 19). That gift is an unspeakable gift (2 *Corinthians* 9 : 15). Before such an act of love, in face of such a splendour of generosity, there is nothing left for man but silent and grateful adoration. The Incarnation in its essence is an act of God on behalf of man.

Paul saw the Incarnation from the side of Jesus Christ, the Son. Here Paul saw the Incarnation in a way that is uniquely his own. He did not think of the sacrifice of Christ as beginning upon earth. He did not think of the sacrifice of Christ in terms only of the terrible things which happened to Him in this world, and which ended in the breaking of His heart by men's disloyalty, and the breaking of His body on the Cross. Paul thought of the sacrifice of Christ as beginning in eternity. Paul was haunted by the thought of what Jesus Christ gave up in order to become man. He could never forget how Jesus Christ laid aside His glory for the humiliation of manhood. With a wonder which throbs through even the written word, he says: " Though He was rich, yet for your sakes He became poor " (2 *Corinthians* 8: 9). To Paul the sacrifice of Jesus Christ was a sacrifice which began before time and the world; it was something which had its beginning in eternity.

The theologians call this the kenotic theory of the Incarnation. The Greek verb *kenoun* means *to empty;* and the noun *kenōsis* means *an emptying.* And the idea is that, Jesus Christ, the Son of God, deliberately and sacrificially emptied Himself of His divine glory in order to become man.

The thought of Paul finds its fullest expression in *Philippians* 2: 5-11. There Paul speaks of Christ Jesus who had equality with God as a right, and not a thing to be snatched at; but He gave it up and did not hug it to Himself, and He became a man. Then Paul goes on to heap up the things which show the extent of this self-emptying. If God had come into this world, He might have been expected to come as a great king in power and might and glory, and with all the magnificence that the world could give. But Jesus became of no reputation; He became, not a king, but a servant. He came, not to order, but to obey. He became obedient unto death; and that death was not only a natural death, it was the death of the Cross. As every piece in the pattern of this passage falls into place, it stresses the extent and the completeness of the self-emptying of God which the Incarnation involves.

The strange thing about this *kenōsis* theory is that it baffles the mind and yet moves the heart. It baffles the mind to see how God could abandon His essential attributes and still remain God. God is omniscient, and yet it is clear that in His earthly life there were things which Jesus did not know. He often asked questions, and when He did so we dare not think that He was simply play-acting. He said Himself that not even He knew the day and the hour when the Son of Man would come in His glory (*Mark* 13: 32).

God is omnipotent; and yet it is clear that there were things which Jesus in His earthly life could not do. Even that gospel which contains the highest view of Jesus, still shows us Jesus tired and weary and physically exhausted with the journey (*John* 4: 6). Mark tells us how, when they crossed the lake in the fishing boat, Jesus was asleep on a pillow in the stern of the boat (*Mark* 4: 38), and the eternal God neither slumbers nor sleeps.

God is omnipresent; and yet it is clear that during His earthly life Jesus was subject to the laws of space and time, and like any other man could only be in one place at one time.

When we try to grapple with this idea of the self-emptying of God in the Incarnation, the mind cannot grasp it. We may make it a little easier for our minds to think of, if we say that in the Incarnation God emptied Himself of His purely metaphysical attributes, such as omniscience, omnipotence and omnipresence; but not of his moral attributes, His goodness, His justice and, above all, His love.

The self-emptying of God in the Incarnation is the supreme demonstration of His love, for it was of His love that He wished to tell men, and it was about His love that men above all needed to know.

It may be that this Pauline idea of the divine *kenōsis*, the self-emptying of God is something which the mind cannot grasp and cannot explain; but for the heart it does set out, as no other doctrine does, the unimaginable sacrifice of love which God made in becoming man at all. It sets out what God had to give up in order to come into this world for us men and for our salvation.

More than once Paul stresses the reality of the Incarnation. We have already seen how in *Philippians* 2: 5-11 Paul stresses the completeness of the Incarnation. In *Romans* 1: 3 he speaks of Jesus being made of the seed of David according to the flesh. The actual physical descent of Jesus is laid down at the very beginning of the letter. In *Romans* 8: 3 he speaks of God sending His Son in the likeness of, in the guise of, as Moffatt puts it, sinful flesh. We find this same insistence on the reality of the Incarnation in John's First Letter. John writes: " Every spirit that confesseth that Jesus Christ is come in the flesh is of God: and every spirit that confesseth not that Jesus Christ is come in the flesh is not of God " (1 *John* 4: 2, 3).

Both Paul and John were directing their teaching against a heresy which is known as Docetism. We have seen how the Gnostics believed that matter was essentially flawed and essentially evil. If that be so, then quite obviously the body must be essentially an evil thing. These Gnostics taught that Jesus had not a real body at all; that He was a kind of ghost or phantom with a body which was made of spirit and not of flesh. *Dokein* means *to seem;* and these Gnostics taught that Jesus seemed to be a man, had the appearance of being a man, but in reality had no human body at all.

The Gnostics produced many books which purported to be lives of Jesus. One of them is called The Acts of John and it was written about A.D. 150. In it John is represented as saying about Jesus: " Sometimes when I would lay hold on Him, I met with a material and solid body, and at other times again, when I felt Him, the substance was immaterial and as if it existed not at all . . . And often-times when I walked with Him, I desired to see the print of His foot, whether it appeared on the earth; and I never saw it."

To these Gnostics Jesus was a phantom figure who looked like a man but who was not. Paul would have none of that; He insisted that Jesus was really and truly man. As we shall see, in Paul's thought it was completely essential that Jesus must be completely man, if ever He was to redeem man. And Paul would have nothing to do with any of these theories which tried to honour the divinity of Jesus by destroying His humanity.

Paul regarded the Incarnation as an act of the love of God; he regarded the Incarnation as involving the beginning of Jesus Christ's sacrifice in eternity and before time; he regarded the Incarnation as involving the full and complete humanity of the Son of God. For Paul the manhood of Jesus was of supreme importance, because Paul was quite clear that we are saved as much by the life of Jesus as by His death. For Paul the life of Christ is every bit as necessary an element in salvation as the death of Christ. We must look in detail at this idea in Paul, for it is the key to one of the most difficult chapters that Paul ever wrote.

Twice this idea of the efficacy of the life of Jesus in the work of salvation emerges. It emerges briefly in 1 *Corinthians* 15: 21, 22: " Since by man came death, by man came also the resurrection from the dead; for as in Adam all die, even so in Christ shall all be made alive." But this idea emerges most fully in *Romans* 5: 12-21. The basic idea of that passage is stated in verse 19: " As by one man's disobedience many were made sinners, so by the obedience of one shall many be made righteous."

The argument of this passage is that all men sinned in Adam. We must note carefully that Paul is not saying that all men sinned in the same way as Adam sinned. He is not saying that from Adam men inherited the tendency to sin. He is saying that all mankind literally and actually sinned in Adam. The fact that Adam sinned constituted all men sinners.

To a twentieth-century western mind that is a very difficult, if not an impossible idea. We find it very difficult to understand how all men, how we, sinned in Adam. At the back of it there is the Jewish idea of solidarity. This is an idea which is characteristic of the primitive thinking of most nations. The Jew never thought of himself as an individual; he always thought of himself as the member of a family, a clan, or a nation. Apart from that family, clan, or nation he had no separate existence. He existed not as an individual, but as a unit in a society. To this day it is said that an Australian aborigine, on being asked his name, will give, not his own name, but the name of his tribe. He thinks of himself first and foremost as a member of a tribe. This is most clearly seen in action in the blood feud. Suppose a man of one tribe is injured or killed by a man of another tribe. Then it becomes the duty of the whole tribe of the injured man to take vengeance on the whole tribe of the injurer. The whole tribe is thought of as involved in the injury: and the whole tribe is thought of as inflicting the injury. The matter is not a matter of individuals at all; it is a matter of tribes; that is solidarity in action.

We have a vivid example of this principle in action in the Old Testament in *Joshua* 7. At the conquest of Jericho, Achan had kept to himself certain of the spoils in direct disobedience to the commandment of God that all the spoils should be destroyed; and at first no one knew of Achan's secret disobedience. After the fall of Jericho the Israelites moved on to take Ai, which should have fallen without any trouble at all. It did not; the siege of Ai produced disaster. Why? Because Achan had sinned by disobedience. The sin of Achan had constituted the whole nation one corporate sinner and on the nation God was sending His punishment. Achan was not an individual; he had no separate existence apart from the nation; he was part of the nation; and in his sin the whole nation had sinned, and for his sin the whole nation was being punished. What the individual did, the nation did. Further, when it was discovered that it was Achan who had sinned, not only was Achan executed, but his whole family was also executed with him, for they were involved in his sin. Here then is solidarity.

Paul begins with the idea that quite literally all men sinned in Adam; all men were involved in Adam's sin; because Adam became a sinner all the descendants of Adam were constituted sinners.

But it might well be said to Paul: "How can you prove that? That is an extraordinary statement to make. Can you advance any proof that in fact all men did sin in Adam?" It is that proof which Paul seeks to advance in *Romans* 5. In Paul's argument there are certain basic steps.

1. Basic to Paul's argument is the insistence that death is the consequence of sin. Death came by sin (*Romans* 5: 12). Had there been no sin, there would have been no death. Death is the result of sin.

II. Adam broke a positive commandment of God, the commandment not to eat of the fruit of the forbidden tree. Thereby Adam sinned; and thereby Adam became liable to death (*Romans* 5: 12).

III. But how can Paul prove that in that particular sin of Adam all sinned? The Law did not come into the world until the time of Moses. Now, if there is no Law, there can be no sin, for sin is a breach of the Law. Therefore before Moses there could be no such thing as sin. Between Adam and Moses the Law did not exist; therefore sin did not exist. *And yet men died.* That is the argument of *Romans* 5: 13, 14.

IV. Why then should men die, if there was no Law, and therefore no sin? The answer is that they died because they had sinned in Adam; they were involved in Adam's sin; by one man's offence death reigned by one (*Romans* 5: 17).

It is Paul's argument that the fact that men continued to die before the beginning of the Law, and therefore before there could be such a thing as sin, is the proof of the fact that they had sinned in Adam. By the sin of Adam all men were constituted sinners.

And now we come to the other side of the argument. Into this world came Christ. He brought to God the perfect righteousness and the perfect obedience (*Romans* 5: 18, 19). And just as all men were involved in Adam's sin, so all men were involved in Jesus Christ's perfect obedience, and perfect goodness, and perfect holiness. By that perfect obedience of Jesus Christ, the evil and unending chain of sin and death was broken; the deadly series was interrupted; the new holiness entered in. And just as men had been constituted sinners by Adam's sin, they were constituted righteous by Jesus Christ's obedience. In view of the conception of solidarity mankind was involved in the sin of Adam; and in view of the conception of solidarity mankind is involved in the holiness of Christ. The sin of Adam made all men sinners; the obedience of Christ made all men righteous.

Now it is completely clear that the argument of Paul rests on the fact that Jesus Christ was fully man. The whole argument collapses unless Jesus is as human as Adam was human. For the argument to be valid the Incarnation must be absolutely real. Mankind must be as fully identified with Christ as once it was with Adam.

To our modern minds all this is a strange argument. We find it hard to grasp, and, if we are honest, many of us will have to say that we do not find it very convincing. But in this argument there is one great flaw and there is one great truth.

The flaw lies in this. Suppose we take the Adam story quite literally. Suppose we assume that it is literally true that Adam was the first man, and that we are all his descendants. Then the conclusion is that our connection with Adam is a physical connection. It is something which we can neither choose nor reject. We have no choice whatever in the matter. It is simply an inevitable matter of physical descent. But on the other hand, our connection with Jesus Christ is a spiritual connection. It is by no means an

69

inevitable relationship; it is something which we can either accept or reject. The connection is quite different. No man can reasonably be condemned because he is physically connected with his ancestors; but any man must bear the responsibility for accepting or refusing his connection with Jesus Christ. That is the flaw in Paul's argument.

But there is also in Paul's argument an eternal truth. The truth is this. Man was involved in a situation from which he could not free himself; he was dominated by sin; he was helplessly in the grip of sin. Into this situation came Christ, with a power which could break into this hopeless situation and introduce a new element of release. What is true is that man was hopelessly and helplessly involved in sin, and that Christ liberated him from that tragic and impotent situation. Through Jesus Christ, man the sinner becomes potentially man the righteous. As Paul would have said, the sin of Adam made men sinners; the holiness of Christ can make men holy.

VIII

THE WORK OF CHRIST

As WE study the writings of Paul we come upon picture after picture of what Jesus Christ has done for man.

In the very forefront of Paul's thought was the fact that Jesus Christ brought to men a knowledge of God which without Him they could never have possessed or entered into. Jesus Himself said: " He that hath seen me hath seen the Father " (*John* 14: 9) and that was an essential and primary part of the belief of Paul. To put it at its simplest, Paul believed with all his heart that Jesus has shown us what God is like. God commanded the light to shine out of the darkness " to give the light of the knowledge of the glory of God in the face of Jesus Christ " (2 *Corinthians* 4: 6). Jesus is the revelation of the glory of God; He is the incarnate glory; in Him men see the glory of God.

It is in the letter to the Colossians that this idea emerges in all its splendour. That letter was written to combat a heresy which held that Jesus was certainly great, but that He was only one stage on the way to the knowledge of God. Paul will have none of that. For him there was nothing partial about Jesus Christ. Jesus was the full revelation of God. "It pleased the Father," he writes, "that in Him should all fulness dwell" (*Colossians* 1: 19). He speaks of Christ "in whom are hid all the treasures of wisdom and knowledge" (*Colossians* 2: 3). And then he goes on to make the statement beyond which no statement about Jesus Christ can go: "In Him dwelleth all the fulness of the Godhead bodily" (*Colossians* 2: 9).

It is not so much that Jesus came to bring the full revelation of God. It is not that He came to write a book, or to give a course of sermons or lectures on what God is like. Rather He came to *be* the full revelation of God. It is not as if Paul said: "Listen to Jesus Christ, and you will learn what God is like." It is as if he said: "Look at Jesus Christ, and you will see what God is." That seeking for sinners, that care for sufferers, that feeding of the hungry, that comforting of the sorrowing, that sacrificial love for men is a demonstration in time of the eternal attitude of God to men.

But it would not be enough simply to show men what God was like. That in itself might even be a torturing and haunting thing. It might be like allowing a man a glimpse of some warmth and splendour into which he himself could never enter. It might simply be to tantalise a man with a vision of beauty which could never be anything other than something seen at a great distance. As Paul saw it, Jesus Christ came to open the way to God for men, to give men access to God.

Paul speaks of the access we have to grace through

Jesus Christ. He speaks of those who were far off being brought near (*Ephesians* 2: 13). He says that through Him we have access unto the Father (*Ephesians* 2: 18; 3: 12). The word which Paul uses for *access* is of supreme interest. It is the noun *prosagōgē*, which is connected with the verb *prosagein*. In the Greek version of the Old Testament, *prosagein* is the word which is used of bringing men to God that they may be ordained as priests for His service (*Exodus* 29: 4).

Even the heathen world would see the greatness of the meaning of this word. The main form of Greek religion in the time of Paul was the Mystery Religions. They were like passion plays; and the worshipper was only allowed to attend them after a long course of instruction and training and discipline had prepared him to become an initiate. When he was so prepared, it was the duty of an official called a *mustagōgos* to bring him in, and the word for bringing in such an initiate is *prosagein*.

It is perhaps even more suggestive that this word had a use which was connected specially with the court of kings. *Prosagein* is the regular word for introducing a person into the presence of a king. Xenophon tells for instance how Astyages the king had a trusted official called Sacas, who was his cup-bearer, and who had the responsibility of introducing (*prosagein*) to the king those whom he thought to have a right to that privilege, and of keeping out those whom he did not think fit for it. There was in fact at the Persian court a court official whose title in Greek was *prosagōgeus*, the introducer, the person who was responsible for ushering others into the presence of the king. So then, to Paul, Jesus was the person who was able and willing to introduce men into the presence of God.

Behind that thought of Jesus Christ as the introducer into the presence of God there were in Paul's mind two thoughts. The first is that men by their sin had erected a barrier between themselves and God, and Jesus removed that barrier and opened the way. We must leave the fuller discussion of that until later. But Paul would have agreed with all his heart that the love of Christ had broken every barrier down.

But in Paul's mind there was certainly another idea. We have already said that Jesus Christ came into this world to show men what God is. The fact is that until Jesus came into the world men had a wrong idea of God. They thought of God as the task-master, the lawgiver, the judge. They thought of God as that awful purity before whom every man is in default, and from whom every man can expect nothing but condemnation. They thought of God as that inexorable justice, which was bound to utter sentence of condemnation. They thought of God as the implacable hunter bent on the destruction of the sinner. Clearly men who held that idea would have but one idea—not to approach God, but to flee from His presence and to escape from His wrath, an obviously impossible task.

But the coming of Jesus Christ showed God in an entirely new light. His life of service and His death of love gave men a completely new idea of God. It showed God to men as the lover of the souls of men. It showed

God as seeking love. It showed God as the God whose one desire is to forgive and to gather men to Himself in fatherly love. It banished the fear of approaching God from the hearts of men. It opened a way to God for men whose one desire and instinct had been to flee from God. Apart from Jesus Christ men never could have known the love of God. And that new revelation, and that new discovery opened a door of access to God, for it made men able to cast themselves on the love of God instead of fleeing for ever from the wrath of God.

In the course of his writings Paul uses six great metaphors to describe the work of Jesus Christ. He takes six great pictures from ordinary life everyday to show to men what Jesus Christ has done. These pictures would be very vivid to those who heard them for the first time, for they came from spheres which they all knew and understood; and they are still capable of becoming real for us to-day.

The first great metaphor is *the metaphor from the law courts*, the metaphor of *justification*. Christianity, like Judaism before it, is essentially an ethical religion. That is to say, Christianity insists that a man should live a certain kind of life and be a certain kind of person. It is God's will and God's commandment that he should do and be so. An ethical religion must always have sanctions. That is to say, there must be a difference between what happens in eternity to the man who has fulfilled the ethical demand of his religion and the man who has not. To put that in another way, it means that there must be judgment. Some day man must stand his trial before God; he must appear before God's judgment seat; he must give account for the things done in his body (*Romans* 14: 10, 12). If that be so, every man must stand in default, for no human being can possibly fulfil the demands of the perfection of God.

It is just here that justification comes in. Justification pictures a man on trial before God. Paul says: " Being justified by faith, we have peace with God through our Lord Jesus Christ " (*Romans* 5: 1). He says that it is true that we have all sinned, but we are justified freely through His grace (*Romans* 3: 24). We are justified by faith (*Romans* 3: 28). God, says Paul in a magnificent phrase, justifies the ungodly (*Romans* 4: 5).

In the New Testament, especially in Paul, the verb *to justify*, when it is used of God, has a very different sense from that which it has in English. In English to justify a person means to produce reasons why he was right, to bring forward arguments which prove, or attempt to prove, that he was perfectly correct, to act as he did. If I justify myself, using the word in its English sense, it means that I seek to produce reasons in defence of any action that I have taken. But that is not at all what the word means in the New Testament. In Greek the word for *to justify* is *dikaioun*. Greek verbs which end in *-oun* do not mean to make a person something; they mean to treat, to reckon, to account a man as being something. And when Paul speaks of God justifying the sinner, he means that God, instead of punishing the sinner, instead of issuing penalty like a righteous but merciless judge, treats the sinner as if he had been a good man.

This is exactly what shocked the Jews to the very core of their being. For any judge to treat a bad man as if he was a good man was to the Jew the acme of injustice and wickedness. The Old Testament has it: " He that justifieth the wicked is an abomination to the Lord (*Proverbs* 17: 15). God says: " I will not justify the wicked " (*Exodus* 23: 7). In face of that Paul comes with the audacious and the tremendous paradox that God is characteristically the God who justifies the ungodly (*Romans* 4: 5).

The whole essence of the gospel which Paul came to preach is that God, in this astounding mercy, treats the sinner as if he had been a good man. Instead of smashing the sinner, He welcomes him with open arms. Instead of outpouring the mighty vials of His outraged holiness, He pours out the cleansing waters of His sacrificial love.

When the American Civil War was in progress, and when the South had rebelled against the North on the question of slavery, someone once asked Lincoln: " When this war is over, and when the South has been subdued and conquered, and has come back into the Union, how are you going to treat these rebellious southerners, what are you going to do to them? " Back came Lincoln's answer: "I am going to treat them as if they had never been away." That is precisely what Paul means by justification; he means that in that astonishing love, God treats men as if they had never been away.

We so often think of justification as a theological and even a remote, conception; but the perfect picture of justification lies in the Parable of the Prodigal Son. The son has planned to come back with his confession of sin against heaven and his father; and with his request to be made a hired servant. He is never allowed to make that request (*Luke* 15: 18, 19, 21). His father welcomes him back, not to the status of servant, but to the status of son, as if he had never been away.

A Sunday school teacher was once telling the story of the Prodigal Son to a class in a slum mission in Scotland. She told the story of the son's rebellion, of his terrible fate in the far country, of his resolution to come home. And she went on, " What do you think his father would do to him when he got home ? " From that class of slum children, who knew life at its toughest, back came the immediate answer: " Bash him ! " That is the natural answer; that is what anyone would expect; but that is the wrong answer, for the glory of God is that God justifies the ungodly. He treats the bad man as if he had been good.

Of course there is more to it than that; the process does not stop there; justification has to be followed by *sanctification*. The sinner who has been so freely received back has to go on to clothe himself with the lost holiness. But the first step in the process of salvation is the simple, yet utterly tremendous, fact that God justifies the ungodly, treats the rebellious as if he had never rebelled.

But, we must go on to ask, why justification *by faith*? What is the meaning of the words *by faith*? The answer to that lies in another question: How can we believe that God is like that? All our instincts would make us think of God as the judge, God dealing out strict and impartial justice, and of ourselves standing at the judgment seat of God as criminals condemned, and justly, for their misdeeds. How can we know that God is not like that, that in fact His one desire is to welcome the sinner home? We can only know that because Jesus told us so. We have to put our whole faith in the assumption that Jesus was right when He told us that God is like that. Faith is staking everything on the fact that God is like Jesus, that Jesus was right when He told of the God who welcomes sinners home. Faith is accepting Jesus at His word when He brings to men the offer of God.

That then is the first great metaphor which Paul uses to describe the work of Christ. It is the message that the just shall live by faith (*Galatians* 3: 11); that by works of the law shall no flesh be justified (*Galatians* 2: 16). It is the message that we receive a right relationship with God, not through our own efforts to achieve the hopeless task of pleasing God, but by accepting just as we are, the offer of His love. When Paul speaks of the man who is just, he means the man who is in a right relationship with God. That relationship cannot be won; it must be accepted in the certainty that God treats the bad man as if he had never been away.

Here is the metaphor from the law courts. It shows us man standing before God with the right to expect nothing but utter condemnation; and suddenly discovering through the message of Jesus Christ that God is not threatening him with austere justice but is offering him amazing love.

The highest thought of the Jewish Rabbis had faint

glimpses of this. One Rabbi heard God say: " Return as far as you can, and I will come to you the rest of the way." God is always ready to meet the sinner more than half-way. Another Rabbi said: " Beloved is repentance before God, for He cancels His own words for its sake."

Such is the love of God that He cancels the demands of His own justice upon men. That is what justification means. It means that the sinner is not a condemned criminal; he is a lost son, whom God will treat as if he had never been away, if he will only turn and come home.

The second of the great metaphors which Paul uses to describe the work of Christ is the *metaphor from friendship*. This picture is contained in the word *reconciliation*. The Greek verb for *to reconcile* is *katallassein*. It is not that Paul uses this metaphor very often, but, when he does use it, it is at the very heart of his gospel.

He speaks about us being enemies to God, and being reconciled by the death of His Son (*Romans* 5: 10). In *2 Corinthians* 5: 18, 20, there are three occurrences of this word and of this idea. God has reconciled us to Himself by Jesus Christ. God was in Christ reconciling the world unto Himself. And Paul's appeal is: " Be ye reconciled to God." In *Ephesians* Paul speaks of how God reconciled Jew and Gentile to each other, and both to God (*Ephesians* 2: 16). In *Colossians* he speaks of it being God's aim to reconcile all things unto Himself by Jesus Christ (*Colossians* 1: 20). " You," he says, " who were sometime alienated and enemies in your mind by wicked works, yet now hath He reconciled" (*Colossians* 1: 21).

The key to this idea is the restoration of a lost relationship. Because of man's sin and disobedience and rebelliousness the relationship which exists between man and God is a compound of estrangement, enmity and fear; but because of what Jesus Christ has done that grim relationship is replaced by a relationship of trusting love. It is the removal of the barriers, the substitution of a relationship of love for a relationship of fear, a relationship of intimacy for a relationship of distance.

One thing has to be noted, Paul never speaks of God being reconciled to men, but always of men being reconciled to God. The breach was not on God's side, but on man's side. It is as if God sent Jesus Christ into this world to live, to suffer and to die, as if to say: " I love you like that. Surely you cannot shut your heart to me and resist me any more."

This is the simplest of all the pictures. Reconciliation means bringing together again two people who have become estranged; and Jesus Christ brought man and God together again.

The third of Paul's metaphors is the *metaphor from slavery*. The ancient world was built on slavery. It may be that most of the Church's members were slaves or had been slaves, and this picture would be very real to them. It is the picture in the words *redemption*, and *purchase at a price*. This picture has two backgrounds which share equally in giving it its meaning.

It has a Hebrew background. In the Old Testament this idea of redemption (*lutrōsis*) is intimately bound up with the thought of the emancipation of the people from Egypt. To the Jews that liberation from their slavery in Egypt was the supreme event in their history, and the supreme intervention of God. " I will redeem you," said God, " with a stretched out arm " (*Exodus* 6: 6). " Thou in Thy mercy hast led forth Thy people whom Thou hast redeemed " (*Exodus* 15: 13). " The Lord hath redeemed you out of the house of bondmen " (*Deuteronomy* 7: 8). Again and again the text occurs in one form or another: " Thou shalt remember that thou wast a bondman in the land of Egypt and the Lord thy God redeemed thee " (*Deuteronomy* 15: 15; 16: 12).

Through this picture there throbs the joy of the slave set free. The Jews never forgot how God had interposed to liberate them from slavery in Egypt. This is the metaphor of liberty regained by the intervention of God.

But this picture has also a Greek background. It was possible in Greece for a slave with a great effort to purchase his own freedom. The method by which he did so was rather a lovely thing. The slave would decide to make the great effort. In the little spare time he had he would take any job that he could get in order to earn a few coppers. By the laws of slavery he could not keep even all the little that he did earn. His master was entitled to claim a percentage of it. The little he did keep the slave deposited in the temple of some god. The years passed by and the day came when the slave had accumulated enough to pay for the purchase price of his freedom. The slave then took his master to the temple, and the priest paid over the money to the master; the result was that the slave became the property of the god, and therefore free from all men.

It is that picture which is in Paul's mind when he says: " Ye are bought with a price" (1 *Corinthians* 6: 20). " Ye are bought with a price; be not ye the servants of men " (1 *Corinthians* 7: 23). The slave was free of all men because he had become the possession of the god who, it was held, had paid his price.

There is no doubt that that picture of the way in which a slave obtained his liberty by becoming the possession of a god was in Paul's mind; but it is clear that that metaphor is not to be overpressed. In that kind of liberation and emancipation the slave saved until he had amassed his own purchase price; in a sense he was his own liberator. Paul would not for a moment have held that we could pay our own purchase price. This is a good example of a Pauline metaphor which must be taken in its general idea, and not pressed overmuch in detail.

Whatever its background this picture of freedom, of emancipation, of liberty regained is much in Paul's mind. He writes to the Romans of the Christian being justified freely by God's grace, through the redemption that is through Jesus Christ (*Romans* 3: 24). To the Corinthians he writes that Jesus is made by God righteousness, and sanctification, and redemption (1 *Corinthians* 1: 30). To the Ephesians he writes of the Christian having redemption through the blood of Christ, and forgiveness of sins according to the riches of His grace (*Ephesians* 1: 7). To the Colossians he speaks of Jesus Christ in whom we have redemption through His blood, even the forgiveness of sins (*Colossians* 1: 14).

Here indeed is a metaphor and a picture which speaks to our condition. In so many cases, and so often, life is a slavery, bound in the chains of our own forging. For many of us it is true to say that the only reason why we are not better than we are is that we cannot make ourselves better. There are weaknesses within us that we cannot conquer. There are habits that we cannot break. There is a past which has us in its shackles. There are ingrained things which we cannot escape. We have incurred a condemnation from which there can be no acquittal that we could ever win.

Jesus Christ liberates us from ourselves. Eric Linklater called his autobiography *The Man Upon My Back*. For so many of us our greatest handicap is our own selves; and Jesus Christ gives us the strength and power to conquer ourselves.

Jesus Christ liberates us from frustration. Another way of putting that is that the tragedy of the human situation is that we know what is right, and we cannot do it. We have seen the dream and we cannot achieve it. We are haunted by the impossibilities of life. Jesus Christ gives us the power which makes the impossible possible.

Jesus Christ liberates us from fear. So many people live in a fear-haunted life; but Jesus offers us His continual presence in which fear must die, for with Him we can face and do anything.

Jesus Christ liberates us from sin. Through what He

has done the sin of the past is cancelled, and into life there comes a strength in which the temptations of the future can be conquered. Sin's penalty is removed and sin's power is broken by the work of Christ. Redemption is the metaphor of liberation from slavery. Jesus Christ is the great emancipator of all mankind.

There is one picture of the work of Jesus Christ which for Paul was very near the heart of things. It is the idea which the Authorized Version renders by the word *propitiation*. The central passage is in *Romans* 3: 25 where Paul speaks of Jesus, "whom God sent forth as a propitiation through faith in his blood." This is an idea which is at the very heart of Jewish religion and at the very centre of the experience of Paul. The word for *propitiation* is *hilastērion*, the precise meaning of which we shall have to go on to discuss. But first of all let us try to penetrate to the idea which lies behind it.

The word *hilastērion* is connected with the verb *hilaskesthai*, which in turn is connected with the adjective *hileōs*. We shall best get at its meaning if we start from the adjective. *Hileōs*, the adjective, means *gracious, well disposed to*. So, then, the verb *hilaskethai* means *to make*, or *to become, gracious to*. It means to make expiation for sin, and when it is used of God it means quite simply to forgive.

The basic idea is the turning of wrath into graciousness, the change from being hostile into being well-disposed to a person.

Behind this word there lies all the meaning of the whole institution of sacrifice. The basic idea of sacrifice is this

—there are certain things that a man must not do, for if he does them he invades the prerogatives of God; he transgresses the law of God; he rebels against God. Clearly, if a man is guilty of any such action, the relationship which should exist between him and God is broken and interrupted. The problem then is, how can that relationship be restored? That is where sacrifice comes in. Sacrifice is that which restores the lost and broken relationship between man and God. It is to be clearly remembered that in any real religion, and certainly in Jewish religion, it was not the sacrifice itself which restored the relationship; it was the penitence of which the sacrifice was a sign, a symbol, a guarantee and a proof.

The idea is quite simple. A man sins; a man realises what he has done; a man repents. But how can he guarantee and prove that that penitence is real and genuine? He can only do so by offering to God something precious in order to show how really and truly sorry he is. That is the true idea of sacrifice. The important thing is not the sacrifice itself; the important thing is the real penitence and sorrow of which the actual sacrifice is only the outward expression.

So, then, Paul says that Jesus is our *hilastērion*. What is the meaning of that word? If the word be taken as a noun, there are two suggestions. (*a*) It is suggested that *hilastērion* means *a sacrifice to expiate sin*. This would mean that Jesus is the sacrifice who expiates the sin of man. Nowhere in all Greek literature does *hilastērion* mean a sacrifice, nor is it possible that the word can mean sacrifice.

That is a meaning of the word which we shall have to discard.

(*b*) There is one thing which *hilastērion* can mean, if it is a noun, and which, in fact, it does regularly mean both in the Old and in the New Testament. All Greek nouns which end in *-ērion* mean *the place where something is done*. *Dikastērion* means the place where *dikē*, justice is done, and therefore a law court. *Thusiastērion* means the place where *thusia*, sacrifice is done, and therefore the altar. Therefore *hilastērion* can certainly mean the place where *hilasmos*, expiation, is done and made. Because of that, both in the Old and New Testament, *hilastērion* has a regular and a technical meaning. It always means the lid of gold above the ark which was known as *the mercy-seat*. In *Exodus* 25: 17 it is laid down of the furnishings of the tabernacle: " Thou shalt make a mercy-seat (*hilastērion*) of pure gold." In only one other place in the New Testament is the word used, in *Hebrews* 9: 5, and there the writer speaks of the cherubim who overshadow the mercy-seat. The word is used in that sense more than twenty times in the Greek Old Testament.

Now there were two special ideas attaching to the mercy-seat. The mercy-seat as we have seen was the golden lid of the ark which rested in the Holy of Holies. Into the Holy of Holies only the High Priest might enter, and there the High Priest, representing the people, held communion with God. It was God's promise: " I will meet with thee, and I will commune with thee from above the mercy seat" (*Exodus* 25: 22). God promised: " I will appear in the cloud above the mercy seat " (*Leviticus* 16: 2). The mercy-seat was above all the place where God and His people met.

But there was another ceremony connected with the mercy-seat. It was on the Day of Atonement that sacrifices were made which atoned for all the sins, known and unknown, of the people. And it was on the mercy-seat that the blood of the sacrifices was sprinkled (*Leviticus* 16: 14, 15). The result of that sacrifice and that sprinkling of blood was that the people would be cleansed from all their sins (*Leviticus* 16: 30). Therefore the mercy-seat was the place where the blood which atoned for sin was shed.

If then we take *hilastērion* to mean the mercy-seat, and, if we call Jesus our *hilastērion* in that sense, it will mean, so to speak, that Jesus is the place where man and God meet, and that specially He is the place where man's sin meets with the atoning love of God.

That is a tremendous thought. It is the thought that the death of Jesus Christ, the Cross is the trysting-place where God's justice and God's mercy meet. It means that on the Cross we see the mercy of God offering the sacrifice for the sin of man which His justice demands. That is one way of looking at what happened on the Cross.

There are in God two essential attributes. The first is His love; that love of God demands and insists that God must forgive. The second is His justice; that justice of God demands and insists that man's sin must be punished. Here is what in all reverence we may call the dilemma of God. God's love necessitates the forgiveness of sin; God's justice necessitates the punishment of sin. What can God do? The answer is that on the Cross, in Jesus Christ, God's love pays the penalty and bears the punishment which God's justice demands. On the Cross, in Jesus Christ, God's love and God's justice meet, in the one possible act which could satisfy both that justice and that love. Here, indeed, is a most moving thought on which the mind can feed and the heart can rest.

But there is another way to take this word *hilastērion*. It is possible, indeed it is more likely, that *hilastērion* is not a noun, but rather an adjective (*hilastēros*), which means *able to make expiation for sin*.

If we take it this way, and it is most likely the right way, in *Romans* 3: 25 what Paul is saying is that God set forth Jesus for all men to see, as the only person in all the universe who can bring man back to God, who can restore the lost relationship and, who can make expiation for sin. Cranmer translated *hilastērion* as the *obtainer of mercy;* the Geneva Version translated it as the *pacification.* Jesus is the one person able by His life and His death to bring man and God together again.

We are not bound to interpret this great fact in any one way. We may interpret it by saying that Jesus Christ paid the penalty which man's sins had made necessary. We may interpret it by saying that that infinite and tremendous demonstration of the love of God broke men's hearts and destroyed the last barrier. It does not matter how we interpret it, we are back at the truth which is for ever at the centre of the New Testament. It cost the life and death

of Christ, it cost the Cross, to restore the lost relationship
between God and man.

It was out of the experience of Paul that this idea was
born. Think of Paul's background. He was a Jew, and
as a Jew he had an intense awareness of the sheer holiness
of God. The sense of the holiness of God tortured him with
the sense of his own unworthiness, and of the barrier which
his sin had erected between himself and God. The religion
of his country and his nation believed that sacrifice could
remove that barrier. Paul knew that it could not, for he
had tried it and it had failed. Then, sudden on a moment,
he was confronted with Christ, and the barriers were down,
and Paul was at home with God at last. The enmity was
gone; the estrangement was destroyed; God was his
friend.

Paul, more than once, uses a picture taken from family
life to express what God in Jesus Christ did for men. It
is the picture of *adoption* (*huiothesia*). In *Romans* 8: 15 Paul
says that the Christian has received the spirit of adoption
which enables us to call God Father, and to approach God
as such. In *Romans* 8: 23 he describes the Christian and all
creation as waiting eagerly for the adoption. In *Romans*
9: 4 he speaks of the people of Israel as the adopted people
of God. In *Galatians* 4: 5 he says that God sent His Son
to redeem those who were under the law, that they might
receive adoption as sons. In *Ephesians* 1: 5 he says that
it was God's eternal purpose that the Christians should be
adopted as children through Jesus Christ.

It is clear that this is an idea which was much in the

mind of Paul, and that it was a picture which for him did represent what had happened to the Christian through the work of Jesus Christ.

The idea of adoption would paint an even more vivid picture to the people of the ancient world than it does to us to-day. Adoption was common in the ancient world. It was carried out for three main reasons—to ensure the continuation of the family and of the family name, to ensure that there was someone to whom the family estates might be passed down, and to ensure that the worship of the family and ancestral gods might go on uninterrupted.

The different sections of the ancient world had their different methods of adoption. Amongst the Jews adoption was not common, and there were no special legal ceremonies connected with it.

Amongst the Greeks the practice of adoption was much commoner and the process was more elaborate. Adoption could only be carried out by persons capable of making a will, that is by men; both parties must be of sound mind; there must be no undue influence; before a man could adopt a son, he must have no legitimate son; that is, he could not adopt a son over the head of an already existing legitimate son. The party to be adopted must be a Greek citizen; if he was of age, his own consent was necessary; if he was a minor, his guardian's consent was necessary; neither the adopter nor the adopted must be guilty of anything which affected his citizenship or his legal status. For instance, a person who for any reason was disfranchised could neither adopt nor be adopted.

The method of adoption was simplicity itself. The Greeks were divided into *phratriai*, which were practically clans, and into *demes* for administrative purposes. And the ceremony of adoption was simply a religious and civil ceremony of adoption into the new clan and enrolment into the new *deme*.

The result of the adoption was that the adopted person lost all rights in his old family and gained all rights in his new family. Even if legitimate children were afterwards born, he inherited fully and without question along with them.

But that which is really in Paul's mind is Roman adoption. There was no more dramatic and far-reaching legal ceremony in any law than Roman adoption. The seriousness and the finality of Roman adoption was due to the fact of the Roman *patria potestas*, the law of the father's power. Under Roman law a Roman father had absolute power over his children. He could sell the child and he could enslave the child. That right even extended to the right of life and death. A Roman father was legally entitled to execute his own child. Under Roman law a son could not himself possess anything, or inherit anything. Anything left to him passed at once into his father's power. Still further, under Roman law so long as his father was alive a son never came of age. He might be a man of very senior years; he might have reached high and noble and honoured office in the state, but so long as his father was alive, he remained entirely in his father's power. Dion Cassius, the Greek historian, describes the situation: " The law of the Romans gives a father absolute authority over his son, and that for the son's whole life. It gives him authority, if he so chooses, to imprison him, to scourge him, to make him work on his estate as a slave in fetters, even to kill him. The right still continues to exist even if the son is old enough to play an active part in political affairs, even if he has been judged worthy to occupy the magistrate's office, and even if he is held in honour by all men."

In Rome there were two main methods of adoption depending on whether the person to be adopted was of age or not. If the person was of age, that is to say, if his father was not alive, the process was called *Adrogatio*. The person to be adopted had to appear before the *Comitia Curiata*, which was the most solemn of all Roman Courts. It was presided over by the *Pontifex Maximus*, the High Priest, and had charge of the ordination of magistrates, the administration of wills, and this kind of adoption.

The adoption was in two stages. First, there came the *Detestatio Sacrorum:* this meant that the man to be adopted had in public to forswear his own family and ancestral gods and to accept as his gods the gods of the family into which he was being adopted. It was a public denial of the old gods, and a public acceptance of the new gods.

Second, there followed a process called *Rogatio* in which a full legal bill embodying the adoption was presented before the *Comitia Curiata* and was voted on in the usual way. Obviously all this was a most elaborate and impressive ceremony, representing and ratifying a step than which none could be more serious.

If the person to be adopted was under the legal age the ceremony was equally dramatic. The child had to pass from one *patria potestas* to another. It was carried out by a symbolic sale; the process was called *mancipatio*. Scales and copper weights were used. Twice the father sold his son, and twice he bought him back again. Then he sold him for a third and last time, and the sale was complete. After that, the three parties, the adopted son, his father, and the adopter, all appeared before the Roman magistrate called the *praetor*, and a symbolic lawsuit was carried out, in which the legal claim for the son to be brought into the new *patria potestas* was fully argued, and only when that case was settled was adoption complete.

It can be seen that under Roman law adoption was not an easy affair; it was regarded as the most decisive of steps; it could only be taken after the most searching and dramatic ceremonies had been gone through; and once undertaken, it was finally settled once and for all.

The consequences of Roman adoption were far-reaching. The adopted son completely lost all rights in his old family and completely gained all rights in his new family. In the most literal sense he gained a new father. He became as fully heir to his new father's estate as any normal son. According to the law all the debts and the obligations of his former life were cancelled. He was a new person entering upon a new life. If the adopted person had children of his own, as he well might have, these children also became the children of the adopting father. The family was affected by the adoption just as much as the father was.

In Roman law the adopted person became in the most literal sense the child of the adopting father. How literal this sense was can be seen from the following case. Claudius, the Roman Emperor, adopted Nero, so that Nero could succeed him as Emperor. Nero was no relation. Claudius already had a daughter called Octavia. It was thought that Nero's succession would be still further assured if he married Octavia. Nero and Octavia were not in any way blood relations, but in the eyes of the Roman law they were literally brother and sister because Claudius had adopted Nero; and the Roman senate had to pass a special bill before Nero could marry the girl, who was no relation to him, and who was yet in the eyes of the law his full sister.

It was of all this that Paul was thinking when he spoke of the adoption of the Christian into the family of God. The Christian received a new father—even God. The Christian's family were included with him; the promise was to his children also. All his past life was cancelled and there was given to him a new beginning and a new start, clean from the cancelled sins of the past. He became a full inheritor of the grace and the wealth of the riches of God. He became the kinsman of all the saints of God.

There is one more tremendous fact which is implied in this picture of adoption. So long as we think of religion in terms of law, and of the Christian as being under obligation to satisfy the law of God, then the relationship of the Christian to God is always that of slave to master, and of criminal to judge, and must always be a relationship compounded of distance and fear. But no sooner do we bring this idea of adoption into the picture at all than the relationship becomes a family relationship. By the very word adoption, God becomes Father, and we become child; and the very essence of religion becomes not a struggle to keep an impossible law, but the joy of entry, all undeserved, into the family of God.

IX

THE DEATH OF CHRIST

WE HAVE been looking at the great pictures which Paul used to express the work of Jesus Christ; now we must turn our thoughts to the most important of all parts of Paul's thought. We must ask, for what did the death of Jesus Christ stand in Paul's mind? Where does the Cross stand in Paul's scheme of things?

One thing is certain—for Paul the Cross stood at the centre of the Christian faith. Paul's unbroken insistence is on the essential centrality of the Cross. He writes to the Corinthians: " We preach Christ crucified " (1 *Corinthians* 1: 23). He writes: " I determined not to know any thing among you, save Jesus Christ, and Him crucified " (1 *Corinthians* 2: 2). He writes to the Galatians: " God forbid that I should glory, save in the Cross of our Lord Jesus Christ " (*Galatians* 6: 14). There is no need to seek to prove that for Paul the Cross of Christ stood in the centre of the universe.

It is further clear that to Paul the Cross of Christ had a certain self-evidencing power. The Cross contained its own appeal. To seek to decorate it with fine words was simply to obscure it. To Paul the Cross was something to be shown to men in all its stark simplicity. He will not preach with wisdom of words lest the Cross of Christ should be made of none effect (1 *Corinthians* 1: 17). He did not come with excellency of speech or wisdom (1 *Corinthians* 2: 1). He cannot understand how the Galatians could have slipped back when Christ had been placarded before their eyes (*Galatians* 3: 1).

Paul would have said that first and foremost the Cross is not something to be argued about, but something to be shown to men. He had the conviction that the Cross has a persuasive power of its own, that the story of the Cross simply told will break the barriers down, that the first task of the Christian preacher is without adornment to show to the world the Man upon the Cross. For that very reason it is all the more incumbent upon us to try to see what Paul saw in the death of Jesus Christ.

We may well begin with something about which there can be no possible dispute. Paul was quite certain that Jesus Christ died on behalf of men. We must be careful to get this phrase right. The preposition in the Greek is always *huper* which means *on behalf of*. The preposition is not *anti*, which would mean *instead of*. The Authorized Version usually translates it simply *for men*. We may very well find in the end that there is an element in Paul's thought that Jesus died in place of man, but the fundamental, basic essential thought is that Jesus died on the Cross on behalf of men. He writes to the Thessalonians of the Lord Jesus Christ who died for us (1 *Thessalonians* 5: 10). He pleads for consideration for the weaker brother for whom Christ died (1 *Corinthians* 8: 11). He talks of the brother for whom Christ died (*Romans* 14: 15). He talks about Jesus Christ who loved the Church and gave Himself for the Church (*Ephesians* 5: 25). We may well begin with the simple and basic fact that Jesus Christ died on behalf of us, that His death achieved something for us that by ourselves we could never have achieved.

We may now go on to try to define more fully what this phrase *on behalf of* means and implies. Paul is clear that it was that death of Jesus Christ which achieved *reconciliation* between man and God. It is by the Cross and through the Cross that the relationship which should exist between man and God is restored. The gulf is bridged; the estrangement is healed; the enmity is taken away. He talks of us being reconciled to God by the death of His Son (*Romans* 5: 10). He speaks of men being brought nigh by the blood of Christ (*Ephesians* 2: 13). He speaks about God making peace by the blood of the Cross (*Colossians* 1: 20). The death of Christ is that which achieved the reconciliation of man to God, that which restored the lost relationship of intimacy and of love.

We may pause to note that this in itself does not imply or necessitate a substitutionary, or even in the narrower sense, a sacrificial view of the death of Jesus Christ. Taken by itself, apart from the other great sayings of Paul, it might be interpreted to mean that the death of Christ gave men such an utterly compelling demonstration of the love of God that man is compelled to cease to see God as the

law-giver, the taskmaster and the judge, and is compelled
to begin to see Him as the lover of the souls of men. It
might be interpreted to mean that the Cross says to men as
nothing else in the world does: God loves you like that,
and that that discovery of the love of God was exactly the
fact which produced this reconciliation which gave men
peace with God. There is indeed no possible doubt that
that is part of Paul's thought. " The love of Christ con-
straineth us," he said (2 *Corinthians* 5: 14). There is no
doubt that Paul did see in the Cross a demonstration of that
incredible and amazing love, the sight of which could
break the hearts of men. But it would not be a fair reflection
of the thought of Paul to leave the matter there.

The thought of the Cross, the death of Jesus Christ, and
the idea of *redemption* are inextricably connected in the mind
of Paul. That emerges in a phrase so simple as: " The
Saviour, the Lord Jesus Christ " (*Philippians* 3: 20). The
very use of the word *Saviour* makes it clear that there was
something from which man had to be saved and that that
salvation was wrought by the life and death of Jesus Christ.
In *Galatians* 4: 5 Paul says quite plainly: " God sent
forth His Son . . . to redeem them that were under the
law." In such a phrase there must be two intertwined
ideas. (*a*) God sent His Son to rescue men from their
bondage to the law, to lead them away from that legalistic
outlook which could result in nothing but estrangement
from Himself, to show them that the dominant force in
life must be, not law, but love. (*b*) God sent His Son to
save men from the penalties which under law they had

incurred. If there is a moral law in this world, breach of that law must involve penalty; and God sent His Son to rescue men from the situation into which their sinning had brought them.

In *Ephesians* 1: 7 Paul puts the two things together, as if they were parallel. " In Jesus Christ we have redemption through His blood, the forgiveness of sins." The redemption is redemption from punishment which man has merited and deserved into a forgiveness and grace which he has not merited and which he has not deserved. The sentence is repeated word for word in *Colossians* 1: 14. This redemption, liberation, emancipation, this gaining of freedom is something which has to be achieved by the paying of a price. It was the death of Jesus Christ which achieved this freedom; and it did so in a double way; it achieved present liberation and the blotting out of the handwriting which the sins of the past had produced against us (*Colossians* 2: 14).

We must now approach the crucial essence of the matter. Over and over again Paul connects the death of Christ with *sin*. In this matter there are no hints and implications; the connection is definitely and bluntly made. The very first item of the belief which Paul received was that " Christ died for our sins according to the scriptures " (1 *Corinthians* 15: 3). He writes to the Galatians, at the very beginning of the letter, of Christ who gave himself for our sins (*Galatians* 1: 4). He writes to the Romans of Jesus our Lord who was delivered for our offences (*Romans* 4: 25). He says that in due time Christ died for the ungodly

(*Romans* 5: 6). He says that while we were yet sinners Christ died for us (*Romans* 5: 8).

To Paul there was the clearest possible connection between the death of Jesus Christ and the sin of man. It was not only that the sin of man procured the death of Jesus Christ, although that was true; it was that the death of Christ did something to, and for, the sin of man.

It is necessary that we should pause here for a moment and gather up the materials as far as we have gone. We saw that for Paul the Cross has a strange self-evidencing power and that for him preaching consisted not in arguing about the Cross but in confronting men with the Cross. We saw that put in its very simplest form, Paul believed that Christ died on behalf of men. We saw that the great, basic work which Christ did on behalf of men was to reconcile them to God, that somehow His life, and especially His death, were effective in restoring the lost relationship between men and God. We saw that for Paul the death of Christ and the redemption, the liberation, the emancipation of men from the power and the penalty of sin are inextricably connected. Finally we saw that the death of Christ and the sin of man are bound up together; and we saw that it is not simply the sin of man which caused the death of Christ, but that the death of Christ did something to and for the sin of man.

There remains only one step to take, and in Pauline thought we must take it. Paul thought of the death of Jesus Christ in terms of *sacrifice*. In *Galatians* 2: 20 he speaks of: " The Son of God, who loved me, and gave

Himself for me." In *Ephesians* 5: 2 he uses the actual word, for there he speaks of Christ, " who loved us, and who gave Himself for us an offering and a sacrifice to God." Can we penetrate even more deeply into the meaning which Paul poured into this idea?

There is one sentence in Paul's writings which may well give us the key and the clue to the whole of Paul's thought. In 1 *Corinthians* 5: 7 Paul says: " Christ our Passover is sacrificed for us." What are we to read into, and to understand, by that phrase? There are two possibilities.

The first is to take this phrase in a quite general way. The Passover was pre-eminently the feast which commemorated the deliverance of the people of Israel from bondage in the land of Egypt. The Passover Feast was designed to make it certain that the people of Israel would never forget that deliverance wrought for them by the hand of God. The phrase could therefore mean quite generally that the death of Jesus Christ is a sacrifice which has the effect of delivering men from the bondage to sin in which they are held. Truly that is a great and a true thought; but it may well be that in this phrase there is something more vivid and definite than that.

The essence of the Passover story lies in the name itself. The ancient story tells how the people of Israel were instructed to smear the lintels of their door with the blood of the lamb that had been slain; and when the angel, who had been sent to destroy the first-born son of every Egyptian home, saw that smear of blood, he would *pass over* that house (*Exodus* 12: 22, 23). In later days, when they were asked the meaning of this feast, they were to say: " It is the sacrifice of the Lord's Passover, who passed over the houses of the children of Israel in Egypt when He smote the Egyptians, and delivered our houses " (*Exodus* 12: 27). The essence of the Passover Feast, enshrined for ever in its very name, is the undying memory that the blood of the Passover lamb saved the inmates of the house from the visitation of death.

It is surely that idea that is in the mind of Paul. The death of Jesus Christ was that which saved men from the death in which their sins had involved them. If that is so —and we believe that for Paul it was so—then the death of Jesus Christ is in the most real sense a sacrifice for men, a sacrifice which saved them from the death of the soul which they had merited and deserved.

Paul makes two further statements which underline and stress that idea. They are sayings which emphasise the cost of salvation to Jesus Christ. In *Galatians* 3: 13 he writes: " Christ hath redeemed us from the curse of the law, being made a curse for us: for it is written, Cursed is every one that hangeth on a tree." In 2 *Corinthians* 5: 21 he writes: " For He hath made Him to be sin for us, who knew no sin; that we might be made the righteousness of God in Him." It is not possible to take these sayings as having any other meaning as Paul saw it, than that what ought to have happened to us did happen to Jesus Christ, and that He bore the suffering and the shame which we rightly should have borne.

In any Jewish sin-offering, before the animal was

sacrificed, the Jewish worshipper placed his hands on the victim's head and pressed on them, and then with penitence confessed his sin. The idea was that in some sense his sins were transferred to the animal, and the animal was a substitute for himself. Paul knew about all this. Without a doubt he must often have done all this; and at the end of it he was as far from God, and as estranged from Him as ever. But the moment Christ came into his life, and the moment he was confronted with the Cross of Christ, then the barriers were removed, the estrangement was gone, the sense of separating guilt was taken away. For Paul Jesus Christ did that which all the sacrifices of Jewish ritual had failed to do; and, therefore, Paul saw in the death of Jesus Christ the supreme and the only availing sacrifice for the sin of men—and for his own sin.

One of the most famous passages in *The Pilgrim's Progress* is the passage where John Bunyan tells how Christian lost his burden: " Now I saw in my dream that the highway up which Christian was to go was fenced on either side with a wall, and that wall was called Salvation. Up this way, therefore, did burdened Christian run, but not without great difficulty, because of the burden on his back. He ran thus till he came to a place somewhat ascending, and upon that place stood a cross, and a little below, in the bottom, a sepulchre. So I saw in my dream, that just as Christian came up with the cross, his burden loosed from off his shoulders, and fell from off his back, and began to tumble, and so continued to do, till it came to the mouth of the sepulchre, where it fell in, and I saw it no more." For

Bunyan, as for Paul, the Cross removed for ever the burden of sin.

We can now go back and read all Paul's pictures in the light of the sacrifice of the Cross.

There is *Justification*, the picture from the law courts. God treats the sinner as if he had been a good man, and welcomes him as if he had never been away. But the fact remains that sin must have its punishment; if God is to be true to Himself, sin cannot be dismissed as something which does not matter, or there arises moral chaos; therefore, someone must have paid the penalty which was due; and that someone was Jesus Christ. We are, as Paul put it, justified by His blood (*Romans* 5: 9).

There is *Reconciliation*, the picture from friendship. But the fact remains that no one can draw near to the holiness of God, unless he has clean hands and a pure heart, for God in His very nature is of purer eyes than to behold iniquity. Someone must supply the merits which are necessary for that approach; and that someone is Jesus Christ.

There is *Redemption*, *Emancipation*, the picture from slavery. It is true that man is delivered from the bondage of sin, but no man, in a world of slavery, ever received his freedom unless he paid the price, or unless some generous-hearted soul paid it for him, when he could not pay it for himself. Man's emancipation had its cost; man's freedom had its price; someone had to pay that cost and that price and that someone was Jesus Christ.

There is *Adoption*, the picture from the family. The whole of the adoption ceremony in Roman law centred on the moment when the adopted person passed from one *patria potestas* to another, the moment when he received a new father. But again that ceremony centred in a symbolic sale; someone had to pay the price, and that someone was Jesus Christ.

There is *Propitiation*, the picture from sacrifice. According to Jewish religion, for every sin there was the necessary sacrifice which was the sign and the guarantee of the true penitence of the man who brought it. But Paul's experience was that there was no such thing as a human sacrifice of any animal, however costly, which removed the feeling of guilt and atoned for sin. Such a sacrifice had to be found, if man was ever to be at peace with God; and on His Cross Jesus Christ made and paid that sacrifice.

There is one last picture which Paul uses. It is a picture which is seldom talked about nowadays; but in view of all that we have said it is very close to the heart of Paul. It is the metaphor from the world of *accounting*. It is in the word *logizesthai*, which the Authorized Version translates *to count* or *to impute* or *to reckon* (*Romans* 4: 3, 5, 6, 8, 9, 10, 11). The word *logizesthai* means *to set down to someone's account*. It can be used equally of setting down to a man's debit or to a man's credit.

Paul's ideas is that there is not a man in all the world who has not a vast debit balance in his account with God; he is in God's debt to an extent that he can never pay. But, in the mercy of God, his debt is cancelled and the merits of Jesus are credited to him, and he is clothed with a righteousness which is not his own. To take a very distant analogy—we are sometimes allowed entry into a group of a society or a house, not because of any qualifications of our own, but because of the qualifications of the friend who introduces us. So we are welcomed into the presence of God, not because of anything we are, or can bring, or can do, but because of the merits of Jesus Christ who introduces us into the presence and the family of God.

Paul saw in the death of Jesus Christ an action of God Himself, by which God made it possible for the sinner to come home to Him, and possible for Himself to accept that sinner when he came.

X

THE RISEN CHRIST

TO ANYONE who reads the Book of Acts with even the most cursory attention it is immediately clear that the early Church was characteristically and specifically the Church of the Risen Christ. At that stage the attention of the Church was focused on the Resurrection even more than it was upon the Cross.

There was a reason for that. At that time the Church was still mainly Jewish. Because of that, men were still thinking of Jesus in terms of Jewish Messiahship; and the one thing which was the final guarantee that Jesus was the Messiah was the fact that He had risen from the dead. It was inevitable and right that at that stage the attention of men should be fixed upon the Resurrection.

It is true that in the writings and the thought of Paul the emphasis to some degree changes. It is true that Paul's emphasis is on the Cross, and on the atoning and sacrificial death of Jesus Christ. But to the end of the day it remains true that for Paul, as for the early Church as a whole, the Resurrection was central to the Christian faith.

When we read the Synoptic Gospels and hear the actual

words of Jesus, we find that Jesus never foretold His death without foretelling His rising again. He never thought of the shame without the triumph. The humiliation and the glory were integrally and inseparably connected. The one could not exist without the other. It is Jesus' first announcement of His death to His disciples that, " The Son of Man must suffer many things, and be rejected of the elders, and of the chief priests, and scribes, and be killed, and after three days rise again " (*Mark* 8: 31; cp. *Mark* 9: 31). To Jesus the Cross and the Resurrection were part of the same process and He could never speak of the Cross without speaking of the triumph which lay beyond it.

It was the same with Paul. He speaks of Jesus Christ " who was delivered for our offences and raised again for our justification " (*Romans* 4: 25). He says that though Jesus Christ "was crucified through weakness, yet He liveth by the power of God " (2 *Corinthians* 13: 4). In the great *Philippians* passage (*Philippians* 2: 5-11) the humiliation of Jesus Christ is set out in all its stark terribleness, but the passage comes to its triumphant conclusion, " wherefore God also hath highly exalted Him." Paul was like his Master; he could never speak of the agony and the shame of the Cross without his thoughts going beyond it to the triumph and the splendour of the Resurrection.

How central the thought of the Resurrection was to Paul may be seen from the fact that he mentions it specifically in every letter except 2 *Thessalonians* and *Philemon;* and even in those two letters, although the fact of the Resurrection is not definitely stated, the thought of the Risen Christ still permeates all things.

He writes to the Romans: " Like as Christ was raised from the dead by the glory of the Father, even so we also should walk in newness of life " (*Romans* 6: 4; cp. 7: 4). To the Corinthians he writes: " God hath both raised up the Lord, and will raise up us by His own power " (1 *Corinthians* 6: 14; cp. 2 *Corinthians* 13: 4). His very first words to the Galatians are of " Jesus Christ, and God the Father, who raised Him from the dead " (*Galatians* 1: 1). To the Philippians he writes that God " has highly exalted Him, and given Him a name which is above every name " (*Philippians* 2: 9). To the Ephesians he writes of the power of God " which He wrought in Christ, when He raised Him from the dead " (*Ephesians* 1: 20). To the Colossians he writes of " God, who has raised Christ from the dead " (*Colossians* 2: 12). Paul could not think of Jesus Christ without thinking of Him as the Saviour who died and the Lord who rose again.

This is very important, for from Paul we learn that the fact of the Resurrection was an essential part of the teaching of the early Church. It is to be remembered that the writings of Paul take us back to a time before the writing of the gospels. It is most probably true to say that none of the gospels, as we know them, had come into being before the last of Paul's letters was written. Certainly, if they were in existence, they were not widespread and universally accepted documents of the Christian faith. But there was in existence a body of oral tradition. In an age

in which books were few and hand-written and printing
had not yet been invented, it was in fact by oral tradition
that truth and history were commonly handed down. Very
early this oral tradition was stereotyped and crystallized.
It was the basis of instruction for those who were entering
the Church for the first time; it was the essential raw
material of all the teaching and the preaching of the Church;
and certainly it was the concentrated essence of the teaching
of the first missionaries wherever they went. An essential
element in that first universal tradition was the story and
the facts of the Resurrection.

In 1 *Corinthians* 15 Paul has his fullest teaching about the
Resurrection. He begins with the facts of the Resurrection,
and his first word is: " I delivered unto you first of all
that which I also received " (1 *Corinthians* 15: 3). When He
told the story of the Resurrection, He passed on the standard
teaching of the Church. This is important, for it means
that the story of the Resurrection is not a late and a
legendary development and embroidery of the Christian
story, but that it was embodied in it from the very first
moment of the Christian Church.

But to the evidence of the tradition of the Church, Paul
has something to add—the evidence of his own experience.
He gives his list of the Resurrection appearances of Jesus,
and then he says: " And last of all He was seen by me also,
as of one born out of due time " (1 *Corinthians* 15: 8). For
Paul the Resurrection was not a story which he had to
accept at second hand and on the evidence of someone else.
It was something which he had experienced, something of

which he could give an eye-witness account, something
for which his evidence was independent and at first
hand.

There can have been no time when the Church did not
possess something in the nature of a creed, however bare
and summary that brief statement of the faith must have
been. The Church existed in the midst of a pagan society,
and it must always have been able briefly and succinctly
to tell that pagan society where it stood. In a Church into
which converts from heathenism were pouring in a constant
flood, it must always have been necessary to have some
brief statement of the faith, which converts on baptism
could publicly confess. We learn from Paul that the fact
of the Resurrection was an absolutely essential part of that
first creed, and of that earliest public confession. In *Romans*
10: 9 we read: " If thou shalt confess with thy mouth the
Lord Jesus, and shalt believe in thine heart that God
hath raised Him from the dead, thou shalt be saved."
Clearly that sentence is an extract or an echo from the
confession of faith and creed of the early Church, an echo
of the simple statement on which the early Christians
took their stand. We can therefore clearly see that the
Resurrection is not only an integral part of early Church
tradition, but that it was also an essential part of the first
creed, and an essential element in the first confession of
faith. It is true to say that the Church itself, and the faith
of each individual Christian within it, is founded on belief
in the Risen Christ. This is not a late development which
was added to the Church's faith, it is there from the very

beginning. It was in fact the foundation stone of the Church's faith.

Before we begin to see more of what the Resurrection meant to Paul, we must note one basic act. For Paul in the plainest and most literal sense, the Resurrection was an act of God. It is true that sometimes Paul does say that Jesus rose from the dead; but far oftener he says that God raised Jesus from the dead. For Paul the Resurrection is the product of the power of God, the act of the hand of God. He speaks of God who raised up Jesus our Lord from the dead (*Romans* 4: 24). He says that God has raised up the Lord (1 *Corinthians* 6: 14). When Paul speaks of the Resurrection, his characteristic way of speaking of it is as an act of God. The Resurrection was in fact the complete and final and unanswerable demonstration of the indestructible and undefeatable power of God.

There was one mistake into which the early Church was never in any danger of falling. In those early days men never thought of Jesus Christ as a figure in a book. They never thought of Him as someone who had lived and died, and whose story was told and passed down in history, as the story of someone who had lived and whose life had ended. They did not think of Him as someone who had been but as someone who is. They did not think of Jesus Christ as someone whose teaching must be discussed and debated and argued about; they thought of Him as someone whose presence could be enjoyed and whose constant fellowship could be experienced. Their faith was not founded on a book; their faith was founded on a person.

The whole aim of Paul and early Church was not to tell men about Jesus Christ, but to introduce them to Jesus Christ, and His presence and His power. In the early days—as it should be now—Christianity was not argument about a dead person, however great; it was encounter with a living presence.

We must now go on to see something of what that fact of the Resurrection meant to Paul.

The Resurrection was to Paul the final proof that Jesus was the Messiah. In one case he quite definitely says that. In *Romans* 1: 4 he speaks of Jesus Christ " declared to be the Son of God with power . . . by the resurrection from the dead."

It was inevitable that the Jews should think of Jesus in terms of Messiahship. Always they had been waiting for the Messiah of God. Inevitably they had thought of the Messiah in terms of glory, of conquest, and of power. But in Jesus they were confronted with a Messiah who had died upon a Cross. Something tremendous was needed to convince them that this man, who contradicted all the accepted ideas of Messiahship was indeed the chosen one of God. That one convincing fact was the Resurrection, for the Resurrection was a triumph and a glory beyond any triumph of which men had ever dreamed.

It may be wondered why Paul does not make more of this idea. When he does state it, he states it very definitely; but he does not turn to it very often. The reason is that, for the most part, Paul was dealing with Gentiles in his letters, and this idea was an idea which was more relevant

The Mind of St Paul

to a Jew than to a Gentile. But we do know that, when Paul preached to Jews, he did use this idea as a main part of his preaching. We have in *Acts* 13: 14-43 Luke's account of a sermon of Paul in the Synagogue at Antioch in Pisidia; and in that sermon Paul does seek to convince the Jews of the Messiahship of Jesus by the fact of the Resurrection. To a Jew the fact of the Resurrection was the proof that, in spite of the way in which the Cross contradicted the accepted idea of Messiahship, Jesus really and truly was The Anointed One of God.

The idea of the Risen Christ as the perfect High Priest is an idea which is characteristic of the Letter to the Hebrews. But once at least Paul uses that idea. In *Romans* 8: 27 he speaks of the Risen Christ making intercession for the saints according to the will of God; and in *Romans* 8: 34 he speaks of Christ being at the right hand of God, and also making intercession for us. Paul saw in the Risen Christ the one who even in the heavenly places is still pleading the cause of men, and still opening the door to the presence of God for men.

The word priest has gained at least in some minds a meaning which it ought never to have had. To some minds the word priest suggests a person who shuts men off from God, who bars the way to God, who with his ritual and his claims comes between men and God. But the Latin word for priest is *pontifex*, which means a *bridge-builder;* and a real priest is a man who builds a bridge between his fellow-men and God. Even in heaven the Risen Church as Paul saw it, is still doing the work He did

116

on earth; He is still opening the way for men to God.

The idea of the Risen Christ as Judge is another idea which occurs in the thought of Paul. It appears in *Romans* 14: 9, 10: "For to this end Christ both died, and rose, and revived, that He might be the Lord both of the dead and living. But why dost thou judge thy brother, or why dost thou set at nought thy brother? we shall all stand before the judgment seat of Christ." That same Jesus, on whom men sat in judgment and who was condemned by men, is the Risen Christ before whose judgment seat all men must appear.

There is one idea which is very deeply rooted in the mind of Paul, and very near and dear to his heart. That is the idea of the power of the Resurrection. In *Philippians* 3: 10 Paul describes one of the supreme aims of his life as "to know the power of His Resurrection." In *Ephesians* 1: 19, 20 he speaks of the greatness of God's power to us who believe, that power which was operative in the Resurrection.

Again and again Paul connects the Resurrection with the new life which the Christian is enabled to lead, and the new goodness which clothes the Christian man. In *Romans* 6: 4 he says that, just as Christ was raised from the dead, by the glory of the Father, "even so we also should walk in newness of life." In *Romans* 7: 4 he says that Jesus Christ was raised from the dead that "we should bring forth fruit unto God." In *Colossians* 2: 12 he speaks of the Resurrection and goes straight on to speak of the Christian forgiveness of sins and triumph over sins. In 2 *Corinthians*

13: 4 he tells how Christ was crucified in His human weakness, but lives by the power of God; and then he goes on to say that " we also are weak in Him, but we shall live with Him by the power of God toward you."

Paul saw in the Resurrection a release of divine power, a surging tide of power which cleansed and beautified the life of the Christian. To Paul the Resurrection was not a past fact, but a present power.

There is no incomprehensible, mystic mystery here. If Christ is risen from the dead, it means that it is possible for the Christian to live every moment of every day in the presence and the fellowship of the living Christ. It means that the Christian approaches no task alone, bears no sorrow alone, attacks no problem alone, faces no demand alone, endures no temptation alone. It means that Jesus Christ does not issue His commands, and then leave us to do our best to obey them alone, but that He is constantly with us to enable us to perform that which He commands.

There is a very beautiful saying of Christ which is one of the unwritten sayings which do not appear in the New Testament at all: " Raise the stone and you will find me; cleave the wood and I am there." It means that, as the mason works at the stone, as the carpenter handles the wood, the Risen Christ is with him. The Resurrection means that every way of life can be walked hand in hand with the living Christ. The reservoir of the power of His presence is open for every Christian to draw upon.

But the most uncompromising statement of the utter necessity of the Resurrection is in 1 *Corinthians* 15: 14-19.

There Paul writes: " If Christ be not risen, then is our preaching vain, and your faith is also vain . . . If Christ be not raised, your faith is vain; ye are yet in your sins. Then they also which are fallen asleep in Christ are perished. If in this life only we have hope in Christ, we are of all men most miserable." Why should that be so? What are the great truths which the Resurrection, and the Resurrection alone, guarantees and conserves? The Resurrection is the guarantee of four great truths.

It proves that *truth is stronger than falsehood.* In Jesus Christ God's truth came to men; men sought to eliminate, to obliterate, to destroy that truth, but the Resurrection is the final proof of the indestructibility of the truth of God.

It proves that *good is stronger than evil.* Jesus Christ was the incarnate goodness of God. The sin of man sought to destroy that goodness. But the Resurrection is the proof that goodness must in the end triumph over all that evil can do to it.

It is proof that *life is stronger than death.* Men sought to destroy the life of Jesus Christ once and for all; the Resurrection is the proof that the life which is in Christ cannot be destroyed—and the Christian shares that life.

It is the proof that *love is stronger than hate.* In the last analysis the contest in Jerusalem was a contest between the hatred of men and the love of God. Men took that love and sought to break it for ever on the Cross; but the Resurrection is the proof that the love of God is stronger than all the hatred of men, and can in the end defeat all that that hatred can do to it.

Unless we could be certain of these great truths life would be intolerable.

To Paul the Resurrection of Jesus Christ was neither simply a fact in history nor a theological dogma. It was the supreme fact of experience. To Paul the fact of the Resurrection meant the greatest thing in all the world; it meant that all life is lived in the presence of the love and of the power of Jesus Christ.

XI

IN CHRIST

EVERY MAN who writes or speaks a great deal has favourite phrases. He uses them almost without knowing that he is doing so. Paul had such a phrase, and the phrase is *in Christ*. We have been studying something of what Jesus Christ meant to Paul, and it is fitting that now we should turn to this phrase, which occurs so often in Paul's writings and which clearly meant so much to him.

This phrase is not so much the essence of Paul's theology, as it is the summary of his whole religion. For Paul this phrase *in Christ* was always a compendious statement of the Christian faith. Of all the letters which Paul ever wrote, it is absent only in one—in 2 *Thessalonians*. No one would deny that the passing of the years deepened and enriched and intensified its meaning for Paul; but the fact remains that this phrase and all that it means was no late and sudden development in the mind and thought and heart of Paul. From the beginning to the end of his Christian life it was the centre and soul of his Christian experience.

Still further, we must note that Paul never at any time looked on this phrase as describing a religious experience which was unique and peculiar to himself. It was not something which he enjoyed because he was in a specially privileged position, or because he had risen to a devotional height, which ordinary people could never hope to scale. It was something to be known and experienced by every Christian man and woman. Paul would not only have said that the phrase *in Christ* was the essence of the Christian life in general; he would have said that it is the essence of every individual Christian life also.

Still further yet, we must note that Paul never uses the phrase *in Jesus*; he talks about being *in Christ, in Christ Jesus, in Jesus Christ, in the Lord*, but never *in Jesus*. That is to say, this phrase has to do uniquely and specifically with the Risen Christ. It does not describe or express a physical relationship, which is dependent on space and time and physical contact, a relationship which can be found and lost as presence and absence alternate. It describes a spiritual relationship, which is independent of space and time, a relationship of the ever and everywhere present Risen Lord and everliving Christ. Tennyson came near to expressing it when he wrote in *The Higher Pantheism*:

Speak to Him thou for He hears, and Spirit with Spirit can meet—
Closer is He than breathing, and nearer than hands and feet.

This is not a necessarily limited relationship with a physical person; it is an unlimited relationship with the Risen Lord.

In Christ

We must begin by going to the letters of Paul, and examining in some detail how he uses this phrase *in Christ*.

Paul thought of the Church as a whole, and of each of the Churches, as being in Christ. The Church in Thessalonica is in God and in the Lord Jesus Christ (1 *Thessalonians* 1: 1). The Churches of Judæa are in Christ (*Galatians* 1: 22). The individual Churches may be in different and widely separated parts of the world; but they are all in Christ. The life of the Church is life in Christ.

But not only are the Churches in Christ; the individual members of the Churches, the individual Christians are in Christ. *Philippians* is addressed to the saints in Christ Jesus who are at Philippi (*Philippians* 1: 1). Greetings are sent to every saint in Christ Jesus (*Philippians* 4: 21). The members of the Church at Philippi are brethren in the Lord (*Philippians* 1: 14). The letter to Colosse is addressed to the saints and faithful brethren in Christ who are at Colosse (*Colossians* 1: 2). When Epaphroditus is sent back to Philippi after his serious illness in Rome, he is to be received in the Lord (*Philippians* 2: 29). Those who are set in authority in the Church are over the others in the Lord (1 *Thessalonians* 5: 12).

The fact that all individual Christians are in Christ is indeed precisely the source and origin of that unity which should characterise all members of the Church. All Christians are the children of God by faith in Christ Jesus (*Galatians* 3: 26) and because of that circumcision and uncircumcision are irrelevant (*Galatians* 5: 6). In Christ there is neither Jew nor Greek, male nor female, bond nor free (*Galatians*

123

3: 28). All Christians are one body in Christ (*Romans* 12: 5). It is God's aim to bring unity to a disintegrated universe and that unity can only come in Christ (*Ephesians* 1: 10). This must operate in the most practical way. The two women in Philippi who have quarrelled are urged to come together again in Christ (*Philippians* 4: 2). Because every Church is in Christ, there can never be disunity between real Churches. Because every Christian is in Christ, there can never be any barrier between those who are truly Christian. They may be of different nations and colours and status and class and ability and rank and birth; they may belong to different branches of the Church; they may differ in language, in politics, in methods, in ritual, in liturgy, in administration; these differences do not, and cannot, matter, if men and women are in Christ.

The disunities of the Church would be solved to-morrow, if men realised that Christianity does not mean being in a Church, but being in Christ.

For Paul himself life was lived in Christ. Every action which he did, every word which he spoke, every experience which he underwent was in Christ. His ways are in Christ (1 *Corinthians* 4: 17). He has begotten the Corinthians in Christ, and they are his work in the Lord (1 *Corinthians* 4: 15; 9: 1). He speaks in Christ (2 *Corinthians* 2: 17; 12: 19). He makes his plans and thinks of the future in Christ. In the Lord he trusts to send Timothy to Philippi, and in the Lord he trusts soon to come himself (*Philippians* 2: 19, 24). He sends his love to the Corinthians in Christ (1 *Corinthians* 16: 24). In speaking of himself and of his own spiritual experience, he says that he knows a man in Christ (2 *Corinthians* 12: 2). Even in prison his bonds are in Christ (*Philippians* 1: 13).

It is not only Paul who can write like this. Tertius, the amanuensis who wrote *Romans* to Paul's dictation, sends his greeting in the Lord (*Romans* 16: 22). It is open to any Christian to enter into that relationship with Christ in which his whole life will be in Christ.

It is, in fact, the case that at last sometimes *in Christ* simply means *Christian* in the real and deepest sense of the term. *Romans* 16 is specially instructive in this direction. In that chapter the phrase *in Christ* occurs no fewer than nine times in the compass of fifteen verses. Phoebe is to be received in the Lord (verse 2); she is to be given a true Christian welcome. Priscilla and Aquila are Paul's helpers in Christ Jesus (verse 3); they are his helpers in all Christian work and activity. Andronicus and Junia were in Christ before Paul (verse 7); they were Christians before Paul was. Amplias is my beloved in the Lord (verse 8); he is the fellow-Christian whom Paul loved. Urbane is our helper in Christ; that is, our helper in Christian work (verse 9). Apelles is approved in Christ (verse 10); he is a well-proved Christian. The household of Narcissus are in the Lord (verse 11); they are Christians. Tryphena and Tryphosa labour in the Lord (verse 12); they are engaged actively in Christian work. Persis laboured in the Lord and Rufus was chosen in the Lord (verse 13); Persis is engaged in Christian work, and Rufus was chosen as a Christian by Jesus Christ Himself. It can be seen that in nearly all these

The Mind of St Paul

cases the phrase *in Christ*, or its equivalent, could be translated Christian, although that would be a colourless and inadequate translation.

As Paul saw it, all great Christian gifts and all great Christian qualities are in Christ. We have consolation in Christ (*Philippians* 2: 1). We are bold in Christ (*Philemon* 8). We have liberty in Christ (*Galatians* 2: 4). We have truth in Christ (*Romans* 9 : 1). We have the promise in Christ (*Ephesians* 3: 6). The promises of God are confirmed and guaranteed in Christ (2 *Corinthians* 1: 20). We are sanctified in Christ (1 *Corinthians* 1: 2). We are wise in Christ (1 *Corinthians* 4: 10). We are new creatures in Christ (2 *Corinthians* 5: 17). We are called in the Lord (1 *Corinthians* 7: 22). The high calling of God is in Christ (*Philippians* 3: 14). We are babes in Christ (1 *Corinthians* 3: 1). God has stablished us in Christ (2 *Corinthians* 1: 21). We walk in Christ (*Colossians* 2: 6).

It can be seen that for Paul the whole process and itinerary of the Christian life is in Christ. The call to it is in Christ; we begin by being babes in Christ; we are stablished in Christ; the gifts of nurture and of strength are in Christ; the Christian way is walked in Christ. For Paul the Christian life is begun, continued and ended in Christ.

But special occasions and special demands and special crises demand special powers and gifts, and these special powers and gifts come to us in Christ.

In times of persecution and of peril it is in the Lord that Christians stand fast (1 *Thessalonians* 3: 8; *Philippians* 4: 1). It is in Christ that we find joy in times of sorrow (*Philippians*

126

1: 26; 3: 1; 4: 4; 4: 10). It is in Christ that His servants are faithful. So Timothy is faithful in the Lord (1 *Corinthians* 4: 17); and the letter to the Ephesians is addressed to those who are faithful in the Lord (*Ephesians* 1: 1).

Every good thing that we have experienced, that we possess and enjoy, that we can attain, is in Christ. In the letter to Philemon Paul speaks of every good thing which is in you in Christ (*Philemon* 6); and in Ephesians he speaks of God who has blessed us with all spiritual blessings in Christ (*Ephesians* 1: 3).

There is one way in which it might be possible to simplify the whole matter. The phrase in Greek is *en Christō*. In classical Greek *en* does mean *in;* but in the later Greek of New Testament times *en* is very often commonly used of the *instrument* or *agent*, and very often means *by means of*, or *through the agency of*. Linguistically, it would be possible to take the phrase *en Christō* to mean *through Christ, by means of Christ, through the agency of Christ*. The phrase would then mean that Christ is the enabling power; that it is through His grace and power that we are enabled to live the Christian life. It would be simple to think of being called by Christ; of standing fast in persecution and peril through the help that Christ gives; of receiving wisdom and truth through the agency of Christ.

To take *en Christō* in this sense, certainly in many cases, gives us a perfectly intelligible meaning; and he who looks for easy solutions, and who is impatient of anything that has any kind of mysticism in it, may well be tempted to

accept the meaning; but the fact is that in many passages
we will be compelled to admit that *en Christō* means far
more than this. That key might unlock some doors, but
it certainly would not unlock all the doors; and the doors
it did unlock would lead us to the ante-chambers and the
vestibule of the treasure-house which lies beyond. To say
that the phrase *in Christ* means *through Christ* is true, but
considerably less than half the truth.

It might be possible to argue that this phrase could be
taken in a purely metaphorical sense. We could cite as
some kind of parallel or analogy such a phrase as being
wrapped up in a person. When two people are very near
and dear to each other, when they are very intimate, when
they love each other, and are interested only in each other,
we can and do talk of them as being wrapped up in each
other. There is no doubt that this line of thought does
throw a ray of light on this matter, because it is a metaphor
taken from the sphere of love, and it is only in the sphere
of love that we can express Paul's relationship to Christ
at all. But the cumulative effect of all Paul's uses of the
phrase *in Christ* demands something even more than this.
Something even more intimate and certainly more lasting
is expressed by the phrase *in Christ*.

There are some who would go to the pagan religious
background of Paul's time for the explanation of this
phrase. In Paul's time the outstanding religious phenomenon
of the Graeco-Roman world was the Mystery Religions.
These Mystery Religions were based on what we would
call passion plays. Their central act was the dramatic

presentation of a story of some god who lived and suffered and died and rose again. Greek mythology was full of stories like that. Before the initiate was allowed to be present at such a performance he or she had to undergo a long process of training and instruction and fasting and asceticism; the person to be initiated was worked up to a high pitch of emotional excitement and expectation. The performance itself was given under conditions carefully calculated to drive a person to a kind of hysterical ecstasy. Cunning lighting, perfumed incense, sensuous music were all used to heighten the emotional atmosphere; and the aim of the whole process and presentation was to enable the worshipper to experience a complete identification with the god whose story was being played out. The worshipper became one with the god, sharing his sufferings, his death and his final triumphant resurrection, till in the end the worshipper could and did say: " I am thou, and thou art I."

Beyond a doubt men did undergo an amazing experience in the Mystery Religions. But there are two reasons why this will not do as an explanation of the phrase *in Christ*. First, the experience of the Mystery Religions was ecstatic, hysterical, highly emotional. But there is nothing emotional and ecstatic in the experience which Paul summarises in the phrase *in Christ*. To be in Christ was not a brief ecstasy, induced by deliberately provoked psychological excitement; it was something which was obtained every day in the ordinary business and routine of everyday life. Second, the experience of the Mystery Religions was necessarily transient. It might be very vivid in the brief moment of ecstasy; it might be repeated again under favourable circumstances; but the experience which Paul describes in the phrase *in Christ* is something which is lasting and permanent, something which endures, not for one exotic hour, but for a lifetime of day-to-day living.

We will not find the explanation of Paul's *in Christ* in the Mystery Religions, although the experience they offered may well have been a dim foretaste of the Christian reality.

Deissmann suggested that this phrase can be interpreted by using the analogy of the way in which we live in the air. Just as all men live in the air, and cannot live without the air, so the Christian lives in Christ. And just as the air is inside all living things, in a man's lungs and in a man's body, so Christ is in the man. Just as all men live in the air, so the Christian lives in Christ; just as the air within them gives all men life, so Christ within him gives the Christian newness of life. To be in Christ is to live a life in which Christ is the atmosphere which we breathe. That is undoubtedly a lovely thought, and yet it has in it a nebulousness which is not in the Pauline conception.

There are certain other pictures which Paul uses about the Christian experience of Christ, which will enable us to come nearer to the meaning of his phrase *in Christ*.

(*a*) In *Galatians* 3 : 27 he says that those who have been baptised into Christ have put on Christ; and in *Romans* 13 : 14 he tells his Roman friends: " Put ye on the Lord Jesus Christ." It is as if the Christian is encompassed, enveloped, clothed with Christ as he is with his clothes.

(*b*) In *Galatians* 4: 19 he has a vivid picture. " My little children," he says, " of whom I travail in birth again until Christ be formed in you." In the Christian life, Jesus Christ is born into a man, until the man is filled with the life of Christ.

(*c*) In *Galatians* 2: 20 there is the great passage: " I am crucified with Christ; nevertheless I live; yet not I, but Christ liveth in me." The life principle which was Paul is dead; and Christ has become the life principle in him. The self of Paul is dead, and in its place Christ lives in him.

(*d*) Most vivid of all is the picture of baptism in *Romans* 6 and in *Colossians* 2: 12. We have to remember that baptism was adult baptism, because it was the reception into the Church of men and women coming straight from paganism; and we have to remember that it was by total immersion. What the *Romans* 6 passage is saying is: When a man is immersed in the water, it is like going down into the grave and being buried and dying once and for all. When he emerges from the water, it is as if he emerged a new person, with a new life in him, and that new life is Christ.

Let us remember who and what Paul was. Once he had been a persecutor, pillaging the Church as a marauding army pillaged a city, as a wild boar laid waste a vineyard. Then on the Damascus Road something happened. In one flash of time, Paul the enemy of Christ became Paul the slave of Christ. It is difficult to describe it any other way than to say that in that moment one man died and another man was born. The old Paul was dead and a new Paul was born. And who had been responsible for this change? None other than the Risen Christ. From that moment Paul felt that between him and Christ there was so real, so close, so indissoluble a union that it could not be expressed in any other way than to say that he lived in Christ, and Christ lived in him.

It was not a case of identification with Christ; Paul did not lose his own personality; for Paul could still kneel and look up and worship and adore. But something had happened which brought Christ into Paul's heart and joined Paul's life to the life of Christ in such a way that he could only say that he was for ever in Christ.

We are here trying to describe something which has to be experienced to be understood. It has been said with the greatest truth that Christianity can only be understood from the inside. To the vast majority of people Paul's experience must remain a mystery—and the reason is that no man can enjoy Paul's experience of Christ, unless he has made Paul's surrender to Christ. It is only the completely surrendered heart which knows what it is to be in Christ in the fullest sense of the term.

XII

PAUL'S CONCEPTION
OF FAITH

It is quite clear that there is no word so near the centre of Paul's belief as the word faith. We have only to read his letters to see that for Paul the word faith sums up the very essence of Christianity. It is therefore of supreme importance that we should understand something of what Paul meant by faith, if we are to understand what Christianity meant to him.

It is of primary importance to note that for Paul faith is always faith in a person. Faith is not the intellectual acceptance of a body of doctrine; faith is faith in a person. Sanday and Headlam have laid it down that there are four main meanings of the word faith, and four main connections in which Paul uses it—belief in God, belief in Jesus, belief in the promises of God, and belief in the promises of Jesus. It is indeed probable that all the Pauline usages of the word faith could be fitted into that scheme; but it will be even more illuminating to go direct to the letters themselves, and to examine the way in which Paul uses the word faith in them.

133

We must begin with a meaning which is not theological at all, and which needs no special background of expert knowledge to understand it. Paul uses faith to mean loyalty, fidelity, that which we would more naturally call faithfulness. That is the way in which he uses this word faith when he is talking of the fruit of the Spirit (*Galatians* 5: 22). There faith is simply loyalty and the fidelity which are the most valuable qualities in life. Paul writes regularly to his Churches of the gratitude with which he had heard of their faith, and of the praise which their faith has won them. He says that the faith of the Roman Church is spoken of throughout the world (*Romans* 1: 8). In *Ephesians* 1: 15 he says that he has heard of the faith of those to whom he writes. In *Colossians* 1: 4 he tells the Colossians that he has heard of their faith; and he speaks of the steadfastness of their faith in Christ (*Colossians* 2: 5). He writes to the Thessalonians that the story of their faith has penetrated not only over all Macedonia, but even throughout the whole province of Achaia (1 *Thessalonians* 1: 8). He tells them that, since he had to leave them hurriedly and secretly, he now writes to inquire about their faith (1 *Thessalonians* 3: 5). He speaks of their patience and their faith (2 *Thessalonians* 1: 4). He writes to the Philippians of the sacrifice and service of their faith (*Philippians* 2: 17).

In all these cases the reference is to the loyalty and the fidelity of the young Churches to Jesus Christ, a loyalty and a fidelity which overcame persecution and shone through the darkness of the troubled life which the early Christians had to lead.

Plainest of all cases of this meaning is *Romans* 3: 3. There Paul contrasts the faithlessness of Israel with the faithfulness of God. Shall their unbelief, he demands, make the faith of God of no effect? What he means is that not all the disobedience, the unresponsiveness, the rebelliousness of man, can alter the fidelity of God to His purposes and to His promises. It is exactly the same in 1 *Thessalonians* 3: 6 where Paul says that he has received good news of their faith. His information is that they are standing fast.

The Second Book of Samuel has a moving instance of this fidelity (2 *Samuel* 15: 19-23). David had fallen on evil days. Absalom his son had turned against him and the hearts of the people had gone out after Absalom. For David nothing but flight was left. Amongst his bodyguard David had a soldier called Ittai, who was a soldier of fortune. Ittai was not even an Israelite; he was a Philistine; he was one of those men who fought for the love of fighting, a mercenary who would sell his sword to the highest bidder. David saw that Ittai was preparing to follow him into exile and misfortune, and he told Ittai that he was under no obligation to come with him. He was a stranger and a foreigner; there was no call on him to involve his fortunes with the fallen fortunes of David. Ittai answered: " As the lord liveth, and as my lord the king liveth, surely in what place my lord the king shall be, whether in death or life, even there also will thy servant be." That is precisely what Paul meant by faith at its simplest. Faith at its simplest is unshakable and unalterable loyalty to Jesus Christ.

Closely connected with this is the idea of faith as belief, the unalterable conviction that certain things are true. Paul writes to the Corinthians that their faith should not stand by wisdom (1 *Corinthians* 2: 5). The meaning is that their belief in the power of Christianity, their conviction that Jesus Christ is Lord, should not be something which is dependent on and bolstered up by fine-spun and rhetorical human arguments. In 1 *Corinthians* 15: 17 he says that if Christ is not risen from the dead, then their faith is vain. That is to say, if there is no Resurrection, then all their convictions have collapsed, the bottom is knocked out of all that they have accepted as true.

There were two stages in the religious life of John Bunyan. At first he could only say that the Jews think their religion the best, and the Mohammedans think their religion the best, and ask: "What if Christianity be but a think-so too?" And there was the stage when he could run out crying out: "O now I know! I know!" It is that conviction which to Paul is faith.

This meaning comes out well in Paul's use of the verb *to believe*. And one of the most interesting things in his letters is the connection of this unshakable belief and conviction with preaching. Preaching is the medium by which men come to this conviction. He writes to the Corinthians that it was God's purpose to save them that believe through the foolishness of preaching (1 *Corinthians* 1: 21). He speaks of Cephas and Apollos and himself as ministers by whom ye

believed (1 *Corinthians* 3: 5). "So we preached," he says
to the Corinthians, "and so ye believed" (1 *Corinthians*
15: 11). In 1 *Thessalonians* 1: 7 he speaks of all that believe
in Macedonia. In 1 *Thessalonians* he writes, "If we believe
that Jesus died and rose again . . ." (1 *Thessalonians*
4: 14), that is to say, "If we accept the fact of the Resurrection of Jesus Christ." In 2 *Thessalonians* 1: 10 he writes:
"Our testimony was believed," that is to say, it was accepted
as true.

To Paul preaching and belief went hand in hand. How
could a man be moved to belief and to faith unless he was
presented with the Christian message? "How then shall
they call on Him in whom they have not believed? How
shall they believe in Him of whom they have not heard? And
how shall they hear without a preacher?" (*Romans* 10: 14).

Here, then, are two great Christian facts.

I. Conviction is an essential part of Christianity.
Christianity may begin, but cannot ultimately end, with
a kind of vague, nebulous emotional response and reaction
to the wonder of Jesus Christ. It must go on to try and
to test things and to hold fast to that which is good. "The
unexamined life," said Plato, "is the life not worth living,"
and the unexamined faith is the faith not worth having.
Where the heart has gone the mind must follow.

II. Preaching is the medium which produces conviction.
Preaching is therefore the proclamation of certainties, and
the confirmation of belief. Preaching is designed, not to
produce questions, but to answer questions; preaching is
designed, not to awaken doubts, but to settle and to conquer

doubts. The preacher who uses the pulpit to air his own intellectual doubts is doing his people a grave disservice. He will have to state the doubts and the difficulties; but he will have to state them to answer them, not to leave them unresolved. " Tell me of your certainties," said Goethe. " I have doubts enough of my own."

It is often said that the idea of faith as faith in a creed does not occur in the New Testament until as late as the Pastoral Epistles. In a sense that is true, and it is true because the creed of the early Church was quite simply: " Jesus Christ is Lord " (*Philippians* 2: 11). But quite often faith stands in the letters of Paul for what we can only call The Christian Religion. Christianity is The Faith. It is Paul's advice to receive him who is weak in the faith, but not to doubtful disputations (*Romans* 14: 1). That is to say: Welcome the man whose Christianity is not yet firmly based, but not to debatable things, which can only shake his faith. In *Galatians* 1: 23 he tells them that the Palestinian Christians were bewildered that he was preaching the faith which once he had sought to destroy; that is, that he was preaching the religion which once he had tried to wipe out. In *Colossians* 1: 23 he urges his friends to continue in the faith, grounded and settled. In *Colossians* 2: 7 he speaks of being stablished in the faith. In 1 *Corinthians* 16: 13 he urges the Corinthians to stand fast in the faith. He writes to the Thessalonians to tell them that he is glad that their faith is growing exceedingly (2 *Thessalonians* 1: 3). In 2 *Corinthians* 13: 5 he advises his opponents to examine themselves to see if they are in the faith.

In these passages the faith means the Christian religion. But the very use of the word is suggestive; Christianity is not allegiance to a creed; it is faith in a person, Christianity is not a system; it is a faith. Jesus' own practice on earth will illuminate this. When he came to men, He did not say to them: "I have a system that I would like you to examine; I have a philosophy I would like you to discuss; I have a theory I would like to lay before you." He said: "Follow me." That is far from saying that the day would not come when the implications, and the whys and wherefores would not need to be thought out and examined until intellectual conviction followed on the heart's response; but it is to say that the moving force of Christianity is in fact this act of personal faith in Jesus Christ.

Faith in the sense of confident hope is a conception which is more characteristic of the writer to the Hebrews than it is of Paul. His great definition of faith was: "Faith is the substance of things hoped for, the evidence of things not seen" (*Hebrews* 11: 1). But this idea does occur in Paul. On one occasion at least, Paul comes near to making faith and hope one and the same thing, when he says: "We walk by faith, not by sight" (2 *Corinthians* 5: 7). Their faith is a sure and certain hope by which they can walk, even when the path is dark. As Donald Hankey had it: "Faith is betting your life there is a God." Faith is the hope which has gone beyond hope and turned to certainty, even when the evidence and the facts seem all against it.

It is true that all these things of which we have been thinking are included in the Pauline conception of faith;

but it is also true that, although they are to Paul vital parts of faith, they are not the real centre and soul of faith. We shall come nearer to the Pauline idea of faith, if we go on to see the things which Paul believed could come by faith, and in no other way.

Justification comes by faith. "Therein," he writes, "is the righteousness of God revealed from faith to faith;" as it is written, "The just shall live by faith" (*Romans* 1: 17). In *Romans* 3: 28 he writes: "Therefore we conclude that a man is justified by faith." In *Romans* 5: 1 he speaks of the peace with God which comes to those who are justified by faith. In *Galatians* 3: 8 he speaks of the scripture foreseeing that God would justify the heathen by faith. The great key passage is in *Galatians* 2: 16: "Knowing that a man is not justified by the works of the law, but by the faith of Jesus Christ, even we have believed in Jesus Christ, that we might be justified by the faith of Christ, and not by the works of the law: for by the works of the law shall no flesh be justified." Let us stop to remember what *justification* means. The Greek word to justify is *dikaioun*. Greek verbs which end in *-oun* never mean to make a person something. They always mean to treat, to reckon, to account a person as something. So when it is said that God justifies us, it does not in the first instance mean that God makes us righteous; it means that God treats us as if we were righteous, even when, in fact, we are sinners. It means that in his amazing and incredible mercy and grace God treats the bad man as if he had been a good man. If we were to receive our deserts, if there happened that which we have every reason to expect would happen, we would stand as criminals before the bar of God's judgment and leave it utterly and completely condemned without defence. But in point of fact the amazing thing is that God accepts us and loves us and welcomes us and receives us, sinners as we are.

The condition which results from that is what Paul calls *righteousness*. Righteousness to Paul is not in the first instance moral excellence and rectitude. It is being in a right relationship with God. If we received our deserts, the only possible relationship between us and God would be utter enmity and utter estrangement; but again in this incredible grace of His, sinners as we are, God has put us in a relationship of loving fellowship with himself. That is what Paul means when he speaks of the righteousness of God which is by faith of Jesus Christ (*Romans* 3: 22); when he speaks of righteousness which is of faith (*Romans* 10: 6); when he speaks of the righteousness which is through the faith of Christ, the righteousness which is of God by faith (*Philippians* 3: 9). In all these cases by righteousness Paul means that right relationship with God which ought humanly speaking to have been impossible for sinners, but which in the mercy of God is made available for us.

How can we say that all this happens by faith? Here we come to the essence of the matter. We have just been saying that God treats the bad man as if he were a good man; that God opens the way to a relationship with Himself which we could never have deserved, and which we could never have achieved. But surely the blazing question is: How do we know that God is like that? How do we know that God treats men like that? How can we be certain that these amazingly incredible things are true? The answer is: Because Jesus told us that God is like that. Our whole relationship with God is based on unquestioning faith that what Jesus said about God is true. That is what justification by faith, righteousness by faith, means. It is only through faith in Jesus Christ that we can believe these things.

But another blazing question arises. How could Jesus know that God is like that? Where did Jesus get His special knowledge of God? How can we be sure that Jesus was right about God? The answer is that we are certain that Jesus was right because we believe that Jesus is so closely identified with God, if you like to put it so, that Jesus knows God so well, that we can only call Him the Son of God. Our whole relationship with God is dependent on the faith that what Jesus said is true, and the faith that Jesus is the Son of God, and therefore not mistaken.

In *Galatians* 3: 26 Paul puts this in another way. He says that by faith we become children of God. Left to ourselves we could not conceive of God being anything other than our enemy. On any human grounds we could not conceive of ourselves as receiving anything other than condemnation from God. With such power of thought as we can bring to bear upon this it is incredible that the holiness of God should ever welcome any approach from the sin of man. That is precisely the Old Testament position. Moses heard God say: "No man shall see me and live" (*Exodus* 33: 20). When Manoah discovered who his heavenly visitor had been, his terrified cry was: "We shall surely die, because we have seen God" (*Judges* 13: 22). Into this terror and estrangement and distance and enmity there comes Christianity with the message that God is eager to welcome men to himself, just as they are. How can anyone believe that? It can only be believed when we take Jesus absolutely and completely at His word; and when we believe that He has the right to speak because He is who He is.

That is what faith means for Paul. We shall go on to develop this still further, but here we are already at the heart of the matter. Faith is complete trust and complete surrender to Jesus Christ. It is the total acceptance of all that He said, of all that He offered, and of all that He is. It is the approach to God in complete confidence that all that Jesus said and taught about God is true, and that we can rest our souls in it.

We will understand even more about what Paul means by faith, if we go on to see the other things which Paul says come by faith. *Romans* 3: 22 lays down the great truth about which we have been thinking: "Righteousness is by faith unto all that believe." That is to say, the only way to a right relationship with God is to take Jesus at His word, and to cast ourselves on the mercy of God, believing utterly that what Jesus says about God is true.

But in *Romans* 3: 25 Paul introduces another idea. We have propitiation through faith in His blood. What then is propitiation? A propitiation is a sacrifice which restores the lost relationship between God and man. A man commits a sin; that sin causes a breach between him and God. That breach is healed when a sacrifice is brought with a humble and a contrite heart. So what Paul is saying is: It cost the life-blood of Jesus Christ, it cost the Cross, to restore the lost relationship between God and man. Faith is the complete trust that that which Jesus Christ has done in His life and in His death opens for us the way to God.

We may put this in another way, and in a simpler way. It may be that for us the idea of sacrifice is difficult to understand, because, unlike the Jews, we have not been brought up in a sacrificial system. But Paul has another way of putting this which is a much more universal way. In *Romans* 5: 2 he speaks of access by faith; in *Ephesians* 3: 12 he speaks of access with confidence through faith. As we have already seen, the word for access is *prosagōgē*, which is the technical Greek word for access to the presence of a king. Obviously ordinary people do not have access to the presence of an earthly king; an earthly monarch is fenced around with guards and courtiers and palace officials. In the ancient world there was actually an official called the *prosagōgeus*, whose function it was to ward off the undesirable and to introduce the acceptable into the presence of the king. Quite clearly no one would ever dream that sinning men should have access to the presence of the holiness of God; anyone would assume that the sinner is shut out from the presence of God. But the wonder of Christianity is that Jesus Christ came to tell us of the

God whose heart and whose door are wide open to the sinner. Once again, apart from Jesus Christ we could never have believed that God is like that; we could never have guessed that God is like that. We can only approach God at all because we believe that God is as Jesus Christ told us that He is. That for Paul is access by faith.

But there is still another connection which is very close to the heart of the thought of Paul. In *Ephesians* 2: 8 he writes: " By grace are ye saved through faith." This is a highly compressed saying. We shall later on in our studies have to think much more fully of what Paul means by grace; but at the moment we note this. In the Pauline idea of grace there are invariably two elements. Grace is something which is very lovely, and grace is something which is entirely free.

It is the second of these ideas which is always dominant in Paul's thought. Grace is something which we could never deserve, which we could never have earned, something which is given generously and freely for the accepting. Here is the very essence of Pauline religion. The Jew would have said: You must earn the favour of God; you must keep the Law, you must live a life entirely obedient to the Law's commands; and then you will earn and receive the favour of God. The whole duty of a Jew was to earn God's favour. Paul would have said—and he said so because he had tried it—that it is utterly impossible for any man ever to earn the favour of God, that man's imperfection can never satisfy God's perfection, that in relation to God the best man in the world, and the best man who can ever be, is always in default. What then is the consequence? The consequence is that what we cannot earn, we must freely accept and trustingly take. We cannot earn God's love; God's love is offered to us freely and for nothing. That is what grace means.

But again the salient question arises—How can I know that? How can I possibly believe that? How can I believe that God's love is not to be earned, but to be freely and wonderingly accepted? The answer is the same again— apart from Jesus Christ we could never have known that. It is because we believe that Jesus told us the truth about God that we believe in the grace of God.

There is still one other way by which Paul comes at this. He says first of all that Jesus is the power of God unto salvation to everyone that believes (*Romans* 1: 16). That means that apart from Jesus Christ, we would be strangers, enemies, criminals in the sight of God. When we accept all that Jesus Christ says as true, then there comes into life the power which makes us friends with God again. Paul has one other way of putting this, and it is the greatest way of all. In *Ephesians* 3: 17 it is his hope and prayer that Christ may dwell in our hearts through faith. His prayer is that we will never at any time doubt what He says, that we will never at any time question His offer, that we will absolutely and without argument or doubt take His word about God, and so enter into this new relationship of fellowship with God.

With all this in our minds, let us turn to the man who was Paul's perfect illustration of faith. Paul knew quite well that very few people can grasp abstract truths and abstract ideas; he was a wise teacher and he knew that nearly everyone thinks in pictures and that, if we want to present a person with an idea, that idea must become vivid and concrete and dramatic in a picture. So Paul turns the word faith into flesh; he turns the idea of faith into a person, and that person is Abraham. It is in *Romans* 4 and *Galatians* 3 that this idea is most fully worked out. Abraham was justified; that is to say, Abraham was in a right relationship with God. How did Abraham arrive at that right relationship? It was certainly not by keeping the Law, for the simple reason that the Law was not given until four hundred years after Abraham was dead. It was certainly not through circumcision because Abraham was in his right relationship with God years before he was circumcised. The promise and the blessing and the right relationship came to Abraham quite independently of the Law and of circumcision.

Wherein then lay Abraham's faith? Put at its very briefest—Abraham went out not knowing whether he went. Put in another way—Abraham took God absolutely and completely at His word. Let us put it in still another way—Abraham's faith was compounded of perfect trust and absolute obedience. Abraham took God at His word when God promised and when God commanded, and that is faith.

On any reasonable and logical view of the matter there can be nothing but distance between God and man. Measuring the matter by human standards, man could expect nothing but judgment and nothing but condemnation from God. But the very essence of Christianity is that the relationship between man and God is not distance, but fellowship; and the attitude of God to man is not condemnation, but love.

But we ought to remind ourselves again and again and again that we could never have known that, we could never have guessed that, we could never even in our wildest dreams have hoped for that, apart from Jesus Christ. Everything we know of the mercy and the love of God goes straight back to Jesus Christ. That is what all Christianity is founded on, faith in Jesus Christ. We would never possess even the beginnings of the religion we possess unless we took Jesus Christ at His word when He tells us the good news about God. And it is that taking of Jesus at His word which is faith. Let us now see if we can develop that a little further.

The first element in faith is what we can only call receptivity. In *Romans* 10: 17 Paul uses a very significant phrase when he speaks of " faith which comes by hearing." An offer has first to be heard and then to be received. A man can confront the message of Jesus Christ either with a blank and blunt refusal to listen to it at all, or else with a shut and closed mind which refuses to take it in. In both cases faith is impossible. Faith begins with the consent to listen to Jesus Christ with an open mind. In any event, apart altogether from the religious side of the matter, no honest and honourable man condemns anyone without giving him a hearing. Faith begins with giving the message of Jesus Christ a hearing—and an honest man is bound to do that.

The second element in faith is what we might call the assent of the mind. There can be no faith without the belief that God exists; there can be no faith without the belief that Jesus Christ did come to this earth and that He was who He was.

Every now and again we are confronted with an attack on Christianity which seeks to prove that Jesus never existed, that He is in fact nothing but a myth or a legend. That attack must always collapse on one basic fact. Suppose we assess the evidence for the Battle of Hastings, wherein does the strength of that evidence lie? In the last analysis it does not lie in the history books and the chronicles and the annals. It lies in the state of this country to-day. The Norman arches of the most ancient cathedrals and churches, the government and the administration of this country, the racial characteristics of the people, the whole way of life which we have inherited and which we live, apart altogether from anything that chronicles and stories and history books may say, demonstrate the truth of the fact that the Normans did conquer this country; and the evidence for the historical existence of Jesus Christ lies not in the gospels or in any history book; it lies in the state of this world to-day.

We have simply to compare the world before and the world after Christ. Whence came that new code of sexual purity? Whence came that new passion for social justice? Whence came that new respect for women, that new love of children, that new care for the weak and the sick and the deformed and the aged and the poor? There was one world before and another world after the emergence of Jesus Christ in history. The evidence for the existence of Jesus Christ lies in life itself.

But further, not only must we believe that Jesus did live and die, and rise again, we must also believe that He is the person He claimed to be. We need not express that in any one way, but we must assent to the uniqueness of Jesus Christ; we must assent to His unique right to speak of and to speak for God. Jesus is not one voice among many speaking about God; He is not even the greatest of the voices who spoke about God; He is in a unique sense the voice of God.

Faith then begins with receptivity; it goes on to an assent of the mind to the basic facts. But faith goes far beyond that. We can put this third step this way—faith is not only assent to the facts; faith is still more assent to the significance of the facts. Or may we put that in another way—faith is not merely the assent of the mind to Jesus Christ; it is the assent to the whole man to Jesus Christ.

Intellectual assent by itself is not nearly enough. James put this matter most bluntly: " Thou believest that there is one God; thou doest well: the devils also believe, and tremble " (*James* 2: 19). Let us see how Paul himself puts it: " If thou shalt confess with thy mouth the Lord Jesus and shall believe in thine heart that God hath raised Him from the dead, thou shalt be saved " (*Romans* 10: 9). This is a belief, a faith, which resides, not only in the mind, but in the heart.

Let us take the simplest of simple illustrations of the two kinds of belief. I believe that the square on the hypotenuse of a right-angled triangle equals the sum of the squares on the other two sides. I am intellectually convinced of that—but it makes no difference to me. But—I believe that six and six make twelve, and I will therefore resolutely refuse to pay one shilling and two pence for two sixpenny bars of chocolate. The one kind of belief was quite outside my active life; the other kind of belief dominates my active life. In the one case I assent to the facts, but that is all that is to it; in the other case, I assent to the significance of the facts, and the significance of the facts permeates my every action. That is something like what Paul means when he speaks about believing with the heart. Faith is not simply receptivity of the facts; it is not simply assent to the facts; it is assent to the significance of the facts for life.

But there is one other saying of Paul which must be woven into this pattern. In *Galatians* 5: 6 Paul speaks of faith which works, which is set in motion, through love. Here we are getting very near to the heart of things. This final kind of faith is set in motion through love. It is not possible to make a hard and fast, cut and dried, analysis of human thoughts and motives; but in Christian faith at its fullest and best there are three steps.

1. A man is confronted with the Christian message, either through the word of a preacher, or through the study of God's book. He comes to the decision that he must

believe what Jesus tells him about God; and that He must believe Jesus' own claims. He has made his first act of assent.

II. He is then confronted with what it cost Jesus to bring this messsage of the love of God, and thus to open the way to God for men. It cost Jesus every sorrow of body, mind and heart which can come to the life of any man. It cost him the hatred of the orthodox churchmen of His day; it cost Him the breach with His own nearest and dearest; it cost Him the disloyalty of His closest friends; it cost Him the scourging, the crown of thorns, the Cross and death. In view of all that a man is bound to say: I am bound to love Him who made such a sacrifice for me; such love demands my love. In simple gratitude I cannot do anything else but love this Christ. Faith is now energised by love. First there came the assent; then there came the realisation of what it meant even to make the facts known; and assent kindles into love and passionate devotion.

III. Then there comes the third step which sets the coping-stone on faith, and without which faith is incomplete. A man receives the facts and assents to them; he sees what the facts cost and his love runs out to Jesus Christ. Then he is bound to go on to say: Because I must answer love with love, I will make a complete self-surrender and a complete submission to this Jesus Christ.

Any tremendous gift involves tremendous obligations. No man can in honour take everything and give nothing back. And the coping-stone of faith is in fact obedience. It is the acceptance not only of the offer of grace, but of the obligation of grace.

So now we have complete the three elements in faith. Faith is receptivity; faith comes from hearing the message of Jesus Christ. Either to refuse to listen or to listen with a shut mind makes faith impossible. Faith goes on to assent that this message is true; that God is as Jesus proclaims Him to be, and that Jesus has the right to make that proclamation because He stands in a unique relationship to the God of whom He speaks. Faith passes from assent into the realisation of the wondrous love which bore the sacrifice that the proclamation of these facts involved, and faith surrenders in perfect trust and perfect submission and perfect obedience to Jesus Christ. Faith is the total assent of a man's total being to Jesus Christ.

We may sum it up in this way: Faith is the response of trust of a man's total personality to the love of God as shown to us in the life and death of Jesus Christ.

XIII

THE ESSENTIAL GRACE

JAMES MOFFATT in his book *Grace in the New Testament* has succinctly laid it down that the very essence and centre of Pauline faith and religion can be summed up in one brief sentence: " All is of grace, and grace is for all." For Paul grace is the essential grace.

We must begin by noting two general facts about grace. These two facts are not exclusively Pauline; they belong to the very nature of the idea of grace. We shall have to return to them more fully, but at the moment we state them briefly.

First, grace is in essence a lovely thing. The Greek word for grace is *charis*, and *charis* can mean *physical beauty*, everything that is contained in the word *charm*. Grace always moves in the realm of winsomeness, of loveliness, of attractiveness, of beauty and of charm. The word has in it all the beauty of holiness. There are certain Christian terms which inevitably have in them an idea and an atmosphere of sternness and of severity. But grace, in the Christian sense, is a thing of such surpassing beauty that the heart bows down in wondering adoration before it.

There is an old hymn which has the line: " Grace 'tis a charming sound," and there is a world of truth there.

Second, grace has always in it the idea of a gift which is completely free and entirely undeserved. The ideas of grace and merit are mutually exclusive and completely contradictory. No one can earn grace; it can only be humbly, gratefully and adoringly received. Grace is something which is given, as we say, *gratis*. The fundamental idea of grace is a gift, given out of the sheer generosity of the giver's heart, a gift which the receiver could never have earned and could never have deserved by any efforts of his own.

When Paul laid such stress on grace, he set out on a road of thought which was quite strange to the orthodox Jewish teaching of his day. It is true that in its highest and most devotional moments Jewish religion did rest in the mercy of God and in nothing else. From the daily prayer book of the Jews there comes the prayer which every Jew still knows: " Sovereign of the worlds, not because of our righteous deeds do we present our supplications before Thee, but because of Thine abundant mercies." On this prayer Abrahams, comments: " Rewards and punishments were meted out in some sort of accordance with a man's righteousness and sin, yet nothing that a man with his small powers and finite opportunities can do constitutes a claim on the favour of the Almighty and the Infinite. In the final resort, all that a man receives from the divine hand is an act of grace." There speaks the highest and most devoted thought of Judaism; but that is not representative of the teaching of the orthodox Rabbis in the days of Paul.

Much more representative of orthodox Judaism is the passage in the *Sayings of the Fathers* (3: 22 ff): "The world is ruled by goodness, yet everything is according to the amount of work." That saying is closely followed by a kind of parable or allegory: Everything is given on pledge (i.e. on pledge of repayment) and the net (i.e. of destiny) is spread all over the living. The shop is opened and the shopman (or money-lender) gives credit; the account-book is opened and the hand writes; everyone who desires to borrow comes and borrows; but the collectors (i.e. the angels) go round continually every day and exact payment from a man, whether he knows it or not (i.e. whether or not he is aware that calamity and sorrow and sickness are the result and the payment of the debt); and they (the collectors) have that on which they rely. And the judgment is a judgment of truth (i.e. accurate and fair); men have to pay what they owe but no more.

That is the accounting and the legalistic idea of religion. It looks on the relationship between God and man as a relationship of debit and of credit; it looks on religion as something which either earns so much credit, or incurs so much debt.

In the *Mishnah* there is the sentence: "It was because the Holy One wished to give Israel an opportunity to acquire merit that He gave them so much *Torah* (Law) and so many commandments." The Law was designed to enable a man to amass and to acquire credit in the sight of God. Moffatt quotes Marmorstein as summing the matter up: everything depends on the assumption that, " Man has got the ability to acquire merits before the heavenly Father." However weak and frail man may be, physically and morally, he is in a position to gather merits in the eyes of God.

Nothing could be more diametrically opposed to the conception of Paul. To Paul the essential idea of all religion is grace, and grace means that no man can ever acquire anything in the sight of God; that all that man can do is wonderingly to accept that which God freely and generously gives.

We may see the position that grace held in the mind of Paul, when we see that every single letter that Paul ever wrote begins and ends with grace. It is worth while to list Paul's beginnings and endings:—

Romans 1: 7. To all that be in Rome, beloved of God, called to be saints: Grace to you and peace from God our Father, and the Lord Jesus Christ.

Romans 16: 24. The grace of our Lord Jesus Christ be with you all.

1 *Corinthians* 1: 2, 3. Unto the Church of God which is at Corinth . . . grace be unto you, and peace, from God our Father, and from the Lord Jesus Christ.

1 *Corinthians* 16: 23. The grace of our Lord Jesus Christ be with you.

2 *Corinthians* 1: 1, 2. Paul, an apostle of Jesus Christ by the will of God . . . unto the Church of God which is at Corinth . . . Grace be to you and peace from the Lord Jesus Christ.

2 Corinthians 13: 14. The grace of the Lord Jesus Christ, and the love of God, and the communion of the Holy Ghost, be with you all.

Galatians 1: 1-3. Paul, an apostle . . . unto the churches of Galatia, grace be to you and peace from God the Father, and from our Lord Jesus Christ.

Galatians 6: 18. Brethren, the grace of our Lord Jesus Christ be with your spirit.

Ephesians 1: 1. Paul, an apostle of Jesus Christ . . . to the saints which are at Ephesus, and to the faithful in Christ Jesus, grace be to you and peace, from God our Father, and from the Lord Jesus Christ.

Ephesians 6: 24. Grace be with all them that love our Lord Jesus Christ in sincerity.

Philippians 1: 1. Paul and Timothy . . . to all the saints in Christ Jesus which are at Philippi . . . grace be unto you, and peace from God our Father, and from the Lord Jesus Christ.

Philippians 4: 23. The grace of our Lord Jesus Christ be with you all.

Colossians 1: 1, 2. Paul an apostle of Jesus Christ . . . to the saints and faithful brethren in Christ which are at Colosse; grace be unto you and peace from God our Father and the Lord Jesus Christ.

Colossians 4: 18. The salutation by the hand of me Paul. Remember my bonds. Grace be with you.

1 *Thessalonians* 1: 1. Paul . . . unto the Church of the Thessalonians . . . grace be unto you and peace from God our Father, and the Lord Jesus Christ.

1 *Thessalonians* 5: 28. The grace of our Lord Jesus Christ be with you.

2 *Thessalonians* 1: 1, 2. Paul . . . unto the Church of the Thessalonians . . . grace unto you and peace from God our Father, and the Lord Jesus Christ.

2 *Thessalonians* 3: 18. The grace of our Lord Jesus Christ be with you all.

Philemon 1-3. Paul, a prisoner of Jesus Christ . . . unto Philemon . . . grace to you and peace, from God our Father and the Lord Jesus Christ.

Philemon 25. The grace of the Lord Jesus Christ be with your spirit.

Every letter Paul wrote begins by striking the note of grace and ends by leaving the sound of grace ringing in men's ears.

When Paul thought and wrote like this, he was thinking and writing out of the depths and heights of his own religious experience. He knew what he had been, and he knew what he was—and there was no possible explanation of the change other than the grace of God. He knew of the work that once he had been doing, and he knew of the work which now had been given him to do; he knew how the persecutor had become the apostle; and only grace could explain that transformation. He knew what the heathen world was like, and he knew what a man could become in Christ, and the only possible explanation of that recreation was the grace of God. To Paul grace was central because he could never forget what grace had done for him, and daily he was seeing what grace could do for all men who would receive it.

When we read Paul's letters, we see, even on the most cursory reading, that Paul can speak without distinction of the grace of God and of the grace of Jesus Christ. In *1 Corinthians* 1: 4 he writes of "the grace of God which is given you by Jesus Christ." In *Galatians* 2: 21 he says: "I do not frustrate the grace of God." But in *1 Corinthians* 16: 23 he speaks of the grace of our Lord Jesus Christ, as he does in *Philippians* 4: 23; *Galatians* 6: 18; *Romans* 16: 24. And in all his opening addresses in his letters he speaks of the grace of God our Father and of the Lord Jesus Christ. Here again we are reminded of two great Pauline facts which we have often seen before.

First, behind everything is the initiative of God. The grace is God's grace; the offering love is the love of God; the initiative is the divine initiative. From this point of view the passage in *1 Corinthians* 1: 4 is very illuminating; it speaks of the grace of God which is given to you *en Christō Iesou*, which can equally well mean *by Jesus Christ* or *in Jesus Christ*. It was God's grace which was mediated to men by Jesus Christ; or, if we care to put it more vividly, but just as accurately, Jesus Christ is the incarnate Grace of God. Jesus is not only the channel or the expression of God's grace to men, great as that would be: He *is* God's grace to men.

Second, the fact that Paul begins his letters with the message of grace from God the Father and from the Lord Jesus Christ means that the mind of Jesus and the mind of God are one and the same; and the attitude of God and the attitude of Jesus to men are identical. Looking at this, as we might say, from the point of view of Jesus, we may say that Jesus did not come to this world by compulsion or by coercion, not even as one under orders, but because in Him there was the heart of God which is the heart of grace and love. Looking at this, as we might say, from the point of view of God, we may say that in no way did the coming of Jesus change or alter the attitude of God to men, in no way did anything that Jesus did change the wrath of God into the love of God, for the grace that is in Jesus is the grace of God. The love which Jesus demonstrated is the love of God. Grace is the grace of God and of the Lord Jesus Christ.

Let us now seek to bring to light the main Pauline ideas behind the conception of grace.

We must begin with that most basic of all ideas, an idea which we have already mentioned. The basic idea behind the conception of grace is the undeserved generosity of God. The idea of grace is the idea of God's forgiveness of man as a free gift, which man could never have deserved or earned, and which is given in the sheer generosity of God. In 1 *Corinthians* 1: 4 Paul speaks of " the grace of God which is given to you." In *Ephesians* 3: 7 he speaks of the gift of the grace of God. In 2 *Corinthians* 6: 1 he pleads with the Corinthians not to receive the grace of God in vain. Grace is something which can only be received. In 2 *Corinthians* 8: 1 he speaks of the grace bestowed upon the Churches in Macedonia. Grace is something which is

bestowed, not earned. In 2 *Corinthians* 8: 9 the grace of
Jesus is demonstrated by the fact that He who was rich
for our sakes became poor. Grace is this undeserved sacrifice
of the love of God; it is the generosity of God for us and
to us. In *Romans* 4: 4 grace and debt are contrasted.
Payment, contract, debt are something which a man earns
and incurs, and to which he has a right; grace is something
unearned and undeserved. In *Romans* 11: 6 grace and works
are contrasted. If works determine the relationship between
God and man, then grace is no longer grace. The idea of
merit and the idea of grace contradict each other. In
Ephesians 1: 6 it is said that it is by grace that we are accepted
in the beloved. Our acceptance is not something merited;
it is something given. In *Ephesians* 2: 5-9 Paul lays it
down with all the emphasis at his command that it is by
grace that we are saved. Man's salvation is due neither to
any merit nor to any effort of his own, but is dependent
solely on the sheer mercy and love of God. Even the faintest
idea of achievement is ruled out.

All through his letters Paul is entranced and engrossed
with the conviction that grace is the gift of the generosity
of God, which man can neither earn nor achieve, but which
he can only take and receive.

We must further note that for Paul there is a certain
inexhaustible abundance in the grace of God. In 2
Corinthians 9: 14 he speaks of the exceeding grace of God;
in 2 *Corinthians* 9: 8 he tells the Corinthians that God is
able to make all grace abound to them. In *Romans* 5: 20
there is the triumphant claim that where sin abounded

grace did much more abound. In *Ephesians* 1: 7 Paul speaks of the riches of His grace; and in *Ephesians* 2: 7 of the exceeding riches of His grace.

Grace is not a thing of narrow limitations, it is not a thing measured out in painstakingly accurate quantities with just enough and no more, as an ingredient might be in a recipe for some concoction; in grace there is a certain infinity; a certain complete adequacy; a certain inexhaustibility and illimitableness. No demand that can ever be made on it can exhaust it or strain its capacity and its power.

There is a corollary to this. As Moffatt put it in a vivid phrase: " Grace needs no supplement." It is by grace and grace alone that men are saved: nothing else is needful; in fact the introduction of anything else destroys the whole principle of salvation. This is the principle on which Paul insists in two of his greatest epistles.

It is the argument which is at the basis of *Romans*. The idea that Paul is there combatting is the idea which willingly accepts the fact that there is such a thing as grace, but holds that the operation of grace must be buttressed and helped by the performance of works designed to gain merit. In that telegraphic verse in *Romans* 11: 6 Paul lays it down: " And if by grace, then it is no more of works; otherwise grace is no more grace. But if it be of works, then is it no more grace: otherwise work is no more work." To Paul grace and works are mutually exclusive principles. If salvation has anything to do with works, then it is not of grace; it is of merit. If salvation be a thing of pure grace, then works do not enter into the matter, for merit cannot enter into the matter. We cannot set out to save ourselves by works, and then drag in the principle of grace; we cannot accept the principle that we are saved by grace, and then drag in works. The two exclude each other. If salvation is by works, then there is no such things as grace; and if grace is grace, it needs no supplement, but is all sufficient. The same argument recurs in *Galatians*. The Galatians did not deny the existence of grace. Their position was: Grace there is; but the work of grace has to be buttressed by the acceptance of circumcision and the acceptance of the Law. To put it bluntly, they said: A man cannot be saved by grace alone; to God's grace he must add his own circumcision and his own performance of the works of the Law. To God's grace he must add his own merit-winning performance.

In face of this way of thinking Paul flings his great challenge: " I do not frustrate the grace of God; for, if righteousness come by the Law, then Christ is dead in vain " (*Galatians* 2: 21). If a man can be saved by his own efforts, if by the meticulous performance of the works of the Law a man can establish the right relationship between himself and God, then the death of Christ was a colossal mistake, and His sacrifice was a completely unnecessary sacrifice.

Paul's whole position was: Accept the position that works are efficacious for the obtaining of salvation, and you have accepted the position that man by his unaided efforts can acquire merit in the sight of God; and simply to state that possibility is to obliterate the fact and the need of grace. But accept the position that all is of grace, that all is the generous gift of God, and nothing further is needed. To bring in anything further is to deny the full sufficiency and the full adequacy of grace.

Once again it is from personal experience that Paul is speaking. For Paul righteousness consists in a right relationship with God; to put it very simply, righteousness is friendship with God. All his life Paul strove for that friendship. He tried to attain to it by a meticulous performance of the works of the Law, for he could claim that in his performance of the demands of the Law he was blameless (*Philippians* 3: 6). And the only result of all this was that he was as far, and farther, away from God. Then in the face of the Cross he determined to fling himself quite simply on the mercy of God; and the peace of the right relationship with God came to him in a flash. God's grace had done what all his own works were powerless to do. Paul had made the great discovery that divine grace needs no human additions to be effective for salvation. For Paul that was the beginning of the Christian way, although as we shall yet see it was not the end.

Paul was convinced that we are saved by grace; but Paul would have gone further than that. Paul insisted that we are not only saved by grace, but that we are also called by grace. It is not only the final work that is the work of grace; the first movings, the first stirrings, the first faint desirings in a man's heart, are also the work of grace. The grace of God does not only save a man; the grace of God also shows a man his need to be saved and puts into his heart the desire for salvation. *Galatians* 1: 6 speaks of the Galatians as being called into the grace of Christ. *Romans* 11: 5 speaks of the election of grace. Our realisation that we are sinners, our penitence and our contrition are also the work of grace.

Here we have something which is of great importance. We have seen how Paul, especially in the later epistles, thinks in terms of the pre-existent Christ. We have also seen that Jesus Christ may be looked on as the embodiment and essence of the grace of God. Now if Jesus Christ was pre-existent and eternal, it means that God's grace is eternal. God's grace is not a kind of emergency measure which was introduced when a world founded on merit had collapsed; God's grace was not something which came in when the Law had been found to be impossible. The gracious purpose of God is the eternal purpose of God. God's grace was there before all time. God is the God of grace, yesterday, to-day and for ever.

All through his letters Paul makes it clear that he was convinced that not only his eternal salvation, but his whole personal life, his place and task in the world and in God's scheme of things were bound up with grace. This grace was working on him before he could ever have any conception that it was working.

It was that grace which separated him from his mother's womb and called him (*Galatians* 1: 15). In 2 *Corinthians* 1: 1 he says that he is an apostle by the will of God. These two sayings are very suggestive for they say the same thing in different ways. The first says that it was God's grace

which made Paul an apostle; the second says that it was
God's will which made Paul an apostle. That is to say, these
two sayings equate God's grace and God's will. In other
words, the grace of God is the will of God in action on the
lives of men.

It is the grace of God which gave Paul the task of preaching among the Gentiles the unsearchable riches of Christ
(*Ephesians* 3: 8). It is the grace of God which enabled
Paul like a wise master-builder to lay the foundations of
the faith of the Corinthians (1 *Corinthians* 3: 10). It is by
the grace of God that he has his walk and conversation in
the world (2 *Corinthians* 1: 12). It was the evident fact
that the grace of God had been given to him in relation to
his task among the Gentiles which persuaded the leaders
of the Church to accept him and, as it were, to ratify his
special commission (*Galatians* 2: 9). When Paul speaks,
it is through the grace of God that he does speak. "I say,"
he writes to the Romans, "through the grace given unto
me to every man that is among you not to think of himself
more highly than he ought to think" (*Romans* 12: 3). To
sum it up, Paul is what he is by grace and nothing else. "By
the grace of God I am what I am: and his grace which
was bestowed upon me was not in vain; but I laboured
more abundantly than they all; yet not I, but the grace of
God which was with me" (1 *Corinthians* 15: 10).

Here again we have one of these illuminating parallels.
This passage from 1 *Corinthians* is bound to turn our
thoughts to the companion passage in *Galatians* 2: 20:
"I live; yet not I, but Christ liveth in me." In the one

passage it is the grace of God which is in Paul; in the other passage it is Christ who is in him. The principle of Paul's life is grace; and the principle of Paul's life is Christ. Paul equates grace and Christ; both mean the same. Grace is Christ, and Christ is grace.

But it is not to be thought that Paul connected grace with only the great events and the great experiences of life. To Paul grace is the power which enables men to meet with gallantry and with adequacy the demands, the responsibilities, and the tasks of this life.

In 2 *Thessalonians* 2: 15-17 Paul is encouraging the Thessalonians to stand fast in the midst of the persecution and hardship which the Christian life necessary involves; and the ground of his request is that God " has given us everlasting consolation and good hope through grace." It was grace alone which could take them through the threatening stretches of this life.

Still more, it was grace which enabled Paul to carry on the routine business of life when he was up against it. He tells of the thorn in his flesh, and of his prayers that it should be taken away from him. He tells that that release was not to be; but the answer came: " My grace is sufficient for you " (2 *Corinthians* 12: 9). It was by that grace he lived every day; and in that grace he met the routine tasks of every day.

Still further, it is grace that is responsible for any nobility that there is in life. In 2 *Corinthians* 1: 12 Paul attributes his sincerity to the grace of God. In 2 *Corinthians* 8: 7 he attributes the liberality and the generosity of his converts to grace. In *Galatians* 5: 22, 23 the great qualities of the Christian life are called the fruit of the Spirit. The work of grace and the work of the Spirit are the same. The Spirit is the bringer of Grace; and grace is the power of the Spirit on the lives of men.

Grace is that power of God which clothes a man with day-to-day fortitude and strength. Grace is that power of God which adorns a man's life with lovely things. Grace is a man's day-to-day defence and inspiration. Grace is not only the glory of the mountain top; it is the source of strength for the ordinary road of the everyday.

There remains one side of the question still to be considered, and it can only be called the obligation of grace. Twice Paul uses a suggestive phrase, once of himself and once of his converts. In 1 *Corinthians* 15: 10 he says that the grace of God was not bestowed upon him in vain. In 2 *Corinthians* 6: 1 he beseeches his converts not to receive the grace of God in vain. In the latter cases the phrase is *eis kenon*, literally *for emptiness*.

Here is the other side of the question. It is here that the balance is preserved and that works come in. We can say that works have nothing to do with salvation; but we dare not say that works have nothing to do with the Christian life. Paul was far too good a Jew ever to say that, for Judaism was supremely an ethical religion. Christianity was a religion which issued in a certain way of life. Was not its first title The Way?

A man is saved by grace. What is the result of that? The result is that it lays upon a man the tremendous obligation to spend his life showing that that grace was not expended on him in vain. In grace there has reached out to him the love of God; he must therefore be filled with the unutterable longing and the burning desire to show himself, by the help of that grace, worthy of that grace. This is out of the sphere of law altogether; this is no legal obligation; it is not a case of doing good or being good, because the opposite would entail some legal penalty and punishment; it is a case of doing good and being good, because a man cannot bear to disappoint the love which has loved him so.

Here is what is at the back of *Romans* 6. At the back of that chapter there is an argument. The misguided ones say to Paul: "You believe that God's grace is the biggest thing in the world?" "Yes," answers Paul. "You believe that God's grace is wide enough to forgive any sin?" "Yes." Then the misguided ones go on to argue: "If that be so, let us go on sinning to our heart's content. God will forgive. Nay, more, the more we sin, the more chances this wonderful grace of God will receive to abound. Let us continue in sin that grace may get more chances to abound."

The whole essence of that argument is that it is a legal argument. Basically it says that we can go on sinning, because sin will not be punished, and grace will find a way of escape. But Paul's whole position is the lover's position: he cannot make the grace which loved him so of no effect; he must spend all life in one great endeavour to show how much he loves the God who loved him so much. That is the obligation of grace. That is where works come in.

Here is the balance we need. We can never be saved by works; but, if our salvation does not issue in works, it is not salvation. It is not first works, and then salvation. It is first salvation, and then works. We do not become saved by keeping the Law; we can only keep the Law because we are saved. All is of love, and a man cannot accept God's grace, and then go on to break the heart of the God who loved him so much.

XIV

PAUL'S THINKING
ABOUT THE HOLY SPIRIT

W HEN Jesus left this world in the body, it was His promise
that He would send the Holy Spirit to His people (*John*
14: 16, 17, 26; 16: 7, 13). It is therefore clear that the
doctrine of the Holy Spirit is one of the most important
doctrines in the Christian faith. It is quite true that the
Holy Spirit is some one to be experienced, and not some
thing to be talked and argued about. Nevertheless it will
be salutary for us to see the greatness of Paul's thinking
about the Spirit.

We must begin by noting that here, as everywhere else,
Paul leads all things straight back to God. Here as everywhere his uncompromising monotheism and his conviction
of the fundamental supremacy of God dominate all his
thinking.

Paul is certain that the Holy Spirit is the gift of God. In
1 *Thessalonians* 4: 8 he speaks of God who has also given
unto us His Holy Spirit. The Holy Spirit, as Paul sees the
matter, comes to men through the announcement of the
Christian gospel which produces faith in men's hearts. We

may put two of Paul's sayings together. In *Romans* 10: 17 Paul says that faith comes by hearing, and hearing by the word of God. In *Galatians* 3: 2, 5 he speaks of receiving the Spirit by the hearing of faith. The Spirit is received by men as a consequence of their hearing and accepting in faith the gospel which is preached to them. The Holy Spirit is God's gift to men, and comes to men when men react in faith to the message of good news sent by God.

Here, right at the beginning, we are face to face with an essential fact. The coming of the Holy Spirit into a man's life is not something which a man can win or achieve or gain by his own efforts; it is something which a man must accept and receive in faith. It is one of the great and simple facts of the Christian life that we cannot receive the Spirit of God unless we are prepared to wait patiently and prayerfully and expectantly for the coming of the Spirit.

More than once Paul uses a curious and a vivid phrase about the Holy Spirit. In 2 *Corinthians* 1: 22 he speaks of God who has given us the *earnest* of the Spirit. In 2 *Corinthians* 5: 5 he speaks of God giving us the *earnest* of the Spirit. In *Ephesians* 1: 14 he speaks of the Spirit who is the *earnest* of our inheritance.

The word which the Authorized Version translates *earnest* is the Greek word *arrabōn*. This is a word which very frequently appears in contracts and agreements. Amongst the papyri many of these contracts still exist, and this word occurs in them. A woman sells a cow and she receives one thousand *drachmae* as an *arrabōn* that in due time the remainder of the purchase price will be paid. A troop of castanet dancing-girls are engaged for a village festival; they are paid so many *drachmae* in advance as an *arrabōn*, with a proviso that this sum will be taken into account when the final payment is made, after the performance has been duly given. An *arrabōn* was an advance payment; it was a first instalment; it was a part-payment which was a pledge and a guarantee that in due time the full payment would be made.

Here we have a great thought. The gift of the Holy Spirit is the first instalment of that perfect blessedness which God has prepared for those who love Him. The life which is lived in the Spirit is a foretaste and a guarantee of the life of Heaven itself.

Very often Paul uses the conception of the Spirit in a very special way. All through his writings there runs a contrast between flesh and spirit. Often the two words occur in juxtaposition, the one expressing the opposite of the other.

In *Galatians* 3 : 3 Paul protests that those who began in the Spirit now think that they can be made perfect in the flesh. In *Galatians* 5 : 16ff he contrasts walking in the Spirit with fulfilling the lusts of the flesh, and he contrasts the fruit of the Spirit, and the fruit of the flesh. In *Galatians* 6 : 8 he contrasts those who sow to the flesh, and thereby reap corruption, and those who sow to the Spirit, and thereby reap life everlasting. *Romans* 8 is full of this contrast. In *Romans* 8 : 5 he contrasts those who are after the flesh and who mind the things of the flesh, and those who are after the Spirit and who mind the things of the Spirit. In *Romans* 8: 9 he insists that his converts are no longer in the flesh but are in the Spirit. More than once (e.g. *Romans* 8: 1) he urges his converts to walk, not after the flesh, but after the Spirit. For Paul the Spirit stood for all God's goodness and God's power and God's way of things as contrasted with the natural evil and the natural propensity to sin of the man without Christ.

In another vivid phrase Paul speaks of the possession of the Spirit as being the *sign* and *seal* that a man belongs to God. In *2 Corinthians* 1: 22 he speaks of God who has *sealed* us, and given us the *earnest* of the Spirit. In *Ephesians* 1: 13 he says that his hearers are *sealed* with the Spirit who had been promised. In *Ephesians* 4: 30 he urges them not to grieve the Holy Spirit with whom they are *sealed* against the day of redemption.

Just as in the case of the word *arrabōn*, there lies behind this also a trading and commercial and business practice. There were two cases in which a seal was specially significant and important in the ancient world. When a man sealed a document or a will he guaranteed by affixing his seal that it was his, and that he was prepared to stand by the contents and the conditions of it. Further, very frequently goods were sealed. A sack or a package might be closed with a seal placed over the knot in the cord or rope which closed it. The seal was the sender's guarantee that the goods really came from him, and that they were of the standard which he had undertaken to deliver.

The gift of the Spirit is God's seal upon man, guaranteeing

the fact that that man belongs to Him. When we see a
man living with the peace and the power and the joy and
the serenity and the wisdom which only the Spirit can
bring, that is unanswerable proof that that man belongs to
God, and is God's man.

Before ever Christianity came into this world, the Jews
had their beliefs about the Spirit of God. The Jews had
two basic beliefs about Spirit. They believed that the
Spirit was the person who brought and revealed God's
truth to men; and they believed that the Spirit was the
person who enabled men to recognise the truth, and to
understand it, when it came to them.

Again and again Jesus had called the Spirit whom He
promised the Spirit of truth. He had said that the Spirit
would teach men all things; that the Spirit would bring
all things to their remembrance; that the Spirit would guide
them into all truth (*John* 14: 17, 26; 15: 26; 16: 13). It
was then very natural that Paul should look on the Spirit
as the revealer of God's truth to men, as God's agent in
revelation.

In *Ephesians* 3: 3-5 he speaks of the revelation of that
eternal mystery of God which is now revealed by the
Holy Spirit to the prophets and to the apostles. In 1 *Corinthians* 2: 11 he insists that, just as only a man's spirit
knows the things that are in the man, so only the Spirit
of God knows the things of God. He claims that the things
which he himself teaches are not the product of man-made
or man-discovered wisdom, but the result of the revelation
of the Spirit of God (1 *Corinthians* 2: 13, 14).

Paul knew and used the old Jewish idea that the Spirit of God both reveals God's truth and enables a man to recognise God's truth when it is revealed to him. But it was clear to Paul that the man who shut his heart to the Spirit, the man who refused to wait prayerfully and patiently and expectantly until he had received the Spirit, could not possibly receive or recognise God's truth. Even if it came to him, he would not recognise it as God's truth, for the Spirit is revealer and interpreter in one.

We are well aware that over-simplification can be dangerously easy and can in fact drift into heresy; but it is not altogether wrong to say that for Paul God the Father was God in creation, in recreation and in providence; that God the Son was God for ever and through all eternity active in redemption and in the saving of men; and that God the Holy Spirit is God for ever revealing His truth and conveying His power to men. Certainly to Paul the Holy Spirit is God's agent in revelation. We may put it this way. Externally, the Holy Spirit is the agent who brings God's truth to men; internally, the Holy Spirit is the person and the power who prepares men's hearts to receive that truth, and who enlightens their minds to comprehend and to understand it, and who enables and inspires them to pass it on to others.

We may put this in a wider way. The Holy Spirit is God's Mediator; the Holy Spirit is the person who brings and who distributes God's gifts to men. It is the Holy Spirit who sheds abroad the love of God within our hearts (*Romans* 5: 5). It is the Holy Spirit who leads and guides us into true sonship of God (*Romans* 8: 14). It is by the Holy Spirit that we have access to the Father (*Ephesians* 2: 18).

In this connection there are two conceptions of exceeding beauty in the thought of Paul.

In *Romans* 8: 16 Paul writes: " The Spirit Himself beareth witness with our spirit, that we are the children of God." In *Galatians* 4: 6 (cp. *Romans* 8: 15) he writes that because we are sons, God has sent forth the Spirit of His Son, into our hearts, crying, Abba, Father.

There is a most beautiful idea behind this. What gives us the certainty that we are the sons of God? What moves us to look up to God, and to cry, Father? How, even if we have a wistful desire to take it, can we be sure that the way is open to us to God? Even if there are the deepest longings in our hearts that it should be so, how can we be sure that the God to whom we look up is Father? Paul's answer is that the impulse which moves us in the first place to desire these things is the impulse of the Spirit. And the certainty in our hearts that we will not be disappointed is also the work of the Spirit. It is the Spirit who tells us of our need of God; it is the Spirit who starts us on the way to God; it is the Spirit who makes us sure that God is waiting to welcome us, and that He is the Father whom our hearts desire.

Paul's second idea in this connection is perhaps even more beautiful. In *Romans* 8: 26 Paul writes, as the Authorized Version has it: " Likewise the Spirit also helpeth our infirmities: for we know not what we should pray for as

178

we ought: but the Spirit Himself maketh intercession for us with groanings which cannot be uttered; and He that searcheth the hearts knoweth what is the mind of the Spirit, because He maketh intercession for the saints according to the will of God." Moffatt translates that passage: " So too the Spirit assists us in our weakness; for we do not know how to pray aright, but the Spirit pleads for us with sighs that are beyond words, and He who searches the human heart knows what is the mind of the Spirit, since the Spirit pleads before God for the saints." In his commentary on *Romans*, Dr. C. H. Dodd has an exposition of that passage which is one of the noblest and most beautiful that has ever been penned. When we pray, we know too little of the will and purposes of God ever to pray aright. All that we can really offer to God, the highest kind of prayer, is an inarticulate sigh of the human heart and spirit, but the Holy Spirit can take that inarticulate sigh and translate it for us in the presence of God. William James, the famous psychologist, once wrote: " Many reasons have been given why we should not pray, whilst others are given why we should. But in all this very little is said of the reason why we do pray. The reason why we pray is simply that we cannot help praying." As C. H. Dodd so magnificently puts it: " Prayer is the divine in us appealing to the God above us." Paul would have said that it is the Holy Spirit within us who awakens that unutterable longing for God. He would have said that, being men we know not what to pray for; we can only bring to God a deep sigh of the human heart, which the Holy Spirit interprets to God for us.

In every letter Paul makes it clear that it is his conviction that the Holy Spirit is the source of the Christian life. The Holy Spirit helps our infirmities (*Romans* 8: 26). It is through the power of the Spirit that we abound in hope (*Romans* 15: 13). It is by the power of the Spirit that we are sanctified (*Romans* 15: 16; 2 *Thessalonians* 2: 13). The Spirit is the source of Paul's own power (*Romans* 15: 19). In 1 *Corinthians* 6: 9-11 Paul sets out the grim list of sins to which the Corinthians had once been subject; but they are washed, they are sanctified, they are justified in the name of the Lord Jesus and by the Spirit of our God.

The Holy Spirit is the source of the many gifts which are necessary for the administration of the day to day ordering of the Christian Church (1 *Corinthians* 12: 4ff). All lovely qualities which adorn the Christian life are the fruit of the Spirit (*Galatians* 5: 22). Our change from glory into glory until we become like Christ is the work of the Spirit (2 *Corinthians* 3: 18). The fact that Christians can be built and fitted together until their fellowship can become the habitation of God is the work of the Spirit (*Ephesians* 2: 22). The strength of character and of personality that the Christian can achieve is the work of the Spirit (*Ephesians* 3: 16).

It can be seen that for Paul the beginning and the middle and the end of the Christian life all depend upon the work of the Spirit. The development of the individual Christian and the perfecting of the Church both depend upon the Spirit. A man's call, a man's forgiveness, a man's growth in grace are all the product of the power of the Spirit.

There is something very suggestive here. Something

new has been brought into the conception of the work of the Spirit of God. In the Old Testament and in Jewish thought there was much about the Spirit, but for the most part it is true to say that the power and action of the Spirit were connected with extraordinary and abnormal happenings. The great utterances and the great visions of the prophets, sudden manifestations of the splendour of God, were the work of the Spirit; but in the New Testament the Spirit has become even more precious, for the Spirit has become the moving, the controlling, and the upholding power for everyday life and for everyday action.

The heathen philosophers cried out for what they called " the medicine for the sick soul." For Paul the power of the Spirit was that very medicine, for the Spirit cleansed men from sin, broke the chains that bound them, and gave them day to day strength and joy and hope and peace and power.

It is then easy to see how for Paul the great actions and the great qualities of the Christian life are all in the Spirit. The Kingdom of God is righteousness, peace and joy in the Holy Spirit (*Romans* 14: 17). We pray in the Spirit (*Ephesians* 6: 18). Christians love each other in the Spirit (*Colossians* 1: 8). The gospel comes to men in the Holy Spirit (1 *Thessalonians* 1: 5). Even in the midst of persecution, the Thessalonians have joy in the Holy Spirit (1 *Thessalonians* 1: 6). The worship of the Christian is shared and offered in the Spirit (*Philippians* 3: 3).

It is as if the Spirit is the atmosphere and the climate in which alone the great Christian qualities can grow and in which alone the Christian graces can flourish, and in which alone the activities of the Christian individual and the Christian church can be carried on.

It is no surprise therefore to find Paul identifying the Spirit with life. The Spirit is life because of righteousness, he writes in *Romans* 8 : 10. The Spirit is the power by which the Christian enters the Christian life, and the power in which he lives the Christian life. The Spirit is at one and the same time the source and the sustainer of life in the fully Christian sense of the term.

When we think of what Paul says of the Spirit and attributes to the Spirit, it becomes clear that the things which are in the Spirit are the things which are in Christ. Paul was not a systematic theologian but a man whom Christ had found and a man who had found Christ, and who was seeking to share that experience with others. He was not primarily propagating a theology; he was seeking to share a religious experience. It is therefore not surprising to find Paul in the end simply saying: " The Lord is the Spirit " (2 *Corinthians* 3: 17). To him to live in the Spirit was to live in the presence of his risen and ever-living Lord. It would not be too much to say that for Paul the Spirit was the fulfilment of the promise of Christ that He would be with His men alway even unto the end of the world (*Matthew* 28: 20).

XV

PAUL'S THINKING ABOUT SIN

G. K. Chesterton once laid it down that, whatever else is true about man it is certainly true that man is not what he was meant to be. With that dictum Paul would have completely agreed; and the reason for that situation is sin. There are some who would accuse Paul of being, as it were, obsessed with sin. But the fact is this—Paul uses the word *hamartia*, the commonest word for sin, 62 times in his letters; and of these 62 occurrences 48 are in *Romans*; and only 14 in all the other letters; and in the letter to the Philippians the word *hamartia* does not occur at all. It is obviously true to say that Paul saw with intensity the seriousness of sin, but it would be quite wrong to say that he had a morbid obsession with the idea of sin. Let us then see what Paul has to say of sin.

First and foremost, we must note that Paul insisted on the universality of sin. Sin was not to him something in which only some people are involved; it is not like a disease which strikes some, and which others escape. To Paul every man is involved in sin. Both Jews and Gentiles are under sin (*Romans* 3: 9). All have sinned and come short of the glory of God (*Romans* 3: 23). Sin is a universal human predicament.

For Paul that universality of sin was doubly proved. First, it was a fact of human experience. Second, it was a fact of history. To Paul all men were involved in the sin of Adam; that is the whole point of *Romans* 5. It is not that all men sin *as* Adam sinned; it is not that all men inherited from Adam the taint and the tendency to sin; it is that in Adam all men did actually sin. To us this is a strange argument. To a Jew it was perfectly natural. The Jew believed strongly in solidarity. To this day there are primitive tribes, and if you ask a man from one of these tribes his name, he will not tell you his name; he will give the name of his tribe. He is bound up in his tribe; he has no separate existence; apart from the tribe he does not live. Just in that same way, in Adam all men sinned.

Paul's proof of that is simple, and to a Jew quite logical. Because Adam sinned, death entered into the world. Death is the penalty of sin. Adam's sin was a direct breach of a commandment of God. Where there is no commandment there can be no sin. Now the Law was not in the world until Moses came; therefore there could be no breach of the Law; there could be no sin in that sense of the term. And yet between Adam and Moses men still died. They had not broken the Law, for there was no Law to break; and still they died. Why? Because they had sinned in Adam; in him they had actually committed sin.

That is the Pauline argument. For him the facts of human experience, and the facts of history, demonstrated the universality of sin. So then we begin with this fact that all have sinned.

It is inevitable that Paul should closely connect the Law and sin. There are two senses in which the Law, so to speak, produced sin. The Law defines sin; where there is no law there can be no sin; and in that sense the Law creates sin. To take a simple modern example. For a long time it may be quite legal to drive a motor car up and down a street in either direction. Then new traffic regulations are laid down, and a law is enacted whereby that street becomes a one-way street. By the enacting of that law a quite new breach of the law has been created. Before the passing of the law it was perfectly legal to drive up or down that street in either direction; now it is only legal to drive in one direction, and to drive in the other direction is a newly created breach of the law. From the legal point of view a new sin has been created. So then without the law there can be no sin. " By the Law is the knowledge of sin " (*Romans* 3: 20). " Scripture has shut up all under sin " (*Galatians* 3: 22). " Sin is not imputed when there is no law " (*Romans* 5: 13). " The Law entered that the offence might abound " (*Romans* 5: 20). Until the coming of the Law, no one could break the Law, and therefore there is a sense in which the Law created sin.

But there is another, and a much more dangerous sense, in which the Law *provokes* sin. It is a characteristic of human nature that as soon as a thing is forbidden it becomes desirable. It is the grass on the other side of the fence that is always most succulent. That is what Paul discovered by bitter experience: "I had not known sin, but by the Law: for I had not known desire except the Law had said: Thou shalt not covet." Sin "took occasion" by the commandment. "Without the Law sin was dead; for I was alive without the Law once; but when the commandment came, sin sprang to life, and I died." The commandment which was designed for life effected death. It was through the commandment that sin took occasion to deceive Paul and to lead him to death (*Romans* 7: 7-11). Here is the universal dilemma. The Law, which is meant to forbid and to control sin, provokes sin, because of the fatal fascination of the forbidden thing. C. H. Dodd quotes in illustration of this the famous passage from Augustine:

There was a pear-tree near our vineyard laden with fruit. One stormy night we rascally youths set out to rob it and carry our spoils away. We took off a huge load of pears—not to feast upon them ourselves, but to throw them to the pigs—though we ate just enough to have the pleasure of forbidden fruit. They were nice pears, but it was not the pears that my wretched soul coveted, for I had plenty better at home. I picked them simply to be a thief. The only feast I got was a feast of iniquity, and that I enjoyed to the full. What was it that I loved in that theft? Was it the pleasure of acting against the law, in order that I, a prisoner under rules, might have a maimed counterfeit of freedom, by doing with impunity what was forbidden, with a dim similitude of omnipotence? (*Confessions* 2: 4-6).

It is a fact of experience that the human heart desires the forbidden thing; and the law by forbidding a thing awakens the desire for it.

So then in a double sense sin and the law are inextricably connected. The Law defines sin, and, therefore in a sense, creates sin; the Law by forbidding a thing awakens a desire for it. As Paul insists, without the Law there can be no sin.

Since sin and the Law are so closely intertwined, it is clear that sin is disobedience. It was by one man's disobedience that the many were constituted sinners (*Romans* 5: 19). Any man who was capable of rendering to God and to God's law a perfect obedience would never sin. We may put this in another way—sin means listening to oneself instead of listening to God.

As soon as we have disobeyed the voice of God, and sinned, another element enters into the situation. Through sin we *come short* of the glory of God (*Romans* 3: 23). What does that mean? When we go back to the old story of creation we find that God made man in His own image, and His own likeness (*Genesis* 1: 26). That is to say God made man to bear His own image, and therefore to reflect His own glory. Sin therefore is what keeps a man from being what he was meant to be and what he was created to be. Here we come at the basic meaning of *hamartia*. *Hamartia* was not originally an ethical word at all. It was, in fact, a word from shooting; and it meant *a missing of the target*. Sin is the failure to hit the target; sin is the failure to be what we were meant to be; sin is falling below one's own possibilities. The moment a man begins

187

to disobey he begins to lose the image of God, and therefore falls short of what he was meant to be. Here is the very foundation in practice of the universality of sin. To fail to do one's best as workman, to fail to be as good a father, mother, son, daughter as one might have been, to fail to use and to develop the gifts of hand and eye and mind and brain that God has given us, in any way to fall short of the best that we could be is a sin. Disobedience to God means failure in life; and failure to hit the target is sin.

It is characteristic of any disease that when it obtains a grip it spreads; and so does sin. Sin and the offence *abound* (*Romans* 5: 20). Sin is like some trouble which is allowed to gain a grip. Weeds which are not eradicated seed themselves and spread ever more virulently. A source of infection which is not removed is a breeding ground of disease. A cancer, unless it is excised, grows and spreads and develops. There is in sin an extraordinary power of self-multiplication. It sweeps like an epidemic through life, when it has gained the smallest foothold.

As Paul saw it, in a double sense *sin begets death*. It does that in the moral and the spiritual sense. " Sin, taking occasion by the commandment, deceived me, and by it slew me " (*Romans* 7: 11). " The body is dead because of sin " (*Romans* 8: 10). Sin has a killing power. It kills goodness; it kills beauty; it kills human love and human fellowship; it kills conscience and it kills character. If a man allows sin to grip him, the end is that he is dead in sin.

But as Paul saw it, not only does sin beget moral and

spiritual death; sin is also the cause of *physical death*. Paul's teaching is that, if there had been no sin, there would have been no death. Death came into the world by sin (*Romans* 5: 12); sin reigned unto death (*Romans* 5: 21). A man can be the servant of sin unto death or of obedience unto righteousness (*Romans* 6: 16). The wages of sin is death (*Romans* 6: 23). As Paul sees it, it is through sin, and because of sin, that death entered into the world. Sin is the destroyer of moral and spiritual and physical life.

Again and again Paul uses words which stress in vivid pictures the power and the grip of sin. Sin *reigns* unto death (*Romans* 5: 21). The word for *reign* is *basileuein*, which comes from the noun *basileus* which means a *king*. Sin becomes a king, and men become its wretched subjects. Sin is like a *slavery*. The work of Christ is that we should no longer be the slaves (*douleuein*) of sin (*Romans* 6: 6). In his pre-Christian days the Christian was the *slave* (*doulos*) of sin (*Romans* 6: 20). " Sin," says Paul, " shall not *have dominion* over you " (*Romans* 6: 14). The word he uses is *kurieuein* and *kurios* was the title for the emperor, or for the master of a slave, and denotes ownership and supreme power. In his Christless days Paul saw himself as *sold into the power of sin* (*Romans* 7: 14), like a slave, knocked down at an auction, and becoming the absolute property of his owner.

As our own experience has shown again and again there is a tyranny and an enslavement in sin; the grip of sin can become unbreakable; a man may desperately desire, for instance, to free himself from a habit, and be quite unable to do so. He has become the slave, the property, the subject, the creature of sin.

Sin does not remain an external power outside a man. As Paul saw it, sin takes up its residence within a man, and occupies him as an enemy occupies a conquered country. He speaks of the sin that dwells (*oikein*) in him; he speaks of the sin in his members (*Romans* 7: 20, 23). Sin is not simply an influence or a force; it is a kind of personal demonic power which invades a man and takes up its residence within him. It is in fact there that Paul's whole conception of the body and the flesh come in. Any invading enemy requires a bridgehead; it is the flesh which gives sin its bridgehead. The flesh is not simply the body; and the sins of the flesh are not simply the fleshly sins. Idolatry, hatred, strife, wrath, heresy are all sins of the flesh (*Galatians* 5: 20). The flesh is human nature apart from God. And it is just there that sin obtains the bridgehead for the invasion whose end is the occupation of the human personality.

There are two further facts about sin in the Pauline view which we must fit into this scheme. First, sin is that which hinders the work of Christ and the spread of the gospel. Those who hinder Paul from bringing the message of God to the Gentiles fill up their sin, they bring their sin to its summit and to its fulness (1 *Thessalonians* 2: 16). Second, sin is the opposite of faith. "Whatsoever is not of faith is sin" (*Romans* 14: 23). Now faith for Paul was total surrender to God; and therefore sin is anything which hinders a man's total surrender to God. Sin is that which opposes or lessens or obstructs the lordship of God and His Christ in the world or in the human heart.

It is not our task here to examine the words for particular sins, but there are certain general words for sin which Paul uses, each of which has its contribution to make to his total picture of sin.

Sin is *adikia*, and the sinful man is *adikos*. The normal Authorized Version translation of these two words is *unrighteousness* and *unrighteous*. We shall best see the meaning of these words, if we come at them from their opposite. In Greek ethics the good man, the righteous man, the just man is *dikaios*; and the man who is *dikaios* is defined as the man who gives both to gods and to men what is their due. Unrighteousness is the failure to give to God and to men what is their due. The unrighteous man is the man who fails in his duty to God and to men; he is the man who fails to give God his love and his obedience, and who fails to give men his charity and his service. Paul so describes the sinner in *Romans* 1: 18; 1: 29; 3: 5; 6: 13; 9: 14; 1 *Corinthians* 6: 1, 7, 8.

The words *adikia* and *adikos* are not uncommonly joined with the words *asebeia* and *asebēs*. These words describe the *godless* man and his conduct. Sin is godlessness; it is the total disregard of God; it is treating God as if He did not exist. It is not atheism, for atheism does not believe that there is a God. Godlessness knows that there is a God —and totally disregards Him; it is therefore even worse than atheism.

Sin is *anomia;* and the sinner is the *anomos* (*Romans* 6: 19;

2: 12; 1 *Corinthians* 9: 21; 2 *Corinthians* 6: 14). *Nomos* means *law;* and the sinner is the man who disobeys God's law. This word stresses the deliberation of sin; it describes the man who well knows the right, and who yet does the wrong.

Sin is a *parakoē* (*Romans* 5: 19; 2 *Corinthians* 10: 6). The Authorized Version translates this word *disobedience*. But there is a vivid picture in it. It comes from the verb *parakouein*. *Parakouein* originally meant *to mishear* or *to fail to hear*. It could be used of the man who did not catch something that someone else said, because it was indistinctly spoken, or because he himself was deaf. Then it came to mean *deliberately not to hear*, as it were, to close the ears to. In the last analysis a man hears only what he wants to hear; and sin means closing the ears to God in order to listen to oneself.

Sin is *parabasis* and the sinner is *parabatēs* (*Romans* 2: 23; 4: 15; *Galatians* 3: 19; *Hebrews* 2: 2; *James* 2, 9). *Parabasis* literally means *a stepping across*. The picture is of a man stepping across a line across which he has no right to step, of a man invading forbidden territory, and crossing the bounds of that which is right. Sin is the deliberate crossing of the fence between right and wrong.

Sin is *paraptōma* (*Romans* 4: 25; 5: 15, 16, 17, 20; *Ephesians* 1: 7; 2: 1; 2: 5). *Paraptōma* originally meant *a slip*, a trip up, a blunder. Longinus, for instance, the Greek literary critic, uses it for the blunders in style and taste of which even the best authors are occasionally capable. It is of all words for sin the least deliberate. It describes the slip which a man may make when he is off his guard, when he is not looking where he is going, when he takes his eye off the goal. Sin is the failure in concentration, the failure in self-control through which a man is swept or slips into sin.

Sin results in *pōrōsis* (*Romans* 11: 7; 11: 25; 2 *Corinthians* 3: 14; *Ephesians* 4: 18). *Pōrōsis* describes a process of petrifaction, resulting in the complete loss of all sensation and of all ability to feel. As Burns said of sin: " It petrifies the feelings." If a man goes on sinning he kills his sense of decency and honour and goodness; he comes to a stage when regret and remorse and penitence are dead. It is the progressive hardening of the heart, until the heart can no longer respond in obedience to God and in compassion to men.

Finally, there are two things to be put against all this. First, grace is the antidote to sin. Where sin abounds grace still further abounds (*Romans* 5: 20). There is a power which can check sin; and there is a power which can liberate from sin; and that power is grace; and grace is even greater than sin. Second, in spite of sin God has never ceased to love men. God commends His love to us, in that while we were yet enemies, Christ died for us (*Romans* 5: 8). There is a love which will not let us go, and which will go even to the Cross to conquer sin—and therein lies our hope.

XVI

PAUL'S CONCEPTION
OF THE FLESH

ANY examination of the mind of Paul which failed to seek
to understand what Paul meant by the flesh would be very
inadequate, for this expression occurs again and again in
his letters. At the same time the most cursory reading of
Paul's letters makes it plain that it is not easy to understand
just what Paul did mean by this word, for he very obviously
does not use it always in the same way. He uses it in many
different connections and with many different connotations,
although it is true to say that among the many uses of it,
there is one use which is characteristic of the mind and
thought of Paul.

We have only to glance at a saying like 2 *Corinthians* 10: 3
to see the difficulty. There Paul writes: Though we walk
in the flesh (*en sarki*), we do not war *after the flesh* (*kata sarka*).
It is quite clear that in that one sentence Paul is using the
word *flesh* with widely differing meanings, although these
meanings may be inter-related. *To walk in the flesh* is
something which no man can avoid; *to war after the flesh*
is something which every man must avoid. Let us then see

if we can disentangle the various Pauline uses of the word flesh, *sarx*.

Paul frequently uses the word flesh in a quite neutral and literal sense, meaning nothing other than the human body. He tells us that his first visit to Galatia and his first preaching there were due to infirmity of the flesh (*Galatians* 4: 13). That simply means that his first arrival in Galatia was due to some bodily ailment, some physical illness. He speaks of the thorn in his flesh (2 *Corinthians* 12: 7). The overwhelming probability is that the thorn in his flesh was a physical disability which caused him intense and excruciating pain. He speaks of being absent in the flesh (*Colossians* 2: 5), and of those who have never seen his face in the flesh (*Colossians* 2: 1). He is referring there to those who did not know him personally, and who had never seen him face to face in the physical presence. He speaks of living in the flesh and abiding in the flesh (*Philippians* 1: 22, 24). He is referring to the bodily, physical life which he lives. When he speaks of Jesus, he speaks of the body of His flesh (*Colossians* 1: 22) by which he means the natural, physical, human body which Jesus wore in his days upon earth. He speaks of the Christian duty of ministering to those who are poor in carnal things (*Romans* 15: 27). The word is the corresponding adjective *sarkikos*. *Carnal* is an unfortunate translation, because it is a word which in English has acquired a bad connotation. When Paul speaks of ministering to the carnal needs of those who are less fortunate, he simply means the duty of bringing practical help for everyday life and living to those who are poor

and hungry and who never have enough. In 1 *Corinthians*
9: 27 he speaks about keeping his body under, and of bringing it into subjection; and, if that passage be read in its context, its meaning is that throughout the long, weary and
hard years he had taught and disciplined himself to do
without the luxuries and the refinements, the indulgences
and the softnesses, which he might well have had and
enjoyed.

We shall see later that when Paul speaks of the sins of
the flesh he is thinking of far more than sexual sins, that in
fact those sins are a very small part, and not the most important part, of sins of the flesh. But in 1 *Corinthians* 7: 28
he speaks of those who have trouble in the flesh, where the
reference is to the problem of continence in a difficult and
a dangerous situation.

Paul frequently uses the conception of the flesh when he
wishes to speak of things from what we might call the
purely human angle, when he is considering things from
the human and not from the divine point of view. Usually
there is no kind of condemnation, not even any kind of
criticism, involved.

Very often Paul uses the phrase *the flesh* just as we might
say *humanly speaking*. So Jesus was born of the seed of
David according to the flesh (*Romans* 1: 3). That is to say,
looked at from the human angle, Jesus was a descendant
of David. He lays it down that no flesh shall be justified
in the sight of God by deeds of the Law (*Romans* 3: 20).
Here no flesh simply means no human being. He speaks
of Abraham our father as pertaining to the flesh (*Romans*

4: 1). That is simply to say that it is from Abraham that the Jews trace their physical descent. In *Ephesians* 6: 5 he urges servants to be obedient to those who are their masters after the flesh. There he is drawing the distinction between those who are their human masters and God who is their heavenly Lord.

In *Galatians* 1: 16 he says that after his conversion he did not confer with flesh and blood. That is to say, he did not seek counsel and advice from any merely human authority. In 2 *Corinthians* 1: 17 he speaks of a purpose according to the flesh, that is, a purely human purpose. In *Philippians* 3: 3, 4 he claims that, if anyone has grounds for glorying in the flesh, he has more. That is to say, if it comes to a contest on the grounds of human achievement and human qualifications, he can stand comparison with any man, and emerge victorious from the comparison. In 2 *Corinthians* 11: 18 he speaks of those who glory after the flesh, that is, those who stake their claims for honour and for authority on purely human achievements and on purely human grounds.

This is in fact one of the commonest of all uses of the word flesh in Paul's letters. It does not confer or imply any kind of rebuke or condemnation. It merely states things in purely human terms apart from the divine plan and purpose.

Paul has two uses of the word flesh at which we may glance in the passing, because they are interesting and illuminating. In one case he uses the word almost in the sense of *pre-Christian*. In *Romans* 7: 5 he uses the expression

" when we were in the flesh." In its context that means before we met Christ, when we were struggling along defeatedly in our own strength and before we found peace and power in Jesus Christ. It is as if Paul looked at life in two stages. In the first stage he was in the flesh trying to deal with things in his own strength, and meeting with nothing but frustration. In the second stage he was in Christ, and was experiencing all the victorious blessedness which being in Christ brings with it.

The other instance is when he uses the allied word *sarkikos*, which the Authorized Version translates *carnal* in the sense of *sub-Christian*. In 1 *Corinthians* 3: 3 he demands of the Corinthians: " Are you not carnal (*sarkikoi*) ? " The reason of the demand is that they are still living a quarrelsome, divided, sectarian existence, which is far below the standard of the life which those who are in Christ should live. They are living a sub-Christian life.

We now arrive at the characteristically Pauline usage of the word flesh. In the mind of Paul the flesh is inextricably connected with sin. In this sense the word flesh has lost its physical meaning and has acquired an ethical meaning. In *Romans* 7: 14 he says that in the days before he met Christ, he was carnal (*sarkinos*, another allied adjective) and sold under sin. In *Romans* 7: 23-25 there is the agonised cry of the sick soul, which ends with the heart-breaking dilemma: " So then with the mind I myself serve the law of God; but with the flesh the law of sin." In *Romans* 8: 6 to be carnally minded (literally, the habit of mind of the flesh) is death. In *Romans* 8: 7 that same habit of mind is enmity against God. In *Romans* 8: 12, 13 to live after the flesh is to die.

In *Romans* 13: 14 Paul urges his people to make no provision for the flesh and for the lusts thereof. In *Galatians* 5: 13 he insists that the Galatians must not use their freedom as an occasion for the flesh. In *Galatians* 5: 17 flesh and spirit are wholly opposed. In 2 *Corinthians* 7: 1 he speaks of the filthiness of the flesh. In *Ephesians* 2: 3 he speaks of the lusts of the flesh. Here the flesh is integrally connected with sin.

It is here that we must be careful to note one all-important fact. When Paul thinks of the lusts of the flesh, he is by no means thinking only, or even mainly, of the grosser sins, the sins which in our modern terminology are the sins of the flesh. Certainly he includes them, but they are not the principal sins of the flesh. In *Galatians* 5: 19, 20 we have the list of the sins of the flesh. That list includes adultery, fornication, lasciviousness, uncleanness; but it also includes hatreds, variance, emulations, wrath, strife, envyings, murder, drunkenness, and even heresies.

It is quite clear that for Paul it is not only the fleshly sins which have their seat in the flesh; it is there that what we would call the spiritual sins also have their seat and their origin. It is of the greatest importance to note this.

We must bring in here another and a parallel Pauline conception—the conception of the old man. In *Ephesians* 4: 22 Paul exhorts his people to put off the old man which is corrupt according to deceitful lusts. There are two parallel passages which together show how closely interconnected are the conceptions of the flesh and of the old man. In *Romans* 6: 6 Paul writes: " Knowing this, that our old man is crucified with Him, that the body of sin might be destroyed, that henceforth we should not serve sin." And in *Galatians* 5: 24 Paul writes: " They that are Christ's have crucified the flesh with the affections and lusts." The parallelism is so close that it is clear that for Paul the flesh and the old man stand for one and the same thing; they stand for the helpless subjection to sin which dominates life before Christ enters it.

We must now ask what was in Paul's mind when he speaks of the flesh, and when he so closely connects the flesh and sin. Was this connection the outcome of the normal Greek dualism of the world in which Paul lived? The thinking Greeks were dominated by the conviction that matter is essentially evil, that matter as such is flawed and debased. With that conviction the Greeks could not do otherwise than think of the body as essentially evil; they were bound to long for the day when they would be rid of the body once and for all.

For the Greek the flesh of the body is the prison-house of the soul; the whole material universe is evil, and spirit alone is good. That is why the greatest of the Greeks believed in the immortality of the soul but would have been shocked at the idea of the resurrection of the body. To the Greek the body was an unmitigated evil. It was this idea which produced the Orphic jingle in words: *Sōma sēma,* the body is a tomb. Plotinus, the neo–platonist, could say that he was ashamed that he had a body. Seneca could break out; "I am a higher being, and born for higher things than to be a slave of my body, which I look upon as only a shackle put upon my freedom . . . In so detestable a habitation dwells the free soul" (*The Moral Letters* 65: 20). Epictetus could say: "Thou art a poor soul burdened with a corpse."

Is this the basis of the Pauline conception of the flesh? When Paul connected the flesh with sin, was he simply taking over this Greek conception of the essential evil of all material and bodily things, and the essential supremacy of spirit?

The answer to that question must be an uncompromising no. Paul was very far from holding such a view of the body. To Paul the body was a noble instrument made for noble things. The heathen with their unclean ways dishonour the body (*Romans* 1: 24), therefore the body itself is an honourable thing. A fornicator sins against his body (1 *Corinthians* 6: 18). Sexual impurity is a sin against the body which was made for purity. In 1 *Corinthians* 12 Paul works out his greatest picture of the Church, when he calls it the body of Christ. In *Romans* 12: 1 he urges his people to present their bodies a living sacrifice, holy and acceptable to God—an idea which could never have entered the mind of a Greek, and which a Greek would have regarded with revulsion. In 1 *Corinthians* 3: 16 and 6: 19 Paul insists that the body is the temple of the Holy Spirit, and in 2 *Corinthians* 6: 16 that it is actually the temple of God.

1 *Corinthians* 15 deals with the resurrection of the body, an idea which, as we have seen, would be not only

incredible but actively disgusting to a Greek. The Holy Spirit will quicken the mortal body (*Romans* 8: 11). The body itself is to be redeemed (*Romans* 8: 23). The body is to be conformed to Christ's glorious body (*Philippians* 3: 21).

Paul's conception of the flesh comes from no other source than that of human experience. It is, in point of fact, by sense impressions that sin enters in. It is in point of fact the primitive basic instincts of the body which give sin its chance and its means of approach. It is these things, these tendencies which are the weapons and the instruments of sin. The Jewish Rabbis knew this. " The hand and the eye," they said, " are the two brokers of sin." " Passions lodge in the heart only of him who sees." As A. H. McNeile put it, it is true that the body is in actual fact " the handle and instrument of sin."

The New Testament several times uses a very vivid word; once in *Galatians* 5: 13 Paul actually uses it in conjunction with the word flesh; the word is *aphormē*. An *aphormē* is what we would call in military language a bridgehead. An *aphormē* is the point at which an attack can be launched with the greatest possibility of success. *Aphormē* is, of course, frequently used in its literal sense; but it can also be used in a metaphorical sense. Dionysius of Halicarnassus (8: 2, 5) tells how Coriolanus went to Tullus Attius to plot an insurrection which would lead him to power. He suggested how a certain situation could be deliberately provoked, a situation which could be used as a ground (*aphormē*) for just resentment. The situation would supply a bridgehead, a starting-point, an occasion, an opportunity to launch the contemplated attack.

What Paul has in mind when he speaks of the flesh is that the body with all its instincts, mental, emotional and physical, is the bridgehead where sin can launch its attack with the greatest prospect of success. That is why Paul can speak of the body of sin (*Romans* 6: 6); the body of this death (*Romans* 7: 24). That is why the body is dead because of sin (*Romans* 8: 10), and why it is the body of our humiliation (*Philippians* 3: 21).

When Paul spoke of the flesh he was thinking simply in terms of universal human experience. The body is capable of, and meant for, the highest and the greatest and the purest things; yet empirically and in actual practice the body is the seat of the passions and emotions which lead to sin, and which give sin its opportunity.

It is here that we gain our clue to the whole matter. We began by quoting 2 *Corinthians* 10: 3: "We walk *in the flesh* (*en sarki*), but we do not war *after the flesh* (*kata sarka*)." *En sarki*, in the flesh, we must be; *kata sarka*, after the flesh, we need not be. When the old man is crucified with Christ, when we have died to the old life and risen to the new life, we are still *en sarki*, in the flesh, but we are no longer *kata sarka*, after the flesh, for the Spirit of Christ is in us, so that we no longer walk according to the flesh but we walk according to the Spirit. "The life which I now live in the flesh," says Paul, "I live by the faith of the Son of God" (*Galatians* 2: 20). All the instincts, the passions, the emotions, the desires which were the raw material of sin when they were controlled by our own human power become the raw material of goodness when they are controlled by Christ.

For Paul the flesh stood for all the weakness, all the inadequacy, all the liability to sin, which are inherent in human nature without Christ. The idea is the helplessness, the fallibility, even the sinfulness, of human nature without Christ. It is the Christless human nature which is helpless in the face of temptation. It is the human nature which is not only helpless in the face of temptation but which is—to use a Scottish word—thirled to sin. Calvin wrote: " Whatever is not in Christ, Paul calls flesh." C. H. Dodd writes: " The flesh is the common stuff of human nature which we inherit. Paul . . . does not think of it as necessarily evil but as powerless for moral ends." The flesh is man apart from God. Karl Barth asks: " What indeed does flesh mean but the complete inadequacy of the creature when he stands before his creator? "

So in this matter we see Paul doing what he so often and so rightly did. He is arguing from experience. He was not a theologian who had " never looked out of the window." He was not one of these writers who have ink in their veins instead of blood. He was not interested in abstruse and recondite speculations about the body. He never thought and never meant to say that, as the Greeks believed, the body was essentially an evil thing. By his own bitter experience he had discovered—as all must discover—that the Christless man has in his body a bridge-head through which sin can effect an entry into his life with fatal ease. But when a man's old self dies, and Christ springs to life within him, not only is his soul saved but his body also becomes the temple of the Holy Spirit. The man into whose inmost being Jesus Christ has entered is redeemed in body and in soul, and the body which was once the instrument of sin becomes the weapon of righteousness. It was not the destruction of the body, but the redemption of the body, for which Paul hoped and laboured and prayed.

XVII

THE SECOND COMING
IN THE THOUGHT OF PAUL

WE DO well to try to see what place the doctrine of the
Second Coming had in the thinking of the early Church;
for this is a doctrine which has suffered one of two opposite
fates in the thought of the modern Church. For the most
part, it is very largely disregarded; it is but seldom that a
sermon upon it is heard; it is not too much to say that in
many quarters it has come to be looked upon as one of the
eccentricities of the faith, which have been outgrown and
left behind. On the other hand there are some few who
think about hardly anything else; the Second Coming to
them is the most important doctrine in the Christian faith;
it dominates all their thinking and all their preaching.
It is of extreme importance that we should try to adjust
the balance, and that we should see both that the doctrine
of the Second Coming receives its just place in our thinking,
and that it does not usurp a place that is not its own, until
it fills the whole horizon.

It is always of importance to see not only where Christian

thought ends, but also where it begins. To a Jew the doctrine of the Second Coming would have seemed not only completely intelligible, but even completely inevitable. We do not say that the doctrine of the Second Coming is a product of Jewish thought for no one can honestly read the gospels and fail to admit that Jesus did speak of His Coming in power; but we do say that the pictures in which the Second Coming were visualised were very largely Jewish both in their outline and in their detail.

It is possible to regard Jewish thought in two ways. In one sense the Jews were the greatest pessimists in history; but in a far truer sense the Jews were the greatest optimists in history. The Jews never lost the conviction that they were the Chosen People. To them that chosenness necessarily implied world respect, world power, and world domination. It became increasingly clear to them that that triumph to which they looked forward could never happen by purely human means; it must happen by the direct intervention of God into world affairs. Their numbers were too few for them ever to reach world power; there were only about four million Jews in Palestine in the time of Jesus, and that was as nothing compared with the world empires. They had lost their independence. They were subject in turn to the Babylonians, the Persians, the Greeks and the Romans. If God's promise, as they saw it, was ever to come true, it could only come true by direct, supernatural and divine intervention in human affairs. To that intervention the Jew looked forward, and still looks forward.

In the thought of the Jew that idea took a basic and fundamental form. The Jew divided all time into two ages. There was *this present age*, which was wholly evil, wholly wicked, and wholly bad. It was beyond cure; it could only be cured by being destroyed, annihilated and obliterated. There was *the age to come*, which would be the golden age of God.

How was the one age to become the other? How was this fundamental change to be effected? The change was to come through *the Day of the Lord*. The Day of the Lord would be the day of the intervention of God; it would be a day of cosmic agony, the day of the birth-pangs of the emergence of a new universe. Let us look first of all at the Jewish dream of the golden age.

The golden age would be an age of plenty, an age when earth would bring forth her fruits in such munificent and effortless abundance that all would have enough and none would have too little. " Behold, the days come, saith the Lord, that the plowman shall overtake the reaper, and the treader of grapes him that soweth seed; and the mountains shall drop sweet wine, and all the hills shall melt.... And they shall plant vineyards, and drink the wine thereof; they shall also make gardens, and eat the fruit of them " (*Amos* 9: 13, 14). " The wilderness shall be a fruitful field, and the fruitful field be counted for a forest " (*Isaiah* 32: 15). " The Lord will comfort all her waste places; and He will make her wilderness like Eden, and her desert like the garden of the Lord " (*Isaiah* 51: 3).

It would be an age of friendship; in particular it would

The Second Coming in the Thought of Paul

be an age when the enmity between man and the beasts
would no longer exist. " In that day will I make a covenant
for them with the beasts of the field, and with the fowls of
heaven, and with the creeping things of the ground: and
I will break the bow and the sword and the battle out of
the earth, and will make them to lie down safely " (*Hosea* 2:
18). " The wolf also shall dwell with the lamb, and the
leopard shall lie down with the kid; and the calf and the
young lion, and the fatling together; and a little child shall
lead them. And the cow and the bear shall feed; their
young ones shall lie down together and the lion shall eat
straw like the ox. And the sucking child shall play on the
hole of the asp, and the weaned child shall put his hand on
the cockatrice' den; they shall not hurt nor destroy in all
my holy mountain " (*Isaiah* 11: 6-9). In the golden age
there would be a friendship which would cover all living
things throughout all the earth.

In the golden age there would be no more pain; it would
be the land of the ever young, what in Gaelic the High-
landers call Tir-nan-og. " There shall be no more thence
an infant of days, nor an old man that hath not filled his
days: for the child shall die an hundred years old "
(*Isaiah* 65: 20). A man's life would be like the life of a
tree for years (*Isaiah* 65: 22). " The inhabitant shall not
say, I am sick " (*Isaiah* 23: 24). " He will swallow up death
in victory; and the Lord God will wipe away tears from
off all faces " (*Isaiah* 25: 8). There would be no more pain,
and no more death too soon.

The golden age would be the age of peace, the age when

wars would be no more. " They shall beat their swords
into ploughshares, and their spears into pruninghooks:
nation shall not lift up sword against nation, neither shall
they learn war any more " (*Isaiah* 2: 4). " They shall
not hurt nor destroy in all my holy mountain " (*Isaiah*
11: 9). " My people shall dwell in a peaceable habitation, and in sure dwellings, and in quiet resting places "
(*Isaiah* 32: 18). " Great shall be the peace of thy children "
(*Isaiah* 54: 13). The terror of war would be for ever
gone.

We must now go on to ask: What would be the place
of the people of Israel in this new universe of God? There
is no one answer to that question.

It was universally believed that Jerusalem would be
the centre of the world, and to her all the nations would
come to learn the ways of God. " And it shall come to pass
in the last days, that the mountain of the Lord's house shall
be established in the top of the mountains, and shall be
exalted above the hills; and all nations shall flow unto it.
And many people shall go and say, Come ye, and let us go
up to the mountain of the Lord, to the house of the God of
Jacob; and He will teach us of His ways, and we will walk
in His paths: for out of Zion shall go forth the law,
and the word of the Lord from Jerusalem " (*Isaiah* 2:
2, 3; *Micah* 4: 1, 2). Jerusalem was to be the religious
centre of the world. To her all men would come to
find God.

Some few, some very few, of the Jews, had the noblest
of all dreams—the dream that the Jews must go out to the

world to bring to all men the knowledge of God, that the Jews had a missionary duty, that they were meant by God to be a light to the Gentiles. " I will give thee for a light to the Gentiles, that thou mayest be my salvation unto the end of the earth " (*Isaiah* 49: 6). " The glory of the Lord shall be revealed, and all flesh shall see it " (*Isaiah* 40: 5). This was a dream which came to only very few. The missionary task was a task to which the vast majority of the Jews were blind.

The commonest dream of all was the dream of power, the dream of conquest, the dream of a day when all men would be subjected to a world empire of the Jews. " The nation and kingdom that will not serve thee shall perish; yea, those nations shall be utterly wasted " (*Isaiah* 60: 12). " The labour of Egypt, and merchandise of Ethiopia and of the Sabeans, men of stature, shall come over unto thee, and they shall be thine: they shall come after thee; in chains they shall come over, and they shall fall down unto thee (*Isaiah* 45: 14). " And it shall be, that whoso will not come up of all the families of the earth unto Jerusalem to worship the King, the Lord of hosts, even upon them shall be no rain. And if the family of Egypt go not up, and come not, that have no rain there shall be the plague, wherewith the Lord will smite the heathen that come not up to keep the feast of tabernacles " (*Zechariah* 14: 17, 18).

We must now turn our thoughts to the way in which the change would be brought about. Broadly speaking,

Jewish thought envisaged two ways in which this change would take place.

There was a time when the Jews believed that this change would take place under human leadership. In the days before they had realised their own smallness and their own helplessness, in the days before their successive captivities had convinced them that human power would never raise them to greatness, their dream had always been that a great leader and commander would arise from the stock of David, and lead them to world greatness. " And there shall come forth a rod out of the stem of Jesse (David was the son of Jesse), and a Branch shall grow out of his roots " (*Isaiah* 11: 1). " Then there shall enter in by the gates of this house, kings sitting upon the throne of David " (*Jeremiah* 22: 4). " They shall serve the Lord their God, and David their king whom I will raise up unto them " (*Jeremiah* 30: 9). " Behold, the days come, saith the Lord, that I will raise unto David a righteous Branch, and a king shall reign and prosper, and shall execute judgment and justice in the earth " (*Jeremiah* 23: 5). It was of this that men were thinking when in the gospel story they addressed Jesus as Son of David (*Luke* 18: 38; *Matthew* 21: 9).

But, as we have said, the Jews became convinced that no human power could ever bring in the new age, and that it could only come through the direct intervention of God in history. And hence there arose the conception of The Day of the Lord which pervades so much of the Old Testament. The Day of the Lord was to be the day of

God's direct intervention; it was to be a day of concentrated dread, the birth-pangs of the new age. Let us now look at the characteristics which in Jewish thought, marked the day of the Lord.

It was to be a day of destruction and of terror. " Behold the day of the Lord cometh, cruel both with wrath and fierce anger, to lay the land desolate " (*Isaiah* 13: 9). "Alas for the day! for the day of the Lord is at hand, and as a destruction from the Almighty shall it come " (*Joel* 1: 15). " That day is a day of wrath, a day of trouble and distress, a day of wasteness and desolation, a day of darkness and gloominess, a day of clouds and thick darkness " (*Zephaniah* 1: 15): The whole terror of God was to be unleashed on the wickedness of the world.

It was to be a day of cosmic upheaval, when the world would be shaken and shattered to its very foundations. " And I will shew wonders in the heavens and in the earth, blood, and fire, and pillars of smoke. The sun shall be turned into darkness, and the moon into blood, before the great and the terrible day of the Lord " (*Joel* 2: 30, 31). " For the stars of heaven and the constellations thereof shall not give their light: the sun shall be darkened in his going forth, and the moon shall not cause her light to shine . . . Therefore I will shake the heavens, and the earth shall remove out of her place, in the wrath of the Lord of Hosts, and in the day of his fierce anger " (*Isaiah* 13: 10, 13). The day of the Lord would be a violent dissolution of the established world.

It would be a day of judgment, when the wicked would

213

be sought out and finally obliterated. " I will punish the world for their evil, and the wicked for their iniquity; and I will cause the arrogance of the proud to cease, and will lay low the haughtiness of the terrible " (*Isaiah* 13: 11).

So far we have taken all our evidence from the pages of the Old Testament itself. But in the days between the Old and New Testaments, many Jewish books were written concerning this time of terror which would be the prelude to the new age. These books are called Apocalypses; the Greek word *apokalupsis* means an *unveiling* or a *revealing* and these books were visions of the end of this world and the beginning of the new world, visions of the intervention of God. We must remember that they were written in days when Israel was suffering terribly at the hands of her conquerors, and these books were the favourite reading matter of the people, for they foretold the end of Israel's misery and the beginning of her glory. They were books which Jesus would certainly know and which Paul would certainly have read.

In them the Old Testament characteristics of the Day of the Lord are repeated and still further accentuated. They foretold that there would be wars. There would be " quakings of places, tumults of peoples, scheming of nations, confusion of leaders, disquietude of princes " (4 *Ezra* 9: 3). " There shall come astonishment of mind upon the dwellers on earth. And they shall plan to war one against another, city against city, place against place, people against people, kingdom against kingdom " (4 *Ezra* 13: 31).

These books give even more terrifying pictures of the shaking of the world. " From heaven shall fall fiery swords, down to the earth. Lights shall come, bright and great, flashing into the midst of men; and earth, the universal mother, shall shake in those days at the hand of the Eternal; and the fishes of the sea and the beasts of the earth and the countless tribes of flying things and all the souls of men and every sea shall shudder at the presence of the Eternal and there shall be panic " (*The Sibylline Oracles* 3; 363ff). "The horns of the sun shall be broken, and he shall be turned into darkness, and the moon shall not give her light, and be turned wholly into blood, and the circle of the stars shall be disturbed " (*The Assumption of Moses* 10: 5).

One of the most terrible things would be a kind of complete destruction and reversal of all moral standards.

And honour shall be turned to shame,
And strength humiliated into contempt,
And probity destroyed,
And beauty shall become ugliness . . .
And envy shall rise in those who had not thought aught
*   of themselves,*
And passion shall seize him that is peaceful,
And many shall be stirred up in anger to injure many,
And they shall rouse up armies in order to shed blood,
And in the end they shall all perish together with them

(*2 Baruch 27*)

In the thought of the Old Testament and in the writings of the Jews between the Testaments, there is nothing more deeply rooted than the thought of the terrible coming of the Day of the Lord. It was in Judaism that Christianity was cradled; these were ideas on which every Jew fed his mind; it was only natural that there should be a kind of identification of the Day of the Lord and the Second Coming of Jesus Christ; both were the great intervention of God in human affairs. In Christian thought the two became deeply intertwined. To the Christian the Second Coming of Jesus Christ was indeed the Day of the Lord.

With all that Jewish heritage in our minds we now turn directly to the New Testament. The Second Coming of Jesus Christ was always an essential part of the message of the Christian Church. One of the most notable contributions to New Testament scholarship in modern times is C. H. Dodd's reconstruction of what is called the *kerugma*. The word *kerugma* literally means *a herald's announcement*, and it is used to describe the basic elements in the preaching of the early Church. As C. H. Dodd formulated them, on the basis of the sermons of the Book of Acts, and the Letters of Paul, these basic elements were:

The prophecies are fulfilled, and the new age has been inaugurated by the coming of Christ.

He was born of the seed of David.

He died, according to the Scriptures, to deliver us out of this present evil age.

He was buried.

He rose again on the third day, according to the Scriptures.

He is exalted at the right hand of God, as Son of God, and Lord of the quick and the dead.

He will come again as judge and saviour of men.

That is to say, the Doctrine of the Second Coming of Christ was from the beginning an integral and essential part of the Christian message.

The doctrine is there in *Acts* 1: 11 in the announcement of the two angelic figures: "This same Jesus, which is taken up from you into Heaven, shall so come in like manner as ye have seen him go into Heaven." It is there in Peter's sermon: "That He many send the Messiah appointed beforehand for you, Jesus, whom Heaven must receive until the time of the restoration of all things, of which God spake through the mouth of his prophets from the beginning" (*Acts* 3: 21). In *Acts* 10: 42 it is said that Jesus is appointed to be the Judge of the quick and the dead.

In *Acts* there are only these three references to the Second Coming in the account of the early preaching; but with Paul it is different. It is the simple fact that in every one of Paul's letters except *Galatians*, and possibly *Ephesians*, the Second Coming is not only mentioned but stressed as an essential part of the Christian gospel.

Before we go on to examine Paul's references to the Second Coming in detail, we may note two special references to it. In *Romans* 2: 16 Paul speaks of the day when God shall judge the world by Jesus Christ "according to my gospel." The Second Coming was therefore an essential part of that account of the gospel which Paul considered to be uniquely his. When he is writing to the Thessalonians, he beseeches them to live the Christian life by the coming of the Lord Jesus Christ, and by our gathering unto him (2 *Thessalonians* 2: 1). The Second Coming was one of the primary motives for the Christian life. Apart from the many other references, which we shall go on to consider, even these two taken alone would serve to show how central the idea of the Second Coming was to the thought and to the teaching of Paul.

It is commonly said that Paul's conception of the Second Coming underwent a certain development. It is true that Paul's ideas about the Second Coming did change, but it is not true that Paul, so to speak, grew out of the idea, or that he abandoned it. From the beginning to the end of Paul's life the idea was there. Let us go to his letters, and let us take soundings in them from the earliest to the latest. With the possible exception of the Letter to the Galatians, the letters to the Church at Thessalonica are Paul's earliest letters. There the Second Coming is set before men with vividness and with immediacy. One of the things which worried the Christians at Thessalonica was the problem of what was to happen to Christians who had died before the Second Coming arrived. Would they lose the glory which was bound to come to those who remained? Paul assures them that it will not be so: "For this we say unto you by the word of the Lord, that we which are alive and remain unto the coming of the Lord shall not take precedence of them that sleep" (1 *Thessalonians* 4: 15). When Paul wrote that, he obviously expected the Second Coming to happen within his own lifetime and within the lifetime of those to whom he was writing. In 1 *Thessalonians* 5: 23 he writes that it is his prayer to God that their spirit, soul and body may be preserved blameless unto the coming of the Lord Jesus Christ. The significant thing there, is the mention of the body. The obvious implication is that he expected them to be in the body when Christ came; he expected the coming of Christ to be within their lifetime and his.

Let us turn now to *Romans*. In *Romans* 13: 11, 12 there is that great passage in which Paul writes with a certain splendour of words: " And, knowing the time, it is now high time to awake out of sleep; for now is our salvation nearer than when we believed; the night is far spent, the day is at hand; let us therefore cast off the works of darkness, and let us put on the armour of light." In that passage the Second Coming is not mentioned in so many words; but the Second Coming is the whole background of it; and it is the imminence of the Second Coming which is the ground of the urgency of his appeal. But one thing is to be noted. That very passage is the culmination of the long passage in which Paul looks forward to the evangelisation of the whole world, Jewish and Gentile. All men were to hear the gospel; and all were to be given the chance to be gathered in. Clearly a process of evangelisation like that would take time; and we might think that by this time Paul did not expect the Second Coming to happen quite as soon as when he wrote to the Church at Thessalonica. But it is doubtful if we can lay a great deal of stress on that argument.

We now turn to 1 *Corinthians* 7 which is of paramount importance for this matter. The keynote of that passage is in 1 *Corinthians* 7: 29: "But this I say, brethren, the time is short." The passage comes in a discussion of marriage and of sexual relationships. Paul's verdict is that, if a man's natural passions are strong, and, if abstention from marriage is going to drive the man to the risk of immorality, then the man may marry; but, he would be much better not to; he would be better to avoid all earthly bonds and commitments so that he can concentrate the whole of life on preparation for the coming of Christ. The importance of that passage lies in this. Not only does it show that Paul at that time believed in the imminence of the Second Coming, but it shows that his advice to all men was to arrange and order life on the assumption that the Second Coming was going to happen at any moment.

We now turn to the last letters which Paul wrote. When he wrote the Letter to the Philippians the likelihood is that he was in his last imprisonment; and once again in it there comes the warning and the challenge: "The Lord is at hand" (*Philippians* 4: 5). It has been said, and said truly, that the Letter to the Ephesians represents the highest reach of Pauline thought. It is indeed the Queen of the Epistles. Here is the fullest development of the thought of Paul. It is very commonly—almost universally —stated that in *Ephesians* there is no mention at all of the Second Coming, that by this time Paul had outgrown that whole conception. Is that completely true? In *Ephesians* 4: 30 Paul speaks of the Holy Spirit " whereby ye are sealed unto the day of redemption." Is not that at least possibly still another reference to the last great day of victory and of judgment in the Second Coming of Christ?

It is, we believe, demonstrable that from the first to the last letter which he wrote, the Second Coming is always in the mind of Paul, although it is less in the foreground at the end than it was at the beginning.

The Corinthian letters come in the midtime of Paul's ministry for Christ, and for this matter they are very important. In I *Corinthians* 10: 11 he speaks of us on whom the ends of the world were come. In that age men were living—it does not matter how we put it for this purpose— in the last twilight of the old age, or the first dawn of the new. But by far the most significant saying comes at the very end of the first letter to the Corinthians in I *Corinthians* 16: 22. There Paul writes: " If any man love not the Lord Jesus Christ, let him be anathema (accursed) *Maranatha.*" *Maranatha* is the Aramaic for The Lord is at hand, or for, Come, Lord!

Certain extremely important conclusions follow from this sentence. It comes right at the end of the letter, with only the blessing to follow. It is as if it was the culmination, the keystone, the heart of the message of Paul. It is as if he wished to leave the readers of the letter with that phrase ringing in their ears. It is almost as if he said: "Whatever else you remember or forget, never forget that the Lord is at hand." The very position of that sentence sets it, as it were, in bold type. Further, there is this. The Church at Corinth was a Greek Church; it could have had very few Jews in it at all; and yet, writing as he was to Greeks, Paul ends with this phrase in Aramaic. No Greek would know Aramaic; and yet the Greeks of Corinth must have understood this Aramaic phrase. Only one conclusion is possible; the phrase must have been a catchword, a slogan, a battle-cry, a watchword, a motto, which every Christian knew and understood.

This very expectation gave rise in Paul's letters to a phrase which with Paul is a characteristic description of the Christian life. Again and again Paul speaks of the Christian as waiting for Jesus Christ. The Christian life was essentially nothing other than an expectation of and waiting for the coming of Christ. He reminds the Thessalonians " how ye turned to God from idols to serve the living and true God, and to wait for His Son from heaven " (1 *Thessalonians* 1: 9, 10). He prays that the Lord may direct their hearts into the patient waiting for Christ (2 *Thessalonians* 3: 5). He declared that the Thessalonians are to be his hope, his joy, his crown of rejoicing in the presence of the Lord Jesus Christ at His coming (1 *Thessalonians* 2: 19). He speaks of the Corinthians as waiting for the coming of our Lord Jesus Christ (1 *Corinthians* 1: 7). He tells the Philippians that our conversation is in heaven from whence also we look for the Saviour, the Lord Jesus Christ (*Philippians* 3: 20).

We must note another important fact. When Paul did speak of the Second Coming he often used language which he had inherited from his Jewish scholarship and up-bringing. In particular he was much influenced by the twenty-sixth and twenty-seventh chapters of *Isaiah*. We may note certain parallels.

I. The Lord's Coming: *Isaiah* 26: 21; 2 *Thessalonians* 2: 1.

II. The coming of judgment: *Isaiah* 26: 21; 2 *Thessalonians* 1: 9; 2: 8.

III. The Resurrection of the dead: *Isaiah* 26: 19; 1 *Thessalonians* 4: 16.

IV. The Sound of the trumpet: *Isaiah* 27: 13; 1 *Thessalonians* 4: 16.

V. The Gathering and Assembling of the Elect of God, which was an essential part of the Jewish idea of the last days: *Isaiah* 27: 12; 1 *Thessalonians* 4: 17.

It was inevitable that Paul should speak to people in language and in pictures which they could understand; he was bound to take his pictures from the Old Testament and from the imagery of the end with which men were very familiar.

But there is a warning here; it is quite clear that we cannot approach these pictures with a crude literalism, that we cannot take them to be an advance photographic record of the events of the Second Coming. It is clear that they are pictures of prophetic symbolism. The fact of the

Second Coming they stress and lay down; but to take them as literal pictures of the details of the Second Coming is to forget that they come from the minds and the voices of the prophets, who used them only as symbols of the unspeakable terrors and glories which would be.

We have seen how integral the idea of the Second Coming was to the thought of Paul; and we have seen how Paul took many of his pictures of the Second Coming from the prophets and from his Jewish heritage. It will therefore not surprise us to find that one central Jewish idea occurs in Paul's thought in a new guise. We saw what a great part the idea of the Day of the Lord played in Jewish thought. In Paul's thought the Day of the Lord becomes the Day of Christ. He writes to the Thessalonians: " The Day of Christ is at hand " (2 *Thessalonians* 2: 2). It is his confidence that the Corinthians will be blameless in the Day of the Lord Jesus Christ (1 *Corinthians* 1: 8). They are to be his rejoicing in the Day of the Lord (2 *Corinthians* 1: 14). He tells the Philippians that, if they are worthy of their Christian calling, he will have cause to rejoice in the Day of the Lord (*Philippians* 2: 16). The Day of Christ was as essential a part of the thought of Paul, as the day of the Lord was of the thought of the Jews. Let us then see what Paul has to say about the Day of Christ.

Paul believed that the Day of Christ would come suddenly and without warning. " The Day of the Lord so cometh as a thief in the night " (1 *Thessalonians* 5: 2). That was not to say that it would not be preceded by signs (2 *Thessalonians* 2). There would be a time of falling away, and a final contest with evil, but the actual moment of its coming would be shatteringly sudden.

The Day of Christ would be a day when the holy wrath of God would be let loose on a rebellious world. It is Paul's hope that his own people, Christ's people, will be found blameless (1 *Thessalonians* 3: 13; 1 *Corinthians* 1: 8); but for the rebellious, and for those who are at enmity with God, it will be a day of dreadful punishment (2 *Thessalonians* 1: 7-10). In a sense that is why the Christian looks forward to the Day of the Lord. On that day the righteous will find their rest, and their persecutors will find the punishment which their misdeeds have merited (2 *Thessalonians* 1: 6, 7). The Christian hope and joy are in the expectation of that day (1 *Thessalonians* 1: 10); for, when Christ appears, they too will appear in glory (*Colossians* 3: 4).

Here is the place where we must face, not one of the problems, but one of the great facts of Paul's scheme of things. Paul believed intensely in judgment. It does not matter whether Paul believed that that judgment would come at the Day of the Lord, or whether it would be postponed to some later time; the essential fact is that Paul gave a very real place to judgment in the Christian scheme of things. In *Romans* 2: 5 he speaks of that day of wrath and revelation, when God will render to every man according to his deeds. In *Romans* 2: 16 he speaks of the day when God will judge the secrets of men by Jesus Christ. In *Romans* 5: 9 he speaks of the Christian being saved from the wrath by the work of Jesus Christ. 1 *Corinthians* 4: 5

speaks of the folly of judging until the Lord who is to
come will judge the secret things of the hearts of men.
In *Colossians* 3: 24, 25 Paul urges men to do everything as
unto the Lord, knowing that of the Lord they will receive
the reward of the inheritance . . . but that he who does
wrong will receive for that which he has done, without
respect of persons. *Ephesians* 6: 8 counsels fine living, in
the knowledge that whatsoever good thing any man does,
the same shall he receive of the Lord. 1 *Corinthians* 3: 13
declares that every man's work will be judged. 1 *Corinthians* 3: 17 declares that he who defiles the temple
of God will pay the penalty. 1 *Corinthians* 5: 13 extends
this judgment to those who are without; it will be a
universal judgment. 2 *Corinthians* 5: 10 says bluntly that
we must all appear before the judgment seat of Christ, that
every man may receive the things done in his body, whether
they be good or bad. And then Paul goes on to say that it
is knowing the terror of the Lord, that we do persuade men.
In *Romans* 14: 10 he lays it down that we shall all stand
before the judgment seat of Christ.

Judgment is an essential principle of the Christian faith.
This has caused many people difficulty. What has grace
to do with judgment? If Christianity is a religion of grace,
if forgiveness is utterly free, utterly unmerited, utterly
undeserved, the product of nothing other than the love and
mercy of God, and, if this grace is so superabundant that,
wherever sin abounds, it abounds still more, what place is
left for judgment? If a man must be judged by the deeds
done in his body, what has happened to justification by

faith? If no flesh can ever be justified by deeds, how then can a man finally be judged by deeds? These are questions which demand an answer.

First, Paul was cradled in Judaism, and Judaism is an intensely ethical religion. It offered a way of life; as Jesus Himself said: " By their fruits shall ye know them " (*Matthew* 7: 20). Even if he had wished to, Paul could never have escaped from the ethical demands of religious faith. And an ethical religion involves standards of judgment, from which there can be no escape. When a way of life is laid down, failure to live that way of life must have its inevitable consequence.

Second, Paul was a missionary. He lived and preached in a Gentile world which was notoriously immoral; he could not have gone out with any other message than that goodness was demanded from a Christian, and that evil is punished. No message other than the stern demand could have produced results.

Third, it is possible gravely to mis-state the doctrine of grace. Grace is the greatest gift in the world; but grace is the greatest responsibility in the world. Grace is a gift; and grace is a gift of love; to offer that grace to men cost God all He had to give; and therefore there is laid on every man the awe-inspiring obligation of doing all he can to deserve that grace. That he can never do; but he can and must respond to that grace by seeking throughout all his life to be what that grace desires him to be. He must say: " If I have been loved like that I dare not break the heart of that love." A man who fails to see the obligation of

227

grace is a man who is blind to honour and blind to love; he has sinned against the greatest love in the universe. It is true that grace does everything; but to grace a man must respond. And if a man fails to respond, there must be consequences.

Fourth, it must be clearly understood that Justification by Faith is the beginning of the Christian life. Through justification by faith a man is put into a right relationship with God; he learns and realises and glories in the fact that God is his friend and not his enemy. But that new relationship must issue in a new life; it must go on to sanctification, by which a man's life and living are changed. The whole point of that new relationship is to enable a man to live a life, where he can conquer sin and enter into the righteousness of Jesus Christ. He can only prove that he has entered into that relationship by seeking to live a life which fits that relationship. Long ago Nietzsche, the German atheist philosopher said: " Show me that you are redeemed, and I will believe in your redeemer." Justification, like grace, brings a man an immense privilege and lays on a man an immense responsibility. Judgment is an essential part of the Christian faith for the very simple reason that Christianity is meant to make a man a certain kind of man, and enables him to be that kind of man; and, if he fails to be that kind of man, then there is only one conclusion— he is not really Christian; and the fault is his, for the enabling grace was there.

Let us then sum up the ultimate values of the doctrine of the Second Coming.

The Second Coming in the Thought of Paul

It would help a great deal if first of all we would realise that we are in effect forbidden to speculate about its date and time. Jesus said: " Of that day and that hour knoweth no man, no, not the angels which are in heaven, neither the Son, but the Father" (*Mark* 13: 32). To claim, or to aspire to, a knowledge of that of which Jesus Himself was ignorant is nothing short of blasphemy. The fact of the Second Coming we must accept; of the method, the date, the time of it we are forbidden to speculate.

The great value of the doctrine of the Second Coming is that it guarantees that history is going somewhere. We cannot tell how it will happen, and when it will happen. We cannot take as literal truth the Jewish pictures of it which Paul used. We need not think of a physical coming of Christ in the clouds, or a physical trumpet blast. But what the doctrine of the Second Coming conserves is the tremendous fact that there is one divine, far-off event to which the whole creation is moving; there is a consummation; there is a final triumph of God. In his book, *An Arrow into the Air*, John H. Withers has a quotation, from Gerald Healy's play *The Black Stranger*. It comes from the days of the Irish potato famine in 1846. At that time as part of the relief work men were set to making roads which had no purpose whatever. It was simply to give them some work to do. One day in that desperate situation Michael comes home to his father, and says with a kind of poignant disillusionment: " They're makin' roads that lead to nowhere!" When we confess our ignorance, an ignorance which even Jesus shared, of dates and times; when we abandon all the Jewish imagery and pictures, which by this time have become only fantastic; when we strip the doctrine of the Second Coming down to its bare essentials; we are left with this tremendous truth—the Doctrine of the Second Coming is the final guarantee that life can never be a road that leads to nowhere; it is a road which leads to Christ.

XVIII

THE MIND OF PAUL
CONCERNING THE CHURCH

THE letters of Paul provide us with ample material for arriving at a clear idea of his thoughts and beliefs concerning the Church; for in them the word *ekklēsia*, church, occurs about sixty times. Let us first see how, and in what connections, he uses this word.

Paul uses the word *ekklēsia*, both in the singular and in the plural, to describe the body of believers in any given place. So he speaks to the Church at Cenchrea (*Romans* 16: 1); the Church of the Laodiceans (*Colossians* 4: 16); the Church of the Thessalonians (1 *Thessalonians* 1: 1; 2 *Thessalonians* 1: 1). He speaks of the Churches of the Gentiles (*Romans* 16: 4); the Churches of Galatia (1 *Corinthians* 16: 1; *Galatians* 1: 2); the Churches of Macedonia (2 *Corinthians* 8: 1). He calls those who brought the various collections for the poor Christians of Jerusalem the messengers of the Churches (2 *Corinthians* 8: 23); and he urges the Corinthians to show the fruit of their love before all the Churches (2 *Corinthians* 8: 24). He speaks of the care of all the Churches which is upon his own heart (2 *Corinthians* 11: 28).

We know that in the very early days the gatherings of the Christians must have been small, for it was not until the early third century that anything in the nature of Church buildings came into being. In the early days the Christians were still meeting in any house which had a room large enough to give them accommodation. So Paul uses the word *ekklēsia* for any particular part of the Church in any given place. Thus he speaks of the Church which is in the house of Aquila and Priscilla (*Romans* 16: 5; 1 *Corinthians* 16: 19); of the Church in Laodicea which is connected with the house of Nymphas (*Colossians* 4: 15); of the Church which is in the house of Archippus (*Philemon* 2).

Paul uses the word *ekklēsia* as a description of the body of local Christians gathered together in any one place for worship and for instruction. That is a usage which comes very near to our use of the word congregation. He speaks of the unseemly things which happen when the Corinthian Christians come together in the Church (1 *Corinthians* 11: 18). He holds that the prophet edifies the Church (1 *Corinthians* 14: 4, 5, 12), and criticises those who place too much stress on speaking with tongues, because in the Church he himself would rather speak five words with understanding than ten thousand words in an unknown tongue (1 *Corinthians* 14: 19). He speaks of the whole Church being assembled in one place (1 *Corinthians* 14: 23). He lays it down that women are to keep silent in the Church, and that it is a shame for them to speak (1 *Corinthians* 14: 34, 35). He speaks of the things which he ordains and teaches in every Church (1 *Corinthians* 4: 17; 7: 17). In all these cases the word Church describes the worshipping people of Jesus Christ, met together in His name.

Lastly, Paul uses *ekklēsia* to describe the Church as a whole, the whole company of believers in Jesus Christ in every place and in every nation. He says of himself that, as far as zeal went, he was a persecutor of the Church (*Philippians* 3: 6). He talks of the manifold wisdom of God being shown through the Church, and of glory being rendered unto God in the Church (*Ephesians* 3: 10, 21). He speaks of Christ being the head of the Church (*Ephesians* 1: 22). He speaks of the Church being subject unto Christ, and of Christ loving the Church (*Ephesians* 5: 24, 25). He speaks of the Church as being the body of Christ (*Colossians* 1: 24). Paul uses the word Church as an all-embracing word to include all those who have given their hearts and dedicated their lives to Jesus Christ.

Further, Paul frequently makes it clear that he does not regard the Church as a merely human organisation or institution. The Church and the Churches are the Church and the Churches of God. Twice he confesses that he persecuted the Church of God (1 *Corinthians* 15: 9; *Galatians* 1: 13). When he is rebuking the contentious members of the Church at Corinth, he says the Churches of God have no such custom (1 *Corinthians* 11: 16). He tries to make the Corinthians, who are guilty of unseemly conduct, realise that their conduct is the equivalent of despising the Church of God (1 *Corinthians* 11: 22). He speaks of the Churches of God which are in Judæa (1 *Thessalonians* 2: 14); and says that he boasts of the excellence of the faith and conduct of the Thessalonians in the Churches of God (2 *Thessalonians* 1: 4). The Church may be composed of man, but it is nonetheless the Church of God. In the same way he speaks of the Churches of God, which are in Judæa and which are in Christ (1 *Thessalonians* 2: 14; *Galatians* 1: 22). The Church is in Christ and belongs to God.

In the two letters to the Corinthians there is a hint of a development in the thought of Paul. These two letters are addressed to The Church of God which is at Corinth (1 *Corinthians* 1: 2; 2 *Corinthians* 1: 1). The Christian community is no longer the Church of Corinth; it is the Church of God which is at Corinth. Here there is the beginning of the great conception that the Church is not a collection of loosely integrated, or isolated, units; wherever a congregation may be, it is the Church of God in such and such a place. There is now no such thing as a Church of Corinth, or of Galatia, or of Rome; it is all the Church of God.

Two things may well have moved Paul's thinking in this direction. (*a*) In Corinth he had to deal with the problem of disunity; he had to deal with a situation in which the local congregation had been split into fragments who claimed to be of Paul, of Apollos, of Cephas (1 *Corinthians*

1 : 12). It was Paul's conviction that the Church is a unity; that it is not composed of different Churches and sects and parties; that it is not even, in the last analysis, composed of different congregations; that it is all, wherever it is, the Church of God. (*b*) It may well be that Paul's growing experience of the Roman Empire helped him in this direction. All over the world there were Roman colonies. A Roman colony was not a colony in the English sense of the term. It was not a settlement in an unknown and unexplored land; it was not a movement of pioneers out into the unknown. Rome had a custom which she followed all over the world. There were strategic places, which commanded road junctions, and from which whole areas could be controlled. In such places Rome was accustomed to settle little bands of citizens, usually composed of veterans of the army, who had served their time, and who had been granted citizenship. These colonies were the strategic centres which bound the Empire together. Now the characteristic of these colonies was that, wherever they were, the Roman language was spoken, Roman dress was worn; the magistrates had Roman titles; Roman customs were followed; Roman law was observed and administered. These colonies were little bits of Rome planted throughout the world, and they were completely and proudly conscious that it was so. Wherever they were, to the ends of the earth, surrounded perhaps by barbarians, they were Rome. So Paul saw the Church, wherever it was, as the Church of God. The Church was a unity which embraced all nations, and remained the Church of God irrespective of its local

habitation. The idea of the unity of the Church had taken root in Paul's mind, and was, as we shall see, to be greatly and wonderfully developed.

Before we leave the word *ekklēsia*, we have something further still to note. The word *ekklēsia* was not a creation of the Christian Church. When the Christian Church annexed it for its purposes, it was already a word with a history, and a double history. At that double background we must look, in order that we may see the associations which the word *ekklēsia* carried with it, and the memories which it would awaken in the minds of those who heard it.

First, the word had a Jewish background. In the Septuagint, the Greek version of the Hebrew Scriptures, the word *ekklēsia* is regularly for the assembled people of Israel, that is, for the assembled people of God. It is, for instance, used of the assembly of the people on the day when the ten commandments were given by God to Moses. The Book of Deuteronomy speaks of " all the words, which the Lord spake with you in the mount out of the midst of the fire in the day of the assembly (*ekklēsia*) " (*Deuteronomy* 9: 10; 18: 16). Frequently the word is used for the *assembly* or the *congregation* of Israel (*Deuteronomy* 31: 30; *Judges* 20: 2; 1 *Samuel* 17: 47; 1 *Kings* 8: 14; *Psalm* 22: 22). So, then, for a Jew this word had always meant *the assembled people of God*. The very use of this word carries with it the implication that the Church is the people of God. Israel was God's chosen people; but Israel had failed to recognise and to accept God's Son, when He came; Israel had therefore lost her place and her privilege as a nation. The real Israel, the new Israel, the true people of God, the genuine *ekklēsia* was no longer the nation of Israel; it was the Church. The very word *ekklēsia* lays it down that it is the Christian Church which is the true instrument and agent of God.

Second, the word had a Greek background. In the great Greek democracies the ruling body was called the *ekklēsia*, and the *ekklēsia* consisted of every citizen who had not lost his rights as a citizen. It is true that in the days of the oligarchies the *ekklēsia* might be limited to those who had some kind of property qualification; but in the great days of the democracy the *ekklēsia* was composed of all free men who were citizens of their city. It was the *ekklēsia* which elected and deposed the magistrates, which received and sent out ambassadors, and which had the last word in the administration of justice and the making of the laws. So to a Greek the word *ekklēsia* would tell of the glories of citizenship; and, when the Christians took over the word, the member of the *ekklēsia*, if he were a Greek, could think of himself most easily and most naturally as a citizen of the Kingdom of Heaven.

It is seldom that the great historical national ideals of two lines of culture meet as they do in the word *ekklēsia*.

By this time we are able to set down one of the great basic facts about the Church, a simple fact and an obvious fact, yet a fact often forgotten. Nowhere in the New Testament does the word Church mean a building. In the New Testament the Church is never a structure, composed of stones and lime, or bricks and mortar. If the reference were to a building, no New Testament would have understood the phrase " a *beautiful* Church." In the New Testament the Church is always a company of worshipping people who have given their hearts and pledged their lives to Jesus Christ. Since this is so we shall find information as to the true nature and function of the Church in the words which Paul uses to describe the members of the Church. Three titles for the members of the Church constantly recur in his letters.

1. The most frequent title of all is the title *saints*. In Paul's letters the members of the Church are called *saints* almost forty times. The Greek word is *hagios*, and to modern ears *saint* is an unfortunate translation. To very many people nowadays the word *saint* brings thoughts of figures in stained-glass windows, and of people surrounded with a halo of other-worldly goodness. *Hagios* is the word which is also translated *holy;* and the basic idea in it is the idea of *difference* from ordinary things, that of being set apart from ordinary purposes. So the Temple was *holy* because it was *different* from other buildings; a priest was *holy* because he was *set apart* and, therefore, *different* from other men; an animal destined for sacrifice was *holy*, because it was *different* from other animals in that it was *set apart* for a sacred purpose; the Sabbath day was *holy* because it was *different* from other days; and God is supremely the *Holy One* because He is different from men. So, then, to say that the Church member is *hagios, holy,*

a saint as the Authorized Version has it, is to say that he is different from other men.

No sooner have we said that than we must immediately add another thing to it. That difference is expressed, not by withdrawing from the world, but by living differently within the world. Frequently Paul gives a local habitation to the people whom he entitles *hagios*. He writes to all that are at Rome, called to be saints (*Romans* 1: 7). He speaks of the poor saints which are at Jerusalem (*Romans* 15: 26). He writes to all the saints that are in all Achaia (2 *Corinthians* 1: 1). Whatever the difference may be, that difference is meant to be expressed in the everyday life of the place where a man finds himself, and does not consist in a withdrawal from the world after the example of the hermits, the monks and the nuns.

Wherein, then, does this essential difference consist? More than once Paul adds to the word *hagios* a defining phrase. He writes to the saints *in Christ Jesus* who are at Philippi (*Philippians* 1: 1), and in the same letter he sends the closing greeting: " Salute every saint who is *in Christ Jesus* " (*Philippians* 4: 21). He writes to the saints and faithful brethren *in Christ* which are at Colosse (*Colossians* 1: 2). So, then, a saint is one who is in Christ Jesus. The difference which the word *hagios* expresses is that the man who is *hagios* lives his life in the constant presence of Jesus Christ, in the constant awareness of that presence, and in the constant and deliberate attempt to listen to the commands of Christ and to carry them out. His life is lived within the world, and within the affairs of the world, but his whole life is dictated by the standards of Christ, and not by the standards of the world. The word *saints* really means "Christ's dedicated people." Those who are members of the Church are those who have dedicated their lives to Jesus Christ.

11. Almost, if not quite, as common a title for the Christians in Paul's letters is *the brethren*. When he writes to the Christians at Rome, he greets certain people by name, then he adds: " Salute the brethren which are with them" (*Romans* 16: 14). To set a bad example is to sin against the brethren (1 *Corinthians* 8: 12). " All the brethren greet you," he writes to the Corinthians (1 *Corinthians* 16: 20). He speaks of the brethren who came from Macedonia (2 *Corinthians* 11: 9). The Letter to the Ephesians comes to its close with the blessing: " Peace be to the brethren " (*Ephesians* 6: 23). " Salute the brethren which are at Laodicea," he writes to the Colossians (*Colossians* 4: 15), and to the Thessalonians he writes: " Greet all the brethren with a holy kiss " (1 *Thessalonians* 5: 26). Throughout all his letters Paul's commonest and favourite address to the people to whom he writes is: " Brethren ! "

Herein lies the great truth that the Church is meant to be a band of brothers. It is meant to be the family of God in which men are brethren one of another. When a Church is divided in spirit and in heart, when bitterness has invaded its fellowship, when the unforgiving spirit has caused breaches which remain unhealed, the Church ceases to be a Church, for a Church is no Church unless it be a brotherhood. Nelson in his dispatches attributed one of his greatest victories to the fact that he had the happiness to command a band of brothers. The Church is meant by God to be a band of brothers.

III. Less commonly, but still quite often, the Christians are *the believers, those who believe*. God is the Father of all those who believe (*Romans* 4: 11). The Thessalonians in their faith and love are an example to all who believe (1 *Thessalonians* 1: 7).

That is to say, the Church member is the man who accepts what Jesus Christ says as true, and who lives his life on the confident assumption that it is true. The Christian is the man who is convinced that Jesus Christ is the Saviour of his soul, and who has made Jesus Christ the Lord of his life.

So, then, in regard to the world, the Church member is the man who is different, because he lives in the presence of, and according to the standards of Christ. In regard to his fellow men, the Church member is the man who lives in the fellowship of brotherhood. In regard to Jesus Christ, the Church member is the man who has accepted the offer of Christ for his soul, and the demand of Christ for his life.

We must now turn to certain great pictures of the Church which Paul uses in his letters. From them we will learn more of Paul's conception of the Church than from any other source; but, at the same time, we must be careful to remember that they are pictures and metaphors, and that too much must not be read into them, or built upon them. As we study them, the difficulty will always be to be sure when the metaphor is a metaphor, and when it is a literal fact. We shall begin with the greatest of the pictures, the picture of the Church as a living body.

Paul uses the picture of the Church as a body to stress the essential unity of the Church. He writes to the Christians at Rome: " As we have many members in one body, and all members have not the same office, so we, being many, are one body in Christ, and everyone members one of another " (*Romans* 12: 4, 5). So every man must fully use the gift which God has given him, the gift of prophecy, the gift of service, the gift of exhortation, the gift of liberality, the gift of administration, the gift of mercy (*Romans* 12: 7, 8). Now it must be clearly noted out of what situation this Pauline picture arises. He has just been insisting that no man must think of himself more highly than he ought, but that he must think of himself in terms of the gifts and the graces which God has given to him to lay at the common service of the community (*Romans* 12: 3). So, then, the Church is a unity like a body. No man must be conceitedly proud of any gift which God has given to him; no man must think his gift the most important, and magnify and exalt it at the expense of the gifts of others. All gifts must be used in the spirit of humility and of service, in the constant remembrance that we are never in competition with one another, but that we are like the members of one body, all of which must work in harmony and co-operation.

Paul works out this picture even more fully and vividly in 1 *Corinthians* 12. The Church, like the body, is composed of many members. Each member has its function. The foot cannot do without the ear; nor the ear without the eye. The body could not function at all, if it were composed entirely of one member. Even the members which are hidden, and which it would be shameful to mention and to display have a special and peculiar honour of their own. When one member of the body suffers, it does not suffer in lonely isolation, for its suffering affects the whole body, and is of necessity shared by the whole body (1 *Corinthians* 12: 12-27). Once again, it must be clearly remembered out of what situation this picture arose. The Church of Corinth was doubly divided. It was divided into sects and parties who had attached themselves to the names of different people, people who were in no way responsible for the divisions, but whose names, all against their will, had been annexed by these competing parties (1 *Corinthians* 1: 12). Further, as 1 *Corinthians* 14 shows, within the Church there was a kind of piously unholy competition in regard to spiritual gifts. Those with the gift of tongues prided themselves on it; and even the prophets competed with each other for an opportunity to deliver their message. In 1 *Corinthians* 12 Paul, in fact, lists the various gifts. There is the word of wisdom and the word of knowledge; there is faith, there is the gift of healing and of performing miracles; there is prophecy, the discerning of spirits, the gifts of tongues and of the interpreting of tongues (1 *Corinthians* 12: 7-9). Within the functions of the members

243

of the Church there are apostles, prophets, teachers, those with the gifts of miracles, of healings, of helps, of administration, of tongues (1 *Corinthians* 12: 28, 29). The trouble at Corinth was that the gifts of the Spirit were being used in competition instead of in co-operation. Even at the Lord's Supper the Church at Corinth was divided into cliques and parties and sections (1 *Corinthians* 11: 18); and the result was that the whole effect of the sacrament was ruined, because they came together not discerning that they were the Lord's body, not sensitively aware of their intimate unity in Christ.

The immediate purpose which Paul has in using the picture of the body in this great passage of 1 *Corinthians* has nothing to do with the Church at large; and it has everything to do with the life and spirit of the particular congregation. Within their own assembly the Corinthians had never learned to live as one body; they were living as disintegrated and warring fragments and atoms; they were using their gifts for self-exaltation and in competition with each other; whereas they should have been living in as intimate and harmonious a state as the members of the human body. It is needless to say that that picture has in it the germ of a conception which can be, and which was to be applied, to the whole Church of Christ; but that which first produced it was in fact the warfare of a particular Church within itself.

Further, the Church is a body in the sense that it is the begetter of unity. The great letter of the Church is the Letter to the Ephesians. The theme of this letter may be summed up in this way. As we see it, this world is a warring disunity. There is war between nation and nation, between faith and faith, between Gentile and Jew, and within a man's own being. It is the aim of God to reconcile and to gather all men and all things into one in Jesus Christ (*Ephesians* 1: 10). Jesus Christ is God's instrument in the reconciliation of all the warring and divided things and persons into a new unity. By His life and by death Jesus Christ brought to men the means towards that unity. But the means towards that unity have to be brought out throughout the world to all men; and that task is the task of the Church. In the Church there is one body (*Ephesians* 4: 4); Christ is the peace of men; he has gathered together Gentile and Jew within the Church; the middle wall of partition has been broken down; and they are reconciled into one body within the Church. That is to say, to put it briefly, Jesus Christ is God's instrument of reconciliation; and the Church is Jesus Christ's agent of reconciliation. The Church is meant within itself to be one body in its unity, and it is meant to be the begetter of that unity among men.

But Paul does much more than call the Church a body; he calls it by its greatest of titles—the body of Christ. Here is the great phrase which begins in 1 *Corinthians*, but which runs through the later letters to the *Ephesians* and to the *Colossians*. "Now," says Paul, "ye are the body of Christ, and members in particular" (1 *Corinthians* 12: 27). He speaks of the Church which is Christ's body (*Ephesians* 1: 23); he speaks about the edifying of the body of Christ (*Ephesians* 4: 12). He speaks of Jesus Christ as the head of the body (*Colossians* 1: 18); and of Christ's body which is the Church (*Colossians* 1: 24).

Here we come upon one of the very real problems of Pauline interpretation. There is more than one view of what Paul meant when he spoke of the Church as the body of Christ. There are those who believe that this phrase must be taken in a mystical sense, and that when a man enters into the Church of Christ, in a mystical sense he enters into the body of Christ. In a famous phrase the Church has been described as " an extension of the Incarnation," so that just as God was Incarnate in Jesus Christ, Jesus Christ is incarnate in the Church. On the other hand there are those who believe that this phrase is to be taken in a much more practical sense, and in what might be called a functional sense. The work of Jesus Christ must go on; but He Himself is no longer here in the flesh to do it; for He has returned to His glory. If Jesus Christ wants a child taught, He must find a man or a woman to teach that child. If He wants His message brought to people who have never heard it, He must find a man or a woman to take it. If He wants His help and His comfort brought to mankind, He must find those who are willing to be the channels for them. That is to say, Jesus Christ needs the Church as His body, in the sense that in the Church He must find hands to do His work, feet to run upon His errands, a voice to speak His message. The Church must be the body through which Christ acts. It is, of course, true that these two views of the meaning of the phrase the body of Christ are not mutually exclusive, but the direction in which a man lays his stress and his emphasis does make a difference.

Let us for the moment leave the answer to that question of difference of meaning in abeyance, and let us return to Paul's pictures of the Church.

In Ephesians and Colossians Paul has another frequently recurring idea—the idea of Christ as the Head of the Church. God has given Christ to be the head over all things to the Church (*Ephesians* 1: 22). The members of the Church must grow up into Him who is the head, that is Christ (*Ephesians* 4: 15). As the husband is head of the wife, so Christ is head of the Church (*Ephesians* 5: 23). Christ is the head of the body, that is the Church (*Colossians* 1: 18). He is the head by which all the body is nourished and administered and knit together (*Colossians* 2: 19). We may note also that Jesus Christ is called the Saviour of the body (*Ephesians* 5: 23).

Now one thing emerges from all this. If we take the phrase, the Body of Christ, in its mystical sense, if we regard the Church as the extension of the Incarnation, then it does mean that in some sense Jesus Christ is identified with the Church. With Paul that is not so; there is always a clear and definite distinction between Christ and the Church. Christ is the Saviour of the body (*Ephesians* 5: 23). The Church is subject unto Christ (*Ephesians* 5: 24). The body is the instrument through which the decisions and purposes of the head are carried out; the body is the agent of the head. The body is that without which the head is practically helpless. It seems to us to be almost beyond doubt that it is in this sense that Paul calls the Church the Body of Christ. The Church is the instrument, the agent, the weapon, the organism through which the purposes and the plans of Jesus Christ must be carried out. It is through the Church that Jesus Christ seeks to bring life and light and salvation to men. Herein is the glory of the Church, that the Church is the necessary instrument in the hands of Christ.

There are two passages in Paul's letters which specially bear this out. It may be objected that to hold that the Church is the instrument or agent through which and by which Jesus Christ carries out the purposes and the plans of God is nothing less than to say that Jesus Christ is dependent on the Church. Startling as it may seem, that is precisely what Paul does say. Writing to the Colossians Paul says that he rejoices in his sufferings for them and that he " fills up that which is behind (lacking) of the afflictions of Christ in his flesh for His body's sake, which is the Church " (*Colossians* 1: 24). It may seem an extraordinary thing to say that there is something lacking in the sufferings of Christ. What Paul means is this. Christ once and for all found the remedy for sin; but that remedy has to be brought to men and made known to men and offered to men— and that is the work of Paul and the work of the Church. And if the task of bringing the good news of God's offered salvation in Christ to men involves sufferings, these sufferings may well be said to be the completing of the sufferings of Christ. Let us take an analogy. A scientist or a doctor may discover a new cure for some hitherto incurable illness; a surgeon may discover a new technique for some hitherto impossible operation; but the cure and the technique have not only to be *discovered;* they must also be made *available* to those who need them; and the making of them available may well involve labour and sacrifice and toil and thought which are at least comparable with the price paid for the discovery itself. The plain fact is, that what Christ did for men cannot avail for men until men know of it; and they cannot know of it until the Church tells them. " How then shall they call on Him in whom they have not believed? and how shall they believe in Him of whom they have not heard? and how shall they hear without a preacher? " (*Romans* 10: 14). Christ needs the Church to bring to men the knowledge of the salvation He offers, and that which is suffered in that task fills up and completes the sufferings of Christ. Once again we are forced to the conception of the Church as the agent and instrument of Christ.

The second passage is in the Letter to the Ephesians. There Paul writes, as the Authorized Version has it, of the Church, "which is His body, the fullness of Him that filleth all in all " (*Ephesians* 1: 23). Now this is no easy statement, and scholars are not agreed as to what it means. But, as we see it, the simplest and the most natural meaning of it, as far as the Greek goes, is this. The word which the Authorized Version translates *fullness* is *plērōma.* The noun *plērōma* comes from the verb *plēroun*, which means *to fill;* and a *plērōma* is that which results when something is filled. *Plērōma* is used, for instance, for the filling of a cup. Euripides (*The Trojan Women* 823) poetically describes the office of a cup-bearer: " Child of Laomedon, thou hast the *filling* of the cups, an office fair." Again, *plērōma* is often used for a ship's crew or a ship's complement, as it is also used of a ship's cargo. It is used naturally and regularly for a basketful or a handful. Still again, in his *Politics* Aristotle describes how Socrates had outlined the organisation of a city at its simplest (*Politics* 4: 4). Socrates had laid it down that the simplest city must contain six artisans— a weaver, a husbandman, a shoemaker, a builder, a smith, a herdsman, to which must be added a merchant, and a retail dealer. These, says Aristotle, compose the *plērōma* of a city. Without them a city cannot be; with them there is the essential basis of a city. So, then, the simplest, and, indeed, the commonest meaning of the Greek word *plērōma* may be expressed by the English word *complement;* the *plērōma* is that by which something is filled up, or completed. So, then, what Paul is saying is that *the Church is the complement of Jesus Christ.* The Church is that through which the task of Christ is completed. We must make it clear that we are drawing a clear distinction between the work of Christ and the task of Christ. The *work* of Christ was completed once and for all upon the Cross, for there the salvation of men was once and for all secured; but the *task* of Christ remains, and the task is to make known that saving act and all its benefits to all mankind. And it is the task of Christ which the Church must complete; it is in the completing of that task that the Church is the complement of Christ.

We hold that when Paul speaks of the Church as the Body of Christ the main emphasis of his thought is on the function of the Church as the instrument and agent of Jesus Christ, the essential complement through which Christ makes known to all men that which He has already done. It is just here that the other meaning of the Body of Christ comes in. If the Church is to complete that task, if she is to be worthy of that task, if she is to do the work for which Jesus Christ designed her, then she must live so close to Christ, she must be so much in Christ, that her unity with Him is such that she can be called nothing less than the Body of Christ in the mystical sense of the term. In other words, to be the Body of Christ in the practical sense the Church must be the Body of Christ in the mystical sense also.

But we have by no means come to the end of the great Pauline pictures of the Church. One of the loveliest pictures in Paul's letters is the picture of the Church as the *Bride of Christ*. That picture is most clearly painted in *Ephesians* 5: 22-23, where the relationship of husband and wife is said to be the same as the relationship between Christ and the Church. " Husbands, love your wives as Christ loved the Church " (*Ephesians* 5: 25). That conception emerges, on the surface less obviously, but even more vividly when the picture is seen in 2 *Corinthians* 11: 2. There Paul writes to the Corinthian Christians in explanation of the urgency

251

of his appeals " I am jealous over you with godly jealousy; for I have espoused you to one husband, that I may present you as a chaste virgin to Christ."

In a Jewish wedding there were two important persons who were called " the friends of the bridegroom." One represented the bridegroom and one the bride. They acted as intermediaries; they conveyed the invitations to the guests; they generally looked after all the arrangements. But they had one duty which was far more important than any other—it was their duty to guarantee the chastity of the bride; it was their duty to assure the bridegroom of the purity and the virginity of the bride. So Paul thinks of Christ as the bridegroom, and of himself as the friend of the bridegroom, and of the Church of Corinth as the bride who is being prepared for Christ; and Paul sees it as his task that he must present the Church at Corinth a pure and unspotted bride to Jesus Christ.

This is a conception which goes far back, and which has its roots in the Old Testament. The prophets saw Israel as the Bride of God. " Thy Maker is thy husband; the Lord of Hosts is His name " (*Isaiah* 54: 5). " Surely as a wife treacherously departeth from her husband, so have ye dealt treacherously with me, O house of Israel, said the Lord " (*Jeremiah* 3: 20). That is why the Old Testament so often speaks of spiritual infidelity as adultery, and that why, when Israel is unfaithful, she is said " to go a-whoring after strange gods " (*Exodus* 34: 15, 16; *Deuteronomy* 31: 16; *Psalm* 73: 27; *Hosea* 9: 1); and it is that spiritual infidelity to God that Jesus spoke of when He spoke of " an evil and *adulterous* generation " (*Matthew* 12: 39; 16: 4; *Mark* 8: 38). And that is why in the Old Testament God can so often be called a *jealous* God (*Deuteronomy* 32: 21; *Exodus* 20: 5; 34: 14; *Zechariah* 8: 2). God is the lover whe can brook no rival.

Here we have the loveliest of all the pictures of the relationship between Christ and the Church. The Church is the Bride of Christ; the relationship between Christ and the Church is as intimate as the relationship between man and wife. Nothing less than the closest of all ties will suffice as an analogy of the relationship between Christ and His Church.

There still remain certain other titles for the Church in Paul's letters at which we must look.

Christians are *members of the family of God (oikeioi theou)*. Paul writes to the Ephesians that they are no more strangers, but they are fellow-citizens with the saints, and members of the household of God (*Ephesians* 2: 19). It is of the greatest significance to note how the relationship between the Christian and the Church and God is described in terms of the closest and most intimate human relationships, in nothing less than terms of husband and of wife, and of father and of child.

Sometimes in Paul's letters the Church is described in terms of a building, erected by and for God. " Ye are God's *building* " (*oikodomē*) Paul writes to the Corinthians (1 *Corinthians* 3: 9). The whole Church is like a building fitly framed together (*Ephesians* 2: 21).

It is from this conception that we get the idea of *edification*, which literally means *building up*. The words of the prophets build up the Church (1 *Corinthians* 14: 3-5). The reason why the Christians must seek to excel in spiritual gifts is not to glorify themselves, but to build up the Church (1 *Corinthians* 14: 12). Paul always does everything for the building up of his people, and his authority is God (2 *Corinthians* 12: 19; 13: 10; 10: 8). The Christian duty is to build up one another (1 *Thessalonians* 5: 11), and ever to pursue the things which make for mutual upbuilding (*Romans* 14: 19; 15: 2). All offices and gifts are given for no other purpose than the building up of the Church (*Ephesians* 4: 12, 16); and the life and conduct of the Christian must be such that it is good for building up the Church (*Ephesians* 4: 29).

Here we are faced with two great truths. The work of the Church must be always construction, and never destruction. If destruction has to take place, and if old and ingrained ideas and conceptions must be swept away, it must always be to raise something new and better in their place. All Christian teaching and action must be characteristically positive and never merely negative in its aim and object. Again, it means that the Christian must never think of himself as an individual. He is a stone in a building. He is not there to draw attention to himself, but to add strength to the building of which he is a part. He is joined to his fellow-Christians as closely as stone is joined to stone in a well-compacted building.

It is further to be noted that there are passages where this building is more closely defined. The Church is not simply a building; it is a building which is *the temple of God*. " Know ye not," demands Paul " that ye are the temple of God?" (1 *Corinthians* 3: 16, 17). " What agreement has the temple of God with idols?" (2 *Corinthians* 6: 16). The whole building is fitly framed together, and is growing into " a holy temple of the Lord " (*Ephesians* 2: 21).

The idea here is very simple, and yet very great. A temple is the dwelling-place upon earth of a god; and the Church is nothing other than the earthly dwelling-place of the Spirit of God.

There are two further building metaphors in Paul's letters. First, Christ is the foundation of the Church (1 *Corinthians* 3: 11); and, second, Christ is the chief cornerstone of the Church (*Ephesians* 2: 20). It is on Christ that the whole Church is built, and it is by Christ that the whole structure of the Church is held together.

Finally, there is one picture of the Church in Paul's letters from a quite different source. He writes to the Corinthians as the Authorized Version has it: " Ye are God's husbandry" (1 *Corinthians* 3: 9). The word is *geōrgion*, and it means *a field*. The Church is the soil which can become fertile in all good things, by the action of the Spirit of God upon it.

So, when we look back across Paul's thinking about the Church, we see that for him the Church is the company of men and women who have dedicated their lives to Christ, whose relationship to Christ is as close as that of husband and of wife, whose relationship to each other is as firm as the stones within a building, and whose supreme glory is that they are the Body in whom Christ dwells, and through which He acts upon the world.

THE END

D1435937

Let's Stay Healthy

Other books by Adelle Davis

Let's Cook It Right
Let's Eat Right to Keep Fit
Let's Have Healthy Children
Let's Get Well

Foreword by Leonard Lustgarten, M.D.

LET'S STAY HEALTHY

HEALTHY

A Guide to Lifelong Nutrition

ADELLE DAVIS

Edited and expanded by ANN GILDROY, M.Sc.

London
GEORGE ALLEN & UNWIN
Boston   Sydney

**George Allen & Unwin (Publishers) Ltd,
40 Museum Street, London WC1A 1LU, UK**

George Allen & Unwin (Publishers) Ltd,
Park Lane, Hemel Hempstead, Herts HP2 4TE, UK

George Allen & Unwin Australia Pty Ltd,
8 Napier Street, North Sydney, NSW 2060, Australia

First published in Great Britain in 1982
Second impression 1982

British Library Cataloguing in Publication Data

Davis, Adelle
    Let's stay healthy: a guide to lifelong nutrition
1. Nutrition
I. Title – II. Gildroy, Ann
613.2   TX353
ISBN 0–04–641041–4

Printed in Great Britain by Biddles Ltd, Guildford, Surrey

Contents

What Vitamins Can Do for You 105

Air, Water, and Minerals 185

Health for the Family   243

Illustrations

Figures

Tables

Publisher's Note

The professional credentials of the three contributors whose writing is included in this book are listed briefly here:

Adelle Davis

> studied at Purdue University and at the University of California, where she received her Bachelor of Science degree
>
> undertook postgraduate studies at Columbia University, at the University of California, and at the University of Southern California Medical School, where she received her Master of Science degree in biochemistry
>
> worked closely with physicians, first in New York as a dietetic specialist at Bellevue and Fordham hospitals and at the Judson Health Clinic, later in California as consulting nutritionist at the Alameda County Health Clinic and at the William Branch Clinic
>
> as a nutritionist counselor in private practice, she consulted with patients referred to her by physicians and planned diets for more than 20,000 individuals who were suffering from a wide variety of ailments

Ann Gildroy

studied at the University of Wales Institute of Science and Technology, where she received her Bachelor of Science degree in Applied Science

undertook postgraduate studies at Queen Elizabeth College of London, where she received her Master of Science degree in Nutrition

has worked as a technician in the Chemistry and Physics departments of North Gloucestershire Technical College, as a medical photographer at Cheltenham General and St. Bartholomew's hospitals, and in research at St. Bartholomew's Hospital and the University of London

is the author of *Vitamins and Your Health* (Allen & Unwin, 1982)

Leonard Lustgarten

studied at Harvard College, where he received his Bachelor of Arts degree

undertook further studies at Albany Medical College, where he received his Doctor of Medicine degree

completed his internship and residency at Lenox Hill Hospital in New York

held a fellowship in medical neoplasia at Memorial and Sloan-Kettering Institute

is an Attending Physician at Lenox Hill Hospital, a Diplomate in Internal Medicine, and a member of the New York Society of Internal Medicine

Foreword

This latest and most up-to-date Adelle Davis book is classic in form, universal in appeal, and disarmingly simple in its expert descriptions of what nutrition really is and how it works. It leads us with easy expertise through the complexities of the human body; it explains briefly and with understandable diagrams just how the body handles, or fails to handle, those substances it ingests. It demonstrates which substances are used for growth, which for energy, which merely add on fat, and which may hurt or kill us by their toxic actions. *Let's Stay Healthy: A Guide to Lifelong Nutrition* is a fascinating journey into ourselves as animate creatures, always striving (with varying degrees of success) for an ideal state of physical and emotional health, and also a ready reference source, its information easily available through many aptly titled chapters and through indexing.

Less than a generation ago virtually no medical school curriculum in the United States included a single worthwhile course in clinical nutrition. The scene is changing rapidly, mainly because of pressure brought upon the medical community by a public hungry for real nutritional information—not from quacks or charlatans, but from trained nutritionists and their own family doctors. Physicians, young and old, are trying to make up for lost time. Medical students are now studying nutrition in most medical schools. Older practitioners are availing themselves of courses in clinical nutrition that were recently added to agendas of continuing postgraduate medical education.

Much of this change is directly or indirectly a result of the enormous effect of Adelle Davis's work over the past three decades. She, probably more than all other nutritionists, has had a national impact whose reverberations have made an entire culture vastly more conscious of nutrition and its importance to health and well-being.

This book will serve not only to introduce the neophyte into the world of nutrition but will also add refinements and an extra dimension of understanding that will prove valuable even to the knowledgeable. The book's organized approach, its logical sequences in presenting information, the timely and yet timeless quality of its content, make it, I believe, an ideal students' nutritional manual. Any high-school or basic college course dealing in human ecology, growth and development, studies on aging, or the health sciences in general should find a major role for *Let's Stay Healthy: A Guide to Lifelong Nutrition.*

A final, and I think quite important, comment about the book: In going through it most critically, as a practicing physician and one interested in human physiology, I have found it to be conceptually sound, intellectually honest, and factually correct. No reader will be misled by what he or she reads. Rather, the reader will have exposure to many basic truths, distilled from the still-young, sometimes clouded, frequently controversial, and always fascinating world of clinical nutrition.

LEONARD LUSTGARTEN, M.D.

New York, 1981

Preface

This is Adelle Davis's first and last book. That statement, once explained, will not be anomalous. In 1942, during the Second World War, when nutrition was a new science and food rationing emphasized its importance, Miss Davis was asked to write a manual on nutrition and health. The publication of *Vitality Through Planned Nutrition* inspired her to write four other books relating scientific findings to healthful nutrition. These four were to become international best sellers, their readership in the millions, their durability—with periodic revisions—spanning decades into the present.

When Miss Davis, past seventy years of age, died in 1974, she had completed all her planned writing projects except for the enlarging and revising of that earliest book. She wished it to be a current guide and reference book, easily accessible to anyone interested in understanding and promoting lifelong good health through the application of scientifically based principles of nutrition. The present book, *Let's Stay Healthy: A Guide to Lifelong Nutrition*, follows her wishes.

Some forty years ago, in *Vitality Through Planned Nutrition*, Miss Davis wrote: "Nutrition is a young science and there is still much to be learned. The essentials of nutrition will probably be little changed by future research, but a great deal of new knowledge will be added. You must . . . keep abreast of this new knowledge as it becomes known and realize that the information given in this book is by no means complete or final." Her words are still true today and my job, as editor, has been made much easier by knowing that she would have welcomed the alterations that have been necessary in updating her original work. Since then, with advanced research, the knowledge of vitamins, minerals, and diet has increased in its own right, but its growth and development have brought, inevitably, many differing views. Crank diets can now be quashed by scientific evidence, but there remain areas of uncertainty and these are a hotbed for conflicting, unproven theories. Anyone seeking nutritional guidance needs facts, not theories. I have endeavored to sift these facts, evaluate them, and draw sound conclusions.

One controversial issue today concerns the benefits, or dangers, of taking large doses of vitamin supplements. Vitamin pills are supplements to a diet, not foods. Opinions about their importance differ among the medical profession, health food manufacturers, and research workers. Since I feel it is important to see these facts in perspective, I have devoted a separate section to this topic (Chapter 41).

I have also added chapters on general physiology, since that information is vital to the proper understanding of nutrition.

The section on diet and health has been expanded to include more information about the medical aspects of diet in the treatment of disease. Some of the illnesses in modern society can be helped as much by diet as by prescribed medication. Unfortunately, dietary terms are not always comprehensible to the layman. I have endeavored to clarify some of the confusion arising from the more common diets, e.g., those controlling diabetes, obesity, and heart disease.

I have kept as closely as possible to the original text, but fashions of style and language alter with each decade and it has been necessary to make fairly substantial changes in some sections. I hope the new structure of the book allows Miss Davis's enthusiasm to be felt by the readers. She was a great pioneer of nutrition and deserves our continuing attention and respect.

I would like to thank all those who have helped me with this book. They include dietitians, librarians, friends, and colleagues. They have been particularly generous with their time and their knowledge.

Special thanks are reserved for Polly Broxup, who read the script (with a keen and critical eye), for Penny Mundy, who typed it (and made order out of chaos), and to Mr. Clive Sandall, who made the beautiful illustrations (after long hours of careful research). Mr. Sandall has asked me to express his thanks to the Royal College of Surgeons in London for their help and advice about his work.

ANN GILDROY

London, 1981

DIGESTION AND ENZYMES

1 · What Nutrition Can Do for You

HEALTH, LIKE HAPPINESS, is difficult to define. When we are ill we long for good health. When we are fit we forget it. A healthy body should be our birthright, but few of us claim it. People have differing ideas on how to attain perfect health. Some feel that exercise is all important; others say, "It's all in the mind." It would be wrong for the nutritionist to claim that food is the most important factor but, since we eat three meals a day for most of our lives, here, surely, is a unique opportunity to put one aspect of health into the right perspective.

This book is not only about nutrition but also about physiology. It is no longer enough to be able to recite a list of the foods we should eat. We need to know why they are important and what happens to them in the body. In the light of this knowledge the rules become more flexible and adaptable. This does not give us a license to switch to bad eating habits, but it does mean we can survive the everyday obstacles to our resolution to eat more healthily. There are many conflicting opinions surrounding health and diet today. These include the advice of well-meaning but often misinformed friends, the sales talk from the food industry, and sometimes the ignorance or skepticism of the medical profession. To be able to sift fact from fiction we need knowledge and we need results. Knowledge is accumulating daily and is there for the taking. The results we can prove for ourselves.

The science of nutrition is relatively new and only within the last few decades has it acquired a respectable place in the college curriculum. But it is not a new subject per se. It is as old as life itself. The subtle distinction between living and nonliving matter which began on this planet many millions of years ago became possible because the essential nutrients were available. This raw material, comprising solids, liquids, and gases, could support a life form capable of growing and reproducing itself indefinitely into the future.

The type of food we eat today is influenced by custom, climate, economy, age, sex, religion, occupation, and many other factors. With such a barrage of external influences, it is not surprising that we do not always select our food for health. In fact, the few of us who do try to do this often meet with opposition rather than approval both in our own homes and when we eat out with friends. Whether you are a housewife trying to introduce new ideas into the family menus or a small voice in the family circle trying to influence the housewife, you must have good arguments to back up your ideas and favorable results to prove them. The diehards of bad nutrition are always with us, but we should accept their challenge. We may even find that we can convert them!

2 · The Right Ingredients

THE BASIC RAW MATERIAL of good nutrition is good food. This may seem obvious but we must remember that this food must be eaten and used by the body before we can benefit from it! It is no good having a plan, writing out a menu, putting labels on the glass jars in the kitchen, or even reading this book unless we follow through by buying the right foods, preparing regular, balanced meals, and eating them.

"Health through nutrition" is a goal for many people. They imagine halcyon days when there will be money to buy expensive foods and time to prepare elegant meals. They believe they will then feel, day by day, fitter, stronger, and more attractive. Life is not like that, and it is never likely to be. We shop, cook, and eat every day and, although there is often less time and less money than we might think ideal, nonetheless there is good food all around us. Supermarkets may stock processed convenience and junk foods, but they also stock fresh food and nourishing food. It is up to us to sort out the good from the bad, to buy the best that we can afford. It is simply a matter of selection. If we know what our body needs then we can supply it with the right foods today. Few foods are "bad," but problems arise because people eat far too many of them. Fat, for example, is labeled as bad for the heart and as a cause of overweight, spots, and acne. Diseases may result when people eat too much fat, or when there is something amiss and the body cannot use the nutrients efficiently, but fat is an essential part of the diet and no one could live on a fat-free diet for very long.

In our study of nutrition and physiology we must consider, first, food: what it is, how much we need, and where we can get it; and second, the body: how it works, how it digests and transports the food, and how it uses it.

Food is energy. It is often compared to the fuel in a car, but it is much more complicated than that. Food supplies the material for the growth and repair of every single part of our body—from bone, muscle, and skin, to hair, teeth, and nails. Even before we were born our bodies were being formed by food. The umbilical cord from our mothers carried the ingredients and balanced nutrients of proteins, carbohydrates, fats, vitamins, and minerals to us. It makes sense to accept the importance of good food and to understand how much and how often we need different nutrients.

As an example of these essential nutrients, we might take a simple cake recipe. The egg included is protein, the flour is the carbohydrate, and butter is the fat. A closer analysis will show that the ingredients are not "pure" substances in that they are not composed of a single nutrient. The egg contains fat as well as protein, the flour contains protein as well as carbohydrate, and butter has been isolated from the rich complex of protein and sugars found in milk. All three foods contribute significantly to the essential vitamins and minerals that we need each day in our diet. A small slice of this plain cake will contain vitamins A, B, D, and E as well as iron, calcium, magnesium, phosphorus, sodium, potassium, and zinc, to name but a few. We do not have to remember all these facts, but we do need to know the proportions of nutrients which go to make up a healthy diet, which foods are rich in one nutrient and which in another. When we know this then we can make some sense of our eating.

We have already stated that the body needs food for energy. The food we eat and the heat and energy that our bodies produce can be calculated in calories. Most people know how many calories they should eat when they are on a diet but without these limitations they usually leave the matter to chance or appetite.

Tables listing the correct calorie intake for different heights, weights, sexes, and ages have been compiled, showing that most adults need between 2,000 and 3,000 calories a day, but what is less obvious from these charts is the way in which the energy is shared among the different groups of foods. For most people on a Western diet, 50 percent of this energy comes from carbohydrates, 40 percent from fats, and 10 percent from protein. This is an "average" rather than an "ideal" distribution, but many people express surprise at the low percentage of protein. We are told how important protein is in our diet and yet this class of food contributes such a small proportion of our energy. Why is this, and shouldn't we be eating more protein? The answer lies in the composition of the human body and how it uses the food it is given. More than half the body is composed of water, about one-third is made up of protein and fat (17 percent and 13 percent respectively), and only 1.5 percent, a very small part of the whole, is made up of carbohydrates. *(See Figure 1.)*

Our needs change with age and occupation. What is right at sixteen years of age is not necessarily right ten years later. The only way to assess our own diet is to know what nourishment the food is supplying and what our bodies need. Understanding the value of food and its function in the body is half the battle and we all have the perfect guinea pig—ourselves! This does not mean we should follow fad diets. It means watching how we feel and how we react to certain types and quantities of food. It means keeping an eye on our weight and checking our calorie intake. Extremes are foolish. No one can live on 400 calories a day, and 4,000 calories a day, unless you are an athlete, are far too many. Somewhere in between is likely to be the right calorie intake.

Having then found how much food energy we need, we can vary the way we supply it in our diet. We can experiment with more protein and less fat, or more carbohydrates and less fat, but the changes must be made very slowly and the benefits observed over a period of time. The body takes time to adjust to new regimes and keeping a record of our weight and general health is

Figure 1

Composition of the Body and the Diet

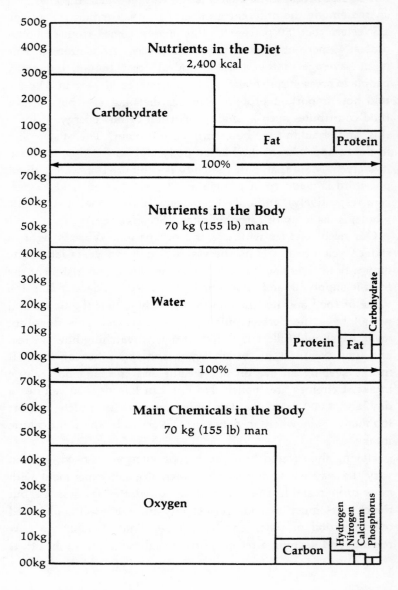

sensible. If you suffer from headaches or allergies, for example, you can observe if one type of diet provokes the problem or alleviates it. In this way, we can plan our diet and eat only the food that is best for us.

3 · What Happens to the Food We Eat?

HUMAN DIGESTION MAY be likened to a vast transport and communications system governed by the vagaries of food supply and demand. When we chew our food and swallow it we send it on a journey. Food at the table has been partly prepared for the journey, but it has not been packaged. In fact any "package" has usually been made to please the eye, the nose, and the taste buds. Once we have swallowed our food, whether it was a feast or a sandwich, it must be reduced to a common workable substance, and this is where the real work begins.

We may make elaborate plans for meals when we entertain our friends, preparing different courses with the colors and textures of the food delicately balanced but, although such social niceties are highly enjoyable, all this is of no consequence to the mechanics of the body. The digestive system is a hollow tube running from the mouth to the anus, but it is by no means a straight road nor is it uniform in width and capacity. The space within this tube is actually separate from the body, with the body wrapped around it. Anything within the tube may be absorbed through its wall into the body or may pass straight through and never actually enter the body. An accidentally swallowed marble, for instance, when finally detected in the feces, has apparently gone through the body but has never been inside the body.

Work starts in the mouth with the help of teeth and saliva. The food is then swallowed and goes straight to the stomach. Here it is mixed with digestive juices and enzymes and subjected to a constant churning and stirring until it is reduced to the consistency of a thick liquid. This substance is called chyme. The churning and stirring continue until every piece of food has been broken down to a size that is suitable for the next stage of the journey. (Children are often told to chew their food thoroughly or they will get indigestion, but lengthy chewing will not affect the ultimate fate of the food in any way.)

If we go back to the analogy of the transport system, we find that the stomach is similar to a spacious packing center compared to the rest of the gut. There is no room for bulky parcels on the next stage of the journey because the tracks are too narrow. Anything over the accepted size that tries to escape from the stomach will be sent back for a further churning. When the food has finally reached the right size, a small amount of chyme is then dispatched through a narrow opening at the end of the stomach to the next region, the small intestine. Here there are three important stations: the duodenum, the jejunum, and the ileum. Each station has a different-sized platform and this is where the passengers (the food we have eaten) alight and "change trains."

Before this can happen the chyme is first mixed with more enzymes and digestive juices which come from the nearby pancreas and gall bladder. These help to reduce the fats, proteins, and carbohydrates to very small particles and prepare them for the next stage of the journey. The carbohydrates are reduced to simple sugars called glucose, galactose, and fructose; the fats are reduced to tiny droplets described as micelles, and protein is broken down into small units called amino acids.

All these food particles can leave the "train" at the first station, the duodenum, though the sugars and amino acids prefer the middle station, the jejunum. By the time the chyme has reached the ileum most of the passengers will have left the train. The next job is one of selection and rejection of the passengers trying to pass through the gut wall. To put it in simple terms, it as as though there is a special gateway or turnstile for each of these types of food. Some able-bodied citizens can slip through the barriers unaided but some need help and have to be pushed or carried.

Everything that the body can use is unloaded in the hope that it will make its way through the gut wall and journey on to the bloodstream. Anything that is not needed or cannot get through the barrier stays on the original route, joins up with the other unwanted goods, and starts on a slow journey through the large intestine to be excreted through the rectum and anus as feces.

The fate of the foods which manage to pass through the gut wall now takes a new turn. Having been separated and sorted for their selection at the barrier, they all meet up again in the tiny blood capillaries and lymph vessels and continue on their journey. But now they travel more as individuals than as part of the crowd. The next station is the liver. Amino acids and sugars travel directly by the portal vein but most of the fats take a roundabout route, traveling first on the "lymph line" before entering the blood system.

At this point we should take a closer look at some changes that have appeared in the transport system. Food from the stomach traveled within a hollow tube aided by the action of the muscles around it. Once it is through the gut wall and into the bloodstream it can travel faster. Blood is much more fluid than chyme and moves rapidly within the complex network of capillaries and veins, aided by the regular pumping action of the heart. It is important, also, to grasp the change of scale as well as speed that has occurred here. We talked pictorially of a change of track gauge after leaving the stomach and entering the intestines. It was, in fact, a change of about 7–8 centimeters to one of 4 centimeters. The next change from gut to bloodstream is from 3 centimeters (the diameter of the ileum) to one so small that it can be seen only under a microscope. This indicates how small the food particles have become and how minute the blood capillaries are which collect and distribute them. The capillaries are minute vessels that can be likened to the mountain tributaries of a vast river. They flow and join up to form the main river, which in this instance is the portal vein. This leads directly to the liver, the hub of our transport system. This is by no means the end of the journey for our breakfast, lunch, and dinner, but it does serve as a temporary resting place until orders are received about their final destination.

The liver is one of the largest organs in the body and it is absolutely essential for life. We can live without our spleen, appendix, one kidney or one lung, but without the liver our lives must cease. It is supplied with blood from the heart and it collects blood from the spleen, stomach, and all parts of the intestines. (*See Illustration 1.*) It is also in direct communication with the brain through branches of the vagus and splenic nerves. Being such a well-supplied communications center, it is constantly aware of the state of all parts of the body and it is easy to understand why it has been called "the master mind of the body," "the biochemical machine," "the great gland," and other superlatives. Not only can it store, synthesize, dispatch, and collect, but it can also monitor and destroy many harmful substances, drugs, and toxins which may enter it via the central bloodstream (from the lungs and heart) or from the portal bloodstream (from the intestines). There are many other functions of the liver but, at this stage, we will concentrate on the fate of food. (See Chapter 14 for a more detailed discussion.)

Many hormones enter the liver through the bloodstream carrying with them information and commands about the needs of the rest of the body. Simple sugars in the form of glucose, and proteins in the form of amino acids, are dispatched through the small veins of the blood according to this need. These small veins widen and flow together, leaving the liver in a large vein which enters the inferior vena cava. This travels upward through the diaphragm and enters the right side of the heart where the blood is immediately pumped to the lungs. Here the blood releases any waste carbon dioxide, collects a fresh supply of oxygen, and changes from a dark venous color to a bright red oxygenated color. On leaving the lungs, the blood returns to the left side of the heart, where it is given a great thrust from the organ's powerful pumping action and sent sweeping up the main artery, the aorta, which channels it to all parts of the body.

In effect, our food particles are now on the last lap of their

Illustration 1

The portal system from the intestines to the liver

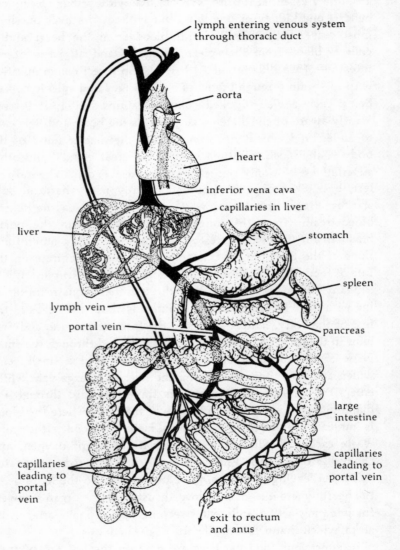

lymph entering venous system through thoracic duct

aorta

heart

inferior vena cava

capillaries in liver

liver

stomach

spleen

lymph vein

portal vein

pancreas

large intestine

capillaries leading to portal vein

capillaries leading to portal vein

exit to rectum and anus

journey. Their final destination is the cell. We are made up of literally millions of tiny cells. These group together to form skin, bone, nerve, muscle, fat, and all the tissues and organs within the body. All the cells vary enormously in shape and function but they are all in constant need of food.

The blood capillaries which deliver food to the cells are too small to be seen except under a microscope, where they can be seen as an elaborate network of fine channels running close to the cells. The capillary walls themselves are made of a single layer of cells which are so thin that food can pass through their pores and junctions, cross a small space, and enter the adjoining cells. The food has now completed its journey. The raw material for building, repairing, and storing has arrived. Here, in the cells, the vital fuel will be used and the waste products collected and discharged back into the bloodstream. These wastes include carbon dioxide, which is removed from the lungs every time we exhale. Other wastes from the cells and from the food are returned to the liver to be recycled or converted to urea and excreted via the kidneys.

This continual delivery and collection service of our food is totally dependent on the circulation of the blood which can be likened to a traffic circle with many exit and access routes. The main highways are the major blood vessels; they are the arteries and arterioles, and the small back roads are the capillaries. These minor roads twist and turn continuously but each one has a point where it curves around and starts to weave its way back to the highway. There is no break in this circuit at any point. The outgoing roads are arteries and the incoming ones are veins. If we decided to follow an artery from the heart to the little finger and back again through the vein it would be possible to do so.

The importance of some sort of coordination within such a complex system is obvious. The need for a particular nutrient may occur quite suddenly in any area of the body. The crisis of a cut finger or a broken bone will need urgent reinforcements of proteins and minerals to promote healing. The right nutrients will be drawn from the liver and carried through the bloodstream. If we go back one stage, we can realize how important it is for nutrients to be available should they be needed. The only way we can ensure this is by eating the right foods regularly. The body stores a certain amount of useful material for emergencies, but these stores are not large and they need to be replenished often.

The analogy of our food's journey shows the main routes and activity centers of the body. We shall look at the different areas in more detail later to show how full health can be achieved only if the network functions as a coordinated whole. A failure or a blockage at one junction or station can cause enormous problems in rerouting and delivery schedules. It is imperative that we use nutrition in such a way that we do not abuse the system by starving it, overloading it, or feeding it useless foods. Instead, we must prove that a plan for nutrition can make each journey useful and profitable and that it can tip the balance away from sickness toward positive health.

4 · Scientific Words

THERE ARE certain words used to describe the physics and chemistry of the body which are familiar to the scientist but can be confusing for the layman. We shall make a brief digression to look at some of these to clarify certain points and make more sense of the dynamics of nutrition and physiology.

A common error often arises in the distinction between atoms and molecules. An atom is the smallest particle of an element that can exist on its own. It is something which cannot be divided any further and still keep its individuality. A molecule is a larger entity and is composed of two or more atoms. These can be made up from the same or different substances. For example, a water molecule is made up of 2 atoms of hydrogen and 1 of oxygen. Its chemical formula is written H_2O. Molecules of gold are made up from gold atoms only and the metal is described as a pure element.

There are nearly a hundred elements on the earth. Humans are made up of 26 of these—with oxygen, carbon, and hydrogen forming over 90 percent of the body. *(See Figure 1.)* Although we are, in effect, a parcel of millions and millions of atoms, most of these are joined together to form many different molecules. These can be relatively simple like the glucose molecule (blood sugar) which contains 6 carbon atoms, 6 oxygen atoms, and 12 hydrogen atoms and is written: $C_6H_{12}O_6$. They can also be very complex, like many of the proteins which consist of coils and chains of many hundreds of atoms linked together in varying sequences.

17

A single atom is very small indeed (approximately $\frac{1}{100,000,000}$ of a centimeter). It cannot be seen even under a powerful electron microscope but it is, nonetheless, a sophisticated piece of matter. A simple plan would show a positively charged central core with electrons circling round it, like planets around a sun. These electrons have a negative charge and they can spin away from their "sun" and join another "planetary system" or they can make room for an additional electron within their own "orbit." When this happens the atom becomes charged with this extra electricity and is described as an ion. It is written with the same chemical symbol but has a plus or minus sign after it to indicate the new electric charge on it.

Table salt is a good example of an everyday substance that demonstrates this ionization. Salt is composed of sodium chloride. The formula is NaCl. If we dissolve it in water the molecule splits into two ions, one of sodium and one of chlorine. These are now written: Na^+ and Cl^-. Ions like these can conduct an electric current and are called electrolytes. Their properties are vital to the proper functioning of nerves and muscles and particularly the heart. They are capable of altering the voltage which always exists between the inside and outside of a cell. This change can cause electric current to flow along a nerve fiber and the current can be measured. The units are in millivolts, and are very much smaller than the volts of a domestic power supply, but the principle of conduction is the same.

Ions are used to calculate the pH of a liquid. This term is used to describe the acidity of body fluids such as blood, urine, gastric secretions, etc. It refers to the number of hydrogen ions (H^+) found in the solution. The values are rated between 1 and 14 with pH1 being the most acid, pH14 the most alkaline, and pH7 neutral.

Blood is slightly alkaline at pH7.4, whereas stomach secretions during digestion are extremely acid at pH2. Urine is normally slightly acidic, with a pH of about 6, but can vary between acid and alkaline values according to the diet eaten and the amount of strenuous exercise taken. (Carbon dioxide in the body can affect the acidity of the blood. This is corrected by the kidneys and a change in the pH of the urine.)

Finally we need to take a look at the different methods the ions and molecules can use to cross the various barriers they will meet in the body. These barriers are usually in the form of cell membranes which surround the cells, and the fine capillary walls which enclose the blood circulating to these cells. When there are no barriers then particles in solution move from areas of high concentration to low concentration. We see this when sugar in a cup of coffee diffuses through the liquid and sweetens it. This is called simple diffusion. Some cell membranes allow water molecules to pass either way through their structure, but other particles, such as sugar and amino acids, are allowed to move one way only and so produce a high concentration on one side of the barrier. Water molecules tend to move toward this concentration in an attempt to dilute it, and this process is spoken of as osmosis.

Osmosis and diffusion work well in transporting food and water in and out of the cells when conditions are right, but when there is an uphill gradient (chemically speaking) and particles in a weak solution have to flow into a stronger one, then help is needed. The push is provided by energy-giving molecules called ATP (adenosine triphosphate; see Chapter 12) and also in the form of special proteins which "fit" the food molecules and take them through the barrier. This last method is aptly described as "active transport."

5 · The Communications Network

THE MOVEMENT of water and food in and out of the cell tissues and blood vessels has a direct effect on all aspects of body metabolism apart from the ones we have looked at concerning digestion. Growth, reproduction, circulation, breathing, and all muscle and nerve functions depend on efficient transport and communication. We have shown that the liver is the hub of the system in food distribution, but it is just part of the whole and, like the rest of the body, comes under the influence of the brain and nervous system.

Only in the last 150 years has the brain received its eminent and correct place in science and medicine. Before that time it was considered unimportant compared to the more colorful structures of the chest and abdomen. When the study of anatomy was in its infancy, parts of the body were compared to religious concepts of a heavenly kingdom. Aristotle considered the heart to be the center of the soul and the lungs to be the dwelling place of the spirits. Greek anatomists knew that arm and leg movements became severely affected after spinal injuries, but the fact that the brain and spinal cord were the true center of thought and function in the body was totally unrecognized until the beginning of the last century.

Now we need to know how the brain communicates with the rest of the body. There are two main systems: the nerves themselves and the bloodstream. The nervous system stems from the brain and the spinal cord. Information and orders are carried to and from this center by the nerve cells. This system does not form a closed circuit like the blood but has two distinct tracks.

Affector or incoming nerves run from the skin to the brain carrying information about the environment. They relay pain, pressure, temperature, and touch. The brain reacts by sending effector or outgoing nerves back to the scene to invoke some sort of response. This double action is very rapid. Think how quickly we drop something that is too hot to the touch (perhaps only a part of a second), but in that time a message has gone from hand to brain and back again. Although we may drop a hot object instinctively we are, to a great extent, in control of that movement. The muscles involved are described as voluntary and they work with the nerves of the central nervous system (CNS). Another part of the nervous system controls the involuntary muscles which regulate breathing, heartbeat, digestion, etc., and which are vital to our existence. These nerves belong to the autonomic nervous system and also stem from the brain and spinal cord.

Nerves are fine white threadlike structures composed of millions of cells. These cells possess long filaments which are bound together in a fatty sheath to form a nerve fiber. These fibers leave the bony protection of the spine and run to all parts of the body to innervate the muscles and glands. This response is invoked by electrical and chemical reactions that are generated by the flow of ions and molecules both inside and outside the cells. When this current reaches the end of the fiber, a chemical called a neurotransmitter is discharged which flows across the tiny gap between nerve and muscle. This creates a further response in the muscle causing it to contract. (*See Illustration 2.*)

Impulses from the brain can also cause the release of hormones from glands into the bloodstream. The main glands of the body are the pituitary, the thyroid, the pancreas, the testes, the ovaries, and the adrenals (near the kidneys). The pituitary gland at the base of the skull releases hormones that influence growth, water balance, and sexual development. The thyroid gland controls the rate at which food is "burned" and the pancreas and adrenal glands control the sugar levels in the blood.

Such a variety of reactions can work together only if there is some general communication and some control to stop and start

the operations. The blood acts as a mediator in both these requirements, for example, insulin from the pancreas is released
when blood sugar rises. The system works on a feedback control
and, in the same way that a thermostat turns on or off according
to the information it receives from its surroundings, the blood is
sensitive to changes of pressure, composition, viscosity, acidity,
etc., and reacts to restore equilibrium. If there is too much salt,
sugar, acid, alkali, or base in the blood, the information is received by the brain and a balancing response is invoked.

Illustration 2

A nerve cell showing the nerve fiber leading to a muscle

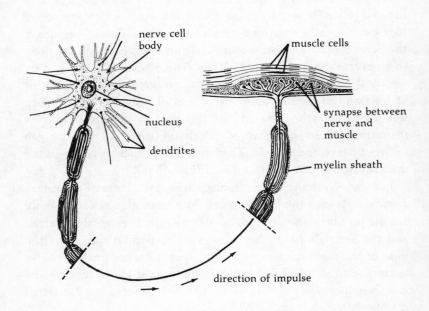

Drugs can interfere with, enhance, or inhibit any of these natural reactions. Medical drugs are aimed at controlling body regulations when they have gone amiss in some way. Similarly, foods can have either an adverse or a beneficial effect. One of the aims of good nutrition—besides supplying energy and raw materials—is to sustain and assist this delicate balance.

6 · The Importance of Enzymes

Early studies in digestion

LONG AGO it was thought that digestion was simply a mechanical mashing of food into small particles. Now we know that this is only one aspect of a much more complicated process. René Antoine de Réaumur contributed to our knowledge of digestion in the early 1700s. He owned a pet hawk to which he fed sponges. Since hawks regurgitate indigestible materials, Réaumur knew that the sponges would soon be returned. He also knew that they would be saturated with digestive juice from the stomach, known as gastric juice. He wrung out the sponges, collected the juice, and dropped various types of food into it to see what would happen. He found that some foods were broken down and some were not.

A few years later an Italian, Lazzaro Spallanzani (1729–1799), used a different method to study digestion in birds, cats, dogs, sheep, cows, horses, and even himself. Foods were tied to the end of strings, then swallowed, and later pulled up. Spallanzani also put bits of food into perforated metal capsules, swallowed them, and later recovered them from the feces. Since the food disappeared, even though the capsules were not crushed, this proved that digestion was dependent on chemical processes.

Thorough studies of stomach digestion were made in 1825 by Dr. William Beaumont, who lived on an isolated island in the St. Lawrence River. He met a French-Canadian soldier, Alexis St. Martin, who had a bullet wound in his stomach which had healed in such a way that there was an opening leading directly to the outside. This gave Dr. Beaumont an opportunity to study the factors which increase the flow of digestive juices and also the extent of stomach digestion. Foods were tied on strings, dangled in the stomach, withdrawn, and observed. Dr. Beaumont found that when he tickled the stomach of his subject with a feather more digestive juices were secreted. On the other hand, anger, fear, and fever all decreased the flow of gastric juices. Alexis St. Martin was not always a willing volunteer in these experiments and he had a tendency to drink. Sometimes he became drunk and escaped into the Canadian woods. Often it took Dr. Beaumont several months to locate his rebellious subject again but he continued his experiments whenever possible and his work contributed much to the study of digestion.

The acid in the stomach was later found to be hydrochloric. Another substance was also isolated from the gastric juice. It was given the name pepsin. It helps in the digestion of protein foods.

The next great contribution to the better understanding of digestion was made by Ivan Pavlov (1849–1936), the eminent Russian physiologist, who used dogs in his experiments. He showed that the flow of stomach juice was stimulated by the mere *thought* of food. If a dinner bell was rung at the time food was customarily given, gastric juice would begin to flow at the sound of the bell even when there was no food in sight. He also found that the larger the amount of food given, the greater the flow of juice, and that certain foods caused greater production of digestive juices than others.

The work of enzymes

Much of the chemistry of digestion is governed by the action of enzymes. Some digestion is possible without them, but only at a slower rate. Enzymes are so important that the process of digestion cannot be understood without a knowledge of their characteristics, how they work, and what conditions influence them.

Enzymes are proteins and are produced by cells within the body. They have the power to combine chemically with other substances. Digestive enzymes combine with a particle of food and break it away from the mother substance. For example, starch is made up of many molecules of glucose. It is first broken down by the action of amylase, an enzyme in the mouth. The product of this first digestion is dextrin. Dextrin usually contains 5 glucose molecules. A further breakdown to maltose (2 glucose units) and, finally, single glucose molecules, occurs in the small intestine. The enzyme is not changed by this process, but is released after each reaction and can take part in further digestion. Eventually the starch is broken down completely and the glucose is absorbed across the gut wall into the bloodstream. There are many different enzymes in the digestive tract which can break down other foods in a similar manner.

Reasons for studying enzymes

A study of enzymes will show how foods are digested and will explain other activities in the body, many of which are governed by enzyme activity. Apart from digestion, enzymes help in the building up of new tissues and in the breakdown of waste products for excretion. They are the key factors in all metabolic processes.

Many enzymes found in both plant and animal cells are extracted and used in the food industry to improve the texture and flavor of foods. Rennin is an enzyme which curdles milk. As a commercial product it is called rennet and is used for making junket. Yeast contains an important enzyme for breadmaking. It breaks down the sugar in the bread mixture, producing carbon dioxide. As the gas is liberated through the dough it causes it to rise. Baking destroys the yeast, so once the loaf is placed in the hot oven it will stop rising.

Other enzymes are found in molds and bacteria. Many cause spoilage of foods. They produce rot and decay in fruits and vegetables. Raw pineapple and papaya juice contain enzymes which break down protein. These can be used to tenderize meats, but their action must be stopped when the meat is sufficiently tender or it will be overdigested. A salesman once tried to make his fortune by selling pineapple juice to the frankfurter trade. He treated some sausages with the juice, cooked them, and presented them to a frankfurter company's executives for tasting. They all voted them tender and delicious and permission was given to treat all the sausages in the factory in the same way. What no one realized was that enzymes continue to work unless destroyed by heat, so the uncooked frankfurters finally dissolved away to useless blobs of jelly. The sample sausages had been cooked at exactly the right moment after partial digestion of the meat, but the salesman had not understood this.

Enzymes are involved in many processes in the body. They are important in the synthesis of body tissues. They combine with particles of food, brought to the site by the blood, into substances which form the actual body structure. They are also responsible for the breakdown of fat and glycogen (animal starch) in the body to provide heat and energy for metabolic processes.

The action of some enzymes is reversible. This means that if an enzyme is capable of breaking down a substance into two smaller components then the same enzyme may be used to reconstruct the original material. But here the versatility ends. Enzymes can act only on one material. For instance, the fat-splitting enzymes in the digestive tract cannot affect sugar. They can only break down fats. Sugar-splitting enzymes cannot digest protein. Some protein-splitting enzymes can digest only proteins with a particular structure. Each enzyme is, therefore, said to be specific: it must fit the material upon which it acts just as a key fits a lock. Also every enzyme has a specific temperature at which it works best. Enzymes in humans are most efficient at body temperature. During a fever, enzyme activity is increased and when the body temperature falls below normal the activity is decreased. Both these conditions are incompatible with good health. This change in the body's metabolism produces weakness and loss of appetite. A return to normal temperature allows the enzymes to work at their correct rate.

Table 1.
Important Enzymes in Digestion

Position	Source of Secretion	Enzyme	Secretions	Function	End Products
mouth	salivary gland	amylase	mucus	part-digestion of starch	maltose and dextrin
stomach	fundus glands	pepsin	mucus and hydrochloric acid	digestion of protein	polypeptides
duodenum	pancreas	lipase, amylase, trypsin, chymotrypsin	water, bicarbonate ions, salts	digestion of fats, dextrin, and protein	maltose, fatty acids and glycerol, polypeptides, amino acids, fat droplets
	liver		bile	emulsification of fats	
ileum	crypts of Lieberkühn	amylase enterokinase		starch and maltose activates protein enzymes	maltose and glucose, amino acids
	cells of gut mucosa	maltase, sucrase, peptidase	water and mucus	final digestion and absorption of amino acids, maltose, sucrose	amino acids, glucose
large intestine	mucus glands		mucus	lubrication	

Enzymes need moisture and the correct degree of acidity or alkalinity to work efficiently. Pepsin, in the stomach, needs an acid medium. The enzymes in the duodenum and the small intestine work best in alkaline solution. The naming of the different enzymes is usually quite simple. They are given the name of the substance they act on followed by the ending *ase*. Thus the enzyme that works on maltose, the malt sugar, is called maltase. The names of the common enzymes in the human digestive system are listed in Table 1.

7 · Digestion

Hunger and appetite

HUNGER HAS BEEN studied in many experiments, with one, for example, in which students swallowed balloons connected to recording instruments. In this way it was possible to trace the muscular contractions of the stomach wall on a graph. Although the stomach contracts to a certain extent all the time, the movements of the empty stomach are more vigorous and, when they are sufficently vigorous, cause discomfort, interpreted as hunger. A fall in our blood sugar can contribute to appetite and give us a craving for something sweet to eat. Mental attitudes and associations, such as looking at the clock before lunchtime, can produce the same sensation of hunger.

The mouth

The thought, sight, or smell of food stimulates the flow of saliva and, while the chewing of food causes further secretion, fear or excitement will inhibit the flow, as Dr. Beaumont found in his experiments. Saliva contains an enzyme called amylase which can digest starch. It enters the mouth from three pairs of glands situated in the cheeks and below the tongue and, although food is not held in the mouth long enough for much breakdown to take place, the saliva moistens the food and makes it easier to swallow. The biting and chewing action of the teeth meanwhile breaks down the larger pieces of food to expose a greater surface area to the digestive juices.

If food is eaten too quickly it will be broken down quite adequately in the stomach although the process will take longer. This upsets the traditionalists who insist that food should be chewed thirty-two times but, of course, moderation is the best policy even though our digestive system is able to cope with a variety of abnormal situations.

The esophagus

When we swallow food, it passes down the esophagus. This straight tube is about 25 centimeters long and runs behind the windpipe or trachea into the stomach. The air we breathe and the food we eat both enter our body by way of the mouth and throat. The act of swallowing produces a reflex that shuts off the air passages and allows the food to pass down the esophagus into the stomach. When we choke over a piece of food, we say it has gone down the wrong way. In fact, the food is simply lodged at the top of the windpipe and a further reflex of coughing or back slapping will normally return it to the throat to be swallowed again.

Occasionally this does not work and if food is deeply lodged in the throat the Heimlich maneuver is often the solution. Dr. Henry Heimlich felt that the advice given by the Red Cross of four back slaps and four abdominal thrusts could waste time. "From the onset of choking a person has only four minutes of life remaining unless his airway is cleared." The Heimlich maneuver has three steps: *First,* stand behind the person, wrapping your arms around his waist. *Second,* put your fist, thumb side against the abdomen, slightly above the navel, under the rib cage. *Third,* grasp your fist with the other hand and press into the abdomen with a quick upward thrust. The lodged food should then be ejected.

As the esophagus descends from mouth to stomach it passes through a large dome-shaped muscle which separates the chest

Illustration 3

The diaphragm, heart, and lungs

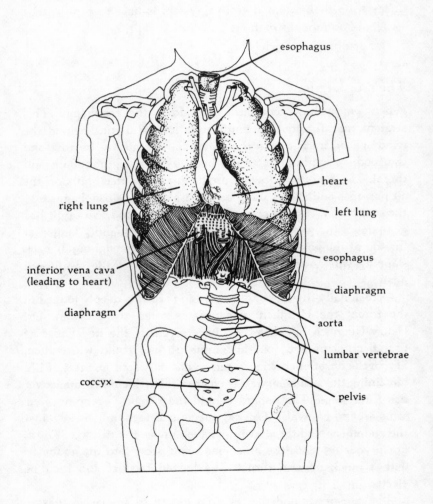

(the thoracic cavity) from the abdominal cavity. The heart and lungs lie above this muscle and the stomach, liver, spleen, pancreas, and intestines lie below it. The early anatomists considered this muscle to be as much a spiritual boundary as a biological one. They thought that the heart was the seat of the soul and the stomach and liver represented the more earthy aspects of the body—hence the diaphragm separated the spiritual from the profane. (*See Illustration 3.*)

The diaphragm muscle relaxes and contracts as we breathe to alter the volume and pressure of air in the lungs and chest. This action can also assist vomiting. Reverse movements of the stomach muscle return food to the esophagus and pressure changes in the chest do the rest.

When digestion is functioning properly, the food's progress is assisted by regular muscular contractions. These start as waves of movement in the esophagus and pass continuously to the stomach, the small intestine, and the large intestine. They are caused by two layers of muscle that run in a circular and longitudinal direction around the digestive tubes. The combined contractions and relaxations of these muscles produce the squeezing and rippling effect known as peristalsis. These muscular contractions are strong, regular movements and even if you ate a sandwich while standing on your head, you would still be able to swallow. Digestion is not dependent on gravity!

The stomach

The stomach (*see Illustration 4*) expands and contracts according to the amount of food it contains but, when it is empty, it collapses into a shriveled pouch, about the size of a clenched fist, and contains only mucus and gastric secretions.

The top of the stomach is often referred to as the cardiac (heart) region although it is separated from the heart by the diaphragm. This cardiac region is a good storage place for food prior to digestion since it is very elastic and able to expand to many times its original size. While food remains in this area,

Illustration 4

The position of stomach, liver, and intestines

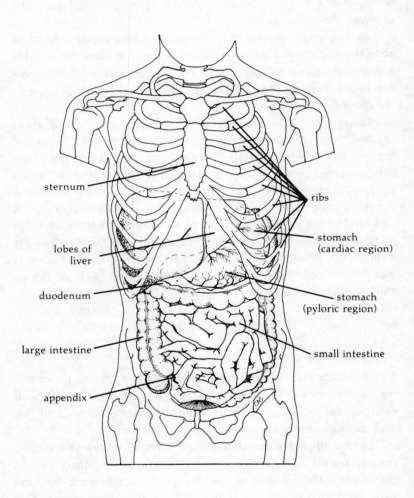

sternum

lobes of liver

duodenum

large intestine

appendix

ribs

stomach (cardiac region)

stomach (pyloric region)

small intestine

some of the amylase from the saliva in the mouth may continue to digest starch but the process is soon inhibited by the high acid concentration of the gastric juices. Most of the food's mixing occurs in the lower part of the stomach, known as the antrum or pyloric region, which lies close to the duodenum. This region contains the strongest muscles which constantly work at reducing the food to a size that will enable it to pass through the pyloric sphincter and into the small intestine.

In the walls of the fundus of the stomach there are many gland cells which produce mucus, hydrochloric acid, and the enzyme pepsin. The glands in the pyloric region of the stomach produce mucus only. This mucus has two important functions. It assists in the mixing of the food and it acts to protect the stomach lining against the strong acid secretions. It is therefore a slightly alkaline substance and can help to neutralize the H^+ ions.

Gastric juice

The stimulation of the flow of gastric juice, like that of saliva, is set up, as noted earlier, by the thought, sight, smell, and taste of food. This flow, controlled by the brain, is reduced if the vagus nerves to the stomach are cut. The flow of gastric juice is also stimulated by the presence of food itself, and chemically by certain foods such as meat extracts and alcohol. For this reason an apéritif may be taken before dinner and meat broth is often given to invalids at the start of a meal.

The flow of gastric juice is also stimulated by a hormone known as gastrin. This is released from the cells in the pyloric region of the stomach and transported by the bloodstream to the gastric-secreting cells in the fundus region. Here it increases the flow of hydrochloric acid and pepsin into the stomach. It also activates a substance called histamine in the fundus cells and this produces a further increase in acid secretion.

The question has been asked, "Why doesn't the stomach digest itself?" It does not do so because the cells in the stomach lining are slightly alkaline. Pepsin can work only in strong acid conditions. The mucus secreted by the gastric cells acts as a protective element both mechanically and chemically. It clings to the cells and neutralizes any acid which comes into contact with it. Pepsin cannot work in this neutral environment and self-digestion of the stomach wall does not take place.

The gastric juice contains some mucus, large amounts of water, hydrochloric acid, and pepsin. Pepsin breaks down protein foods, such as meat, fish, eggs, and cheese, into simpler substances called polypeptides and amino acids so that they can then be acted on by different enzymes found in the intestines. The digestion of protein is never completed in the stomach. There is another enzyme, a fat-splitting lipase, which is also present in the stomach, but lipases can work only in an alkaline medium. The contents of the stomach are always too acid for fats to be broken down at this stage. Many books describe rennin as a stomach enzyme which helps in the digestion of milk. In fact, this enzyme is not found in the human stomach, but is plentiful in the stomachs of young calves. We have a form of pepsin similar to rennin, which curdles liquid milk and aids its digestion. This curdling process delays its passage through the gut so that there is more time for the preliminary protein digestion necessary for such a rich food. This is particularly important in babies, since milk is their only source of food.

Foods leaving the stomach

Solid food in the stomach is mixed with whatever liquid is drunk with the meal. Gastric secretions add a further 100–200 milliliters. The amount of gastric juice produced is largely determined by the size of the meal. The churning of the food and liquids by the stomach muscles produces a semiliquid substance called chyme, as mentioned in Chapter 3. Once it reaches this state the food is ready to pass from the stomach to the intestines for the next stage of digestion.

The length of time the food stays in the stomach depends on the quantity and type of food eaten. A raw egg will pass through

Illustration 5

Passage of nutrients in the intestines and the absorption in the portal vein

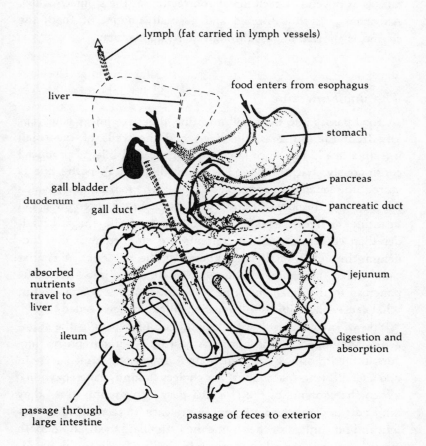

more quickly than a hard-boiled egg. A snack or small meal might take only an hour or two to pass through the stomach whereas a Sunday lunch or a wedding feast could take five or six hours to complete this first stage of digestion. Fats stay in the stomach longer than proteins, and carbohydrates (starches and sugars) have the quickest transit time.

The circular muscle which forms the "door" between the stomach and the intestine is called the pyloric sphincter. This muscle relaxes at the end of each major contraction of the stomach walls. An opening is thus formed and a small amount of food, the chyme, is allowed to pass through to the duodenum.

The small intestine

As food passes into the small intestine, digestive juices pour rapidly from the pancreas, the liver, and the walls of the small intestine itself. The juice from the liver, called bile, is produced continuously, but if no food is being digested then the bile is stored in a small sac, or reservoir, called the gall bladder, which lies between the lobes of the liver. When foods enter the small intestine the liver speeds up the production of bile, the gall bladder then contracts and the contents are emptied into the duodenum through a small canal known as the bile duct. A similar canal called the pancreatic duct carries digestive juices from the pancreas to the small intestine. (*See Illustrations 5 and 6.*) But what causes these juices to appear so quickly when needed?

You will remember that the production of pepsin in the stomach is stimulated by the hormone gastrin. A similar process occurs in the intestines. Here the main hormones are called secretin and CCKPZ (this last is short for cholecystokinin pancreozymin). When the contents of the stomach pass into the intestines they are acidic and this acid triggers the release of secretin. The protein and fat content of the chyme then stimulate the CCKPZ. Both these hormones are released not into the gut but into the bloodstream. They then pass through the circulation to the pancreas and the gall bladder, where they control the release of digestive

Illustration 6

The position of pancreas, gall bladder, and spleen (stomach cut away)

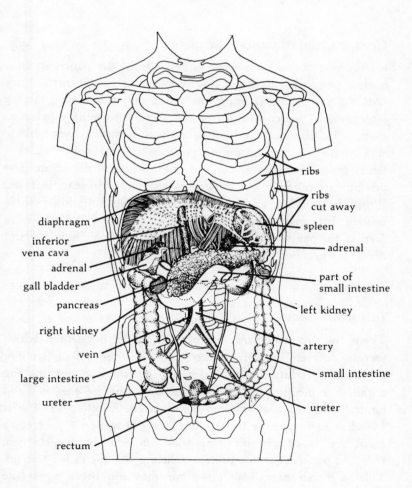

juices. In some diseases there is a shortage or lack of acid production in the stomach which, in turn, upsets the sequence of the hormones that control the release of enzymes. This condition is known as achlorhydria, meaning "without hydrochloric acid," and can cause severe malnutrition because foods cannot be digested or absorbed properly.

Composition of pancreatic juice

Many important digestive juices come from the pancreas. In a normal person as much as 1½ to 2½ pints of pancreatic juice (700–1,000 milliliters) enter the small intestine daily, largely after meals. They contain water and alkaline-forming substances such as bicarbonate ions which can neutralize the hydrochloric acid from the stomach, and enzymes, which can split fats, proteins, and carbohydrates for their next stage of digestion. The principal protein-splitting enzyme is secreted in an inactive form. It must be activated and is then capable of breaking down whole protein. It is easy to understand why it is stored in its inactive form in the pancreas. If it were stored in the active form it would digest the protein cells of the pancreas.

Intestinal juices

There are two important sets of cells in the duodenum which secrete different intestinal juices and enzymes. The Brunner gland cells produce mucus, water, and bicarbonate ions, making an alkaline medium for proper functioning of the enzymes and neutralizing acid coming from the stomach. Another set of cells found in the crypts of Lieberkühn (*see Illustration 7*), secrete a substance called enterokinase. This converts the trypsinogen, from the pancreas, into a protein-splitting enzyme called trypsin. This in turn can activate other enzymes and these digest the larger protein molecules into smaller units known as polypeptides and amino acids.

Illustration 7

The position and structure
of villi in the gut

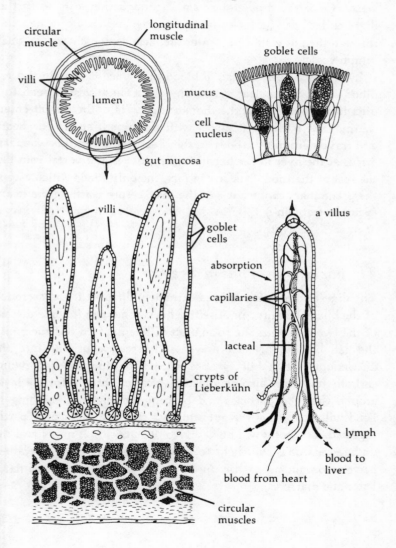

The starch-splitting enzymes break down the large carbohydrate molecules to simple sugars called monosaccharides and disaccharides. Fat is emulsified to very small droplets by the action of the bile and alkaline secretions. This action is similar to the way detergents break down fat on the surface of greasy water. Once the droplets are small enough they can be further digested by lipase, a fat-splitting enzyme, and they can then pass through the gut wall. They enter the lacteals, which are the small lymph vessels.

Lymph is a fluid similar to blood but, since it contains no red blood cells, it is a clear yellowish color. These vessels lead to a duct in the neck called the thoracic duct. Here, the lymph enters the main vein where it mixes with the blood, enters the heart, and travels around the body in the bloodstream. In this way, fats arrive at the liver in the hepatic artery, not in the portal vein like the rest of the food. Fats are, in fact, the only foods which escape the preliminary monitoring of the liver before reaching the heart. (*See Illustration 1.*)

The importance of bile in digestion

The digestion of fats becomes extremely difficult if the secretion of the bile is impaired or absent. This can happen if some disease of the liver prevents the formation of bile or if an obstruction in the gall bladder or duct prevents the release of bile into the duodenum. When bile is absent the digestion of protein and carbohydrate may also be affected since the fat will form a layer around the food particles and prevent the enzymes reaching it. Food will then leave the gut and pass into the colon only partly digested. The body will be deprived of nutrients it needs and the undigested foods will help to support the growth of unwanted bacteria producing gastric upsets in the intestines such as flatulence and diarrhea.

Mechanics of digestion in the intestinal tract

We saw earlier (page 33) how the muscles around the gut help in mixing the food and the enzymes as they move through the intestines. This movement also makes it possible for the enzymes to reach the food in the center of the gut (the lumen) and to pass close to the gut wall (the mucosa). Both these areas are important since the digestion of food by pancreatic enzymes and the emulsification of fats occur in the lumen, and the final stages of amino acid and sugar digestion take place on the surface of the mucosal walls. Some enzymes also act as the carriers through the barrier of the gut wall. This is why the constant movement and mixing in the gut is so important and also why the health of these surface cells is vital for proper digestion and absorption. These cells are constantly replaced by new cells as the old ones are sloughed off and passed out with the waste products in the large intestine.

The time that food takes for digestion varies enormously from person to person and meal to meal but on average the food remains in the small intestine for between 8 and 12 hours, which means that part of the food from two meals will usually be passing through the intestine at the same time. On the extreme ends of the scale, it has been proved that some food may pass into the large intestine after 2 hours while some food from the same meal may remain in the small intestine for as long as 24 hours.

Digestion takes place largely during the first 3 hours after the food enters the small intestine. Studies of the blood and lymph show that at this time they contain increased amounts of sugars, fats, minerals, vitamins, and amino acids. By the time the food mass is ready to pass into the large intestine most digestible material has passed into the bloodstream.

Absorption of foods

Absorption means the passing of foods from the intestines into the blood. The amount of wall space or surface of the intestines, through which the foods must pass, greatly influences the speed at which the food can reach the blood.

The actual surface area of the small intestine is about half a square meter. However, because of the folds and tiny fingerlike projections, called villi, the surface is greatly increased. The villi number between 4 million and 5 million. Just as a radiator is constructed so that a larger amount of surface may give off heat, so do these folds and villi increase the surface through which the food may be absorbed. The increase can be as much as 80 times the apparent surface area. *(See Illustration 7.)* Each tiny projection is supplied with blood capillaries leading to the liver and lacteals leading to the lymph vessels.

In a healthy person there are almost continual contractions of the intestinal wall. The action of the muscular contractions is similar to that of squeezing water out of a sponge. As the wall contracts, the food-laden blood and lymph from the villi flow into the general circulation. The muscular relaxation which follows allows fresh blood and lymph to reenter the vessels ready to pick up more nutrients.

The flow of blood in the capillaries is controlled by the propelling action of the heart. On the other hand, the lymph depends upon contractions of the muscles throughout the body for its circulation. The blood can therefore carry much larger amounts of food than the lymph. Fats are digested more slowly than proteins and carbohydrates. About 60 percent of all the fat eaten is absorbed into and carried by the lymph. The rest goes to the liver by the portal vein.

In the same way, vitamins and minerals, which are freed during the process of digestion, pass from the intestine into both the blood and lymph and hence into general circulation.

The large intestine

Very little, if any, absorption of food material takes place in the large intestine. As the food mass leaves the small intestine it is semiliquid in form. The purpose of the large intestine is principally one of water conservation. Without it it would be necessary to drink great quantities of water to sustain life. For this reason, sea animals, which have no need to conserve water, have no large intestine. Waste material remains in the large intestine for about 24 hours so that the absorption of water may take place. During this time the waste products gradually become more solid and are pushed to the rectum (the lower portion of the large intestine).

In cases of constipation the muscles of the intestinal tract are so sluggish that the food mass remains in the large intestine longer than it should. Too much water is absorbed from it and the feces become hard and dry. On the other hand, when laxatives are taken, water is drawn back into the intestinal tract, little or none is absorbed into the blood and the cells throughout the body are often robbed of much-needed water. Laxatives also force food through the intestines so quickly that complete digestion and absorption of foods cannot take place. Furthermore, laxatives irritate and can damage the delicate linings of the intestinal tract. Exercise, adequate dietary fiber, and water often correct problems of chronic constipation.

The large intestine contains billions of bacteria. Many of these are neither harmful nor helpful. Some may be helpful in synthesizing vitamins that are useful to the body, though it is doubtful if they are produced in very large quantities. Set against this is the fact that the bacteria may utilize other vitamins for themselves. However, *Lactobacillus acidophilus*, found in buttermilk and yogurt, is considered to be particularly helpful. This aids digestion by breaking down milk sugar into lactic acid. The acid environment helps in the absorption of minerals from the intestines and prevents the growth of certain harmful bacteria. For these reasons soured milk products are considered important in intestinal hygiene. Breast-fed babies enjoy a similar advantage as breast milk encourages the growth of *Lactobacillus bifidus* in the gut. This produces lactic acid, which prevents the invasion of disease-forming bacteria and so the baby is less susceptible to minor stomach upsets than the bottle-fed baby.

8 · How Much Sugar Do We Really Eat?

THERE ARE three classes of foods: proteins, fats, and carbohydrates. Fats and carbohydrates are used by the body mainly for the production and storage of energy and heat. Protein is used for building and repair. When people first learn that the body needs carbohydrates and sugar to supply energy they frequently remark, "I eat very little sugar." Mothers often become alarmed, thinking that they should give sugar to their babies or small children. What they fail to realize is that there are many kinds of sugar other than granulated sugar.

Sources of sugar

Everyone obtains a great deal of sugar directly or indirectly from the food he or she eats. This may come from the carbohydrate found in cereals, fruit, and vegetables, where it is stored as starch, or from glycogen (animal starch) found in muscle meats and liver. Even the diet of the Eskimo, which may consist solely of meat, will contain up to 15 percent of indirect sugar.

Plants are nature's sugar manufacturers. Their green leaves utilize the radiant energy of the sun to make simple sugars which are then stored as starch in the seeds and tubers. Animals cannot make carbohydrates in their bodies from water, carbon dioxide, and sunlight in this way. They must eat plants (or animals that have eaten plants) to provide the energy in the diet, and they can only store a limited amount in the form of glycogen. Grain and root crops provide a high percentage of energy in most diets and, in the West, wheat and potatoes are considered our staple foods.

The term *saccharide* is often used to describe the simple units which go to make up the more complex starch and carbohydrate molecules. The name comes from the Latin word *saccharum*, meaning sugar, but there are many different types of saccharides in our diet and only one of these is the true sugar that we use to sweeten our tea or coffee.

Simple sugars, or monosaccharides

The simple sugars, which are the end product of digestion, are spoken of as the monosaccharides. They dissolve quickly in water and are absorbed easily from the intestinal tract and pass into the bloodstream. They are transported to the liver where they may be metabolized, stored, or released, as glucose, back into the bloodstream. There are many sugars which may be classified as monosaccharides, but the three which are of the greatest interest to the nutritionist are glucose, fructose, and galactose.

Glucose, sometimes called grape sugar or blood sugar, occurs in small quantities in the blood of all animals and is also widely distributed in most fruits and vegetables. Sweet potatoes, new potatoes, sweet corn, and onions contain glucose, and this form of sugar makes up more than half the solid matter of grapes and honey. Fructose is found with glucose in most fruits, in many vegetables, and in honey. Galactose does not occur alone in nature but comes principally from the digestive breakdown of milk sugar, a disaccharide. Galactose, combined with other sugars and starches, occurs in plants. These are called polysaccharides. In brain and nervous tissue galactose is found combined with fats and proteins. Mannose is another monosaccharide found in some plants, but it is not so widely distributed and is less important in the diet.

The double sugars of disaccharides

There are three double sugars which are of interest to us. These are sucrose, maltose, and lactose. Sucrose occurs mixed with fructose and glucose in almost all fruits and vegetables. For example, half of the solid matter in ripe pineapples and in the sweeter variety of carrots is sucrose. Maple and cane syrups and molasses are largely sucrose. Commercial sugar is pure sucrose and comes from sugar cane and sugar beet. Sucrose is broken down in digestion to the monosaccharides fructose and glucose.

Maltose is formed during the sprouting of plants. It is also formed in the digestive tract from the breakdown of starch. Maltose itself is further divided into two units of glucose. Since many foods contain starch, which changes into maltose, this sugar is extremely important as a source of heat and energy to the body.

Lactose, or milk sugar, is found in the milk of mammals. Human milk contains 6–7 percent lactose and cow's milk about 4–5 percent. Lactose is less sweet than the other sugars and dissolves in water less easily. Lactose is split into glucose and galactose by the action of the enzyme lactase. This enzyme is produced in the intestinal wall and is plentiful in babies and growing children. Adults tend to have little or no lactase in the small intestine. For this reason some people are unable to tolerate milk and milk products. The undigested lactose passes into the large intestine and may cause diarrhea. The persistence or loss of the enzyme in adult life seems to be determined partly by the type of diet eaten and partly by racial and hereditary factors.

Many sugars, or polysaccharides

Since starch is made up chemically of many molecules of glucose, it is known as a polysaccharide. Starch is our principal source of energy. It is found in all cereals and breads, dried beans, peas,

Figure 2

Fate of Carbohydrates in the Body

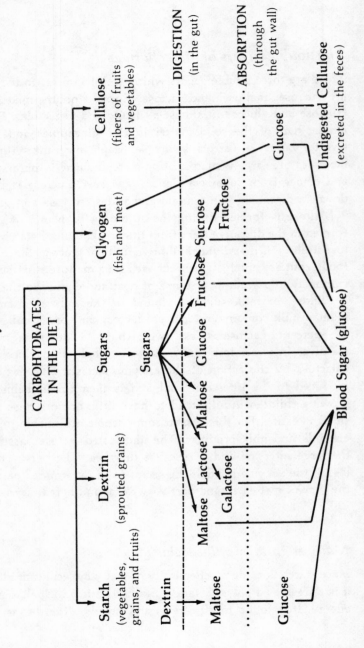

potatoes, and many other roots and tubers. Three-quarters of the solid material in most cereal grains and in mature potatoes is starch. Unripe bananas and apples contain starch, but as the fruit ripens the starch is changed to sugar. The process is reversed in young sweet corn and new peas, for the sugar changes into starch as the foods mature.

Dextrin is another polysaccharide. It is formed from starch when grains sprout. It is also formed when starchy foods are submitted to very high temperatures (about 212°F). In the digestive tract dextrin is broken down first to maltose and then to glucose.

A third polysaccharide is glycogen. This is a form of starch stored in animal bodies to serve as a source of energy. When we eat meat we get sugar from glycogen. The amount varies greatly and depends on the quantity of starchy foods eaten by the animal before it was slaughtered. Liver is the principal storehouse for glycogen or animal starch and is therefore the richest food source for this polysaccharide. Glycogen from meat is broken down into glucose in the digestive tract.

Cellulose, another polysaccharide, is broken down to glucose in the digestive tract of cows and goats and other ruminants. We lack enzymes to digest cellulose, but it offers a valuable service by forming bulk which improves intestinal hygiene. Examples of cellulose are the peelings of fibrous parts of fruit and vegetables and the bran or coating of grains. These were once spoken of as roughage, a misleading term which caused people to visualize sandpaper scraping the walls of the digestive tract. Actually cellulose is quite tender and smooth. Even bran flakes become soft when soaked for a few minutes. The term dietary fiber is used today to describe cellulose.

All sugars, starch, dextrin, glycogen, and cellulose are made of carbon, hydrogen, and oxygen. For this reason they are spoken of collectively as carbohydrates. All, except cellulose, are broken down during digestion to the three simple sugars—glucose, fructose, and galactose—which pass directly from the intestine into the blood.

Other sources of sugar

About 10 percent of digested fat consists of glycerol. The glycerol may be burned in the body, as sugar is, to carbon dioxide and water, thereby producing energy; or it may be changed first into glycogen by the liver and later into sugar. When proteins, which are broken down to amino acids during digestion, are used to supply energy, many of these acids are first changed into sugar. It is from these sources, glycerol, glycogen, and protein, that the meat-eating Eskimo gets his supply of natural sugar.

There are certain acids in foods which are not broken down by enzymes. They are carried in the blood combined with alkaline minerals and can be burned directly to produce energy or used to form glycogen which, in turn, is broken down into sugar. For this reason these acids may be listed as sources of carbohydrates. Malic acid occurs in apples, pears, peaches, tomatoes, and many other vegetables. Citric acid is even more widely distributed and is found in milk, meat, vegetables, and grains as well as in citrus and in other fruits. Lactic acid is obtained in appreciable amounts from buttermilk, sour milk, and cottage cheese. Others such as oxalic acid and benzoic acid occur in foods but these are not easily used by the body and are excreted by the kidneys.

Fate of sugars in the body

Glucose, which occurs liberally in most fruits and vegetables, passes directly into the blood during digestion. It is also formed from the breakdown of starch, dextrin, glycogen, sucrose, maltose, and lactose. (Figure 2 illustrates what happens to carbohydrates in the body.)

The body cannot change galactose and fructose directly into energy. These sugars are first carried by the blood to the liver, where they are converted to glycogen, which in turn may be changed to glucose as it is needed. On the other hand, glucose,

Table 2.

Percentage of Carbohydrates in Vegetables, Cereals, and Fruits

%	Vegetables and Cereals	Fruits
3	asparagus, Brussels sprouts, celery, chard, cucumbers, eggplant, kale, leeks, lettuce, summer squash, pickles, tomatoes	rhubarb
5	beets, cabbage, carrots, cauliflower, onions (dried), green peppers, pumpkin, radishes, string beans, watercress	
7		avocados, grapefruit, lemons, strawberries, loganberries, watermelons, olives
10	celery root, onions (fresh), parsnips, peas, turnips, squash (Hubbard)	blackberries, cantaloupes, melons, oranges, peaches, pineapples, raspberries cranberries
15	fresh garden peas, lima beans (canned)	apples, apricots, cherries, currants huckleberries, pears, grapes
20	lima beans (fresh), macaroni, spaghetti and rice (cooked), potatoes (baked), sweet potatoes, yams	bananas, figs (fresh), plums, prunes
30		persimmons
65		dried fruits (figs, apricots, apples, raisins, peaches)

which is called blood sugar, may be burned directly by the cells to produce energy. The glucose which is not needed immediately is stored in the liver and muscles as glycogen. There is a limit to how much can be stored in this way and when the liver and muscles contain all they can hold then excess glucose is changed into fat and stored in the adipose tissue. Once changed into fat it is never turned back into glucose. There is a very small part of fat which can be used to form sugar and glycogen. This is the glycerol fraction referred to previously, but for practical purposes it is wrong to think of fat as a source of carbohydrate. It is oxidized for energy, but initially it follows a different chemical pathway from glucose in producing this energy.

The sugar content of foods

With a few exceptions fruits and vegetables are composed largely of water, cellulose, starch, and sugars. Some contain a high proportion of fat, such as olives and avocados. Table 2 gives the carbohydrate content of fruits, vegetables, and some grain products in percentage of total weight. For example, 3 percent of a pound (450 grams) of tomatoes is sugar. This is equal to about half an ounce (15 grams). There is 10 percent of carbohydrate in a pound of turnips, the equivalent of approximately 1.8 ounces (50 grams) of sugar. Dried fruits contain a very high percentage of their weight as sugar. A pound of sultanas contains nearly two-thirds of a pound (300 grams) of sugar.

Ample supply of sugar without refined sugar

Almost every food we eat forms sugar either directly or indirectly during or after digestion. A person in the habit of choosing his food wisely may never taste jams, jellies, chocolates, or refined sugars in any form. Instead he receives all the sugar he needs from natural sources. Unfortunately we tend to rely too much on refined sugar to satisfy our hunger since it is absorbed rapidly into the bloodstream and gives a temporary boost to the blood sugar level. However, apart from being used in the body to provide energy it has no other value; it contains neither vitamins nor minerals.

Table 3.

Grams of Sugar Eaten in One Day by a Boy Who "Never Ate Sugar"

	grams of food	grams of sugar
BREAKFAST		
orange juice	200	18
prunes	40	20
porridge	30	20
cream	90	2
egg	50	—
2 slices toast	60	26
1 glass milk	200	10
LUNCH		
sliced tomatoes	100	3
baked potato	100	20
2 slices bread	60	30
raw apple	100	12
4 crackers	40	30
1 glass milk	200	10
AFTER SCHOOL		
peanut butter sandwich	110	35
banana	140	30
1 glass milk	200	10

	grams of food	grams of sugar
DINNER		
macaroni and cheese	150	30
canned peas	100	10
carrots	100	3
lettuce salad	150	2
2 slices bread	60	30
1 glass milk	200	10
pear	120	10
6 dates	50	37
TOTAL	2,650	408

Table 3 shows (in grams) the actual amount of sugar eaten in one day by a boy who claimed that he never ate sugar. The serving of porridge at breakfast is approximately one ounce (28 grams) and this will form about two-thirds of an ounce of sugar (20 grams or 4 teaspoons). The boy's total sugar for the day is nearly one pound. This is formed from natural sources, foods rich in vitamins and minerals. For a growing boy this type of diet is good for his health. However, if he took the same amount of energy as table sugar it would not contain any nutritional value and might well lead to problems of overweight and metabolic disorders.

The daily intake of refined sugars has grown steadily for years and is alarming. It is believed that the average diet contains one teaspoon of refined sugar per hour. While this may seem an exaggeration, the labels on many foods confirm the possibility. Besides the obvious content there is sugar in cold meats, sausages, cured ham, ketchup, many cereals, soups, snack foods, juices, beverages, and most prepared foods. Refined sugars do not improve health; they are more likely to impair it.

9 · How Much Fat Do We Need?

FATS, TOGETHER WITH sugar, serve as a source of energy for the body. They are especially important for giving a feeling of satisfaction during meals. People on fat-free diets suffer much more keenly from hunger than those who can eat a liberal amount of fat.

Sources of fat

Pure fats, such as lard, butter, and edible oils, contain about 100 calories per tablespoon. Whether from animal or plant sources, they are all equally valuable in supplying energy.

Fats rarely, if ever, occur alone in nature. Pure fats are separated from the protein and carbohydrates of plants or animals. With the exception of most fruits and vegetables the majority of foods we eat contain fats. So-called vegetable fats come from nuts and seeds. The principal sources of fats are:

ANIMAL	VEGETABLE
butter	almonds
cheese	Brazil nuts
eggs	filberts
cream	peanuts
bacon	coconut
pork	avocado
fatty fish	olives
(herrings)	

ANIMAL   VEGETABLE

fish liver oil   vegetable oils:

meat fats   sunflower, safflower,

   (lard, mutton fat,   sesame, olive,

   etc.)   corn, cottonseed

Chemical composition of fats

Like carbohydrates, fats are composed of carbon, hydrogen, and oxygen. They are made up of glycerol combined with 3 molecules of fatty acids. The glycerol molecule is constant in all fats but the structure and length of the fatty acid chains attached to it vary considerably. These chains consist of carbon atoms linked together, with the hydrogen atoms attached along their length. Carbon atoms have a capacity to join with 4 other atoms. In fatty acid chains the link between adjacent carbon atoms takes care of two of these bonds and the remaining two are free to combine with hydrogen. When we speak of unsaturated fats we are referring to the fact that the free links on the carbon chain have not all combined with hydrogen. There is still room to add more hydrogen to the composition of the fat. When all the spaces have been filled, the fat is said to be saturated.

Margarine is manufactured by saturating fats with hydrogen and forming a hardened oil, or fat. This is suitable for use at the table or for baking cakes and pastries. Most vegetable oils contain a high percentage of unsaturated fats and are liquid at room temperature, whereas animal fats contain more of the saturated kind, and are solid, like margarine. Modern research has shown that unsaturated fats are beneficial in the diet, particularly in lowering blood cholesterol, and they may protect against heart disease. These should be used in preference to saturated fats when possible. Margarine is now manufactured to contain more vegetable oils and the addition of hydrogen to the chains is kept to the minimum. The resultant fat is much softer but more beneficial to health than earlier margarine. It is usually described as being "high in polyunsaturates."

"Poly" means "many," and an oil or margarine that is high in polyunsaturates indicates that there are many unsaturated bonds in the molecule. Articles about dietary fat often refer to the P/S ratio—a term that is used to describe the proportion of polyunsaturated fat to that of saturated fat in the diet. If we obtain too much fat from dairy foods and meat, and take in very little vegetable oil, the P/S ratio will be low. Ideally we should be eating more vegetable oils than animal fats and this would give a high P/S value.

For example, let us suppose that 75 percent of our dietary fat is from meat, eggs, and butter and only 25 percent from vegetable sources. The P/S ratio would be written:

$$\frac{25}{75} = 0.33 \quad \text{(low)}$$

If, on the other hand, we are eating 75 percent from polyunsaturated fat and only 25 percent from saturated fat then the P/S ratio would be:

$$\frac{75}{25} = 3.0 \quad \text{(high)}$$

Oxidation of fat is often confused with *saturation* of fat. Oxidation is a chemical reaction which affects the same part of the fat molecule, namely, the fatty acid chains but, instead of hydrogen being added on to the carbon atoms, oxygen takes up the free position on the chain. This causes the chain to break and new products are formed. This is the main process which occurs when fats become rancid and the byproducts called hydroperoxides form the smell we associate with rancid fats. Some oxidation of fats is a normal process and will occur when the surface of the fat is in contact with oxygen in the air. Enzymes and bacteria, which may be present at the surface of the oil, speed up the process. Light and heat will also increase this natural oxidation.

A small amount of oxidation in the fats we eat is quite acceptable and will do no harm, but when rancidity becomes

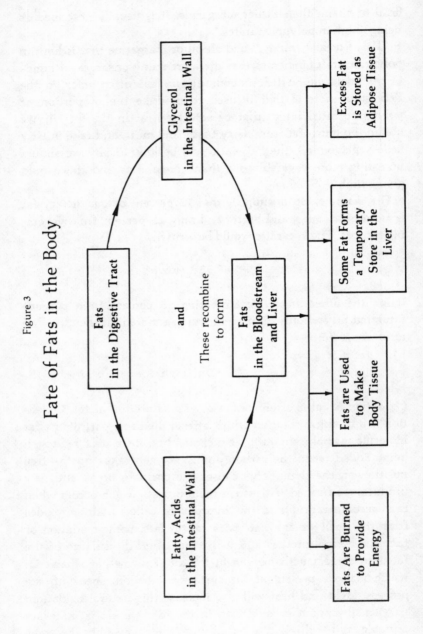

Figure 3

Fate of Fats in the Body

marked then the fat should be discarded. Rancid fats and oils destroy vitamins A, D, and E. They also contain products that may be harmful to the body. When fats are used repeatedly for frying at high temperatures these substances build up in the oil. If the oil becomes dark it should be discarded. Cooking oil is expensive and it is often difficult to justify throwing it away but in terms of real health for the family it is worth it.

To offset the deterioration in fats and oils, we should always try to keep them in a dark container with a lid. Butter and margarine can be kept in the refrigerator but vegetable oils should be kept cool and above freezing point. The reason for this is that hydroperoxides, which can form in vegetable oil, will last longer and do more damage to the vitamins when they are stored in the cold. At room temperature, however, the hydroperoxides change into less harmful substances which do not destroy the vitamins. Vegetable oil is, in fact, one of the few foods that benefit by being kept away from the cold.

Figure 3 illustrates what happens to fats in the body. During digestion fats are broken down into glycerol and fatty acids by enzymes and bile secreted in the pancreatic and intestinal juices. Most fatty acids are unable to pass alone through the intestinal wall but must first combine with the alkaline substances in the bile.

Glycerol from digested fats passes simultaneously into the cells of the intestinal walls where it combines with the fatty acids to form fat again. The fat which is formed is characteristic of each animal. The fatty acid chains vary from species to species but may be influenced by the type of fat eaten in the diet.

Fat is not dissolved in the blood or lymph as sugars are, but is carried as tiny droplets. Following a meal, large amounts of fat entering the blood are withdrawn by the liver for use in the near future. If excess fat which cannot be used by the liver pours into the blood after a meal then it will be stored in the adipose tissue of the body. This is similar to the storage of excess carbohydrate, which also ends up as fat. This body fat can be used to provide energy when needed, but it cannot be changed into sugar.

The largest amount of storage fat is deposited around the kidneys, liver, and heart. A thin layer of fat under the skin protects the muscles and nerves whereas the kidneys are supported by a large volume of fat. A small amount of reserve fat is valuable as a source of energy when sufficient food cannot be eaten. Reserve fat has often saved the lives of people during serious illness or starvation, but it is important to realize that an excessive amount of stored fat is definitely undesirable. This is a burden to the body and can lead to tiredness and ill health.

Functions of fat in the body

Fat provides both an immediate and a future source of energy. As we will see later, food fats are involved in the transport of the fat-soluble vitamins A, D, E, and K. Apart from being an excellent source of calories, fat has many other functions in the body. Fat, combined with phosphorus, is an essential component of every body cell and makes up part of the actual body structure, particularly in the nerves and brain tissues.

Certain fatty acids are essential to humans. These are unsaturated fatty acids, of which the most important is linoleic acid. It has been shown to be a factor essential for growth in laboratory rats and at one time it was classified as vitamin F. This terminology is no longer used and essential fatty acids are usually referred to as EFA. The best sources of EFA are found in vegetable oils. Dairy products and meat fats are not a rich source. Some skin conditions are thought to be due to a lack of EFA in the diet. The most common of these are eczema and dermatitis but although some children do respond to an improved diet containing extra linoleic acid, work has not yet shown conclusively that EFA will always produce a beneficial result. The eczema may be due to a factor not influenced by dietary deficiencies.

Characteristics of body fat

As mentioned previously, the structure of body fats is peculiar to different species of animals. Lard from pork tastes very different from mutton fat. The fatty acid chains, which are attached to glycerol, affect the solidity and flavors of fats. Composition of body fats can be altered by diet if one type of fat is fed to the exclusion of others. For example, the Food and Drug Administration discovered that a certain sample of lard had apparently been adulterated with peanut oil. The meat packers were indignant and insisted that the lard was manufactured from pork meat with no additives. Analysis of the lard still showed a very high content of fatty acids normally found in peanut oil. Later it was discovered that the pigs had been fattened in the South by feeding them vast quantities of peanuts. The fat had been stored in their bodies unchanged.

Completeness of fat digestion

A healthy individual will absorb approximately 95 percent of the fat that he eats. A loss of more than 5–7 percent of fat in the feces indicates a lack of bile, or a state of malabsorption in the intestines. The nature of the fat (oil or semisolid) does not affect its digestibility, but some byproducts of high-temperature frying may be an irritant to the walls of the alimentary tract. This high temperature will also destroy some of the heat-sensitive vitamins in the food being cooked.

Waxes with a low melting point, such as beeswax, are not absorbed well, but are not important in the diet. Mineral oil is sometimes used in cooking and for preserving dried fruits. Liquid paraffin is used as a laxative. These mineral oils are not digested by intestinal enzymes and pass quickly through the colon. Excessive amounts will cause diarrhea, and vitamins and minerals will be lost from the body.

Relation of fats to other body requirements

Many of the fats and oils that we eat contain some of the fat-soluble vitamins. Butter contains vitamins A and D. Fish oils are rich in vitamin D. During the Second World War, when butter was in short supply, margarine was enriched with vitamins A and D to ensure that everyone had an adequate amount in the diet. This is still the practice. Fish oils were used as a supplement in infant feeding regimes.

Vitamin D is particularly important in the prevention of rickets. This disease is the result of faulty calcium balance and bone formation in young children. Vitamin D is essential for the absorption of calcium through the intestinal wall. A diet rich in calcium is useless unless this mineral can be properly absorbed into the bloodstream and carried to the bones.

Sugars, of course, provide an instant source of energy. Fats give a longer, more constant source. When sugar is burned for energy, one of the B vitamins, thiamine, acts as an enzyme and is used up in the process. If fat is burned instead of sugar then this vitamin is said to be "spared." Fats are also said to spare protein in times of fasting and starvation. A small amount of the tissues will be broken down during a fast, but the main protein structures and functions will be spared by this preferential oxidation or burning of fat.

The amount of fat needed

As we mentioned in Chapter 2, no one knows the ideal amount of fat needed in a diet. The actual quantity eaten varies enormously among different people, cultures, and races. A cold climate or hard physical labor increases the need for fat in the diet. Fats add palatability to food and there are few places in the world where a normal diet derives less than 15 percent of its energy (calories) from fats and oils. Most Western diets derive between 35 and 45 percent of their energy in this form. Much more than this is seldom to be recommended. A high-fat diet may cause overweight and can predispose one toward heart and circulatory problems.

10 · The Importance of Protein

PROTEIN MAKES UP the largest proportion of the body, apart from water—about 17 percent. Hair, nails, skin, and muscle tissue consist almost entirely of protein. It is so essential to all living cells as the basis of their structure and living matter that without it life cannot exist.

Sources of protein

Proteins occur in nature together with fats and carbohydrates. The purest forms of natural proteins are found in egg white, milk curds, and fat-free meats. Plants can synthesize their own protein but animals must obtain theirs from foods. Protein is found in all living tissues and is particularly important for growth and development. This rule can help you to remember the food sources of protein, such as eggs and milk, designed to support and feed young life, and plant seeds, such as nuts, peas, beans, and grains. The sources of protein from animal tissues include all meat, fowl, and fish.

Variety of proteins

There are 20 amino acids which go to make up the proteins in the body. These are found widely distributed among most plant and animal foods. (See Table 4.) Eight of these are essential for life and growth in humans and must be supplied in the diet. The rest can be synthesized within the body from the foods we eat.

Table 4.

20 Amino Acids

isoleucine*
leucine*
lysine*
methionine*
phenylalanine*
threonine*
tryptophan*
valine*

alanine
aspartic acid
cysteine
glutamic acid
glutamine
glycine
hydroxyproline
proline
serine
tyrosine

arginine†
histidine†

* These 8 amino acids are considered to be essential for adequate nutrition.

† These 2 amino acids are considered to be essential for children but not for adults.

As the name suggests, amino acids contain an amino group and an acid group in their molecule. These are written as NH_2 and COOH. The amount of carbon, hydrogen, and oxygen varies with each different amino acid. Two of them, methionine and cystine, also contain sulfur atoms.

In the same way as thousands of words are made from 26 letters of the alphabet by combining the letters in different sequences, so are thousands of proteins made from different combinations of amino acids. The proteins in milk differ from the proteins in wheat because the number and type of amino acids used to make up these proteins are not the same. The proteins in the body also vary for the same reason and protein in liver is unlike that found in the muscles. Proteins such as those in egg white (albumin) or milk (casein) contain combinations of several hundreds and even thousands of individual amino acids. They are as complex as a word would be that was made up of thousands of letters.

Proteins used for building and repair

We have seen how proteins are broken down by enzymes into amino acids and are then absorbed through the intestinal walls. When they enter the bloodstream they are carried in the blood to all the cells in the body and are taken up by these cells to construct the new protein of living tissue wherever it is needed.

Protein forms the structure and living matter of the cells which make up the liver, kidneys, nerves, brain, ligaments, cartilage, and the walls of the blood vessels and digestive tract. Proteins and amino acids may be likened to building blocks. Just as the construction of a house is dependent on a good supply of bricks and mortar, so the growth of the body tissues depends on adequate protein in the diet to give a wide variety of amino acids.

The need for protein is greatest when the body is growing, but it is also important after growth has ceased. Just as bricks in a building may crumble and need to be replaced, so the proteins in tissues may wear out and need to be replaced. In this case the worn tissues are broken down by enzymes in the cells and the waste products are carried in the blood to the liver.

The chemical reactions in the liver remove sulfur and nitrogen from the amino acids. These byproducts may be used again by the body or they may pass through the kidneys and be excreted in the urine. Analysis of urine and feces for nitrogen is standard procedure when estimating the amount of protein that is being utilized by the body. The remaining parts of the amino acid (carbon, hydrogen, and oxygen) can be changed into fats and sugars and used for energy.

A constant supply of protein in the diet is necessary at all times in life. During growth it is needed for building new tissues; in adulthood it is used for maintenance and repair.

When a diet is rich in protein foods then more amino acids pour into the blood than are needed. Protein is not stored in the same way as sugars and fats (glycogen and adipose tissue respectively), but there is a constant supply of amino acids in the blood and liver which cells can draw on when they need to. This constant supply is often referred to as an amino acid pool.

If no food is eaten, this amino pool can be replenished only at the expense of body tissues. Protein from muscles will be broken down before that of the vital organs such as heart, lungs, kidneys, and liver. The composition of the diet can affect the way the stores of fats, proteins, and carbohydrates in the body are used for energy.

When a diet is short of protein, energy will be produced by using fats and carbohydrates, but the protein will still be required for the formation of enzymes and hormones and for repair and maintenance of the body tissues. The breakdown of muscle without its resynthesis produces the wasted appearance seen in the people of countries where famine and extreme poverty occur.

Other functions of proteins

Figure 4 illustrates what happens to proteins in the body. Apart from growth, repair, and the production of energy, the body uses

Figure 4

Fate of Proteins in the Body

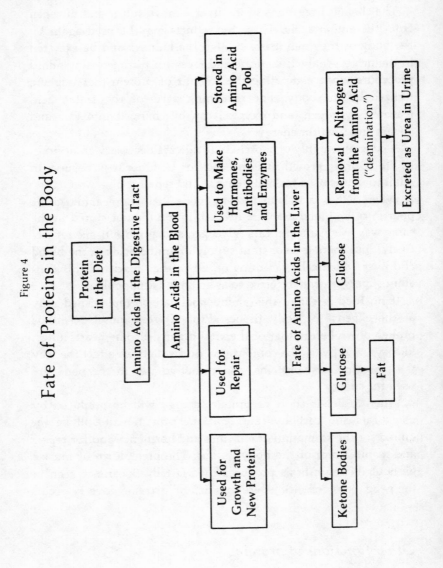

protein in many other ways that are important to health. Hemo-globin, the iron-containing material in the red corpuscles of the blood, is largely protein. Some of the hormones produced by the glands throughout the body are made of protein. Enzymes, which are vital for the biochemical processes of the body, are also made of protein. The transport of substances in the blood; the production of urine and the excretion of waste products through the kidneys; maintenance of the correct acidity of the blood; digestion; absorption and synthesis of tissues—all these and other major functions are dependent on enzymes and there-fore on proteins. The body's defenses against disease and bacteria include such processes as blood clotting and the production of antibodies. Without protein none of these reactions would be possible. It is easy to see why the Greek word *proteios*, meaning "first rank" was adapted to give us "protein."

Finding the right amino acid

When a single protein, such as might be found in milk, eggs, beans, or corn, is fed to experimental animals as the sole source of amino acids, this protein may produce health and growth but, in some cases, it may fail to do so. Certain amino acids are essential for growth but very few proteins contain all these in sufficient amounts. Different proteins are said to complement each other when the amino acids lacking in one are supplied by the other. This is particularly true of vegetable proteins. Origi-nally these were labeled second-class protein until it was realized that the correct combination of different groups of foods—the legumes, cereals, fruits, and vegetables—could supply the equiv-alent of first-class protein.

Eggs, which contain all the essential amino acids, are rated a complete protein and have what is called a biological value (BV) of 100. This means that all the protein can be used by the body. Cow's milk is also a good protein food and has a BV of 75. A low biological value means that the food lacks some essential amino acids. It does not mean that the food is of inferior value. If it can be combined with another food which can provide the missing, or limiting, amino acid, then the resultant meal will have a high biological value. Wheat is short of lysine and peas and beans are short of methionine and cysteine. When eaten together these foods complement each other and the meal then has a high biological value.

We tend to take this information for granted today but the early work which involved isolating and analyzing the different amino acids was long and tedious. Animals were fed diets that were lacking in a single amino acid. If growth was stunted and health impaired, this suggested that the missing amino acid was an "essential" one. By repeating this type of experiment for all 20 amino acids it was established that rats need 10 in their diet, children need 9 and adults need 8. The rest can be synthesized in the body from the foods we eat.

The nutritive value of protein

We have seen that eggs and milk are both good protein foods with a high biological value. Other good sources include glandular meats such as liver, kidneys, and pancreas (sweetbreads). Proteins from muscle meats (steak, chops, and roasts) contain all the essential amino acids but some of these are in short supply and are said to be limiting. This is similar to the situation found in most vegetable protein. If these meats form part of a mixed diet the limiting amino acids will be supplied by other foods and the total protein will have a high biological value. Many everyday combinations of foods complement each other in this way. Porridge and milk (cereal and dairy product), eggs and French fries (dairy product and vegetable), peanut butter on whole-wheat bread (legume and wheat), macaroni and cheese (wheat and dairy product) are all good examples of this principle.

Nitrogen balance

The amount of nitrogen found in animal and vegetable protein is approximately 16 percent. This fact is useful in calculating the protein value of certain foods. If the amount of nitrogen in a certain food is determined by careful chemical analysis, it is possible to estimate the amount of protein in that food. For example, let us suppose that a piece of meat is found to contain 3 grams of nitrogen. We know that this represents 16 percent of the total protein. If we multiply this by a factor of 6.25 ($^{100}/_{16} = 6.25$), we find the answer to be 18.75 grams. This tells us how much protein there is in the piece of meat.

The nitrogen excreted in the urine comes from the breakdown of protein in the body. By multiplying this value by our factor of 6.25 we arrive at the original amount of protein that has been broken down. This may be from food in the diet, or body tissues or amino acids in the amino acid pool.

If a person fasts, the nitrogen excreted represents whatever body protein has been used for energy or broken down by the natural wear and tear of tissues. None has been supplied through diet. The nitrogen output is greater than the input. When this happens the body is said to be in a state of negative nitrogen balance. When the diet supplies all the body needs and the nitrogen intake equals the amount excreted from the body then we describe this as a state of nitrogen equilibrium or nitrogen balance. Young growing animals and children will tend to retain more nitrogen in their bodies than they excrete as they are constantly building new tissues. When this happens there is a positive nitrogen balance.

Careful tests to determine the type of nitrogen balance in the body are helpful in assessing the nutritive values of diets. The state of this balance is also a good indicator of certain diseases. Continuing negative nitrogen balance is acceptable only during medically supervised fasting. At any other time it is a sign that all is not well either with the diet or with the health of the subject. Similarly a positive nitrogen balance is to be expected in growing children, but equilibrium should be the normal for an adult on a healthy diet.

11 · Protein Deficiencies and Requirements

THE IMPORTANCE OF protein in the diet has long been understood, but the amount needed to maintain health and growth has been debated for over a hundred years. Protein foods from animal sources are expensive and there are many countries where poverty excludes this source from the diet of all but the very rich. However, it is possible to obtain adequate protein from vegetable sources, and the addition of small amounts of animal protein, such as milk or fish, can turn the nutritional value of a simple meal from fair to very good.

In the 1930s the League of Nations Technical Commission on Nutrition suggested that a daily intake of one gram of protein for every kilogram (2.2 pounds) of body weight would provide the right proportion of protein in the diet. A person weighing 55 kilograms (120 pounds), therefore, would consume 60 grams a day. There have been many theories and experiments, both before and since that time, which give evidence that more or less than this amount can still support growth and ensure good health, but this standard is a useful yardstick when constructing diets.

Work at the beginning of this century showed that only 40 grams of protein a day would be adequate, yet some athletes today consume 200 or more grams before sporting events, believing that this will give them added strength and stamina. Most observations have shown that *less* rather than *more* protein is beneficial for general health.

This sort of information is difficult to accept when it cuts across a traditional concept of what is good and nutritious. Meat has always been the main part of the meal in America and Europe. Many people are loath to believe that there is sufficient protein for health if meat is missing from the table. However, when it is excluded either because of religious or economic reasons, a well-balanced diet is feasible with the right selection of foods. As explained earlier, it is the balance of amino acids which is important rather than the amount of meat protein in a diet.

Protein deficiency

A protein deficiency is characterized by anemia, lack of muscle tone, fatigue, and poor resistance to infectious diseases. In times of famine and starvation the proteins in the body have to serve as a source of energy. This use by the body of its own protein deprives the blood of important substances called plasma proteins. These have many functions. When nutrients pass from the blood capillaries to the tissues, the plasma proteins remain in the blood vessels. Here they set up an osmotic pressure. This exerts a force which "pulls" the fluid and waste products back into the circulation, where they are carried away to the kidneys and excreted in the urine.

When the body is short of protein this essential process becomes less efficient and fluid builds up in the tissues instead of being drained away. The resulting puffiness of the lower limbs is described as edema. Mild edema can occur for other reasons but the acute condition is often a sign of protein deficiency. It is a typical symptom of severe malnutrition in the developing countries, particularly among young children.

Animal protein and infection

Various experiments on animals have been conducted to establish the connection between resistance to disease and protein content of the diet. Animals fed on incomplete protein, e.g., a source from a single type of cereal or vegetable, tend to succumb to laboratory-induced infections much more easily than animals fed with a complete protein source. This tendency could be due to factors other than the lack of protein, but it is known that plasma proteins called globulins are important in the protection of the body against disease and bacteria. Low-protein intake will reduce the number of globulins in the blood.

This type of experiment cannot be conducted on humans so it is impossible to predict the effects and results of a similar test. However, there is a lot of evidence, past and present, which shows a lowering of resistance to infection after times of hardship and starvation. Epidemics of serious diseases often follow disasters, wars, and periods of famine.

Effects of a high-protein diet

The amount of protein in a diet is often quoted as a percentage of the total calorie intake. One gram of protein is equivalent to 4 calories. In a typical diet in an affluent society about 10–14 percent of the energy comes from protein. Assuming that man needs one gram of protein for every kilogram of body weight, then a 70-kilogram (155-pound) man's requirement will be 70 × 4 = 280 calories from protein. This represents 10 percent of a dietary intake of 2,800 calories per day. The body appears to be capable of adapting to a very wide range of protein content in the diet.

Excessive protein consumption

Although there is little value in eating excessive protein when there are other foods available, there are places in the world where climate and conditions favor an exclusive fish and meat diet for part of the year. Careful studies of Eskimos have shown that a high-protein diet does not predispose to kidney disease, hardening of the arteries, or high blood pressure, as was originally thought. The Arctic explorer, Vilhjalmur Stefansson, and his assistant, lived for a year on meat alone. During that time there was no increase of blood pressure in either of the two men.

Proteins and vegetarianism

Vegetarianism is practiced in many countries and is endorsed by some religions, particularly Buddhism. When the diet is well balanced and supplemented with some form of animal protein, such as milk or eggs, it can be very nutritious and good for health. Unfortunately, many people who follow vegetarian diets, whether by choice or necessity, do not have sufficient knowledge of nutrition, or the availability of all foods needed in the diet. The diet may be incomplete and less than optimum health will result. It is probably easier for the Eskimo to keep fit on his meat diet than it is for the vegetarian with a greater choice of food. This factor should be remembered by anyone who adopts vegetarianism after being used to a meat diet. Some knowledge of nutrition and food values is imperative if a healthy diet is to be followed.

Mixtures of proteins and other foods

During the 1930s there was a vogue for eating only one group of foods at a time and not mixing proteins and carbohydrates, or fats and protein foods. This idea has proved to be worthless. A good mixed diet is far more beneficial both for the digestive system and for providing the necessary foods for energy, growth, and tissue repair.

Increased need for protein

There are certain times when the the body needs a high-protein diet. This requirement can occur after a severe fever, an operation, a broken limb, or a very bad burn. The body goes into a negative nitrogen balance because so much protein is needed for repair. At such a time it is important to introduce extra protein into the diet.

Digestibility of proteins

The heating and cooking of food can alter its nutritive value. The structure of protein changes with the application of heat. This is called denaturization. This process can help in releasing amino acids for digestion but it can also bind them in such a way that they cannot be utilized in the body, and so they lose their biological value. This happens when certain sugars are found in a protein food. They react chemically with the amino acids. Heating, moisture content, length of cooking time, and the presence of fats and sugars can all affect the value of protein. Milk is slightly affected on heating and becomes an incomplete protein after boiling. Pasteurization (which occurs at a much lower temperature) does not cause this loss. Legumes (the bean and lentil family) are improved by slow, gentle cooking. They become more digestible and nutritious.

The protein in most foods is seldom totally absorbed through the gut and some of the nitrogen is therefore lost in the feces. Of all three foods—fats, proteins, and carbohydrates—the proteins are most poorly absorbed. Milk is quite well absorbed (85–90 percent) but on average only 80–90 percent of other proteins are absorbed. Fat is generally well absorbed (95 percent) and carbohydrates are the best (98 percent). It is important to remember these factors when formulating a diet, particularly when estimating the amount of protein that will be needed. Other factors determining the need for protein in different diets include age, health, and growth rate. There are many tables of protein requirements for different countries but amounts ranging between 54 and 84 grams per day for adults were suggested by the British Department of Health and Social Security in 1979. These figures vary according to occupation and age.

Fulfilling your protein needs

It is a good idea to study food tables with an eye to understanding the protein content of common foods. Few people are aware of the high protein content in whole-wheat flour. It can be as high as 12 percent in a loaf. There are many cheap and easily available sources of protein in everyday foods which we tend to overlook. Many people regard bread and cereals as starches and fail to appreciate their value as a source of protein. Nuts are also a good protein food. They do have a high fat content so, though beneficial for children, they should be used with care in slimming diets. Try to plan the protein content of your meals each day. The more you can learn about the value of foods the easier it is to choose your diet so that you are eating a good balance of nutritious foods and achieving optimum health. Table 5 gives the protein content of some everyday foods. Remember that 4 ounces (120 grams) of meat is not 4 ounces (120 grams) of protein. Part of the weight is water and fat and it may contain as little as 1 ounce (30 grams) of "pure" protein.

Table 5.

Grams of Protein in 100 Grams of Typical Protein Foods

Food	grams of protein per 100 grams	common measures and quantities
Milk	3.5	15 grams in 2 cups milk
Egg	12.0	6.0 grams in 1 egg
Bread (white)	8.7	5.0 grams in 2 slices
Bread (whole-wheat)	10.5	
Cheese (Cheddar)	25.0	
Beef	21.6	
Fish (salmon)	21.7	

Average intake of protein per day for an adult, 50–70 grams.

12 · Calories for Energy

FOODS CAN VARY widely as to the amount of energy they can produce when burned in the body. It is impossible to gain a complete picture of nutrition without some understanding of these energy values. This knowledge is of paramount importance when dealing with the problem of overweight or underweight.

Your energy needs

The most obvious need for energy is while exercising and performing all kinds of muscular work. Yet even when the body appears to be at rest, many types of activity still continue to use up energy. The continuous beating of the heart requires energy; the work of the muscles moving the chest and the diaphragm in breathing uses still more energy; even greater amounts are needed for the muscles to maintain their tension or "tone." This is the constant tension which exists in muscles even when no strain or movement is immediately obvious. Someone standing still or sitting in a chair may appear quite stationary but the muscles are working all the time to maintain the balance and control of the body. Even when someone is unconscious this muscle tone persists. When a patient is under an anesthetic and a muscle is cut crosswise, the ends of that muscle will contract. This is due to the inherent tension in the muscle fibers. Maintaining the tension requires energy. Other activities of the body such as the contraction of blood vessels and the constant movement of the stomach and intestinal muscles (peristalsis) are all dependent on muscle tone and a source of energy.

Energy sources

The sources of energy are fat, carbohydrate, and protein. We know that these substances will burn and give off heat. Everyday occurrences, such as burning the toast or overcooking a grilled lamb chop, prove that these foods can act as fuel. But high temperatures are incompatible with life and when food is burned inside the body this heat must be released in very small amounts. The total energy derived from the food will be unchanged but it will have been used for many different processes besides producing heat.

ATP, energy for the cell

There are many ways that small amounts of energy can be stored and used in the body but the most universal method is by "trapping" and "releasing" it from an ATP molecule. As we mentioned in Chapter 4, adenosine triphosphate is vital for the active transport of sugars and amino acids across the cell membrane. Much of the energy in the ATP molecule is held in the bonds between the two phosphate groups. When one of these phosphates splits off, leaving ADP, adenosine diphosphate, energy is released which can be used in nearby reactions. In any chemical reaction there is always an exchange of free energy. The ATP molecule acts as a go-between by collecting this free energy when foods are "burned" to carbon dioxide and water and delivers it where it is needed for the more creative activities such as synthesizing proteins, carbohydrates, hormones, and enzymes.

Calories, energy for the body

The amount of energy trapped and released by the ATP molecule is infinitesimally small and cannot be calculated in everyday terms. However, since the activity is continual, the total energy produced is considerable and can be estimated in the term that we are all familiar with, namely, the calorie.

The calorific value of any fuel is determined by the amount of heat it produces, the exact definition of a calorie being the amount of heat needed to raise one gram of water through 1° C. However, the *energy* value of foods is calculated by the amount of heat needed to raise one kilogram of water through 1° C, a kilocalorie. Through common usage the correct term has been shortened and calorie has been accepted although it is still sometimes found written with a capital C, as Calorie, or as "kcal."

The energy value of foods is determined in the laboratory by using a bomb calorimeter. This registers the total heat production when food is burned in oxygen. As we have seen, this external heat is the same as the energy that would be released inside the body from the food we eat. One gram of protein and carbohydrate each produces 4 calories of heat, and one gram of fat produces 9 calories.

Foods, as they occur in nature, are usually a mixture of fats, carbohydrates, and protein. The amount of each of these can be determined chemically and they are usually listed in food tables as grams per 100 grams of food. For example, 100 grams of fresh milk contains about 3 grams of protein, 5 grams of sugar, and 4 grams of fat. We know that protein and carbohydrate yield 4 calories on oxidation and fat yields 9 calories, so the total in the 100 grams (3½ ounces) of milk is as follows:

Protein	3 × 4 =	12
Sugar	5 × 4 =	20
Fat	4 × 9 =	36
Total calories		68

If the cream were completely removed from the milk (the fat content) then the total calories would be 32. In this manner the calories in all foods can be calculated and added together to give the energy values of different diets and meals. Appendix III shows calorie and other values for 100 gram portions of everyday foods.

Calories vs. other requirements

As long as there is no scarcity of food the healthy individual who has no tendency to gain or lose weight can usually rely on his appetite to determine the correct intake of calories—correct, that is, for him. People who suffer from overweight or underweight have lost this ability to respond to a natural appetite. This may be due to illness, faulty metabolism, or just bad eating habits.

Statistics from insurance companies indicate that men and women are healthier if they maintain their correct weight-for-height throughout their life. This means that your weight at fifty or sixty years of age should be the same as the ideal weight you enjoyed at twenty-five. Average figures show that this is seldom the case but average figures are not the same as ideal figures. (See Table 6.)

Experiments on animals over the years have shown that a diet that provides all the necessary vitamins and minerals and a correct balance among proteins, fats, and carbohydrates will result in long life and good health. Work done with rats has shown that this can occur even when the intake of calories is below normal. Excess calorie intake is likely to produce obesity and a shorter life span. Calorie intake both for animals and for humans varies with age, weight, activity, and the surrounding temperature. Obviously a very low-calorie diet is likely to be deficient in some nutrients, but it seems that a well-balanced low-calorie diet is more beneficial than a high-calorie one. It is better to be slightly underweight than slightly overweight.

The body is extremely efficient at adapting to circumstances, but long periods of undereating or overeating are likely to upset this efficiency and ill health and disease may result. During starvation the body must draw on its reserves for survivial. Fat is the main energy stored in the body but in extreme starvation protein is also sacrificed and the results can be fatal. Kwashiorkor and marasmus are diseases which claim the lives of many young

Table 6.

Weights of Persons 20 to 30 Years Old*

Height (without shoes)	Weight (without clothing)		
	LOW	AVERAGE	HIGH
	Pounds	Pounds	Pounds
MEN			
5 feet 3 inches	118	129	141
5 feet 4 inches	122	133	145
5 feet 5 inches	126	137	149
5 feet 6 inches	130	142	155
5 feet 7 inches	134	147	161
5 feet 8 inches	139	151	166
5 feet 9 inches	143	155	170
5 feet 10 inches	147	159	174
5 feet 11 inches	150	163	178
6 feet	154	167	183
6 feet 1 inch	158	171	188
6 feet 2 inches	162	175	192
6 feet 3 inches	165	178	195
WOMEN			
5 feet	100	109	118
5 feet 1 inch	104	112	121
5 feet 2 inches	107	115	125
5 feet 3 inches	110	118	128
5 feet 4 inches	113	122	132
5 feet 5 inches	116	125	135
5 feet 6 inches	120	129	139
5 feet 7 inches	123	132	142
5 feet 8 inches	126	136	146
5 feet 9 inches	130	140	151
5 feet 10 inches	133	144	156
5 feet 11 inches	137	148	161
6 feet	141	152	166

* From U.S. Dept. of Agriculture, *Home and Garden Bulletin*, No. 74.

children in the Third World countries, due to a lack of protein and calories respectively.

Determination of calorie needs

We have discussed the way in which calories are determined by the amount of heat produced when a substance is burned. The process of burning or combustion requires oxygen and the end product is carbon dioxide. By careful measurement of the amount of oxygen breathed into the lungs and the carbon dioxide breathed out, it is possible to determine the number of calories burned within the body. This type of measurement is termed calorimetry, and scientists use this method to study the calorie needs of people under all varieties of conditions. It is also of value in the diagnosis of certain diseases.

When the measurement is made of the individual lying awake, relaxed, absolutely quiet, and in a comfortable temperature, 12 hours after the last meal, then the resulting value is known as basal metabolic rate (BMR). This test shows the number of calories used to supply energy for the internal work of the body.

Variation in calorie requirements

Individual calorie requirements vary according to age, sex, type of diet eaten, the amount of exercise taken, body weight, and surface area. During the first year of life an individual uses the highest number of calories per kilogram of body weight. Metabolic processes are performed at a very high rate and new tissues are being laid down all the time. The number of calories per kilogram falls after the early years and then rises again at puberty. In adult life the number of calories per hour per kilogram to maintain basal metabolic rate will remain fairly constant. This requirement is usually in the region of one calorie per hour per kilogram of body weight. This value falls in old age. Women need fewer calories than men. This is partly because they have a larger proportion of fat which helps conserve body heat.

Cold climates increase the need for calories in order to maintain an even body temperature. Heat comes from energy spent in maintaining muscle tone. If this is insufficient, shivering is a natural reaction which converts more energy to heat. Some foods stimulate the production of heat in the body. Protein is the most useful in this effect. All foods produce some heat but protein produces more heat than is expected from its calorific value. This phenomenon is known as specific dynamic action. Books on physiology usually refer to this as SDA.

The energy expended on various exercises is another aspect of calorimetry which has interested scientists for a long time. Heavy work and exercise require a much higher intake of calories than sitting still or sleeping. Tables have been drawn up showing the requirements in calories for most day-to-day activities in people's lives. These range from sleeping to strenuous sports such as swimming and cycling. They also include light activities such as typing, reading, and housework. The basal metabolic rate referred to earlier uses up approximately 1,500 calories in 24 hours. This is often spoken of as the resting metabolic rate and does not include work, exercise, and recreation. Most average people need another 800–1,200 calories for the activities of the day. Women need a total of about 2,200 calories and men need between 2,700 and 3,000 calories. This indicates the amount of food which must be eaten to maintain constant weight in a healthy individual who has a normal BMR. Slimming diets are constructed to supply less than the basic needs, i.e., below 1,500 calories. In this way, the body must draw on its own supplies of fat to provide the energy it requires and so weight will be lost.

It is an interesting task to write down your daily activities for a week or two. Note the time taken for each activity and check the calorie expenditure in Table 7. In this way you can work out the number of calories you should have in addition to those needed for BMR.

Table 7.

Calories Expended by an Average Adult

Activity	Calories per hour
Baking	126
Bowling	250
Climbing stairs	320
Cooking	162
Cycling	400
Dancing	300
Digging	600
Driving a car	168
Driving a motorcycle	204
Eating	84
Exercising	360
Golf	260
Horseback riding	350
Ironing	114
Jogging	500
Mowing lawn	395
Playing tennis	425
Rowing	828
Running	570
Sewing	78
Sitting	100
Skating	550
Skiing	550
Squash	480
Sweeping floor	102
Swimming	600
Typing	180
Walking	180
Walking fast	350
Window washing	210

Calories needed for growth

Calories needed for growth in young children and animals can be calculated in terms of the number needed to increase the body weight by one kilogram. Increase of body weight in an adult constitutes an increase of fat but weight increase in the young includes fat, lean body tissue, muscle, and bone. It has been estimated that an increase of 500 grams of body tissue in a growing child would use up 13,000 calories, whereas the same weight of body fat on an adult would represent an intake of only 4,000 calories. This is why it is important that eating should be sensible and controlled when the body is no longer growing. Too many calories usually means unwanted fat.

There is a popular belief that brain work requires a lot of energy, but this is quite unfounded. Experiments have shown that thinking uses a very small amount indeed. In fact, there is very little change in the resting metabolic rate when you sit down to study. A doctor at Harvard University once calculated that the calories from half a peanut were sufficient to sustain the brain for one hour of intensive work.

It often appears that people lose weight doing mentally difficult work. Actually, such work, perhaps combined with worry, may increase the muscular tension and nervousness not only during the day but also at night. Sleep may be disturbed, food intake less, and digestion impaired. It is this loss in calories which accounts for the weight change, not any extra consumption by the brain.

Simplified calorie standards

Although there are many ways of calculating the number of calories needed by any one person, at best it can only be an approximation. The rate of internal activities (metabolism) varies widely with different individuals. No two people take exactly the same amount of exercise for the same hours with the same intensity.

Relation of calories to gaining and reducing

Food that is not needed for energy will be stored as fat. Anyone who gains weight is taking in more energy (food) than needed for BMR and daily activities. This statement remains true regardless of how little is eaten. It will be remembered that 4,000 calories is equivalent to 500 grams of fat so an excess of calories in the diet can soon become evident as extra fat in the body. To lose weight you must eat less than your body is used to. In this way the body will use its own energy stores to make up for the missing calories.

If a person is underweight, then he or she is taking in fewer calories than the daily requirement. This can be due to faulty digestion and absorption or just too little food. Some people are naturally thin, but a continued weight loss is a sign that all is not well. This condition can take place when someone has followed a low-calorie diet for too long. For anyone who wishes to gain weight or to reduce, the first concern should be for a good supply of vitamins, minerals, and proteins in the diet. The calorie content, as determined by fats and carbohydrates, should be adjusted to individual needs. Most people lose weight on 1,000 calories a day, but to continue in good health it is important that those 1,000 calories contain all the vital nutrients for the body. Further discussion of this topic will be found in Chapter 45.

There is no need to memorize all the food values in the back of this book. Just try to remember which are the high-energy foods and which are the low ones.

13 · The Release of Energy

We have seen how calories are derived from each of the three classes of food—fats, carbohydrates, and proteins; how these foods are broken down by the digestive enzymes to form only four simple substances—fatty acids, glycerol, amino acids, and simple sugars; how fatty acids and glycerol recombine to form fats; how fructose and galactose can be stored in the liver as glycogen and released as glucose when needed, and how part of the amino acid molecules can be used to synthesize fats and sugars.

The body, therefore, can reduce fat, protein, and carbohydrate from any of the hundreds of foods eaten to two simple substances—fat and glucose. In the final analysis, it is these two foods that give us our direct energy and these foods must be supplied to every cell of the body each minute of the day and night from the beginning of life until death.

During the oxidation of fats and glucose, the molecules are reduced to smaller and smaller units. As this chemical "chopping" takes place, energy released is stored in the ATP molecule. Much of this activity takes place in the small structures called mitochondria that are found in all living cells and often referred to as the powerhouse since they provide a continual supply of ATP energy. This powerhouse is of course dependent on sufficient "fuel" entering the cell as fats and sugars.

The ways in which the fat and glucose are oxidized differ in the initial chemical chopping processes. The 6-carbon glucose molecule is reduced to a 3-carbon molecule called pyruvate, and the long chains of fatty acids are reduced to smaller units called acetyl coenzyme A. These 2 molecules can both take the same pathway in the last stage of oxidation by joining a cyclic order of reactions known as the tricarboxylic acid cycle or Krebs cycle (named after its discoverer, Hans Krebs). Oxygen is vital for this last group of reactions. Some ATP can be produced from glucose without oxygen, but lactic acid is formed instead of pyruvate acid. Lactic acid builds up in the muscles and can cause the pain and tension that is frequently experienced by athletes during exercise and competition but when more oxygen is made available by deep breathing, the lactic acid can be converted into pyruvate and enter the Krebs cycle, or it can be transported in the blood to the liver for oxidation.

Replenishing the food supply

As the fats and glucose are withdrawn from the blood and burned, the fuel supply naturally decreases. If no food is being absorbed from the intestines, glucose is first replenished from the breakdown of stored glycogen in the liver. Once this supply has been used up sugar must come from the breakdown of protein, since fat cannot be converted to glucose. When there is no food entering the body then fat tissues will be broken down to provide a source of energy. They travel in the blood as fatty acids and can be used by the muscles.

Although fat can spare protein in this sense, some protein must be broken down to amino acids and then to sugar, which is vital for the proper functioning of the brain. Without blood sugar coma and death can result. This is rare and is only likely in total starvation, or when certain diseases, such as diabetes, are incorrectly treated and all the sugar is withdrawn from the blood by an overdose of insulin.

The production of energy

Fat is a concentrated food which contains much less oxygen than glucose does. When fat is burned alone in the body more oxygen is used up than when glucose is burned alone or when fat and glucose are burned together. The amount of oxygen used and carbon dioxide given off can be measured, as we mentioned in the last chapter. Thus, scientists can determine whether the body is deriving its energy from fat or glucose or a mixture of the two.

When there is a good supply of glucose in the blood (e.g., after a meal of sugar-forming foods), glucose is the chief fuel for energy. However, this supply is used up fairly quickly as the body tends to withdraw it from the blood and store it as glycogen and fat. Sometimes it will happen that fat is the sole source of energy. This can occur on some diets and during fasting, when blood sugar and glycogen have been exhausted. The oxidation of fats without glucose is incomplete. Instead of producing carbon dioxide and water, partial oxidation of fats produces substances called ketone bodies. When sugar becomes available these products can reenter the chemical pathway to produce energy, carbon dioxide, and water, but when carbohydrate is absent from the diet these ketone bodies will build up in the blood and can be removed only through the lungs and in the urine.

Three principal ketone bodies are produced in these circumstances. They are acetone, acetoacetic acid, and b-hydroxybutyric acid. They are found in small amounts in the blood under normal conditions, but when there is an excess, acidosis results. Acetone can be detected in the breath. The smell is similar to the acetone of nail polish remover. Acidosis upsets the acid-alkaline balance in the blood and the body tries to correct this by excreting the ketone bodies in the urine. These can be detected by simple chemical tests and are a useful indicator of certain clinical conditions, particularly diabetes. Urine tests are sometimes used to study the progress of a very stringent slimming regime.

Some diets advocate the intake of a high fat and protein diet with little or no carbohydrate. This will produce temporary acidosis by the end of the first day or two and ketone bodies will appear in the urine. Such diets should never be pursued without the supervision of a doctor. If some carbohydrate is then added to the diet the ketosis will disappear and fat will be completely oxidized without a build-up of the ketones. The body is very adaptable and in a long fast or conditions of food shortage the nervous tissues (particularly the brain) and the muscles learn to oxidize ketone bodies to provide the energy they require for daily activities. This adaptation may take a few days and during this time many people experience headaches, sickness, and tiredness. Addition of sugar-forming foods to the diet can eliminate these symptoms. The mixture of foods in our diet and the time between meals can have a significant effect on the degree of energy or tiredness that we may experience in the course of a day. Many experiments have been set up to determine the type of diet and times of meals which produce optimum efficiency in work and sport.

Efficiency in relation to frequency of meals

Some years ago Dr. H. W. Haggard and Dr. L. A. Greenberg of Yale University set out to study the causes of fatigue. They conducted an experiment in a factory where men and women had to complete a piece of work on manufactured goods. Their efficiency was measured by the number of items completed each hour. The frequency of mistakes and the speed and accuracy of their work were correlated to the number and times of the meals that they ate. Metabolic tests were taken during the day to determine their level of blood sugar and to ascertain if energy was derived from glucose and fat or fat alone. It was found that those who ate breakfast were most efficient during the early part of the morning. This ability wore off before lunch, but reached a peak again about half an hour after the midday meal. Those who had no breakfast were a lot less efficient through the whole morning, but their work improved after lunch. Another group ate a good breakfast, but had no lunch. Their work started well, but got slower and less efficient as the day progressed. The most efficient were those who had some small snack at midmorning and midafternoon as well as breakfast and lunch. Evidence showed that those who had more frequent meals and snacks throughout the day worked the best. Blood sugar falls sharply two hours after a main meal and this is the time when fatigue is felt the most. If some sugar-forming snack is taken at this time energy is renewed as more glucose enters the blood.

Most of us have felt tired when we have gone for a long while without food and perhaps had to do some fairly hard physical work at the same time. This feeling soon passes if we have a break and a meal. One of the problems of this sort of hunger is that it often accompanies the first stages of a slimming diet and can undermine good resolutions. The body has to manage on fewer calories than it is used to and most forms of concentrated sugar are forbidden. The body adapts by burning fat from its own tissues, but the irritability and possible headaches of the first few days occur during this time. However, if this is understood and the diet not abandoned, weight will be lost and a feeling of well-being and greater energy will follow.

Children use up a great deal of energy. They are constantly on the go and often crave sweet things between meals. They are most irritable just before meals, and the car sickness experienced by many children occurs if they have not had breakfast or have been too excited to eat before a journey. The blood sugar is low and the body must burn fat for energy. It is thought that the sort of nausea which is experienced when people are ill and off their food is due to the ketosis in the body rather than the actual illness itself.

All of this points to the importance of a constant supply of sugar for the body cells. For this reason it is extremely important to know how glycogen (the energy store in the liver) is formed and how and when it is changed into glucose.

14 · Why Is the Liver So Important?

Sugar and the liver

GLYCOGEN, a substance similar to starch, is made up of glucose units. It is soluble in water and has an arrangement of glucose units different from granules of plant starch. Its formation in the body is controlled by the action of hormones. One of the most important of these is insulin, which is secreted from the pancreas. When the amount of glucose in the blood is increased above normal by the pouring in of sugar from the digestive tract the healthy pancreas secretes insulin. This hormone travels in the blood to the liver and muscles and helps promote the absorption of glucose into these cells. Once inside the cell, enzymes convert the glucose to glycogen, or burn it for energy.

When the level of glucose in the blood falls below the normal amount (80 milligrams in 100 milliliters of blood) the liver converts its glycogen back to glucose and discharges it into the blood. Muscle cells do not take part in this topping-up operation. They need to conserve glycogen for their own high energy needs. The balance between storage and release of glucose is dependent on proper functioning of the hormones, particularly insulin from the pancreas. People who suffer from diabetes cannot produce sufficient insulin to keep this balance regulated. They need the help of insulin injections or medical drugs.

The liver holds a ready supply of fats and amino acids as well as glycogen and these can be released into the bloodstream as needed. They do not form a store in the same way as glycogen but they are always present in the cells and there is a continuous exchange of material entering and leaving the blood. The liver is in a prime position to receive blood from the stomach and intestines before any other part of the body. This could be considered a mixed blessing as it receives first "pick" of the good things but also first attack from the undesirables, such as toxins, drugs, alcohol, and harmful bacteria.

In Illustration 1 (page 14) you saw that as the portal vein enters the liver, it splits into a network of fine capillaries that traverse the lobes before rejoining as the central vein. This gives both time and space for the metabolic activities and monitoring of the blood as it passes through the liver. The hepatic artery also runs alongside this microcirculation. Coming straight from the heart, it brings the fresh oxygenated blood so vital for all the metabolic activities of the liver.

The liver cells form plates, or sheets of cells which radiate from the central vein. They are called hepatocytes, from the Greek *hepar*=liver and *cytos*=cell. Small canals (canicules) run between them collecting the bile, and transporting it to the gall bladder for storage. The spaces between the hepatocytes are the sinusoids. They are bathed with blood coming from the portal vein and they are lined with special cells called Kupffer cells. These pick up the dirt and bacteria from the incoming blood before it enters the cells or the rest of the circulatory system. (*See Illustrations 8 and 9.*) Drugs, alcohol, and poisons are detoxified by an elaborate system of enzymes found in the hepatocytes. The byproducts from these reactions are usually less harmful and can be used by the body or excreted through the kidneys.

Fats and the liver

Not all fats travel directly to the liver from the intestines. Some, as we saw, travel in the lymph. The lymph vessels join the bloodstream in a large vein in the neck and this leads to the heart. Fats will then reach the liver through the hepatic artery. Much of the fat travels in the blood as fatty acid molecules. These are collected together and formed into fats called triglycerides and lip-

Illustration 8

Formation of bile and the microcirculation of the liver

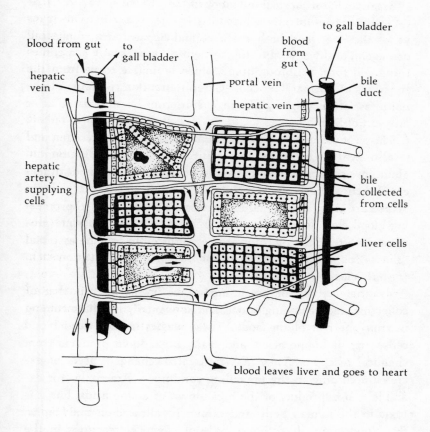

ids which are stored in the liver or sent back into the blood-stream to be used in other parts of the body. The liver manufactures a special coating for fat called lipoprotein. Fat cannot travel in the blood without this coating (oil and water do not mix) so if the process breaks down there is a build-up of fat causing the condition known as "fatty liver." This disease is unlikely to affect anyone eating a normal diet but it does occur in alcoholics on a poor diet and can lead to liver damage and cirrhosis. Excess carbohydrate from the alcohol is turned into fat but the nutrients needed to build its lipoprotein "coat" are lacking so it cannot be transported away from the liver.

Breakdown of normal metabolism in the liver can also be caused by virus infection. Hepatitis is due to a virus which invades the liver, and both cirrhosis and hepatitis can cause cell damage. The liver is able to regenerate its cells but sometimes these will form a fibrous tissue which is unable to perform the functions of normal liver cells. Careful attention to diet is essential in assisting recovery and regeneration of healthy tissue after any sort of liver damage.

The liver stores vitamins and minerals as well as glycogen and it also synthesizes three important plasma proteins: albumin, globulin, and fibrinogen. These are used by the blood for different functions. Albumin maintains osmotic pressure, globulin takes part in preventing infection, and fibrinogen acts in promoting blood clotting when needed. In starvation these plasma proteins are often the first things to be sacrificed to provide essential calories for the body and many of the ills of malnutrition stem from this loss.

Another activity of great importance in the liver is that of collecting and removing waste and unwanted materials coming in from the rest of the body. These wastes include dead blood cells, surplus amino acids, and many breakdown products from chemical reactions. They may be treated, changed, used, or excreted according to the prevailing conditions. Ammonia, for example, is a byproduct of the breakdown of amino acids, but it is toxic in the human body and cannot be allowed to build up in the bloodstream. It enters a cycle of chemical reactions in the liver and is changed to a harmless substance called urea. This can travel to the kidneys and be excreted in the urine. Some waste products are useful and can be recycled. Dead blood cells con-

Illustration 9

Detail of the liver lobules and the blood transport between hepatocytes

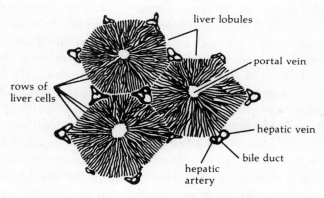

CROSS SECTION OF LIVER LOBULES

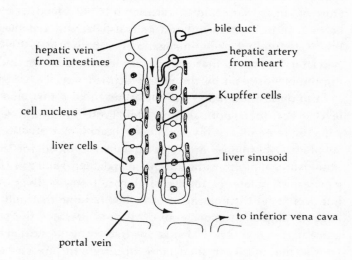

tain iron, a scarce and useful metal in the body. This is extracted and stored for use in making future red blood cells.

The importance of the liver was recognized by the early physicians and anatomists both in the East and West. In early Chinese manuscripts and paintings, for example, the organ was often depicted as a flame in the center of the body as it was considered to be the life force of the body and the provider of all heat to the blood. Early Greek physicians believed that food was burned in the liver and changed into blood to become food for the rest of the body. This is not such an incorrect assumption if we consider the present-day understanding of burning and oxidizing food. A great deal is burned in the metabolic sense and all the by-products do travel in the blood to the tissues even though they are additions rather than constituents of the blood itself. Similarly, the many metabolic processes occurring in the liver provide a good proportion of the body's heat although much of the rest comes from the activities of the muscles.

Claude Bernard, a great French scientist of the last century (1813–1878), was the first man really to understand the workings of the liver, and prove conclusively that the liver contained a store of sugar that could be released into the bloodstream when needed. In his experiments on animals, Bernard fed them diets that were totally lacking in sugar and carbohydrates. An hour or two later, he proved that glucose was leaving the liver and entering the bloodstream by the vein which led directly to the heart.

Even during starvation the liver aims to keep this blood sugar level as near to the normal as possible. Protein is used to replenish supplies if necessary. Everything is geared to maintaining this supply and hormones are released into the blood for this purpose. Adrenaline from the adrenal glands and glucagon from the pancreas stimulate the release of glucose from the liver. Adrenaline acts faster than glucagon. It is the hormone that initiates the "fight or flight" reaction in all of us, and prepares the body for immediate action. The blood is diverted from the skin and intestines so that it can transport more glucose to the muscles where it is needed. This is one of the reasons why we go pale and cannot eat when we are frightened. This reaction of adrenaline can be observed when students are nervous during an examination. The release of glucose into the bloodstream helps to supply the brain with the energy and concentration it needs. It is difficult to set the right balance between anxiety and lack of interest in such a situation, but a certain amount of tension seems to benefit the student.

Certain instances have been recorded where superhuman feats of muscular strength have occurred, for instance, a man lifting a car unaided off the body of a trapped child. This is due partly to the release of glucose by adrenaline but also to the coordination of all muscle fibers in the body acting together. This type of concerted effect does not happen normally.

Sex difference in glycogen storage

Men can store a greater amount of glycogen than women. This is probably because by tradition men have been the protectors and hunters, as most male animals are in nature today. Woman have a smaller store of glycogen so they suffer from low blood sugar more easily than men. It can be argued that this is why women tend to have a sweet tooth and eat more fat-forming foods. For the same reason it is argued that women have more trouble losing weight than men when following a slimming program. Children resemble women in their inability to store a great deal of glycogen. This is why it is important for them to have small but frequent meals to prevent the drop in blood sugar. They crave snacks between meals quite naturally and many schools realize the need for short breaks to produce greater concentration during subsequent lessons.

Our present-day eating habits

We have seen how our energy and efficiency through the day is dependent to a great extent on the glycogen stores in the body. We have also seen that this store is governed by diet, age, and sex, and that the release of glucose is influenced by a number of factors, including hormones, emotions, age, and activity.

The question still remains as to how much glycogen can be stored. A great deal of work and research has been done on this subject and it has been found that the actual store of carbohydrate in the body is very small. This includes glycogen from liver and muscles and sugar present in blood and body. An average 155-pound man has a store of approximately 400 grams which, compared with a fat store of some 9 kilograms, is very small. And this is the first source of energy which the body draws on. It is easy to see why this store is used up so quickly.

A few generations ago many people did strenuous physical work and took a great deal of exercise. To meet their calorie requirements they ate very large meals. Nutrition was not a well-known subject and very few people made any attempt to select the correct foods for health, but the amount of food eaten probably covered most of the body's requirements. The amount of exercise which was undertaken took care of any superfluous fats and carbohydrates. Today people take very little exercise and often eat more than they need. Carbohydrate is stored as glycogen in liver and muscles but, as we have pointed out, this can only accommodate a small amount (usually approximately 250 grams). Excess sugar-forming foods and fats are stored as fat, or adipose tissue.

People who do not wish to gain weight yet take little exercise must adjust their food intake to suit their needs and not take in extra calories. It is important to have regular meals, but they should be small and contain low-calorie foods such as vegetables and some fruit. Ideally, most food should be eaten during the early part of the day, when the activities of work will use up surplus energy. However, by tradition, we tend to eat our heaviest meal at night. This sets up a vicious circle. Glycogen stores are not all used up during the night so we have no great appetite in the morning and tend to skip breakfast. By lunchtime and evening we are hungry for a large meal. Farmers who get up early and eat a big breakfast and a fairly substantial midday meal tend to have a lighter evening meal. This way they have a lot of energy throughout the day and seldom have problems of overweight. The office worker who would benefit from this routine is, unfortunately, usually governed by a habit of little food during the day and a heavy meal at night with no opportunity to work off the surplus fat-forming foods.

Food habits in various countries are often influenced by tradition and by climate. People living in hot climates tend to eat less during the hottest part of the day, but they should always take a small amount of food at midday. Experiments have shown that it is seldom advantageous to go for long periods at work without some form of snack. Just a piece of fruit or a very light meal is sufficient to restore the blood sugar to its normal level and so allow optimum energy for the day's activities.

Objections to between-meal snacks

We are all affected by rules and regulations imposed on us in childhood and many traditions die hard. One of these is being told that eating between meals is "bad for you" and will spoil your appetite. This principle was always supported by various arguments, but these have now been proved wrong. One argument was that the stomach needed to rest between meals. In actual fact the empty stomach contracts more vigorously than a full one. The second objection was that eating between meals caused you to put on weight. This would happen if the snacks were as big as the meals, but if they are kept small and nutritious the total amount of food eaten in one day need be no more than three conventional meals. If you have had a snack between meals you will eat less at the main meals. This way of eating controls the appetite and the first law of a reducing regime is to have small but frequent meals.

This last objection, that snacks spoil the appetite, does deserve rather more attention where children are concerned. Here care is needed in the choice of snacks and the timing of them. The snacks should consist of fresh or dried fruits, fresh fruit juice or milk, and occasional wheat crackers or plain biscuits. Sweets and sugary foods should be discouraged. These are appetite spoilers and they are high in calories. A small bar of chocolate is 300 or more calories whereas apples and pears are only 50 or 60 calories each. Children tend to eat larger snacks than adults because they use so much energy all the time, but they should be encouraged to take these snacks at least two hours before a main meal.

Practical application

We have seen how and when we eat can affect our energy and the efforts we put into our daily activities and work. What rules must we apply to put this knowledge to good use? First, remember that all fruits, vegetables, bread, cereals, and foodstuffs made from grains supply sugar to the body *after* digestion. If you are tired, fruit can give you the quickest lift as it contains fructose and glucose, which can pass straight to the blood and liver without further breakdown. These are the instant energy foods.

If you wish to lose weight, go for the low-calorie sugar-formers, such as fresh fruit and vegetables, and avoid fats and concentrated refined sugar foods. Always try to start the day by eating something, even if you don't like breakfast. If you are ill and have no appetite you can drink fruit juice and have occasional light snacks of wheat crackers or fresh fruit.

As explained earlier, it is important to have a small amount of carbohydrate between meals to help the body to produce energy efficiently. This principle can be applied with advantage for women and children, weight reducers, and those in particularly active occupations. "Don't eat between meals" is out. "Eat little and often" is in.

WHAT VITAMINS CAN DO FOR YOU

15 · How Vitamin A Can Help You

Vitamins are chemical substances essential for health and normal development. They cannot be made in the body in sufficient quantities and must come from the food we eat. Unlike fats, proteins, and carbohydrates, they cannot serve as sources of energy although many are essential to the processes which release energy. During the early part of this century, vitamins were treated with skepticism and people refused to believe in their existence because they could not see them. Today, vitamins can be extracted and crystallized from foods or synthesized from the appropriate chemicals, but there is still room for a more general understanding of their importance.

The nature of vitamin A

Vitamin A, like fats and sugars, is composed of carbon, hydrogen, and oxygen. It is a colorless substance that is found in liver, milk, butter, eggs, and fish-liver oils. Its chemical name is retinol. It is formed in the liver from a substance called carotene which must be supplied in the diet. Carotene was so named because it was first separated from carrots but it is also found in yellow fruits and vegetables and dark green leafy vegetables. In its concentrated form, carotene is deep orange-red, but in the amount in which it normally occurs in foods it appears as yellow-orange. It gives color to apricots, peaches, sweet potatoes, carrots, and yellow sweet corn. Green foods often contain more carotene than

Figure 5

Molecular Structure of Carotene and Vitamin A

CAROTENE
The Provitamin

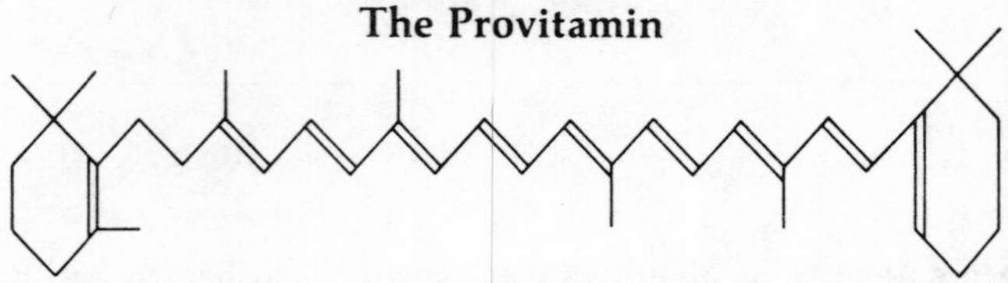

RETINOL
(Vitamin A)

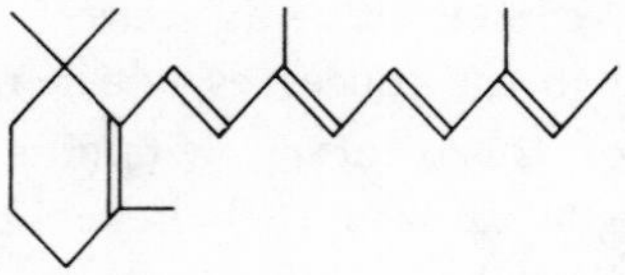

the yellow ones, but the color is obscured by the green of the chlorophyll in the leaves and tissues of the plant. The paler vegetables such as turnips and cauliflower contain very little carotene.

When carotene is eaten, the molecule is broken down to form vitamin A. This occurs in the lining of the intestine (gut mucosa), in the liver, and in some other tissues in the body where special enzymes act on the carotene. If we look at the molecular structure of carotene it is logical to expect it to split into 2 molecules of the vitamin A. (*See Figure 5.*) In fact, it is not as simple as this as there are different kinds of carotene found in fruits and vegetables. These are called provitamins and some produce less vitamin A than others and are poorly absorbed from the intestines. Beta-carotene, found in carrots, is the best precursor of the vitamin.

When we say that carrots are a rich source of vitamin A, we really mean they contain a high concentration of the provitamin carotene. The change from the provitamin to the pure vitamin can only occur in the body but many food tables list total vitamin A as "retinol equivalents" to include this source from the carotenes.

Almost enough vitamin A

A shortage of vitamin A in the body can affect our sight since vision depends on a substance called rhodopsin (visual purple) which is made up of protein and vitamin A (retinol). The ability of the eye to adapt to seeing in a dim light after exposure to a bright light is largely due to the availability of vitamin A in the retina where the vitamin combines with protein to form rhodopsin. When light falls on the eye, it passes through the lens to the retina where it is absorbed by the rods and cones. (*See Illustration 10.*) Chemical changes which occur set up electrical impulses which are transmitted to the brain and interpreted as vision. Both rods and cones are operative in the daylight. The cones interpret the colors we see around us, but the rods can discern only blues and greens. In dim light (such as moonlight) we can detect only light and dark objects. When the rods absorb light, the rhodopsin is broken down. This process is often described as bleaching. The protein and retinol then recombine to form the visual purple again. The rods are then ready to receive and absorb more of the incoming light. This recovery period is dependent on the availability of retinol which is brought to the eye by the bloodstream. A healthy eye, well supplied with vitamin A, will adapt quickly to vision in a dim light while a marked deficiency of the vitamin will result in slow adaption, a conditon that is referred to as night blindness.

A test for vitamin A

Various tests have been devised to estimate the recovery time for the resynthesis of rhodopsin after bleaching. One simple test requires little more than a darkened room and a light source. The person to be tested is put in the darkened room for ten minutes.

Since he sees nothing, the vitamin A remains bound to the protein in the rhodopsin. He then looks into an instrument called a photometer and a bright light is thrown into his eyes for a short time. This light bleaches the visual purple and breaks down the retinol-protein complex. The field of vision is then made dark again, but this time one small light source, often in the shape of an arrow, is present in the room. When the subject can detect the direction of the arrow, sufficient rhodopsin has been re-formed in the rods to absorb the light. The time taken for this to happen varies enormously from person to person. The healthy eye may adapt within three minutes whereas another subject, who may be suffering from a severe shortage of vitamin A, can take as long as fifteen minutes before he sees the arrow.

It would be wrong to conclude that a test always gives a good indication of the total vitamin A in the body since there are many other factors which can affect sight and the ability to see in a dim light. Experiments have shown, however, that people who normally have good night vision show a poor response to a test after a prolonged period on a diet that is almost devoid of vitamin A.

A shortage of dairy products and fresh green vegetables can produce symptoms of night blindness after three to six months. This was seen in the Second World War when Europeans in the occupied countries had little or no dairy products, but vitamin A deficiency was most marked after a particularly hard winter when green vegetables were also unobtainable. With the coming of spring and the availability of early spring greens the condition of night blindness soon improved.

Vitamin A and night vision

Apart from the clinical condition of night blindness, there are many milder states which we all experience during the course of our daily lives. On entering a movie house after walking in bright sunshine, for example, a momentary "blindness" occurs so that we tend to trip over imaginary steps, bump into people, and are unable to tell if a chair is vacant or not. After a few moments in

Illustration 10

Cross-sectional diagram
of the eye

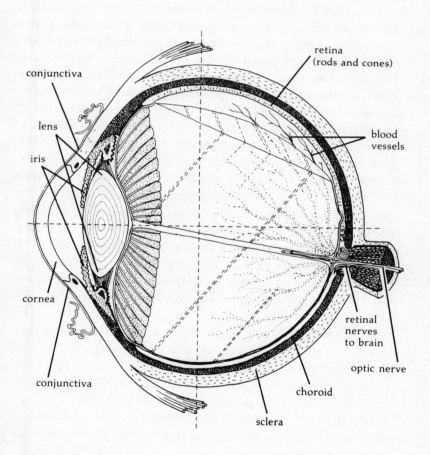

the dark, however, we can see all around us quite clearly. This is a perfectly normal phenomenon since the bright sun in the street bleaches the visual purple in our eyes and when we enter the movie the cones (color-sensitive areas) cease to operate and we must wait until sufficient rods have re-formed the rhodopsin before we can see in the dim light. The time taken for this adjustment will be minimal if the body is well supplied with vitamin A.

This same principle applies to night driving, flying, and any occupation which may involve working in a low light. If you are driving at night, the lights from an oncoming car will bleach the visual purple in your eyes and you will find it difficult to see the edge of the road immediately after the car has passed. Anyone suffering from vitamin A deficiency will take longer to "see" again and on a dangerous or busy road it is often this temporary blindness that leads to accidents. There are many degrees of night blindness and some people are unaware that they suffer from it at all. It is interesting to note that when a driving license is applied for, only daylight vision is tested since it is assumed that if day vision is satisfactory, night vision will also be adequate. This is an optimistic attitude, but not very scientific. Many people wth good day vision have poor night vision. The importance of this became obvious during the war when night flying and blackouts in towns and cities affected everybody's lives. By that time, the use and need of vitamin A was well understood and diets were supplemented with cod-liver oil and carotene-rich foods.

Many people find that bright lights and day vision tire their eyes. They may try to rest the eyes by wearing dark glasses. Models and actresses who work under bright studio lights and draftsmen and typists faced with bright lights shining on white paper may also complain of eyestrain and headaches. To attribute all these conditions to vitamin A deficiency would be risky, but it has been shown that this type of problem is often relieved when a diet rich in vitamin A is administered. Problems with eyesight can be due to genetic factors, disease, drugs, or a temporary illness. However, no harm is done in keeping the correct balance of vitamin A in the body.

An extensive study in the U.S.A., which took three years to conduct, and which considered all socioeconomic levels of society, proved that up to 60 percent of those involved in the survey lacked adequate vitamin A in their diets. The findings were identical nine years later and the conclusions drawn were that such deficiency contributed to increased incidence of many health problems. The continuing deficiency is associated with poor food choice, a problem that is of increasing international concern.

Effect of vitamin A on skin and hair

A diet poor in vitamin A will affect the hair and skin as well as the eyesight since the vitamin is essential for the growth and maintenance of the epithelial layers of the skin. This includes the lining of the gut and respiratory tract, the formation of the enamel layer on teeth, and the growth of hair and nails. When vitamin A is scarce or lacking in the diet the skin tends to become dry and flaky. Oil glands become plugged with keratin and the lining of the respiratory tract loses its layer of fine hair and mucus which protect the lungs from infection. Dandruff and dry hair, broken nails and poor teeth can all result from a low vitamin A content in the diet.

Most of these conditions are reversible if the right foods are introduced into the diet. A survey of school children showed that those living in the country who had more dairy products and fresh fruit and vegetables to eat had fewer deficiency diseases than city children. Many of the city children came from poor homes where dairy products were too expensive to buy and fruit and vegetables were scarce or costly. Most of the city families with more money tended to eat a better diet, but this was not always the case. Education in planning a well-balanced diet is needed for both the rich and the poor. The right selection from the foodstuffs available is more important than the need to buy expensive foods. Carrots and green leafy vegetables can give as much vitamin A as butter and milk when eaten regularly.

16 · Vitamin A and Natural Resistance

WHY DOES ONE PERSON stay well under the same conditions of fatigue, exposure, and lack of sleep which cause another to be ill? We say that the resistance of the first person is high but what do we mean and how can this quality be attained? One of the body's ways of building natural resistance depends on an abundant supply of vitamin A. Let us see how this natural resistance is maintained.

History of vitamin A

The earliest reference to the use of a food rich in vitamin A is the treatment of eye disease recorded on an Egyptian papyrus dated about 1500 B.C. A translation reads: "A treatment for the eyes: liver of ox, roasted and pressed, give for it, very excellent." The Greek physician Hippocrates, who was born in 460 B.C., advised giving ox liver in honey as a remedy for eye disease.

Early medical literature of many countries mentions conditions we now know to be due to a vitamin A deficiency. Many references are made to sore eyes, films over the eyes, and dimness of vision occurring most often in the late winter. Herbs are suggested as a remedy and one that was particularly effective was given the name of "eyebright."

Xerophthalmia, a condition of chronically dry eyes, derived from lack of secretion of mucus and tears by the glands of the eye, may be caused by a prolonged lack of vitamin A. It is common in Third World countries where famine, drought, and poverty produce a very poor diet. It is a disease which has been known to exist in Africa, India, and China for many years, but its association with vitamin A deficiency has been understood only relatively recently. The symptoms, which may start with night blindness, proceed to the blocking of the tear ducts and the build-up of the epithelial layers on the conjunctiva around the eye, causing dryness and swelling. As deficiency continues, the epithelial layers of the cornea are attacked and blindness due to infection and breakdown of the cornea will result. The disease is given the name keratomalacia at this stage and even if it can be arrested there is permanent scarring and damage to the eye.

Knowledge gained from animal experiments

Animals whose diets are adequate in all respects except for sufficient vitamin A are especially susceptible to infections. These infections develop in the nose, throat, bronchial tubes, ears, kidneys, and bladder. Many animals, particularly dogs, develop stones in the urinary tract. There is no evidence that all these symptoms will occur in humans but infections of the eyes and the lungs appear more frequently as a result of vitamin A deficiency.

Many people today believe that vitamin A has an important role in the prevention of the common cold. There have been no clinical trials that prove this to be true but, like many dietary principles, a well-balanced diet will bestow greater resistance to infection than one which is ill balanced and short of important vitamins.

Relation of bacteria to vitamin A deficiency

During the latter part of the last century, the discovery that germs caused disease and infection led medical men to believe that all ills could be explained by the invasion of the body by bacteria. Vitamin deficiency diseases were not properly understood until the twentieth century, when biochemists began to isolate vital food factors from diets.

Xerophthalmia, as we have seen, is a deficiency disease which affects the cornea. Secondary infections which invade the affected eye are caused by bacteria, but the condition which allows this invasion is due to lack of vitamin A. No antibiotic will cure the disease permanently until the cause is corrected.

The body's first line of defense

You will remember that vitamin A is important in the growth and maintenance of the epithelial layers of the skin. These include the outside covering and the inside lining of the body. Many of the body cavities are lined with a tissue that is called mucous membrane. The inside of the mouth is a typical example of this type of membrane surface. Similar tissue covers the inside of the ears, the sinuses, the digestive tract, the bronchial tubes, and the air passages in the lungs. Other important cells line the gall bladder, the urine and genital tracts, and the canals in the kidney which lead to the bladder and then to the outside of the body.

Both the outer skin layers and the membrane linings are constantly producing fresh cells and sloughing off the old ones. Normal cells of the mucous membrane secrete moisture in the form of a thin mucus. This moisture and the presence of fine hairs in many of the internal tracts help to keep the passages clear of debris from dead cells, dust, and bacteria. The nose is a good example of this type of mechanism which we take for granted; it is only when we have a cold and the process breaks down that we become aware of this important function.

Surface layers of our external skin are removed by washing, the rubbing action of clothes, and general movements and activities of the body. Cells are such small particles that we do not see them being rubbed off each day although the process is occurring all the time both internally and externally. When the body is short of vitamin A this natural process may go wrong. Sometimes there is an overproduction of cells and the dead cells accumulate too fast and block the secretory cells of the membranes. Mucus production is affected and the waste products and dead cells together with bacteria that feed on them remain in the tracts and on the skin surfaces. These circumstances present ideal conditions for infection and disease.

When we consider how bacteria are cultivated in the laboratory with constant temperature, food supply, and moisture, it is easy to understand why they can thrive in the human body. All these conditions are on tap. A healthy body can defend itself against this invasion with a healthy skin and mucous membrane and by the production of specific enzymes and blood cells which can destroy the harmful bacteria. However, in an unhealthy body this line of defense is weakened. Changes occur in the mucous membrane when the body is short of vitamin A, and the natural cleansing processes of the tracts become less and less efficient. Bacteria become established and infection and disease soon follow.

Recovery from vitamin A deficiency

When vitamin A is introduced into the diet the tissues lining the body cavities become healthy again. Experiments with animals fed a deficient diet and then an adequate one show an improved condition in only five days. It is more difficult to measure the effect in humans, but tests have shown that the improvement is usually dependent on the extent of the original deficiency and the quantity of vitamin A given with the new diet.

Some experiments were carried out among groups of people exposed to adverse working conditions, such as working in a coal mine. The damp and the dust in the air are conducive to respiratory complaints. Administration of vitamin A in the form of cod-liver oil to half of the workers resulted in a greater resistance to lung infections. The miners who did not receive the supplement suffered pneumonia and chronic ill health in the same period and some of them died.

This type of experiment does provide useful evidence of the effects of diets, vitamins, and food supplements, but it also presents problems of ethics. Is it wrong to use the ill health and suffering of one group of people to prove the benefits bestowed upon another by a particular addition to their diet? Skeptics would suggest that the first group might have refused the supplement in the first place, so were not being deprived of a benefit. This type of argument is open-ended but the problem remains with us. Much research with modern drugs and food additives presents the same dilemma today. The moment comes when animal experiments must be transposed to humans and all such trials involve two groups of people. One group is liable to reap the benefits (or failures) of a new drug, while the control group must continue on an unchanged path without the drug.

Fortunately, many of the early experiments with vitamin A proved conclusively that it was beneficial in helping the body to build up a high resistance to infection so all that was needed was to persuade people to include vitamin A and carotene-rich foods in their diets.

One point that is important to remember is that it is the well-balanced diet which has the greatest effect on our health. It is no good adding vast quantities of vitamin A to the diet in the hope of a cold-free winter when the rest of the food eaten is lacking in adequate protein, minerals, and vitamins, and is far too high in fats and refined sugars. Always try to think of your diet as a composite whole and not a frantic attempt to load up with some of the items you have been missing.

17 · What You Should Know About Vitamin A

We have studied the changes that take place when the body is deficient in vitamin A, but it is also important to know the positive advantages of adequate vitamin A. Assuming that the diet is well balanced and contains the right amount of all essential factors, then vitamin A benefits should include healthy, shining hair, sparkling eyes, clear skin, a freedom from eyestrain and infection, a feeling of good health.

Vitamin A growth

Adequate vitamin A is absolutely essential for normal growth and development. A stunting of growth does not necessarily imply a lack of vitamin A, but if there is a lack of this vitamin during the growing period poor development will result. This has been shown repeatedly with animal experiments. Vitamin A must never be looked upon as essential only to the young. At any age inadequate vitamin A will cause weakening, fatigue, low resistance to infection, and poor vision.

Storage of vitamin A

Vitamin A and carotene are both soluble in fat. Adequate fat in the diet is important both for their absorption through the intestinal walls and for transport to the liver. They can also be stored in the body in the same way that fat can but most of the retinol in the body is stored in the liver. Some is found in the lungs and the kidney and a small amount in the retina of the eye. Vitamin A and carotene are transported in the blood to various parts of the body. The amount of these vitamins found in the blood is now considered the best form of estimating the stores in the body, rather than relying on tests for night vision and dark adaptation.

The fat-soluble vitamins have an advantage over the water-soluble vitamins in that they can be stored in the body and are therefore available in times of shortage. It was once thought that all excess vitamin A ingested would be stored against a rainy day but it has been shown that too great an intake of retinol is toxic. Cases are rare but they do show that it is not a good idea to bombard the system with something just because it is beneficial in smaller quantities. Some mothers, believing that vitamin supplements could only help their babies, gave them too much of the fish oils which contain vitamins A and D. The results were nausea, a dryness of the skin, and swellings at the wrists and knees. These symptoms disappeared once the dosage was properly controlled. Poisoning from excess vitamins has also been reported by Arctic explorers who ate polar bear liver. This liver is particularly rich in these vitamins. The explorers suffered severe nausea and giddiness and the skin became dry and flaky. These conditions abated when the diet returned to normal. Halibut-liver oil is richer than cod-liver oil in vitamins and it is for this reason that small children sometimes receive an overdose of the supplement.

Seasonal variation in vitamin A needs

Most people have a richer store of vitamin A in the body in the summer than the winter. There is a greater supply of fruit and vegetables in the shops and dairy products will contain the benefits of the rich grass crops that the herds feed on rather than the hay and turnip diet of winter in some parts of the world. It is important to bear these factors in mind when you plan your diet.

Food tables often give summer values for vitamin contents in fruits and dairy produce, or they may give an average figure for the year. The amount of milk and green vegetables you eat in summer might not supply the same amount of essential nutrients in the winter. So it is wise to increase the fruit and vegetables, eggs and milk, and liver and fish on your shopping list in the winter months.

The unit of Vitamin A

With the importance of vitamins in the diet now recognized, tables of recommended daily allowances of proteins, vitamins, and minerals have been drawn up. (*See Appendix IV*). These allowances may vary from country to country and of course will vary from person to person, but they do provide an approximation of the amount of a particular vitamin or mineral which will prevent any deficiency disease. Most well-balanced diets will supply all that is needed in basic nutrients. Some religions forbid meat in the diet and some stipulate vegetables and cereals only, with no dairy products in any form. These diets certainly can provide adequate nutrients and sustain good health, but often ignorance of food values makes them dangerous, and some deficiency diseases and anemic conditions can build up over the years.

Recommended daily allowance tables set out the quantity of vitamins and minerals that should be consumed each day. Few of us follow a perfect diet day after day, but these tables do provide a useful guideline. We do not suffer instant ill health if we omit the suggested 750 micrograms (3,750 international units) of vitamin A occasionally, but it is a good idea to be aware of the requirements of the body and try to achieve the right amount when possible.

When vitamin A was first discovered it could not be isolated and weighed. Its activity was determined by the amount of a known substance that would support growth and prevent deficiency diseases in experimental animals. However, carotene, known to be a precursor of vitamin A, could be crystallized from foodstuffs and weighed. The international standard of vitamin A activity was set as 0.6 microgram of carotene. Later, when vitamin A was isolated, it was found that this unit of activity was equal to 0.3 microgram of retinol. For mathematical purposes the potency of carotene is now taken to be one-sixth that of vitamin A. This has led to the term "retinol equivalent" which you will find in food tables. One retinol equivalent is equal to one microgram of vitamin A, or 6 micrograms of its precursor, betacarotene. A microgram is one-millionth of a gram, but in some tables an I.U. (international unit) is used for fat-soluble vitamin allowances. (One I.U. retinol equals 0.3 microgram of retinol.)

In simple terms this means that the carotene source of vitamin A is not so concentrated as the pure vitamin. You need to eat a quarter of a pound (115 grams) of carrots or a large helping of green vegetables each day to get the same amount of vitamin A into your system as that contained in a teaspoon of cod-liver oil.

Requirements for vitamin A vary with size and age. Growing children need a good supply of retinol in their diet, but in terms of body weight their total requirements are smaller than those of adults. The British Department of Health and Social Security recommends between 450 and 575 micrograms for children up to the age of ten. Teenagers onward should have 750 micrograms of vitamin A each day. Special conditions, such as lactation, need 1,200 micrograms. In times of illness and infection the natural store of the vitamin in the body is used up more quickly and a small extra supplement is beneficial. However, it is important to remember that too much vitamin A is harmful. Take only what you need.

Absorption of vitamin A

Sometimes it happens that a person who is taking a correct amount of vitamin A appears to have a low level of it in the body. This indicates absorption is poor. As explained previously, fats are important for the absorption of fat-soluble vitamins. If the digestion of fats from the intestine is faulty or the production of bile from the liver is impaired, many of these vitamins will be lost in the feces and never reach the bloodstream. Mineral oils, used as laxatives, will also cause a loss of vitamins. They act as a solvent for vitamins A and D but cannot themselves be absorbed across the gut wall. They pass out through the body in the feces and take the vitamins with them. Some reducing diets cut down on all fats. This may produce the desired result as far as weight loss is concerned, but it is wise to step up natural vitamin intake to ensure that you are receiving adequate supplies of carotene and vitamin A. Green vegetables are particularly useful for this and are usually prescribed in such diets.

18 · The Source of Vitamin A

Vegetable sources of Vitamin A

CAROTENE is closely associated with the green coloring of plants, called chlorophyll. The darker the leaves of the plant the greater the carotene content. Outer leaves of cabbage and lettuce contain a great deal more carotene than the pale inner leaves. The carotene content of plants increases in the early growing stages. When the plant flowers and produces fruit the carotene in the leaves decreases. The leaves usually become brown and dry at this stage.

Greens such as watercress, spinach, and parsley are very rich in carotene. Similarly, green pods such as peppers and beans and snow peas are all good sources. The color of fruits is a good gauge as to their carotene content. Apricots, peaches, and yellow melons are good. White vegetables like potatoes, white turnips, cauliflower, and butter beans have little or no carotene. Cereals are a poor source, though yellow sweet corn is the exception. Some vegetables which have been bleached or dried and lost their color will also be devoid of vitamin A. White beans, celery, onions, and asparagus are examples. All these vegetables provide other nutrients and vitamins, but they should not be thought of as supplying vitamin A to the diet.

Animal sources of vitamin A

The amount of vitamin A in animals will depend a great deal on the diet and the age of the animal. Animals fed fresh green grass will have a greater store in their bodies than those fed on cereals and dried grass and white root crops. The liver of all animals is the richest source of the vitamin, but significant amounts may also be found in the kidneys, heart, lungs, and pancreas. Muscle meats have little or no vitamin A as they do not store this vitamin.

Vitamin A in dairy products

Eggs and milk always contain some vitamin A. Again the amount will depend on the food that is fed to the animals at the time of year. Usually, if a diet is inadequate, hens will produce fewer eggs and cows a smaller yield of milk, but in farms today food-stuffs are formulated to produce a maximum yield from livestock. Care is taken to see that it is adequate in all respects. The diet can affect the color of egg yolks and the degree of yellow in cream and butter. However, these factors are also influenced by the breed of animal, and a change in feed can significantly alter the total vitamin A in farm produce. Fish oils in the feed can increase the A content in the milk. This will not increase the color, but it will increase the total retinol content in the milk and butter.

Effect of oxygen on vitamin A

Vitamin A and carotene are destroyed on contact with oxygen at high temperatures. Normal cooking methods do not affect the vitamin A content in foods, but frying produces a temperature well above 212° F. and damage to the vitamin can occur then. Also, many fats are susceptible to oxidation and rancidity which will harm the vitamin and render it inactive. Vegetables prepared and cooked quickly for a short period of time in boiling water will have a maximum content of the vitamin, but frying in butter and other high-boiling-point oils will cause a loss.

Vegetables should be cooked until only slightly soft. The Chinese, who fry vegetables for only three or four minutes, were probably the first to master the art of vegetable cookery. Canning and freezing have very little effect on the vitamin A content of foodstuffs. Carrots canned in 1824 for an Arctic voyage and opened in 1939 were found to have retained their carotene content over all those years. Bright sunlight can cause destruction of the vitamin. This is shown in the difference between sun-dried and commercially dried fruits. Sun-dried foods have a much lower final vitamin A content. Fish oils stored in colorless glass bottles lose their potency when left in bright sunlight.

Your garden and vitamin A

Every garden should be planned to produce as much vitamin A as possible. Carrots, spinach, green beans, peas, and other vegetables rich in vitamin A should be planted in larger amounts than parsnips, white turnips, and beets. Celery and asparagus should be left green rather than covering and blanching them. Whenever the right conditions exist watercress should be grown.

Every year new green and yellow vegetables should be added to the list. Too many gardens lack the dark green vegetables such as broccoli, spinach, and kale. No garden is complete without its row of parsley. Each person in the family should develop the parsley habit. One tablespoon of parsley daily (in soups, on salads, or in sandwiches) can make the difference between health and sickness. Not only is it rich in vitamin A and calcium but it provides a good source of iron in the diet. During the winter months parsley should be grown in large flowerpots and kept in the house and given the care and attention demanded by more exotic indoor plants.

If you are lucky enough to live in an area where summers are long and the sun is bright and warm, then you can grow some sweet corn. You should aim to plant the yellow varieties as these contain more vitamin A than the paler varieties. Other vegetables which are useful in any garden include Brussels sprouts, lettuce, and carrots. If you have room to grow beets and turnips, then you should eat their greens. These are a particularly good source of vitamin A but there is little or none in their roots.

Every intelligent gardener who is interested in his family's health will make a special effort to supply as many of the vitamin-rich vegetables as possible. He will also aim to add some new tastes to the diet and experiment with lesser-known vegetables. There are many salad vegetables which can be grown with just a little extra care and attention. These include endive and chicory and outdoor cucumbers. Herb gardening is a fascinating hobby and there are many varieties of common herbs which will grow in cooler climates. A well-planned garden can produce an abundant supply of vitamin A. The wise person who plants such a garden is generously rewarded by the good health of each member of the family.

19 · Your Need for Thiamine

THE VALUE OF thiamine in the diet was first discovered by Christiaan Eijkman, a Dutch doctor working in a military hospital in Java in 1897. Patients there suffered from a disease known as beriberi. Eijkman fed food scraps from the kitchen to his chickens and they soon developed symptoms similar to beriberi. A new routine in the kitchen put a stop to the availability of food for domestic fowls and Eijkman went to the local market to buy grains and unpolished rice for them. When the birds recovered from the illness Eijkman realized that their recovery must have been due to the change of diet. He then proceeded to isolate the factor that had caused the change. He extracted a substance from the part of the rice grain which was normally removed in the milling. This extract was given the name vitamin B. Later, it was discovered that the extract contained other vital food factors besides the one that cured beriberi. These factors were designated vitamin B_2 and vitamin B_3, etc. As more and more of these factors were found and the chemical structure and properties became understood, the nomenclature changed so that each was given its chemical name.

In this section, we shall examine three of these B vitamins—thiamine, riboflavin, and niacin. They are grouped together because many are found in the same types of food. They are all water-soluble vitamins which differentiates them from vitamins A and D (the fat-soluble vitamins). Another property common to many of the B vitamins is that they are involved in important biochemical processes in the body. They act as coenzymes (enzyme activators) in the metabolic pathways. Thiamine is particularly important in the oxidation of glucose to provide energy for the body.

Sources of thiamine

Thiamine is necessary for the sprouting of seed and is therefore found, together with other members of the complex, in all foods which are seeds. These include nuts, cereal grains, legumes (peas, beans, and lentils), and the foods prepared from these raw materials such as peanut butter, whole-wheat bread, and cereals. Thiamine is found in meat, particularly liver, kidneys, and heart, and it is most plentiful in pork. Other sources include brewer's yeast and wheat germ.

Beriberi

Although thiamine was first used as a preventive factor against beriberi, this is not a disease which is common in developed countries where diets are generally varied and adequate. It is found most often in Third World areas of poverty where malnutrition is prevalent and the diet may be monotonous and lacking in many other factors besides thiamine. However, it is important to understand the physiological conditions which occur in all cases of thiamine deficiency as these can lead to symptoms which are also seen in the early stages of beriberi.

Thiamine forms part of an enzyme which is essential in the oxidation of glucose to energy in the body. The brain and the nervous tissue are dependent on this type of energy. If the enzyme is in short supply (due to lack of thiamine) the metabolic pathway is interrupted. The supply of energy fails and two intermediary products, lactic and pyruvic acids, build up in the bloodstream. Both these substances can be harmful when they occur in high concentration. Lactic acid causes pain and fatigue in the muscles and pyruvic acid dilates the blood vessels and puts an extra strain on the heart. When thiamine is added to the diet these conditions are soon corrected. The lactic acid and pyruvic acid can reenter the metabolic pathways and energy is produced from glucose and made available for the brain and nervous tissues of the body.

In cases of mild thiamine deficiency the patient complains of muscle pain and weakness and neuritis (inflammation of the nervous tissue). There may also be changes in the rhythm of the heartbeat and pulse rate. There is a feeling of general fatigue, loss of appetite, and nausea. Secretions of hydrochloric acid in the stomach become abnormal. All these conditions are reversible once thiamine is added to the diet.

In cases of beriberi these early symptoms have been neglected and therefore become acute. Muscle-wasting and chronic neuritis cause great disability but the deaths due to beriberi occur because of the collapse of the heart. The build-up of pyruvic acid in the system and the added strain of a malfunctioning organ cause the heart to enlarge, but it is unable to function normally because of poor muscle tone and loss of energy. Now that so much is understood about diet and beriberi, it has become possible to wipe out this crippling disease in many areas where it was once rife.

Human volunteers have eaten thiamine-deficient diets for several weeks and recorded their reactions. Many complained of digestive disturbances, constipation, and depression. Tests showed changes in heartbeat and pulse rates and high pyruvic-acid levels in the blood. These conditions were reversed once thiamine was added to the diet. (Severe thiamine deficiency is sometimes seen in alcoholics. Their diet is usually very poor as nearly all their calories come from alcohol and they have little or no appetite for the nutritional foods they need.)

It is difficult to envisage a diet that would be totally deficient in thiamine, but there are varying degrees of mild deficiencies which can occur if the diet is high in carbohydrate. Such a diet requires more thiamine for oxidation of the glucose produced. Recommended daily intakes are calculated on the average calorific needs of different age groups. It has been estimated that 0.4

milligram of thiamine is needed for every 1,000 calories consumed. Assuming that most adults eat between 2,000 and 3,000 calories a day, it is reasonable to expect one milligram to cover daily requirements. Some of the diet will consist of fat and protein, but for practical purposes thiamine requirements are related to total calories.

Because thiamine cannot be stored in the body it must be supplied in the diet. This means planning your meals so that you have some foods rich in B vitamins each day. A small supplement of the B complex vitamins is sometimes recommended to combat fatigue. It is also useful in helping athletes to get maximum energy from a high-calorie diet (see Chapter 43). Most supplements ensure that daily requirements will be met and the dose is often as high as five times the recommended intake. Any excess of the B vitamins will be lost in the urine within a few hours of taking the supplement. With careful selection of foods there should be plenty of thiamine in the diet and extra vitamins are not required. Many vitamin supplements are expensive. If you do not need them, use the money to buy foods to enhance the nutrients in your diet. Buy whole-wheat bread, brewer's yeast, blackstrap molasses, liver, and wheat germ. Your money will be well spent.

20 · Your Need for Riboflavin

IN THE 1920s it was found that if foods rich in vitamin B were heated under pressure for a number of hours they no longer cured beriberi but were still valuable in clearing up other conditions. The vitamin not destroyed by heat was given the name B_2 or G. In 1934 this vitamin was synthesized in the laboratory. It is now known by its chemical name, riboflavin.

Like carotene, riboflavin is a coloring pigment. It is the yellowish-green substance that can be seen in egg white, whey, and powdered milk. When people sometimes describe skim milk as blue it is because the carotene of the cream has been removed and this allows the yellow-green of riboflavin to show through the liquid as a "cold" color.

Sources of riboflavin

Generally, riboflavin is found in the foods which are rich in the other vitamins of the B complex, such as liver and brewer's yeast. It is different from thiamine, however, in that it is not abundant in cereals, but is found in useful amounts in dairy products. Riboflavin is formed in green leaves during growth and, like vitamin A, is lost when the leaves become dry and withered. It is found in moderate amounts in roots and tubers. Among the vegetables, beets and turnip greens, carrot tops, broccoli, and kale are the richest sources. Mustard greens, spinach, and watercress are less rich, but are still excellent sources. The leaves of vegetables contain twice as much riboflavin as the stems. The inside leaves of cabbage and lettuce contain only about one-fifth of the amount found in the outside, darker leaves.

The limited amount of riboflavin which does occur in grains is mostly lost when they are made into white flour and refined cereals. Riboflavin can also be destroyed by exposure to light. Milk can lose up to 50 percent of this vitamin if it is left exposed to the sunlight for two or three hours. This is why it is important that milk should be packed in cartons or dark glass bottles.

Functions of riboflavin

Like thiamine, riboflavin aids the "burning" of sugar to produce energy. It combines with protein and phosphates to form important enzymes called flavoproteins. When riboflavin is in short supply many metabolic processes are affected.

Riboflavin deficiency in humans

Experiments have been conducted on human volunteers to establish the deficiency symptoms that arise when riboflavin is withdrawn from the diet. The most pronounced effects include soreness and cracking of the skin at the corners of the mouth, red swollen eyelids, and an inflamed tongue. The symptoms are similar to those found in the early stages of pellagra (a niacin deficiency disease), but they do not respond to treatment with the vitamin niacin alone (see next chapter). Experiments with animals show a wider range of diseases and abnormalities, including loss of hair, anemia, and severe eye infections. When riboflavin is added to the diet these conditions are usually cured.

A lot of work has been done in assessing the importance of riboflavin in preventing certain eye ailments. For some people suffering from eyestrain the addition of riboflavin to the diet seems to relieve the symptoms. Some physicians recommend trying this vitamin to help an eye condition before glasses are prescribed.

Losses of riboflavin

Like the other vitamins of the B complex, riboflavin is soluble in water. It cannot be stored in the body but is lost in the sweat and the urine. When excess riboflavin is taken, either in the diet or as a supplement, it is rapidly excreted from the body. Riboflavin is not affected by cooking but it is lost in the water when vegetables are boiled.

The recommended daily intake is 0.5 milligram per 1,000 calories. Most people consume at least 2,000 calories a day so a normal allowance would be just over one milligram. There should be no difficulty in obtaining this amount in most diets.

21 · Your Need for Niacin

NIACIN IS THE name given to another of the B-complex vitamins. It occurs as an acid (nicotinic acid) and as an amide (nicotinamide). It was isolated chemically long before its vitamin properties were understood. Later it was found to be active in the treatment of pellagra and it became known as the PP, or pellagra-preventive, factor. This term is no longer in use, but may still be found in some earlier works on nutrition.

Niacin is found in an important set of enzymes, the nicotinamide dinucleotides. These are involved in many metabolic processes but, like thiamine and riboflavin, are particularly involved in the production of energy from glucose. Pellagra is the deficiency disease which is most commonly associated with a lack of niacin in the diet. It is prevalent in communities where the staple food consists of a single cereal such as maize and where poverty prevents the addition of extra protein and dairy goods to the diet. It is found today in Africa and parts of India. Originally, it was a disease of the southern states of America and also became widespread in the Mediterranean when maize-growing was introduced to southern Europe. Today it has been largely controlled with the addition of niacin to bread and maize products, together with an improved and more varied diet.

Pellagra is an extreme case of niacin deficiency and is unlikely to be seen or experienced by most people living in the industrialized countries. However, the signs and symptoms of the disease do give us an insight into the type of complaint which may indicate a milder deficiency of this important vitamin.

The work of Dr. Goldberger

The knowledge that pellagra is a deficiency disease is largely due to the work of Dr. Joseph Goldberger. While traveling in the South in 1918 he noticed that pellagra never occurred in homes where there were vegetable gardens and where chickens and cows were kept. In hospitals, nurses and doctors who ate a superior diet did not contract the disease although many patients did. Proof that pellagra was a deficiency disease came from a classic experiment when volunteers from a state prison were fed a diet similar to that eaten by the poor who were so susceptible to the disease. This consisted of fat pork, maize, and sweet potatoes. After a few months the prisoners developed all the symptoms of pellagra. The condition was then cured by adding liver, yeast, and dairy products to the diet.

Early work on vitamins showed that niacin occurred in the same foods as thiamine, but when isolated it could not be used alone to cure beriberi. Later, when it was found to be plentiful in liver and yeast (thiamine-rich foods), experiments were conducted to see if it would cure pellagra. Results were dramatic and improvements were noted within a few days of administering the vitamin.

Two mysteries remained unsolved in the cure of pellagra. Why did the addition of certain proteins to the diet (particularly milk) effect a cure when there was already a good protein source in the maize grain; and why was pellagra almost unknown among the Mexicans, whose staple diet was maize? The answer to the first question came when it was realized that the protein foods that cured pellagra contained an amino acid called tryptophan. This amino acid could be changed to niacin in the body. This meant that even if niacin was lacking in the diet, but protein was plentiful, the body could make its own supply of the vitamin from the amino acid. Tryptophan is found in protein from dairy foods, but not in maize. (You will remember from Chapter 10 that proteins are composed of many and varied amino acids, but not all proteins contain *all* the amino acids.)

The puzzle over the Mexican diet was resolved when it was found that the traditional method of cooking maize is to soak the grain overnight in lime water before using it to make tortillas. This releases niacin from a compound called niacytin found in the grain. Niacytin is a bound form of the vitamin and cannot be used by the body. However, once it is released by the lime water it provides an adequate supply and prevents the symptoms of pellagra.

Mild deficiency conditions can occur even in affluent societies where the diet is lacking in niacin. Alcoholics are a group who are particularly at risk. Symptoms are similar to those found in the very early stages of pellagra, with gastric disturbances and diarrhea being the most common. Lack of niacin can cause changes in the gut mucosa and alter the normal secretions of hydrochloric acid and enzymes. Niacin is extremely important in keeping the tissues of the body healthy and normal. It must never be thought of solely as a factor for curing pellagra. If ideal health is to be obtained this vitamin must be amply supplied in the diet at all times.

Sources of niacin

Liver and brewer's yeast are the two richest sources of niacin. It is also plentiful in fish, fowl, peanuts, lentils, and soybeans. Milk, buttermilk, and cheese contain generous amounts but much of this comes from the tryptophan, which is counted as a niacin equivalent.

Niacin is not harmed by heating, but it is lost in cooking water because it is water-soluble. It is important to use this water as stock for soups and gravies whenever possible. Much of the niacin in whole grains is lost in milling and refining. If your diet includes whole-wheat bread, liver and glandular meats, black molasses and milk and cheese, your niacin needs should be amply supplied.

The recommended intake of this vitamin is calculated according to total calorie requirements. This has been set by the U.N.

Food and Agriculture Organization as 6.1 milligrams for every 1,000 calories in the diet. This value includes the niacin equivalent derived from tryptophan: 60 milligrams of tryptophan can supply one milligram of niacin. As an average figure the daily requirement of niacin is quoted as 15 milligrams for women and 18 milligrams for men.

22 · Other Vitamins in the B Complex

IN THE LAST three chapters we have looked at three important vitamins in the B complex which are involved in the oxidation of glucose to energy, and the deficiency diseases that can result when the process is interrupted. This next group does not fall into quite such a neat category, but acts as coenzymes or intermediaries in other essential metabolic pathways. These vitamins also differ from the first group in that they do not produce such acute conditions of deficiency either because they are abundant in most diets or are required in such small quantities. Some diseases which may occur are often the result of malabsorption, avoidance, or addiction to certain foods rather than to the lack of the item as dietary factor, but these are not on the same scale as beriberi and pellagra.

Pyridoxine was first named vitamin B_6 and was isolated as a vitamin essential for growth in experimental animals. It was the factor that cleared up a particular form of dermatitis in rats. It has been found to be an important factor in the metabolism of amino acids and synthesis of hemoglobin and as a coenzyme in the production of niacin from tryptophan. However, deficiency diseases are seldom specific. Depression, anemia, and neuropathy are often attributed to a lack of pyridoxine and sometimes patients respond to vitamin therapy, but these conditions may occur for other reasons. It appears to be an essential vitamin for young children; deficiency symptoms include convulsions and muscle twitching. Babies fed overprocessed milk feeds lacking in pyridoxine have been known to suffer in this way. In adults, deficiencies may become apparent under drug treatment. The current drugs for tuberculosis are prescribed with extra B_6. The action of the drug speeds up the use of a normal intake of pyridoxine so that extra supplies may be needed. The same type of reaction occurs with some women on estrogen pills. Again, enzyme activities in the body are speeded up and pyridoxine stores are used faster.

Pyridoxine is found in both animal and vegetable foods. Liver, vegetables, brewer's yeast, and whole grains are all good sources.

Folate and B_{12}

It is convenient to pair folate and B_{12} as they are closely associated with the prevention of a condition labeled pernicious anemia. This is a blood disease which occurs when red cells (produced in the bone marrow) are released into the bloodstream before they have been properly formed. These imperfect cells cannot perform all the functions of healthy red blood cells that the body relies on for the transport of food and oxygen.

Pernicious anemia was fatal until the 1920s, when a diet of raw liver effected a cure. Much of the credit for this discovery must go to William B. Castle, who discovered that the curative factor in liver, now known as vitamin B_{12}, was useless without another substance which he called "intrinsic factor." This proved to be an essential element found in gastric juice which aided the absorption of the vitamin across the gut wall. Without this intrinsic factor, the B_{12} from the liver extracts could not cure anemia. Castle's discovery led to further investigations and experiments.

Vitamin B_{12} is needed for synthesis of all new cells and its lack is soon felt in areas where cells normally multiply very quickly, as in bone marrow. The process of forming these cells involves another B vitamin, namely, folic acid (folate). This vitamin was first thought to be the same as B_{12}. It was isolated from green leaves and found to cure anemia in chicks. Trials with humans showed that it produced a sudden cure in pernicious anemia, followed by a relapse. Later it was discovered why this had happened. Folate helped in the production of red cells, but it did nothing to alleviate other chronic symptoms of the disease, e.g., the degeneration of the protective myelin covering of nerve cells. These needed B_{12}. The sudden uptake of B_{12} by new blood cells depleted the body of the small supply it did have and made the nerve tissue condition worse than before.

When these facts were finally understood, the whole picture made sense and B_{12} and folate are now used together in the prevention of pernicious anemia. The condition is rare and is usually a result of malabsorption. B_{12} is found only in animal foods, so although most people are unlikely to go short of the small requirement, some strict vegetarians and the vegan group, who do not eat meat, fish, or dairy produce, may develop anemia. Some do take a supplement, but others refuse this and believe that certain molds and fungi provide all they need in their diet. This needs further investigation. Other possibilities are that the intestinal flora may produce sufficient B_{12} so that some is absorbed from the gut. Folate is usually abundant in all green leaves and vegetables and deficiency is unlikely except in very poor diets. It is also plentiful in peas, beans, and liver. There is a greater need for folate during pregnancy and this is often pre-scribed together with an iron supplement. The combination of this vitamin and mineral can help to prevent a temporary anemia which is fairly common in the last three months of pregnancy. This is not the same as pernicious anemia and the supplements are prescribed by doctors after careful blood tests to confirm the diagnosis.

Vitamin B_{12}, which contains cobalt in its molecule, has the chemical name cyanocobalamin. Folic acid, or folate, is some-times referred to as folacin.

Another B vitamin which should be mentioned is pantothenic acid. Since it is found in most foods we are unlikely to be short of it. Some experiments with animals show that a deficiency can occur on certain diets. These deficiencies produce a form of der-matitis in chicks, a loss of pigment in rats, and premature graying of the hair in black rats. However, similar results have not been produced in humans and, unfortunately, extra pantothenic acid in the diet does not prevent graying of hair. Extravagant claims by some commercial companies who add it to hair oils and other preparations are not scientifically proven.

Rich sources of pantothenic acid are found in eggs and liver. Pantothenic acid forms part of an enzyme called coenzyme A. Just as thiamine is important in glucose oxidation and pyridoxine in amino acid metabolism, pantothenic acid is involved in the synthesis and oxidation of fats.

Biotin is yet another B vitamin. Deficiency can produce certain types of dermatitis but, again, this is rare. The vitamin is found in liver, brewer's yeast, vegetables, nuts, peas, and beans. It is also believed to be synthesized in significant amounts by the gut flora, so a deficiency is unlikely. There is, however, an antagonist to this vitamin, a substance known as avidin, found in raw egg white. When raw eggs are eaten in excess, the avidin binds with any biotin in the diet and there is then a shortage of this vitamin. Occasional cases have been reported on unnatural diets of raw eggs, but these are few and far between. They do, however, illustrate the fact that biotin is a vitamin in the true sense of the word and is essential to our diet.

The final group of food factors often listed as part of the B complex are not strictly vitamins. These include choline and inositol, which are concerned with the transport of fat from the liver. Choline can be synthesized in the body. Inositol is a true vitamin for mice, but not for humans. Para-aminobenzoic acid is part of the folic acid molecule but, although it is listed as a vitamin and shown to be a growth factor for chicks and rats, its claim as a vitamin for us is doubtful.

23 · The Vitamin B Complex as a Whole

WHEN NATURAL FOOD sources supplying the entire B complex are used instead of chemically made vitamins, better results have been consistently obtained in both animals and humans. This cannot be overemphasized since each year millions of dollars are spent on vitamin pills and tablets. Many preparations supply only small amounts of the common vitamins and omit the important ones. The compound may be unbalanced or incomplete. Many people take these products believing them to be a remedy for all ills, but this is far from true.

Reasons for using the entire vitamin B complex

There are two good reasons why you should supply yourself with all the B vitamins. First, since most of these vitamins occur together in foods, no one can be deficient in one of them without being deficient in some of the others as well. This is true even though the deficiency of one may seem more prominent than any other in the group. Second, the efficient action of one often depends on the presence of another in the group. Their functions are interrelated. Vitamin B_{12} and folic acid are a typical example.

Reasons for using natural sources

Natural sources of the B vitamins such as liver, brewer's yeast, whole grains, and dairy products provide the best therapy. It is as illogical to treat a B-complex deficiency with one vitamin as it is to treat a protein deficiency with a single amino acid. If you are short of the B vitamins then you must plan your diet to include the whole complex of this important group. Full health can only be built from fresh natural foods which come from the garden, the health food shop, and the grocery store.

Vitamin B complex and infections

No single vitamin has been proved to be an antidote to infection. Tests with experimental animals have shown a greater resistance to infection in those given a good diet with all the B vitamins supplied than in those with a similar diet but some of the B complex missing. General health is consistently better with the complete complex, and resistance to infection is a natural accompaniment to good health.

B-complex deficiencies and the death rate

Many of the B vitamins are found in wheat, rice, maize, rye, and oats. Ripened grains contain a high percentage of carbohydrate in the form of starch. This is found in the inner part of the grain and is called the endosperm. The outer layers of the grain and the germ of the seed contain protein, fats, vitamins, and minerals. When flour is milled by modern methods the outer husk and the wheat germ are removed, and the fine white flour contains very little of these natural nutrients. White flour is said to have a "low extraction rate." This means that if you start with 100 pounds of wheat and make 70 pounds of flour then it will have a 70 percent extraction rate; 30 pounds of bran and wheat germ have been removed. A high extraction rate of between 80 and 90 percent denotes a whole-wheat flour with much of the natural bran and germ still in the flour. Whole-wheat bread is made from this type of flour, but many loaves which are sold as brown bread may have been made from white flour with some bran, wheat germ, and coloring added. This is seldom made up to the high vitamin and mineral content of the original wheat grain but does contain more nutrients than a white loaf.

In England during the Second World War, when wheat was in short supply, it was imperative that bread should be made with high extraction flour and wastage kept to a minimum. To make the loaf acceptable to a public more used to white bread than brown, the extraction was brought down to 80 percent and then enriched with thiamine, niacin, iron, and calcium. This produced a light brown loaf with a high nutrient content, the "national loaf."

With the return of peace and adequate food supplies, white bread again became the bread of choice, although it was inferior, nutritionally, to the wartime loaf. Since the end of the war there has been a marked increase in the death rate from many diseases. These include cancer of the colon, heart disease, and diabetes. Many people like to attribute this rise of modern ills to the eating of white bread instead of brown. This assumption needs careful consideration before it can be accepted or rejected. During the war there was a marked decline in deaths from heart disease and diabetes and the general health of the nation improved. However, it must be remembered that this was a time when sugar was rationed and sweets and chocolate and many refined carbohydrate foods and fats were hard to obtain. Rationing helped to keep most people at their ideal weight or below it. Gardens, parks, and railway sidings were used to grow vegetables so that most households had an opportunity to obtain fresh fruits and vegetables. All these factors helped in improving health and reducing the incidence of many common diseases.

Since the war we have also returned to white sugar, a high consumption of refined carbohydrate foods and fats, and for many people, less exercise. Recent research has shown that there is a correlation between the incidence of heart disease and cancer of the colon with the amount of fiber in the diet. There is also evidence to show that overweight and overconsumption of sugar can increase the incidence of a form of diabetes known as "maturity onset diabetes." (See also page 280.)

There is much to recommend the 100 percent whole-wheat loaf. It contains vitamins and minerals and it has a much higher fiber content than white bread, but it is important not to lose sight of the picture as a whole. A healthy diet must include all foods. The war years were full of stress and yet they still remain a rare example of what a diet should contain and show how a well-balanced diet can have an immediate impact on the health of a nation even in a time of limited food supplies.

Today most of us can choose from a wide variety of foods, but we should aim to select and buy only the foods that will improve our health. It is often easier to follow a fashion and eat the wrong food than to spend a little extra time planning the menu. And yet it is this attitude which can make or break the chances of enjoying good health.

Body requirements of the B-complex vitamins

These requirements have been dealt with in the different sections on the vitamins. Tables drawn up may vary from country to country, but general standards were laid down by the United Nations World Health Organization committee in the 1960s.

The need for thiamine is judged by the calorie content of the diet, but this in turn is influenced by the carbohydrate eaten. All food in a diet is a source of energy, but when extra food is taken to provide more energy, as in the case of athletes and manual workers, extra thiamine should be included so that energy can be released.

Requirements for growth

Growing children will need varying amounts of thiamine relative to their age and food intake. Teenagers usually need the same amount as adults.

Requirements during illness

Many illnesses speed up the metabolic activities in the body. Fever accelerates the heat production in the body and this increased energy requires extra thiamine, but appetite is often poor. Diarrhea and faulty digestion and absorption may also be present. Careful planning of light nutritious meals with emphasis on the easily digested B-complex foods (wheat germ and brewer's yeast) will help to make up the exhausted supply of these important vitamins.

Losses and destruction of the vitamins of the B-complex

Of the known vitamins in this group only thiamine is easily destroyed by heat. No food should be overcooked and reheating should be avoided when possible. Whole-grain and quick-cooking cereals are preferable to slow-cooking ones. Bread is nutritionally richer if untoasted. Slightly undercooked meats contain more thiamine than overdone joints and steaks.

All the B vitamins are soluble in water. Therefore, they are lost in the water in which the food is cooked unless this is saved and used in soups and sauces.

Daily need for vitamin B

Since water is not stored in the body (over and above what is needed) none of the B vitamins can be stored. If the supply of B vitamins is inadequate, those in the body are quickly used up. It is for this reason that careful planning of your vitamin supply with each day's food is important. Buy whole-wheat flour and whole-grain cereals. Use wheat-germ bread, pumpernickel, black rye bread, and rye and soya flour bread when possible. Buy raw wheat germ from your health shop. This may be cooked or eaten raw added to whole-grain cereals. Eat only a little at first if you are unaccustomed to the taste. Increase the amount as you learn to enjoy it. Use raw wheat germ in place of some of the flour in your favorite recipes. Make waffles, muffins, biscuits, and breads with at least a quarter of the flour in the form of raw wheat germ. You can also add it with advantage to meat loaf and bread crumbs.

Blackstrap molasses is an excellent source of all the vitamins of the B complex with the exception of thiamine. Molasses is a byproduct of the sugar-cane industry. It is now used largely for fattening cattle, but may also be purchased from health shops. Cane juice contains the vitamins and minerals necessary for the life of the plant. In making sugar this juice is boiled down until some 30 gallons are concentrated to about one gallon of molasses. Therefore the nutrients not harmed by the heat are concentrated to thirty times that of the original juice. At this stage the syrup is dark. Sugar, a pure substance devoid of vitamins and minerals, is then crystallized out of the molasses and removed. The molasses remaining is extremely rich in nutrients. Thiamine has been lost by heating, but this can be replaced by fortifying the molasses with a supplement of B-complex vitamins. Molasses is rich in minerals and many of the B vitamins.

Blackstrap molasses may be taken directly from a spoon, stirred into milk, spread on bread, or added to yogurt. If you have never tasted it, then expect to dislike it. Take no more than half a teaspoonful at first, but eat this amount daily. In this way you will cultivate a taste for it and in about two weeks you will probably consider it delicious.

Whole-wheat spaghetti, macaroni, and noodles should always be purchased in preference to those made from white flour. Brown rice should replace white. Include buckwheat in your diet. Boil it for twelve minutes by putting it to cook in twice as much water as grain. It makes an excellent hot cereal or it may be served as a vegetable. Use soya beans baked, or in a loaf, as a meat substitute. Cultivate a taste for liver, heart, and sweetbreads, and use them more frequently than other meats.

Peanuts are a good substitute for sweets and provide a useful source of B vitamins. Brewer's yeast is often used in cattle feed, but it is so rich in B vitamins it should really form an important part of our own daily diet. It can be bought in powdered form in health food shops and should be taken stirred into fruit juices or water. A heaped tablespoon contains a day's allowance of thiamine, so it is an excellent way to get a good supply of the B vitamins into your diet.

Whole grains such as wheat, oats, barley, and rye can all be bought inexpensively. They are high in B vitamins, protein, and minerals. Use them plain or mixed to your taste in preference to the less nutritious and more expensive processed cereals. Prepare by washing, covering with hot water, and soaking overnight. More water or milk can be added and the mixture heated for a wholesome, tasty breakfast.

Whatever your source of the B vitamins, they must be generously used, day after day, if you are to achieve good health. Unless the nation's "normal" diet changes radically it is unlikely that we will receive the full complement of the B vitamins without careful planning and control of our own food.

24 · Ascorbic Acid and Scurvy

ALL FRESH and growing foods contain ascorbic acid, also known as vitamin C. Our richest sources are citrus and tomato juice, cabbages, green peppers, rose hips, and strawberries. Whenever people have been unable to get fresh foods, the ascorbic acid deficiency disease, known as scurvy, has resulted. This condition, which is rare today, has played an important role in the history of nations.

History of scurvy

Hippocrates was the first to write of the disease now recognized as scurvy. He described how large numbers of men in the army suffered from pain in the legs, gangrene of the gums, and loss of teeth. Records dating back to the Crusades of the twelfth and fourteenth centuries tell of ravages of scurvy among the men that caused hundreds to die. It was especially severe during Lent, when the men often gave up the few available foods which might have contained some ascorbic acid.

Many historical records and reports show a definite seasonal relationship with outbreaks of scurvy. The condition was most likely to occur after from three to six months on a deficient diet. A long hard winter, with no fruit and vegetables available, produced symptoms of scurvy. These would clear when green crops could be picked in the spring and added to the diet. Long hard winters are common both in northern Europe and northern Canada. The early French Canadian settlers are said to have lost so many of their members from scurvy during the winter months that they considered abandoning their settlements. In Newfoundland, the English suffered intensely from scurvy and were forced to give up their plans for colonizing the Hudson's Bay region.

Army records show that over 3,000 cases occurred in the Civil War and many thousands of cases were reported in troops of all nations in the First World War. The knowledge and understanding of a vitamin often comes many years before its practical application in the field of nutrition. The need for fresh fruit and vegetables was recognized as a necessity for good health, but it was not until the Second World War, when the vitamin had been isolated and synthesized, that it was possible to supplement the diet of civilians and soldiers and prevent outbreaks of scurvy.

Hindsight is easy and, looking back, it is surprising that we did not understand the need and the source of this important vitamin sooner. Scurvy was common in times of siege, famine, and crop failure. Cases were recorded during the nineteenth century and the beginning of the twentieth in institutions, asylums, and prisons. Such places provided poor diets for the inmates. Bread and water was the basic meal with the occasional addition of meat or bacon. Fresh fruits and vegetables were luxuries and unlikely to fit into meager budgets. Health, unfortunately, was not the aim of those who dispensed the small rations of food.

Wherever it has been difficult to produce natural food supplies scurvy has occurred, and often it has determined the future course of events. In Ireland, where the potato was the staple crop, the famines of 1847–1849 brought untold misery to the Irish. Most people died from starvation but, among those who survived, few escaped from some form of scurvy. The potato is not a rich source of ascorbic acid but it does contain a small amount of the vitamin. This becomes a significant addition to the diet when the potato is eaten in large quantities. In Ireland, where the soil and climate favored its cultivation, most of the land owned by the peasants was used for growing potatoes. With the devastation of the crops in the 1840s, due to a fungal disease, there was no staple food and nothing else to eat.

Before the introduction of the potato, small farms and gardens had grown a variety of vegetables, but the potato provided a greater return in food per acre and it could be stored and used throughout the winter. The Irish therefore switched to this one main crop, with fatal results.

Scurvy at sea

The early voyages of world exploration focused attention on scurvy and eventually led to its cure and prevention. During long trips at sea there were often many months when little or no fresh vegetable or animal food was obtainable. Within three or four months after the ships left port, most of the crews were incapacitated with scurvy.

The records of the journeys of Vasco da Gama, Ferdinand Magellan, Francis Drake, and many others contain accounts of the ravages of scurvy. Jacques Cartier, who in 1536 set out to explore the St. Lawrence River, arrived with his entire crew sick and twenty-six men already dead from scurvy. Several of his men, helplessly ill, were set ashore to die. A few days later the captain, going ashore, found these same men miraculously cured. The Indians had given them a tea made with the young green shoots, the "needles," of the spruce tree.

Other accounts exist in which men, put ashore to die and unable to walk, ate grass. Within a few days they were well again. One sea captain carried a cargo of onions which sprouted during the trip. The crew ate the sprouts, rich in ascorbic acid, and their scurvy was cured. The treatment seemed so successful that on subsequent voyages this same captain fed onions generously to the crew with varying results. Unless the onions sprouted, they failed to prevent scurvy.

In 1747, James Lind, a Scottish naval surgeon, conducted a scientific experiment on the effect of different diets on members of his crew who had developed scurvy. He fed each group a different type of diet and watched to see which foodstuff produced the fastest and most permanent cure. Of the diets chosen, one included fresh oranges and lemons. The men eating this food were quickly cured and able to return to their duties in only a few days. This positive proof of the curative properties of oranges and lemons was not put into effect until some fifty years later. It then became compulsory for sailors in the navy to have a daily ration of citrus juice. This was often made from lemons or limes; hence the nickname of "limeys" for British seamen which is still used today.

One of the reasons for the long delay between the discovery of the cause of scurvy and the application of its cure was the superstitions and prejudices of the day. Illness at sea was believed to be due to evil spirits, salt meat, sea breezes, and so on. The idea of a deficiency disease was a long way ahead. One enlightened sea captain of the eighteenth century was James Cook. On his three-year voyage round the world he always bought fresh fruit, vegetables, and meat for his crew when they stopped at various ports. He also gave his men a tea made from sprouted barley grain. This contained generous amounts of vitamin C. On the entire voyage there was not a single death from scurvy.

The importance of fresh food on a long sea journey was underlined only a few years ago. When Francis Chichester sailed round the world, single-handed, in his yacht *Gypsy Moth,* his cargo included mustard and cress seeds. He grew these at intervals during his voyage and so had a continual supply of fresh green food.

Scurvy in infants

Science can help solve many problems but it can also bring new ones in its wake. Food technology in the nineteenth century encouraged the production of artificial foods and canned milks which could be fed to infants. Many of these foods were devoid of vitamin C because ascorbic acid was destroyed by high temperatures and long cooking times. Breast milk and cow's milk contain small amounts of vitamin C and the babies fed on this for the first few months of life had all the nutrients they needed, but the child weaned onto canned milk or boiled milk, without any vitamin supplements, soon developed scurvy. The boiling of cow's milk was encouraged at the time because an eminent scientist, Louis Pasteur, had discovered that this destroyed harmful bacteria in milk. What was still to be discovered was that boiling also destroyed useful nutrients. Today vitamin-C supplements are usually given to babies in the form of orange juice from the first few days of life.

Symptoms of scurvy

The most common symptom of scurvy is spongy, bleeding gums. Teeth become loose and infections and ulcers develop in the mouth. (These symptoms may be missing from old people who have no teeth or in babies whose first teeth have not erupted through the gums.) Other symptoms include swollen joints and small hemorrhages beneath the skin. Bruising occurs easily and sometimes there is a weakness in bone growth which may lead to easy fracturing. Cases of scurvy are rare but old people, living alone, may eat a poorly balanced diet with little or no fruit and vegetables and they will show signs of the disease unless given simple advice about the need for fresh foods.

Others who may show signs of early scurvy are alcoholics. Just as we have seen how they often suffer from vitamin B deficiencies owing to their poor diet, so they may lack ascorbic acid. In fact, the alcoholic so frequently presents a picture of all the deficiency diseases that, in a sense, he contributes to medical research. We no longer conduct experiments on humans to discover the effects of a deficient diet, but alcoholics often provide the information we need. The difficulties arise when a cure is suggested to the long-term alcoholic. Vitamin supplements can help general health but a cure can be achieved only when good foods replace alcohol in the diet.

25 · The Need
for Ascorbic Acid

EARLY WORK on ascorbic acid posed something of a problem. It seemed impossible to produce the deficiency disease in animals. Experiments on rats, goats, dogs, and other animals had no effect. Eventually, two Norwegian scientists who were trying to produce beriberi in guinea pigs on a rice diet found the animals developed scurvy. Later it was discovered that guinea pigs, monkeys, and men are the only animals who cannot synthesize ascorbic acid in their bodies and so must obtain it from their diet. Other animals possess all the enzymes necessary for its synthesis from simple sugars so they cannot be made deficient by dietary means. Since monkeys are expensive both to breed and to keep, guinea pigs have become the standard experimental animals for the study of ascorbic acid deficiencies.

Early work established the curative effect of citrus fruits on diet-induced scurvy, but it was many years before the substance was isolated from the foods that contained it. Eventually two scientists, Charles S. King in America and Albert von Szent-Györgi working at Cambridge, England, isolated and crystallized ascorbic acid from cabbages, citrus fruits, and adrenal glands. Szent-Györgi was looking at the oxidative properties in various biological tissues and did not realize that the substance he had isolated was the same ascorbic acid that King was trying to find. Once it was identified as the antiscorbutic substance (antiscurvy) it was only a short time before it was synthesized in the laboratories. Initially, ascorbic acid was measured in units that would effect a cure in scorbutic guinea pigs, but once the substance could be synthesized it was possible to weigh it. The pharmacological units were then dropped and the dosage was described in milligrams.

Functions of ascorbic aid

All the millions of cells which make up the body are cemented together just as bricks are held together by mortar. One function of ascorbic acid is to aid the body in maintaining strong cement-like material between the cells. This material is spoken of as connective tissue. The same cementlike substance is used to form the supporting tissue. These tissues include cartilage, ligaments, the walls of arteries, veins, and capillaries, and the basis or "matrix" of bones and teeth which contain important minerals. In the same way that mortar depends on cement for its strength so the substances between the cells and in the supporting tissues depend on ascorbic acid for strength. Conversely, too little vitamin C will produce a weak binding material.

Apart from its extreme importance in this cementing process, many of the functions and properties of ascorbic acid are not completely understood. Many claims have been made that it will cure the common cold and guard against infections. In times of illness ascorbic acid disappears from the blood and tissues, which suggests that it is indeed a necessary item for speedy recovery, but there has been no positive proof that it works to prevent infection in the first place. Dr. Linus Pauling advocates a large daily intake of ascorbic acid to saturate the body with this vitamin and so provide protection against the stress of modern life and as a safeguard against infection. Work at the Common Cold Centre in England, however, has shown no protective properties in large doses of the vitamin against the respiratory infections which their human guinea pigs are subjected to. Among some doctors there is concern that overmedication with vitamin C may produce excess oxalate in the urine. This in turn predisposes to stones in the kidneys.

The recommended daily allowance of vitamin C varies among

countries. In England 30–40 milligrams are considered adequate for general good health. As little as 10 milligrams can cure scurvy and a dose of between 20 and 30 will prevent the disease. In the U.S. in the 1940s the figure of 75 milligrams was proposed as a desirable intake, but this was reduced to 60 in 1963 and then to 45 in 1973 but was raised to 60 milligrams in 1979. This last figure is now the accepted minimum, but still well above the recommended English figure of 30 milligrams. Ascorbic acid is important in all growing tissues. Experiments with guinea pigs have shown that a diet lacking in vitamin C will produce malformed teeth in young animals. The enamel is thin and extensive decay of the pulp and dentine occur when the enamel becomes broken or worn away and bacteria invade the tissues of the tooth. Obviously a similar type of experiment cannot be conducted on children, but it is reasonable to assume that ascorbic acid is important in the formation of new teeth. Their structure depends on a supporting matrix for the deposition of minerals. When children have a low intake of ascorbic acid and subsequently show poor teeth it is important to remember that strong teeth require other vital nutrients besides ascorbic acid. We shall see in later chapters the proven importance of vitamin D and calcium in building strong teeth.

Vitamin C can play a very important role in the maintenance of healthy gums. You will remember that one of the early signs of scurvy is bleeding gums. To a lesser extent this condition is a sign that your body may not be receiving adequate vitamin C. When the gums become unhealthy the mouth is subject to many infections. These infections provide an abnormally high number of bacteria which feed on food and dead cells in the mouth and produce the acid which attacks tooth enamel. Once the enamel is gone, the bacteria can invade the soft tissues of the tooth and produce damage which can be corrected only by treatment by a dentist or, at worst, by extraction of the tooth. Vitamin C is not only important to the visible part of the teeth and gums but it also helps to supply the special "cement" which keeps the root of the tooth fixed in the gum. The only time teeth should be loose in the mouth is when the milk teeth are being pushed out of position by secondary teeth. These secondary, or permanent, teeth should stay firm and healthy in the gums for the rest of your life.

Ascorbic acid and bones

Ascorbic acid plays a similar role in bone formation. The connective tissue or matrix of the bone provides the framework on which the essential minerals, calcium and phosphates, can be deposited. If this structure is weak or inadequate the bone that is formed on it will be weak and inadequate also and could fracture easily. A great deal can be done to correct this with a better diet. Many people believe that bones stop growing and become static, "dead" structures once we reach the age of eighteen or twenty. This is not so. There is a constant breaking down and building up of bone structure our entire lives. Bones will not grow longer, nor will crooked bones become straight, but their basic material will remain alive and functional just like all other tissues in the body. A fracture starts to heal soon after a break and this can occur only in live tissue well supplied with blood, food, and oxygen. From this you can understand that ascorbic acid is important to both growing bones and mature bones.

Ascorbic acid and changes in blood vessels

The walls of blood vessels throughout the body depend on ascorbic acid for their strength. The capillaries are the smallest of these vessels and they have the thinnest walls. These may be only one cell thick, but in a healthy person they are strong enough to contain the blood and fluids which supply and drain the tissues of the body. Their strength lies in the quality of the cementlike substance that binds them together. This connective tissue can be properly formed only if there is an adequate supply of ascorbic acid. Someone who suffers from a lack of vitamin C will bruise easily. This is because the capillaries break quickly under pressure and spill their blood into the neighboring tissues. This can occur in all parts of the body but when it occurs near the surface of the skin it is visible as a bruise. With the breakdown of the capillaries and small blood vessels bacteria can enter the bloodstream and invade the tissues of the body. Internal bruising causes much of the pain and swelling in joints, typical symptoms of the deficiency disease.

During the 1930s when Szent-Györgi and King were working on the isolation of vitamin C, another factor was discovered which proved successful in promoting strong, healthy capillaries. This was isolated from lemon peel and first called citrin. It appeared to correct the permeability of weakened capillaries and was given the name vitamin P. Later this term was abandoned as it could not be proved that citrin was an essential food factor. However, its properties in speeding up the healing and construction of connective tissues have been the subject of much research and it was discovered that foods which are naturally rich in ascorbic acid usually contain substances called flavonoids similar to this obsolete vitamin P. Flavonoids assist in the synthesis of connective tissue indirectly by preventing the oxidation of ascorbic acid. Once oxidized, ascorbic acid can no longer help in the formation of collagen (connective tissues). The debate as to whether flavonoids should be classified as vitamins can be argued from both sides. What it does illustrate is that if you take the vitamin in its natural form you will get a better balance of the nutrients your body needs. Many health stores and vitamin manufacturers are beginning to realize this and try to incorporate these nearly essential factors in their preparations. Vitamin C tablets are often made from rose-hip extracts now, and these are usually rich in flavonoids. The list of ingredients on the label will tell you that the preparation contains not only ascorbic acid but also small amounts of rutin and hesperidin. These are the flavonoids. If you do need a supplement in your diet then try to obtain these natural extracts.

Ascorbic acid and healing

Ascorbic acid is essential for proper formation of all connective tissue in the body. It is equally essential for healing wounds and fractures when they occur, by forming new tissue over the damaged area. This must be strong enough to knit the older tissues together, and it must be particularly strong when formed in tissues such as bone, which are subject to pressure and mechanical stress.

In times of war and disaster, wounds heal slowly when there is little or no ascorbic acid in the diet. Extra vitamin C should be supplied to aid in healing after accidents, burns, and operations. This is surprisingly little understood today. A supplement to patients after operations can help to speed up the healing processes, especially in simple cases such as removal of appendix or tonsils. There have been very few large-scale trials to verify this therapeutic use of ascorbic acid although there are many reports of success among small-scale and individual experiments. In view of our understanding of the role of ascorbic acid in wound healing, it would seem logical to ensure that an adequate supply be given to patients after surgery or accidents, particularly when food intake is likely to be low. Yet this is seldom routine practice in hospitals. Perhaps this is a present-day example of the time lag between gaining knowledge and applying it.

Detection of ascorbic acid deficiencies

Various methods have been used to estimate the amount of ascorbic acid in the body. Early workers believed that the strength, or fragility, of capillaries was a good index of the amount of vitamin C. Pressure was applied to the arm just above the elbow (where capillaries are near the skin surface). The type of instrument used was similar to the kind used to test blood pressure. After a few minutes the pressure was removed and the area inspected for tiny blemishes called petechiae. This type of marking indicates minute breaks in the capillaries. They are very small and soon disappear but the initital counting gives some indication of the state of the capillary walls and hence the ascorbic acid in the system. More than five or six of these in an area of about two square inches suggests that the walls are a little thin. Later estimations were made of the amount of ascorbic acid in the blood and urine. This was found to be a fairly constant figure in a healthy person. In times of illness and infection ascorbic acid disappears rapidly from the blood and little or none is excreted in the urine. However, although adequate as a rough guide, this type of test is exposed to many experimental errors such as fluctuations in diet and body metabolism.

The present-day method determines the amount of ascorbic acid present in leukocytes (the white blood cells). This quantity does remain constant and reflects the content of ascorbic acid in the body. Leukocytes act as scavengers in the blood, engulfing harmful toxins and bacteria. It has been reported that their activity is increased when the body is saturated with ascorbic acid. This lends support to the argument that massive doses of vitamin C will prevent infection.

We can expect to hear many more theories and arguments about vitamin C before all its uses and activities are resolved, but there is no doubt about its importance in the growth and maintenance of body structures and connective tissues.

26 · Requirements and Sources of Ascorbic Acid

Ascorbic acid requirements of babies

A NEWBORN infant has a good supply of ascorbic acid at birth. A breast-fed baby receives a further supply from its mother's milk but a small supplement is advised when the child is a few weeks old. This should be given as diluted fresh orange juice. Vitamin syrups with a high sugar content are not advised. Unsweetened orange juice is usually well tolerated by babies. In England the Department of Health and Social Security recommends 15 milligrams a day of ascorbic acid, but most babies receive more than this. An intake of 35 milligrams is recommended in the U.S. and appears to have only beneficial effects, although massive doses are not recommended because there is a possibility that they can alter bone metabolism and also produce excess oxalate in the urine.

Older children need more ascorbic acid than babies. Their intake is sometimes calculated according to body weight but 45 milligrams are recommended for children. Pregnant and nursing mothers need 60 milligrams daily.

Requirements for the aged

There is no evidence that old people need more vitamin C with age. What *is* known is that they certainly do not need less. They should be taking at least 45 milligrams daily, and 60 would be better. This may seem a small amount but even this low minimum may not be met when either cooking or shopping is difficult, or fresh fruit and vegetables are disliked or are too expensive. Arthritis of the hands makes food preparation difficult and dental problems make chewing painful or impossible. Old people living alone will tend to prefer soft foods which are pre-cooked and/or canned. These may be short of more than just ascorbic acid. The health of old people should become the concern of all of us rather than the health visitor or welfare worker only. Much ill health could be alleviated or avoided if we could find a way of helping senior citizens to eat a better diet. Nutrition is a relatively new science and those of us who are young are fortunate to be able to reap the benefits of this knowledge. But we should also pass the knowledge along to others whenever possible.

A condition that tends to develop in old people is called osteoporosis. This is often referred to as softening of the bone. Fractures and painful joints are typical symptoms. The connective tissue of the bone becomes less dense and calcium salts are lost from the tissues. This is affected by vitamin D and calcium in the diet but it is also thought to be affected by a low ascorbic acid content in the body. Vitamin C may not cure, or completely prevent osteoporosis, but an adequate intake is believed to slow down the development of the disease.

Sources of ascorbic acid

Among the richest sources of this vitamin are oranges, lemons, grapefruits, tangerines, and limes. There is some ascorbic acid in other fruits, but only the berry fruits such as rose hips, black-currants, raspberries, and strawberries have a content comparable with the citrus fruits. Green vegetables such as watercress, spinach, peppers, cabbage, kale, broccoli, and turnip tops are all good sources. Other fruits and vegetables which may not contain high amounts of vitamin C nevertheless contribute to the daily intake because they are common or popular foods. These include potatoes, green beans, lettuce, apples, bananas, and pears.

All grains, cereals, dried beans, and lentils lack ascorbic acid, but once the seed has sprouted the new shoot contains vitamin C. Bean sprouts can be eaten raw, added to salads and cooked as a vegetable. *(Unsprouted beans should always be cooked before eating.)* Many supermarkets today sell bean sprouts and bamboo shoots. These are a regular feature in Chinese and Japanese cooking.

Meat is not a very rich source of vitamin C but there is a useful amount in sweetbreads, heart, brain, kidneys, and liver. Raw meat contains much more of the vitamin than cooked meat. Eskimos eat a lot of their meat raw and so obtain enough vitamin C to prevent scurvy during the long winters when all forms of green vegetables are unobtainable. There is very little ascorbic acid in dairy products, although there is a small amount in cow's milk. This will fluctuate according to season and to the breed of cow.

Effect of climate, soil, and ripening on ascorbic acid

The ascorbic acid content in fruit and vegetable crops can vary enormously from year to year according to the climate, soil, and harvesting. Rainfall and sunshine will contribute both to the yield and quality of the crop. The use of natural and artificial fertilizers will affect the vitamin content of many crops. There is also an optimum time for harvesting any crop. Fruit should be allowed to ripen on the tree to provide maximum vitamin C, but many green leafy vegetables and legumes such as peas and beans have a greater vitamin C content when they are still growing. Mature seed and pod crops tend to increase their carbohydrate content so that there is ample food for the embryo plant in the following season. If beans and peas are picked when young and tender more of the plant can be eaten. We are used to eating the pod of string beans but in many countries the pod of the garden pea is also considered a delicacy. The older, tougher plant contains more cellulose, and weight for weight there is more wastage in these crops. Much of the plant is discarded in preparation— pods and stalks—and the high cellulose content of the part eaten is not absorbed from the intestinal tract. Obviously the commercial gardener must strike a happy medium between picking a crop that is too young and lightweight to sell economically and too old to be attractive or useful to the housewife. However, if you are lucky enough to have a garden of your own you can break the rules and pick some crops when they are young and enjoy the delicious texture and flavor of sugar snap peas as well as having a vitamin-packed meal.

Effects of handling food

Storage and temperature greatly affect the ascorbic acid content of foods. Green leafy vegetables kept at room temperature until they are wilted will lose at least half their ascorbic acid content. If they are stored in the refrigerator the loss is minimal. Fruits vary in the amount of vitamins they lose when kept in cold storage. Citrus fruits lose very little but apples and root vegetables lose up to half their vitamin C when stored for a year. If the food is bruised and broken at all during preparation and harvesting before storage the loss will be even greater. Freezing of fruit and vegetables is one of the best ways of preserving their ascorbic acid content. Some of the vitamin may be lost during preparation, e.g., during washing, shelling, or blanching, and there will be a loss when the food is thawed before cooking, but if the food is carefully handled and cooked when it is needed then losses can be kept to a minimum.

All vegetables and fruits contain an enzyme which, when released by cutting and bruising, immediately starts to destroy the ascorbic acid in the tissues. This enzyme is inhibited in the presence of acid. Boiling water will also inactivate it. This is another reason why it is important to cook your greens as soon as you have cut them and prepared them. Do not leave shredded and finely chopped vegetables in cold water or on the kitchen table for an hour or two before it is time to cook the meal. By doing this you lose nearly all the natural vitamins from the food. Chop and plunge all your greens straight into boiling water. Do not use soda in the water. This creates an alkaline solution and destroys the vitamin. Avoid the use of copper pans when cooking vegetables or preparing fruit and salads. Copper tends to oxidize ascorbic acid and once this has happened the vitamin is of less use to the body.

Overcooked and warmed-up foods lose nearly all their vitamins. This is why so many meals in schools and institutions which may have been planned with maximum vitamin content lose all their goodness if they have to be kept hot for an hour or more. Ideally all vegetables should be picked, cooked, and eaten within as short a time as possible. This is seldom possible without a vegetable garden outside the kitchen door. There is bound to be a delay between the picking and the delivery of the produce. However, once it has reached your kitchen, see that it is cooked and eaten in the minimum time and, if it must be stored, remember to handle it as little as possible and keep it under refrigeration.

Vitamin C dissolves out of the food into the cooking water in the same way as the B-complex vitamins do. Try not to waste this cooking water. Use it in soups, stews, and gravies. It can be used as a hot drink with a yeast extract or tomato juice added to it. If you have no immediate use for it, put it in a cup and keep covered in the refrigerator till the next meal. It is a real waste of valuable vitamins to strain the water off the vegetables straight down the kitchen sink.

Canning

Canned fruits and vegetables do lose some of their ascorbic acid because of the various processing procedures which must be used at the factories, but some of the vitamin is retained and certain products, particularly fruit juices, have extra ascorbic acid added to them to make up for these losses. It is best to have the fresh produce whenever you can but, if this is not practicable, then go for the naturally vitamin-rich canned fruits and juices, e.g., orange and tomato juice. Try to avoid the ones that are preserved in a high-sugar syrup and check the label to see just how much vitamin the product does contain.

Effects of drying and pickling

Drying is a time-honored method of preserving food. Traditional methods relied on sun and wind, or smoke and heat from an open fire. Today modern technology offers a wide range of alternatives and drying is a shorter process. This produces food with a higher nutrient content and a more attractive and acceptable appearance. Some nutrients are lost, however, and vitamin C is the first of the vitamins to suffer when fruits are dried. A pound of fresh grapes contains about 20 milligrams of vitamin C but the same weight of raisins contains none. Other preserving processes, such as pickling, salting, curing, and fermenting foodstuffs, produce a similar loss of ascorbic acid. These foods may provide a good source of other important nutrients but should not be thought of as supplying vitamin C. Even rich sources such as citrus fruits will lose their vitamin content when subjected to this type of treatment for preservation.

Importance of careful preparation

With a little care and attention to the selection and preparation of our food it is usually possible to obtain sufficient vitamin C in our diet at all times of the year. Remember when you refer to food tables that the values given for fruit and vegetables are only approximate and will vary with the condition of the food, the season, and the picking conditions. Try to shop for the freshest foods available and eat as much as you can of them in this fresh, raw state. If you do cook the vegetables, keep the cooking time and liquid to a minimum and remember to save the small amount of cooking water as a vegetable stock. If you try to follow these methods of cooking and preserving vitamins you will certainly feel the benefits and you need never be short of your daily requirement of ascorbic acid.

27 · The Need for Vitamin D

VITAMIN D, by tradition, is always listed among the fat-soluble vitamins. It was found to be an essential factor in the prevention of rickets, a disease that causes softening and malformation of the bones in young children. Recent evidence has shown that the way in which the vitamin assists in the absorption and control of calcium and phosphorus in the body resembles the action of a hormone rather than a vitamin. Hormones are substances which travel in the blood from a gland to the site of action. Insulin, for example, is a hormone that travels from the pancreas to the cells to promote the uptake of glucose.

Vitamin D can be taken into the body as part of our food and it can also be formed in the skin by the direct action of sunlight on natural oils. It is needed for the absorption of calcium and phosphorus from the diet. To understand the importance of vitamin D it is necessary to learn something about the formation and maintenance of bone in the body.

Bone is a strong supporting tissue. It is similar to other tissues in the body in that it is constantly changing and renewing its cells. The length of bones is determined in the early years. The structure starts as cartilage and later becomes calcified. This calcified cartilage is slowly replaced with bone in the adult. It consists of an intricate matrix of connective tissue or "collagen" onto which calcium and phosphate are deposited. The strength and density of this bone will depend on the availability of these minerals in the body. Both calcium and phosphate are found in many foods and most diets provide an adequate supply of these minerals. The trouble is not in selecting the right foods so much as ensuring that they are absorbed effciently.

Most people in Europe and North America take in nearly one gram of calcium in their food each day (the recommended allowance is 500 milligrams). However, it is quite usual for 70 percent of this calcium to be excreted in the feces. The small amount that is absorbed from the gut into the bloodstream is sufficient to keep a healthy calcium balance in the body but, if the diet is poor or absorption is faulty, the formation of bone and teeth will be impaired.

Approximately 99 percent of the body's calcium is found in the bone. The remaining 1 percent occurs mostly in the blood. This small percentage is very important for proper functioning of nerve and muscle, particularly for the heart muscle. This balance between the minerals in the bone and the blood is controlled by vitamin D and hormones from the parathyroid gland in the neck. When blood calcium is low, the mineral is withdrawn from the bone. When it is plentiful it will be laid down in the matrix of the bones and teeth.

If calcium is withdrawn from the bones too often their strength and structure will suffer. Growth becomes irregular and the shape of the bones is then easily altered by the weight of the body and the stress of daily activities. Typical symptoms of bone defects are irregular growth and swellings at the end of the long bones (wrists and knees) and bowing of the bones of the legs. When vitamin D is added to the diet calcium will be properly absorbed and there will be sufficient for the needs of the blood and bone.

Dietary sources of vitamin D are generally poor. The richest source is found in fish oils. There is a small amount in dairy products but little or none in grains and vegetables. Fortunately, we can obtain vitamin D in a nondietary form. This occurs when the skin is exposed to sunlight. The ultraviolet rays of the sun act on the provitamin which is found in the natural oils of the skin. This is changed to active vitamin D and then transported to the liver.

History of rickets

Rickets has been known from antiquity. Many early paintings of infants show them with typical symptoms of rickets, indicating that the disease must have been prevalent and that these deformities (which are described today as rachitic) were not uncommon. Early writings often refer to the treatment of this disease with fish-liver oils. As with many deficiency diseases, the cure was discovered long before the cause was understood.

The first important work on vitamin D and rickets took place after the First World War. Four years of famine and near-starvation, together with bad living conditions, had caused the increase of many diseases and epidemics in Europe. Scientists working at that time were aware that nutrition, or lack of it, was as much a cause of disease as the existence of infection from bacteria and viruses. In 1918 Edward Mellanby, an English scientist, discovered that cod-liver oil cured rickets in dogs. At about the same time, Harriette Chick, who was working in Vienna, found that sunshine or cod-liver oil could produce a cure in young children suffering from the disease. Vitamin D was finally isolated in the 1930s when its chemistry and mode of action in the body were better understood.

Vitamin D is formed from a class of compounds called sterols. These sterols are found in plants and in the adipose tissue of animals. When they are irradiated with ultraviolet light (present in sunshine) these substances change to an active form of vitamin D. In plants ergosterol changes to ergocalciferol and in animals dehydrocholesterol changes to cholecalciferol. It is the natural animal form of the vitamin that is important to us. It is called vitamin D$_3$ and is stored in the liver. People living in a sunny climate are seldom short of this vitamin but those who live in colder climates or smoky cities must obtain more of the vitamin from their diet.

Before all this was understood, rickets was a common disease among children living in dark, smoke-polluted towns, particularly in the overcrowded industrial towns which sprang up throughout northern Europe in the nineteenth century. It was most prevalent among the poor, who could seldom afford sufficient dairy products to supplement their diet. Breast-fed babies, who received sufficient calcium and vitamin D from their mother's milk, avoided early rickets but, since weaning foods were usually lacking in vitamin D, a child who did not get the benefit of sunlight would soon develop rickets. The eradication of rickets in many northern countries in the 1920s and 1930s was a direct result of introducing cod-liver oil as a supplement for infant feeding, together with an improvement of housing conditions and alleviation of atmospheric pollution in industrial towns.

Rickets attacks infants and young children. It deforms growing bones. Lack of vitamin D in adolescents and older people produces a similar condition known as osteomalacia. This is caused by the loss of minerals from the bones, resulting in spongy, weak bones which break easily. There is also swelling and pain at the joints. The groups most at risk with this type of disease are often determined by climate and customs. Women who observe purdah in Muslim countries remain in the seclusion of their homes from early adolescence. If they venture out into the streets even their faces must be covered. Their diets are usually lacking in vitamin D, particularly if they are poor, or if local custom excludes milk and eggs. Their legs become deformed and their teeth do not grow properly. Ignorance and suspicion may preclude the use of cod-liver oil and vitamin supplements in their diet. Women who marry and have children tend to keep their children indoors during the early months of their lives in the mistaken belief that they are protecting their skin from the harmful rays of the sun. Early rickets usually clears once children get out into the sunlight.

Extent of rickets today

Although rickets is now a rarity, isolated cases are still seen, particularly with the widespread migration of dark-skinned people from tropical countries to the colder sunless climates of the north. Dark skin is a natural protection against the strong ultraviolet rays of the sun in tropical climates. In northern climates, this natural barrier is a disadvantage as it tends to prevent what little sunlight there is from reaching the provitamin in the skin. Some immigrant children in Britain have shown signs of rickets. Many of them are vegetarians and will eat no fish and very little dairy produce. Children of school age show typical symptoms in malformation of the leg joints. They may, however, appear reasonably fit so that the disease, which is unfamiliar to many doctors, is hard to diagnose. Vitamin D supplements must be given but these must be from commercial products manufactured by irradiating plant sterols. Fish oil is quite unacceptable to the strict vegetarian.

Vitamin D and teeth

Edward Mellanby's wife carried out extensive surveys on the relationship between the development of children's teeth and the incidence of rickets. Her surveys showed that children suffering from defective teeth were most often short of vitamin D and also suffering from a mild form of rickets. Poorly developed teeth were always the ones that were most susceptible to tooth decay. When children had an adequate supply of vitamin D their teeth grew normally and they had far fewer cavities and dental problems. The formation of a tooth is similar to that of bone and is therefore dependent on an adequate supply of calcium and phosphorus. It is essential that the correct amount of calcium should be available for the growing period of children's teeth. The shape and strength of young bones can be altered to a certain degree with an improved diet in the early years, but a decayed and broken tooth cannot be replaced.

The shape and alignment of teeth in the mouth depend on the development of the jaw bones. A child deprived of vitamin D in the early years may grow up with protruding or misplaced teeth due to faulty bone development. Now that rickets is a comparatively rare disease it is easy to dismiss it from the mind altogether but, as with all deficiency diseases, there are a great many degrees and stages in its development which must not be overlooked. The child who is short of vitamin D may feel tired and unable to enjoy sports, games, and all the activities that need so much energy. This type of fatigue may be due to a shortage of other vitamins and nutrients, but vitamin D is probably the one that needs most attention in the diet. Very few foods provide a rich source of this vitamin and there is not such a large store of vitamin D in the body as there is of vitamin A.

At the end of the winter the reserves may be very low. When the sun becomes stronger more of the vitamin is formed in the skin and the stores can be replenished. Cows and chickens, living and feeding in the open air, will also form more of the vitamin in their bodies with a corresponding increase of it in the milk and eggs they produce.

Each spring many of us experience a feeling of well-being and easily forget the aches and pains of winter. Apart from the psychological aspect of longer, sunny days and the prospect of vacations, much of this can be ascribed to the increase of vitamins in the food we eat. Fruit and vegetables provide a richer source of vitamin A and C and the sun adds to the vitamin D in our bodies. Theoretically it should be possible to keep up this higher intake throughout the winter but it does need careful planning. A winter diet should aim at compensating for the decrease of vitamin content in the foods we buy.

28 · The Value of Sunshine

FROM THE EARLIEST times a few physicians recognized the healthful effects of sunlight. In 1890 a study was made of rickets throughout the world. Freedom from that disease was found in areas of greatest sunshine. To obtain the maximum benefit from sunbathing, washing should be cut to a minimum. Cleansing the skin with oil is really the best method of retaining the vitamin. This is particularly true when letting small babies enjoy the benefits of sunbathing. Sometimes their skins are very sensitive to ultraviolet rays and so they should only have short periods in the sun until they become used to it.

You should try to spend as long as possible in the open in the wintertime to get some benefit from the sun. If this is impracticable, because of work hours, climate, and so on, then it makes sense to check the vitamin content of your diet by food tables and take a supplement if necessary. You should be taking approximately 10 micrograms of vitamin D a day. This small supplement will help to keep you fit, with healthy bones and teeth. However, remember that it is a fat-soluble vitamin and that any excess is stored in the body and not easily lost like the water-soluble vitamins, so don't take more than you need. Too much of a good thing becomes a bad thing with this type of supplement. An overdose of vitamin D can be toxic and cases have been reported of illness and death when the dose has been seriously exceeded.

Symptoms of poisoning with excess vitamin D in children are loss of appetite, pain in the head and limbs, vomiting, and diarrhea. Clinical tests will show a sharp rise of calcium levels in the blood. Provided the symptoms are recognized and the vitamin withdrawn from the diet, there is no permanent damage. Cases of hypercalcemia (too much calcium in the blood) were reported in England in the 1950s. This led to an inquiry on the fortification and enrichment of baby foods. It was agreed that the amounts of vitamin D added to baby foods should be reduced. A child receiving a cod-liver oil supplement as well as rusks, milk, and special foods enriched with vitamin D can soon have a very high intake. Care should be taken to read the list of contents on bottles of baby foods to check just how much extra vitamin the child is receiving each day.

29 · Sources of Vitamin D

You will see from the food tables at the end of the book (*Appendix III*) that vitamin D is not abundant in many foods. We have mentioned that it occurs in fish-liver oils and dairy products. It is useful to know how much we can expect from these sources and whether they will supply our daily requirement of this important vitamin. The oils of sardines, herring, salmon, and tunafish contain some vitamin D. People who eat large amounts of fish are therefore unlikely to be short of the vitamin. Eskimos seldom suffer from rickets although they may see sunshine only for a few brief months in the summer. Milk contains a small amount of vitamin D. One quart supplies approximately one-tenth of the day's needs. Eggs and butter contribute another small amount but the content of all these foods is dependent on the time of year and the type of feed the animal is receiving.

Fish-liver oils

These are by far the richest sources and one teaspoonful of cod-liver oil contains 10 micrograms (400 international units) of the vitamin, which is sufficient for a day's supply. Halibut-liver oil is a rich source but it also contains a very high content of vitamin A and so must be taken only in very small doses. Babies are given this type of oil in drops, rather than in teaspoons.

Many people find that the taste, or lingering smell, of cod-liver oil is unpleasant. They often prefer to take capsules or malt extracts, enriched with cod-liver oil. Care should be taken when giving these special foods and supplements to children. If they taste good and look like sweets children may be tempted to eat more than they need. See that the child has the correct amount and then lock up the bottle or tablets well out of their reach.

Stability of vitamin D

Vitamin D is stable in cooking and is not lost by heating and processing. It is affected by rancidity in oils. If they become rancid the active vitamin is destroyed.

Absorption and excretion of vitamin D

When vitamin D is absorbed from the intestine it is carried first to the liver and then to the kidneys. It is then transported back to the cells lining the gut wall, but it is now a slightly different chemical compound. The dehydrocholesterol has changed to a substance called 1, 25-dehydroxycholecalciferol. This substance encourages the production of a calcium-binding protein in the gut mucosa and it is this protein which helps in the transport of calcium across the cells and into the bloodstream. When there is plenty of calcium in the body the absorption rate slows down. The calcium balance in the body is affected by hormones, diet, and availability of vitamin D.

Storage of vitamin D

Vitamin D is stored in the liver and the adipose tissue. The body does not have as large a reserve of this fat-soluble vitamin as it does of vitamin A. Early symptoms of a lack of this vitamin are hard to recognize. Rickets may take a year or more to show. If diet and sunshine are not adequate, then some form of dietary supplement should certainly be taken, particularly in the winter.

30 · Requirements of Vitamin D

VITAMIN D is required at all ages but it is most important in the early years when bones are growing and developing. It must be remembered that most people will receive some sunshine throughout the year and this will raise their natural production of vitamin D in the skin. Requirements in sunny tropical countries are likely to be lower than in colder northern countries where the sun is lower in the sky and may not shine so often.

With the exception of fish-liver oils most foods are poor sources of this vitamin. You would need to drink about 20 quarts of milk to get the same amount of vitamin D in a teaspoon of cod-liver oil. Eggs are a reasonable source. One egg contains one microgram of vitamin D and fortified margarines contain 2 micrograms per ounce. Fish such as salmon, sardines, and herrings supply between 5 and 20 micrograms per 4 ounces. Other fish, particularly white fish, are a poor source of the vitamins, though cod roes do have a high content.

It is easy to see why the vegetarian is slightly at risk with regard to the dietary intake of vitamin D, especially if no eggs, butter, or milk are consumed. Supplements of vitamin D can be recommended at all ages if dietary sources and sunshine are in short supply. However, the difference between a health-promoting dose and a toxic dose is much less with this vitamin than with any of the others. Poisoning has been reported among infants taking as little as 70 micrograms a day. It is important to check the amount of the vitamin which has been added to baby cereals and milk feeds and adjust the cod-liver oil dosage accordingly.

31 · Vitamin E and Vitamin K

Vitamin E

VITAMIN E was first discovered by Dr. Herbert M. Evans and a colleague, Dr. Bishop, at the University of California in 1923. They noticed that rats reared on a diet of lard, cornstarch, and casein (milk protein) produced no offspring. Later, when vegetable oil was added to the diet, they grew normally and were able to reproduce.

The factor that was isolated from the wheat-germ oil (vegetable oil) proved to be pure vitamin E. This was given the chemical name "tocopherol." Later it was found that other tocopherols existed in the oil. Eight have been identified to date but only three of them are of nutritional significance. They are classified as alpha-tocopherol, beta-tocopherol, and gamma-tocopherol.

The first, alpha-tocopherol, is the most potent. The vitamin is fat-soluble and is found in vegetable oils, particularly wheat germ, sunflower, and safflower. It is also plentiful in whole-grain cereals, eggs, butter, and many green vegetables.

The problem with vitamin E is that, although much is known about its chemistry and its effect on rats, very little is known about the way it works in humans. It does not appear to affect reproduction, abortion, or sterility, but it does have an influence on the amount of oxygen that is used by the muscles. Less oxygen is needed for normal oxidation purposes if the body is well supplied with vitamin E. Dr. Evan Shute, working in Canada, has conducted some successful treatments of patients with heart disease by administering regular doses of vitamin E. Other benefits from the tocopherols include preventing the oxidation of polyunsaturated fats in the body. Without ample supplies of the vitamin these fats are oxidized and some of the byproducts accumulate as a pigment in the tissues. This is thought to accelerate the aging processes; therefore vitamin E has been heralded as a substance which prevents aging of the skin. There are claims that there are many other conditions which are helped by this vitamin, ranging from diabetes and muscular dystrophy to simple skin disorders. The problem is that there have been very few well-conducted scientific experiments which support these claims. Vitamin E appears to bestow different benefits on different people. It is difficult to assess individual reports on these merits but there seems little doubt that it is a useful nutrient. More research is necessary before we can determine the exact functions and benefits of this vitamin.

The tocopherols are found in small amounts in many foods and it is unlikely that many people would find themselves deficient in them. The average diet contains about 10 milligrams of vitamin E per day and this is thought to be adequate for most people. Vitamin E has been praised by so many enthusiasts that it has become one of the most popular vitamin pills in the health shops. It is also incorporated into cosmetics and soaps though again there is no definite proof that it is a useful skin treatment. There is no evidence, to date, of adverse effects from large doses of vitamin E, but it should be remembered that it is a fat-soluble substance and is likely to be stored in the body rather than excreted in the urine. Moderation in the administration of this vitamin seems sensible until we know more about its reactions in the body.

Vitamin K

Vitamin K was discovered in 1934 by a Danish biochemist, Henrik Dam. He was working on a disease found in chickens, which produced bleeding. Normal clotting of the blood failed to take place until certain foodstuffs were added to the diet.

Processes involved in the clotting of blood are very complex. There is a sequence of events, each of which requires certain elements and factors. Calcium is one of the necessary elements and vitamin K is also required at one of the stages.

There is a substance in the blood known as fibrinogen which can change to a fibrous, cobweblike structure called fibrin, which holds the clot together. This change from fibrinogen to fibrin is controlled by an enzyme called thrombin. Thrombin is normally inactive in the circulating blood (blood clotting in the arteries and veins would cause thrombosis and death). However, when the skin is broken and bleeding occurs, the inactive enzyme becomes active and promotes clotting at the site of the wound. The enzyme is synthesized in the liver and requires vitamin K for the process. When the vitamin is in short supply the time taken for the blood to clot is longer than with healthy blood.

Vitamin K is a fat-soluble vitamin and requires bile to ensure adequate digestion and absorption. When the secretion of bile salts from the liver to the intestines is abnormal, as in disease, vitamin K is poorly absorbed. Faulty blood clotting can be very dangerous, particularly in surgery or after an accident, and in such cases the vitamin is administered by injection.

The best sources of vitamin K are alfalfa grass and dark-green leafy vegetables. It is found in cereals; liver also provides a good supply. Although it is an essential food factor it seems unlikely that we could become deficient in this vitamin. It has been found that it is synthesized in the gut by intestinal bacteria and we can absorb some of this supply. There is no specified daily requirement, and a well-balanced diet should supply all our needs.

Other vitamins

It seems highly probable that there are still more vitamins to be discovered. Some animals given apparently perfect diets fail to thrive when kept in sterile conditions. They do not develop any "intestinal flora" and so fail to synthesize certain vitamins in their gut. Even though all known vitamins are administered in the diet, it seems there is some other factor missing. It could be that there are other vitamins produced by bacteria which are essential for proper health and growth. The discovery and isolation of vitamins is a relatively new field. There is still a great deal of work to be done. The story of vitamins is by no means complete.

AIR,
WATER,
AND
MINERALS

32 · Air and Water

AIR AND WATER are essential to life; without air we cannot live for more than a few minutes and without water we would die in a few days. Yet these two vital factors are seldom listed as essential nutrients or minerals and, since they do not fit into any neat category, we tend to take them for granted. Our dependence on air and water goes right back to the time when life first began on earth a billion years ago. The earth evolved from a swirling cloud of gases that cooled and condensed to form mountains, rocks, and volcanoes, leaving an atmosphere of "air" of the lighter elements—hydrogen, nitrogen, carbon, and oxygen. The hydrogen and oxygen then condensed to form water, seas, and lakes and the rains washed the minerals from the rocks and soil into the sea. All these events were natural processes with the gases changing to liquids and solids and the chemical elements forming compounds which became part of the soil and rocks. But the rocks and sea remained inanimate and nonliving. After many millions of years a more subtle change took place. Molecules appeared in the sea which did not conform to the inanimate pattern. They could grow and reproduce themselves and they could use the energy of the sun to make these changes possible. Life had begun.

Scientists believe that these first living molecules were simple collections of sugars, amino acids, and fatty acids. They were formed from the same elements that we find in our bodies and our food today—oxygen, hydrogen, carbon, and nitrogen. The minerals in the sea included the phosphates, calcium, sodium, potassium, magnesium, and many more, all essential for life as we know it. Today air is composed of nitrogen and oxygen. When life first began hydrogen was the dominant gas in the atmosphere. Oxygen, so vital for growth and metabolism, was dissolved in the seas. It was the evolution of plants, not man, which released this oxygen into the atmosphere. Plants use sunlight, water, and carbon dioxide to form simple sugars. This process is called photosynthesis. The water molecule is split during the reaction releasing the oxygen. We are totally dependent on this property in plants for two reasons. Since we cannot use sunlight to form our own foods we must eat plants or animals that have eaten plants for energy, and since we must breathe oxygen we rely on plants to return the oxygen to the atmosphere.

Our dependence on water is easy to understand as it was the first provider of all materials for life, and it was the home for the first cell which developed in that primordial sea. As the cells developed from the early "live" molecules, it is believed they were able to construct a membrane or protective covering around themselves which enabled them to hoard the nutrients and minerals in short supply and reject the ones they did not need. Today, living cells in animals have retained this property and work to maintain a distinct distribution of minerals inside and outside the membrane. Cell fluids (the cytoplasm) contain potassium and magnesium ions while the fluids that surround them contain sodium and chloride ions and calcium. It would seem that although we have left the sea and become land animals we have in a sense "brought the sea with us." More than two-thirds of the body is composed of water distributed among the cells, the tissue fluids that surround them, and the blood plasma. It is the tissue fluids and the blood plasma which so closely resemble the composition of the sea.

Many people have tried to use science and logic to unravel some of the mysteries of the intervening millennia. Much of the reasoning before Darwin published his theory of evolution in 1858 was completely distorted by religious dogma. God created the world in six days and rested on the seventh, the church claimed, and anyone foolish enough to question that was considered a heretic. Today we can trace a much slower development from those first molecules and single cells to the vastly complicated multimillion-celled animal that is present-day man. Apart from their dependence on the sun and the sea those early cells were independent creatures. They were very small and could absorb, digest, and excrete all they needed from their surroundings by simple diffusion. They could use oxygen to metabolize their food, they could react to stimuli such as light and heat, and they could grow, divide, and reproduce. They were a jack-of-all-trades and had, within their cell, all that constituted life.

This singular existence progressed to a multicellular community and gradually certain cells within the community became specialized. Some were responsible for feeding and digestion; some developed into nerve cells sensitive to their surroundings; others formed reproductive glands and tissues. With this increase of size it became imperative to find new methods for the transport of food and oxygen and the removal of wastes. Since diffusion is only effective through short distances, how was the sea to be brought to the central cells? The specialized cells that developed to overcome this problem were the forerunners of our heart, lungs, and kidneys.

The heart, lungs, and kidneys

The heart acts as a pump to distribute the blood with its nutrients to all parts of the body. The lungs extract oxygen from the air and pass it to the bloodstream, and the kidneys filter and cleanse the blood, keeping a constant balance between water retention and excretion. All these organs work together to produce an environment for the cells of the body which resembles the composition of the sea from which we evolved so many millions of years ago.

The primitive development of the heart and kidneys can be seen in many small land and sea animals, such as worms. These have a number of contracting blood vessels which can circulate fluid to all parts of the body. The kidneys are made up of small units called nephrons which collect waste from the fluid and pass it to the outside. They have no special organs for respiration since all the oxygen they need can diffuse through the wet surface of the skin. Fishes show a more advanced form of heart and kidneys and they have also developed gills to extract oxygen from the water around them. Land animals must obtain oxygen from the air and have developed efficient lungs for the purpose.

The lungs

In man the lungs consist of spongelike tissues which form lobes (*see Illustration 11*) that are encased in two layers of membranes called the pleura. They lie on both sides of the heart in the thoracic cavity. The bronchi, extensions of the windpipe, enter the lobes where they divide into smaller branches called bronchioles. They lead to tiny air sacs called alveoli that are surrounded by a lacelike net of blood capillaries. The bronchi are held open by small rings of cartilage to facilitate the entry of air into the lungs, while the air flow in the smaller passages is controlled by the constriction and relaxation of muscles around their walls. The bronchioles and alveoli are lined with a moist mucous membrane which helps the absorption of oxygen from the air. The cells in the bronchioles possess tiny hairlike structures called cilia, which sweep away dust and dirt particles back into the bronchi and windpipe.

Oxygen dissolves in the moisture of the mucous membrane and passes through the adjoining capillary walls and into the bloodstream. In a healthy individual this exchange of gas is continual, but if the lung is diseased then this surface is damaged and the cells cannot absorb gas or remove dirt and bacteria. Too little oxygen reaches the blood and this causes a feeling of breathlessness and exhaustion. This type of condition occurs in cases of pneumonia or bad chest infections. Sometimes a nervous condition can induce an involuntary muscular constriction around the bronchioles and prevent sufficient air from entering the lungs. This is why drugs that are administered to asthmatic patients are

Illustration 11

Trachea, bronchi, bronchioles, and the lobes of the lungs

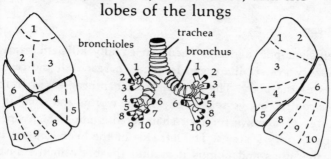

The bronchioles and alveoli of the right lung

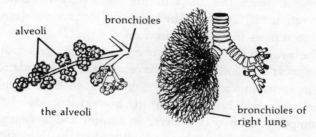

The interchange of oxygen and carbon dioxide

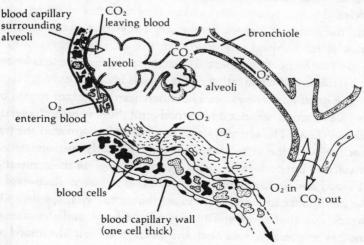

usually intended to relax the muscles in the chest and air passages.

The heart

An efficient pair of lungs needs an equally efficient heart and circulatory system if oxygen is going to reach all the cells and tissues of the body. The human heart has progressed from the simple contracting vessels we saw in the worms and small marine creatures to a powerful four-chambered pump which operates two circulatory systems. The left side of the heart collects blood from the lungs and pumps it around the body in the systemic circulation and the right side collects blood from the veins and pumps it round the lungs in the pulmonary circulation. (*See Illustration 12.*) Valves in the heart and blood vessels ensure that the blood flows in the right direction.

The heart is made up of strong muscular tissue but, unlike other muscle cells, these cells have no definite boundaries. They are in constant contact with each other so that impulses can travel more quickly throughout the heart. Each side of the heart is composed of two chambers, an atrium and a ventricle. The rhythmic beating of the heart is initiated in the right atrium and impulses are conducted simultaneously to the left and right ventricles. These two muscular chambers contract and pump blood into the systemic and the pulmonary circulation. As soon as the muscles relax, blood can flow from the atria into the ventricles ready for the next heartbeat. The active pumping phase is known as systole and the relaxation of the muscle is diastole.

The heart has always been considered an important organ, but its true function was not understood until the seventeenth century when William Harvey, physician to Charles I, discovered the pure mechanics of the circulatory system. The early anatomists and physicians put forward various theories to explain the connection of blood and air in the body. Oxygen had not been discovered so the importance of air to life was attributed to "vital spirits." One theory was that these spirits entered the heart and the arteries; another suggestion was that the heart made all the blood we

Illustration 12

The pulmonary circulation
(lungs partially cut away)

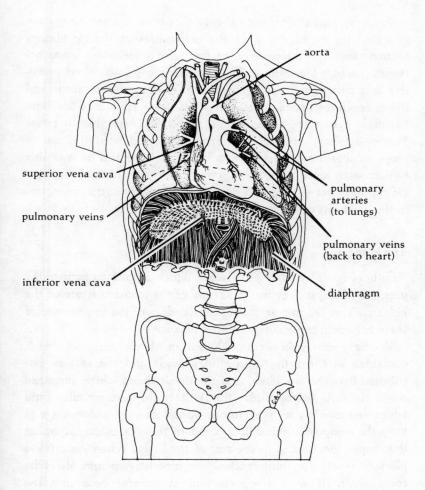

aorta

superior vena cava

pulmonary veins

inferior vena cava

pulmonary
arteries
(to lungs)

pulmonary veins
(back to heart)

diaphragm

needed and allowed this to seep away continually into the tissues. Harvey used simple mathematics to calculate that around 5 liters of blood left the heart every minute. He realized that such a staggering amount of blood could not just seep away and he proved that the heart acted as a pump to recycle the blood. This principle also satisfied the theory that the blood could circulate through the lungs and be revitalized by the air before returning to the heart.

The only part of Harvey's theory that he was unable to prove was that the capillaries were the extremities of the circulatory system where an interchange of food and water took place between the blood and the cells. The microscope was then primitive and although it had been used to examine minute cells and living creatures, it was not until some years later that Marcello Malpighi (1628–1694), an Italian physician, was able to prove Harvey's theory completely correct. Malpighi used the microscope to obtain more detail from his dissections and he was able to demonstrate the capillary system. *Illustration 13* shows a typical capillary network. Blood flow is regulated by small sphincters at the junctions of the vessels.

The kidneys

Another aspect of Malpighi's work which helped to further the progress of physiology was his study of the microstructure of the kidneys. This led to a greater understanding of the importance of these organs in controlling the fluid balance.

We have nearly 45 liters of fluid in our body. Much of this is contained in the cells (intracellular fluid) and the rest is distributed between the blood and the tissue fluids which surround the body cells (extracellular fluid). It is this extracellular fluid which represents the "sea" in our bodies and the kidneys act to keep the composition and the volume of this sea exactly right for the proper functioning of the rest of the body. When we drink a glass of water the fluid reaches our bloodstream and alters its composition. If we eat a meal new substances pour into the

Illustration 13

The circulation
and capillary systems

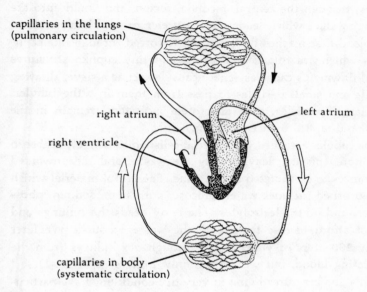

capillaries in the lungs
(pulmonary circulation)

right atrium

left atrium

right ventricle

capillaries in body
(systematic circulation)

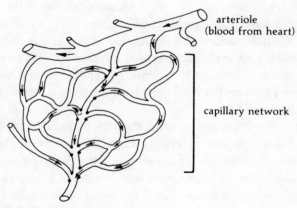

arteriole
(blood from heart)

capillary network

venule (blood return to heart)

bloodstream and the tissues. The kidney works unceasingly to restore equilibrium.

We have two kidneys (*see Illustration 14*), which are supplied with blood from the renal arteries. Urine is formed in small tubules which run from the edge of the kidneys, known as the cortex, through the central, medulla, region, and finally into the collecting duct which leads via the ureter to the bladder. When the blood first reaches the kidney it is forced through fine capillaries which are folded and knotted in tiny cuplike structures called Bowman's capsules. These capsules act as a sieve, allowing liquids and small particles to pass from them into the tubules. The larger particles, such as protein molecules, remain in the blood and return to the circulation.

The tubules are lined with special cells which actively reabsorb the filtered plasma, leaving only the wastes and the unwanted substances to be excreted in the urine. The useful material which is reabsorbed includes water, glucose, potassium, sodium, phosphates, and other electrolytes. The body needs these things and cannot afford to lose them with the waste products. We filter nearly 200 liters of water a day through our kidneys from the circulating blood, but we excrete only 2 liters as urine. Desert animals and creatures living in very dry conditions have particularly long tubules in their kidneys, allowing time for nearly all the water to be reabsorbed, causing them to excrete a very concentrated urine. The movement of water out of the tubules and back into the bloodstream is effected by diffusion, osmosis, and active transport. A network of capillaries surrounds the tubules and collects the materials designated for conservation. (*See Illustration 15.*)

Hormones also control the loss of fluid from the body. Antidiuretic hormone (ADH) from the pituitary gland encourages the reabsorption of water when the body needs it. If we have had a lot to drink then this hormone is not released and the excess liquid passes out in the urine until the balance is restored. Another hormone called aldosterone controls the amount of salt in the body by altering the absorption rate from the kidneys. The pH of the blood can also be controlled by the acidity of the

Illustration 14

The kidneys and adrenal glands

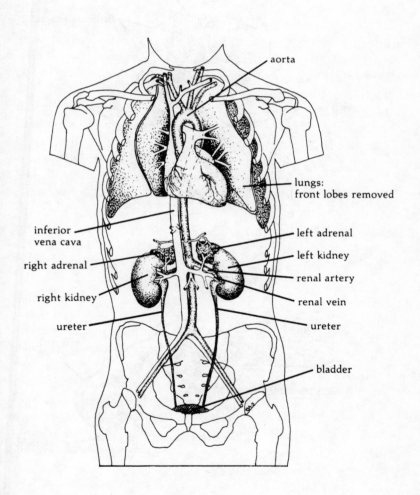

aorta

lungs:
front lobes removed

inferior
vena cava

left adrenal

right adrenal

left kidney

renal artery

right kidney

renal vein

ureter

ureter

bladder

Illustration 15

The structure of the kidney and nephron unit

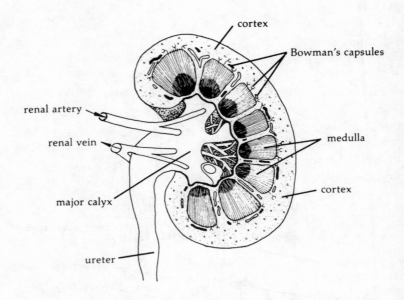

NEPHRON UNIT OF KIDNEY

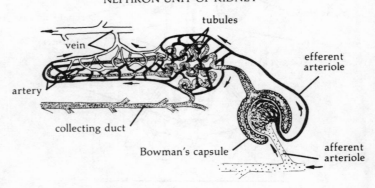

urine. If the blood is too acid then more hydrogen ions will be excreted.

A certain amount of water must be excreted every day to carry away the wastes from the bloodstream. These include urea, the breakdown product from protein, and other unwanted substances and excess electrolytes. We need at least a pint of water a day for the kidneys to be able to function efficiently. This is called an obligatory water loss. We also lose water from the lungs and the skin. Most of us drink more than enough to replace this loss.

People who have to survive in accidents at sea or in the desert with a minimal water supply can live as long as there is sufficient liquid to remove body wastes. Drinking salt water in such a situation can cause severe dehydration and death because the body needs extra fluid to remove the extra salt, and it can only find this by drawing water from the body cells and tissues. Heart

Table 8.

Percentage of Water Found in Foods

Food	% of Water
Bread	36
Cereals	10
Cottage cheese	79
Cheddar cheese	35–50
Fish	50–80
Flour	10–12
Fruits	75–90
Meats	50–70
Milk (whole)	88
Milk (skimmed)	92
Nuts	5–8
Soups	85
Vegetables	75–95

conditions can often upset the water balance in the body. Changes in blood pressure can affect the flow of plasma between the blood vessels and the tissues. The fluid does not drain away from the tissues and a state of edema can result. This shows as a puffiness in the lower limbs. Drugs can alleviate these conditions by controlling blood pressure, and diuretics are often prescribed to encourage the kidneys to produce more urine.

Many of the foods we eat contain a great amount of water, especially fruits and vegetables, but even the foods we think of as dry, such as cereals and beans, still have a relatively high percentage of water. (*See Table 8.*) We also produce water when we metabolize our food. When we burn fats, carbohydrates, and protein in our bodies we produce carbon dioxide and water.

33 · Functions of the Blood

THE FAMOUS PHYSICIAN and chemist Szent-Györgyi, who received the Nobel Prize for Physiology in 1937, said that, when he was studying medicine, everything about the body always seemed to be wrong. There were so many hundreds of diseases to be learned that it seemed impossible for him to remember them all and he failed his examinations. Later, when he took up the study of chemistry, he was amazed at the miraculous perfection of everything in the body—at the dozens of delicate mechanisms by which it was possible for life to continue.

The best monitor of these mechanisms is undoubtedly our bloodstream. The heart pumps 5 liters of blood around the body every minute. This ensures that all parts of the body are in direct communication with each other. Changes in the blood sugar after a meal will be felt in the liver and the brain almost as soon as the glucose has crossed from the gut mucosa into the circulation. Physiologists study the mechanism of the heart and measure blood flow, oxygen content, and many other parameters. The biochemist is interested in the composition of the blood, its chemistry and its effect on the body's metabolism. Some knowledge of both these aspects of blood and circulation can help in our study of nutrition. A healthy bloodstream is essential if we are to benefit from a healthy diet.

The work of hemoglobin

Hemoglobin is the substance that gives blood its red color. One of its most essential functions is to carry oxygen to the tissues. Hemoglobin can also affect the acid/alkaline balance in the body. It acts as a stronger acid when it is carrying oxygen to the tissues. Once it has given up the oxygen it becomes a much weaker acid.

The blood may be thought of as divided into two parts. The fluid part (or plasma) carries dissolved food, vitamins, and minerals. The solid part (the red cells) carries the oxygen. As the blood flows close to the tiny air sacs in the lungs, the hemoglobin combines chemically with the oxygen in the air. (*See Illustration 11*.) This blood is then returned to the heart where it is pumped to all the living cells in the body. No cell can live and perform all its metabolic functions without this constant supply of oxygen. Nor can it survive unless the waste materials and carbon dioxide are removed from it at the same rate.

Blood coming from the heart, arterial blood, is a brighter red than the blood returning to the heart, the venous blood. This is because the hemoglobin and oxygen (oxyhemoglobin) are bright red in color but the oxygen-free hemoglobin appears blue. Physiologists refer to partial pressures of gases when they are speaking about respiration and circulation. Air is a mixture of gases; it is not pure oxygen. The pressure of oxygen in the lungs is only part of the total pressure which we call atmospheric pressure. The rest is made up of nitrogen, a small part of carbon dioxide, and other gases. The partial pressure of the oxygen in the lungs is sufficient to cause it to cross the fine border between the alveoli (air sacs) and the blood to combine with the hemoglobin. When the blood reaches the capillaries, the partial pressure of the oxygen in the surrounding tissues is very low and this enables the oxygen in the blood to pass out from the capillaries into the tissue fluids. The return of carbon dioxide to the lungs is governed by the same principle. When the capillaries reach the tissues where carbon dioxide partial pressure is high, the gas can enter the bloodstream and return to the lungs. Here the partial pressure of carbon dioxide in the air is so low that the venous blood can release its excess carbon dioxide. It is then ready to pick up more oxygen. There is a lot more chemistry to the process than this but the basic fetching and carrying principle is the method by which we get a constant flow of oxygen to all parts of our body.

Gas poisoning upsets this system and if not treated instantly results in death. Carbon monoxide poisoning from car fumes and faulty furnaces occurs when carbon monoxide, not carbon dioxide, is formed in the air around us. Carbon monoxide combines with the hemoglobin in the blood more readily than oxygen and quickly blocks the sites for oxygen transfer. Oxygen does not dissolve easily in the fluid part of the blood. It must have the hemoglobin for its transport. The only way to prevent the death of someone suffering from this type of poisoning is to give him pure oxygen to breathe. Here the partial pressure is so high that it pushes the carbon monoxide off the hemoglobin molecule and allows oxygen to travel to the tissues once more.

Early workers investigating the process of respiration were surprised to find that the greater part of carbon dioxide returning to the heart traveled in the plasma of the blood and not in the red corpuscles. Further work showed that although it does go first to the red cell, further changes occur within the corpuscle. These changes are due to an enzyme called carbonic anhydrase. This splits the dissolved gas into two charged ions. One is called a bicarbonate ion and the other is a hydrogen ion. The concentration of bicarbonate ions is much greater in the red cell than in the surrounding plasma and therefore they tend to move out of the cell to neutralize this imbalance. This movement of ions upsets the balance between negative and positive charges in the cell. The balance is restored by chloride ions moving back into the red cells. This phenomenon is known as the "chloride shift."

One of the reasons for this changeover is that the hemoglobin and the bicarbonate ion help to control the acidity of the blood. The acid/alkali balance of the blood is very important. Human blood has a pH (the amount of positively charged hydrogen ions in the blood) of 7.4, as discussed earlier. This value scarcely ever changes. The lowest and highest values that might be found range between 7.0 to 7.8. This is a very fine control in the body and the movement of bicarbonate and chloride ions between plasma and red cells is just part of this control. Exchange of ions in the kidney tubules is another of the body's mechanisms for adjusting pH.

34 · A Healthy Bloodstream

A HEALTHY BLOODSTREAM can be defined in many ways. The biochemists will tell you how many red cells and white cells as well as how much iron, calcium, protein, and glucose it should contain. Someone with little or no knowledge of blood analysis might look at you and say, "You look well," or, "You look pale." Both reactions have one thing in common. They are remarking on the amount of hemoglobin in the blood. Good health depends on good blood. We have seen how the hemoglobin in the red cells transports oxygen to the tissues. When these cells are in short supply then the body tissues cannot receive all the oxygen required. The tissues cannot burn the food they receive and they cannot produce energy. The amount of hemoglobin in the blood varies slightly between people, particularly between the sexes. Men usually have a higher content than women but the average amount remains fairly constant. When we have too little hemoglobin in the blood the deficiency is described as anemia. The literal meaning of the word is "without blood." This, of course, is an exaggeration, but it does refer to the fact that the important part of the blood is in short supply.

Normal blood formation

A healthy red blood cell has a life span of approximately 120 days. These cells are formed continually throughout life. It has been estimated that there are some 25 trillion red cells in the 5 liters of blood in our body. As each cell survives for only 120 days it is important that the production of new cells be continuous and efficient. The synthesis of these cells occurs in the bone marrow and is controlled by various factors. Vitamin B_{12} is vital for the formation of the cell and iron is needed to form the hemoglobin that it carries. The actual number of cells produced is controlled by a hormone from the kidney called erythropoeitin. When there is a need for more cells to carry oxygen (as in high altitudes where oxygen is scarce), more cells are formed to carry this oxygen efficiently.

Under normal circumstances, 45 percent of our blood is composed of red cells. The remaining 55 percent is composed of the white cells and liquid plasma. About one-third of the mass of red cells consists of hemoglobin. By measuring the hemoglobin content in a small quantity of blood it is possible to estimate the amount in the circulating blood. In a healthy person 15 grams of hemoglobin in 100 milliliters of blood is an average amount. This figure can drop to 11–12 grams in women but below this figure there is a strong indication that the subject is suffering from anemia. Sometimes a quick test is made by comparing the color of the blood against a standard. The standard is the color of blood containing 15 grams per 100 milliliters. The blood to be tested is rated against the color. A very pale color indicates a low hemoglobin value and is usually a sign of anemia.

Anemia

Anemia is a disease which may develop very slowly and does not always give positive evidence. Symptoms include tiredness, listlessness, and general lack of energy. Light-skinned people may show a very pale complexion. Loss of memory or forgetfulness is often attributed to anemia. There are many causes. Lack of iron in the diet can be a major cause, but other factors can produce the same condition. Disease can destroy red cells and also slow down their synthesis in the bone marrow. Disease of the bone marrow and the use of some drugs can cause a drop in the number of cells circulating in the blood. These cells may have a low hemoglobin content so they can carry only very little oxygen around the system.

Iron deficiencies

The body conserves iron very efficiently. When red cells are destroyed and removed from the circulation, the iron is retained for use in the new cells. Some iron is lost from the body in the sweat and skin cells but the absorption of one milligram a day is usually sufficient to offset this loss and prevent anemia. Women of childbearing years are more at risk. Iron is lost during menstruation and childbirth and unless this is replaced there will be a marked fall in the hemoglobin levels. Extra iron is often prescribed for women during pregnancy and while they are breastfeeding.

Iron is present in many foods but it is not easily absorbed into the body. It is similar to calcium, another important mineral, in this aspect. Only about 10 percent of ingested iron is absorbed across the intestinal wall. The best sources include red meat, liver, kidney, egg yolk, and soya beans. Iron from grains and vegetables is less well absorbed. Children who are weaned to foods which are lacking in iron or who are eating poor diets may become anemic. Their performance at school will suffer if they are constantly tired and inattentive.

Other needs for iron

Iron is found in all body cells in the form of a substance called cytochrome. The prefix *cyto* means cell and *chrome* means color. Literally it means cell color. Cytochromes are extremely important in the production of energy from oxidation processes. Muscle tissues also contain an iron-rich substance known as myoglobin (*myo* means muscle). Its function is similar to that of hemoglobin in the blood. It supplies oxygen to the muscle tissues.

Storage iron

The body contains 4 grams of iron and about 3 grams of this is found in the hemoglobin of the blood. The remainder is found in storage and transport iron (ferritin and transferrin respectively) and it also forms part of many enzyme systems. The storage iron is found in the liver, spleen, and bone marrow. This supply can be drawn on at any time it is needed. The body loses approximately one milligram of iron each day, but this is replenished by iron from the diet.

Need for copper

Some types of anemia do not respond to an increase of iron in the diet. Experiments have shown that copper is an important mineral in the mobilization and use of iron in the body. When copper is lacking, the body cannot release iron from the storage iron, ferritin. Many iron supplements and tonics contain small amounts of copper to prevent anemia from a lack of copper.

Copper is referred to as a trace element. This is because only tiny amounts are needed in the body. Fortunately, many foods which contain iron also contain copper. These include molasses, liver, nuts, egg yolk, cocoa, chocolate, mushrooms, and wheat bran. Chocolate-covered nuts and sweets made with dark molasses are far more nutritious for children than many of the oversugared and artificially colored varieties on sale today. They can satisfy a craving for sweets and also help to prevent anemia.

Absorption of iron

There is often some confusion as to the type of iron that is found in the blood. There are two distinct types. One is the iron that is transported from the gut. It is the dietary iron and it is transported in the blood in conjunction with a carrier protein called transferrin. The iron is taken to the bone marrow and is incorporated into the new red cells. The second type is the iron which is part of the hemoglobin in these new blood cells. The first type of iron is the new supply of iron. The second type is the working iron.

The absorption of the iron from the gut to the transferrin in the blood is not always a simple process. It is dependent on many factors. The iron atom has the ability to change the number of electric charges on its ion. The iron we eat is usually in its "ferric" state, Fe^{+++}, but it is absorbed best as a "ferrous" ion, Fe^{++}. This change can occur when the surrounding fluid is acidic. Unfortunately, most food is digested in the duodenum and ileum where secretions from the pancreas and liver are alkaline. It has been found that when iron foods are eaten with some acid foods, particularly those that are rich in vitamin C, this can help the digestion and much more iron can be changed to its ferrous state and absorbed across the gut wall. Acid foods are found mostly among the fruits such as apples, oranges, gooseberries, and so on. Buttermilk is slightly acid. The use of lemon juice and vinegar over salads and vegetables can help iron absorption; side salads of fruit and lettuce should accompany a main meal. Slices of orange and apple in a green salad are just as acceptable as the time-honored tomato and can certainly help to prevent anemia.

The iron that is found in the hemoglobin in animal meats is more easily absorbed than that of vegetable origin. This explains why some of the vegetarian communities in the Third World tend to be more anemic than meat eaters. They must rely on iron from vegetables and cereals. Early work with experimental animals showed how some foods were more effective in curing anemia than others. The most useful were liver, kidneys, apricots, and eggs. These foods did not necessarily have corresponding results when given to human subjects. Absorption rates were dependent on general health, the store in the body, and the rate of blood cell formation in the bone marrow.

Our standards of iron requirements

Standards for daily requirements of iron vary enormously from country to country. The absorption rate of iron from the diet is governed by the iron stores in the body and the composition of the meal. Absorption is often increased when there has been an excessive loss of iron from the body as in cases of childbirth, hemorrhage, or accident. The intake recommended in England is 10 milligrams daily. In the United States the figure is given as 18 milligrams for women. This higher figure is suggested in order to compensate for a poor absorption rate and thus prevent anemia. If the body can regulate its intake according to its need then theoretically this higher intake is unnecessary. Ninety percent of ingested iron is lost in the feces. The conditions for maximum absorption of dietary iron should be thought of as equally important as total intake.

Anemia can be helped with therapeutic doses of ferrous sulfate preparations but, once the condition is cured, careful attention to the diet is particularly important in order to prevent a further iron deficiency. A general feeling of good health is the best guide to assessing the possibility of anemia. If you look pale, feel tired, and are forgetful, plan your nutrition to contain many of the iron-rich foods. Don't expect overnight results. The blood will take a few weeks to build up to the correct number of cells and the right amount of hemoglobin. But if you persevere you should soon feel the benefit.

35 · Why We Need Calcium

Just as iron is important to blood so calcium is vital for proper bone formation. The adult body contains about 3 pounds of calcium (1⅓ kilograms) and 99 percent of this is found in teeth and bones. It is not surprising, therefore, that the development of the skeleton is affected by the supply of calcium received during the growing period.

Calcium and stature

The tallest races in the world are found among those who have a high intake of calcium in their diet. These are usually the people who eat a considerable amount of dairy produce, particularly milk and milk products. The Scandinavian and Germanic races are usually tall. The climate and geography of their countries are ideal for dairy farming. Farther south, where the climate is dryer and pasture land is scarce, the natural diet does not include so much fresh milk, butter, and cream. The southern Mediterranean races are shorter in stature. We tend to think of height as a hereditary and racial trait but in recent years it has been shown that a change in environment and diet in early years can affect growth and development more than genetics. The Japanese have, until recently, been thought of as a people of short to medium height but since many have gone to live and work in the U.S.A. their children have grown up to be the same size and stature as American children. Their diet has been richer in many

211

nutrients, especially calcium. This change has been a natural phenomenon. Similar changes have been observed with animals. Shetland ponies, normally thought of as the smallest type of domestic horse, grow to a normal height when bred in calcium-rich pastures. This may take two or three generations, but the characteristic features of the pony are soon lost with the new diet.

Recognizing calcium deficiencies

The early stages of calcium deficiency can be difficult to detect. The small amount of calcium needed by the blood and soft tissues, only 1 percent of the total, is extremely important for the proper functioning and well-being of the body. If calcium is in short supply it is drawn from the store in the bones. If this continues the bone becomes rarefied and growth is stunted. These changes in bone structure will show on an X-ray if they are very severe but the early stages may not be easy to diagnose. X-rays cannot penetrate bone but they can penetrate the tissues at the end of the long bones. In healthy growth the cartilage at the end of the growing bone becomes calcified and replaced by bone. When calcium is lacking the tissues will not register on the radiograph. This type of diagnosis is unlikely to be used unless symptoms are severe.

Lesser deficiencies may be indicated by nervousness and irritability in children. Muscle weakness accompanies the bone deficiencies and children with rickets are often slow in sitting and walking. When blood calcium falls to a low level a form of tetany or muscle-twitching may become evident. Cramp is another symptom of calcium deficiency. This is often seen in older children and adults when there is a lack of calcium in the diet or if there is a pronounced malabsorption due to some stomach trouble, diarrhea, or vomiting. Experiments on isolated animal hearts show that calcium is vital to proper functioning of the heart. Heartbeats cease altogether if the specimen is placed in a calcium-free medium.

Some calcium exists as charged particles (ions) in the blood. They are important in conducting electrical impulses for the functioning of nerves and muscles. When these electrical impulses are restricted, poor muscle tone will result. Children will have bad posture or tire easily. The need for calcium in growing children is easy to understand. The increase in size and weight of a growing body must be accompanied by good growth and tone in the supporting muscles. Teenagers often have bad posture as they grow, and tend to stoop. This can be the result of a variety of factors other than diet, but it is easier to correct general posture when the muscles are strong and functioning properly.

Calcium and blood clotting

Calcium is necessary for the clotting of blood. When you cut yourself blood starts to clot within a minute or two of the accident. If your blood is short of calcium this clotting time will be delayed. This could be serious after a major accident as it can make a big difference to the amount of blood that is lost from the body. Blood clotting is a complicated process, but it occurs very quickly in a normal healthy person when the skin is broken. The final clot which forms over the wound and promotes the healing contains a protein called fibrin. There are many reactions in the blood which lead to its formation but one important stage is dependent on the presence of calcium.

Calcium and tooth decay

A good supply of calcium is essential for the proper formation and growth of teeth. Children's teeth are forming in the gums long before they become visible. The secondary, or permanent, teeth are also being formed long before they erupt through the gums. Adequate diet is extremely important during these early years. Vitamin D must be supplied if calcium from the diet is to be properly absorbed and used to promote strong bones and teeth. Vitamin C, as we saw in Chapter 25, is also needed. Strong teeth, well cared for, are far more likely to resist decay than malformed teeth with thin enamel. Health can be promoted in many ways by adopting a nutritious diet at any age, but the raw materials for healthy bones and teeth must be supplied in the early years. No supplements of calcium and vitamin C can re-form teeth once they have grown. A good diet will help tc preserve teeth, but it cannot alter their structure. This is one of the reasons why correct infant feeding is so important. We leave so much to chance and often blame defects on our parents. Heredity is a powerful tool but nutrition can be powerful too. Many of the health problems that recur in families could be minimized, or cured, by closer attention to diet.

Absorption of calcium

Absorption of food is a factor so important in nutrition that it cannot be overemphasized. To see that there is sufficient calcium in the diet is not enough. It must be able to pass through the intestinal wall and into the bloodstream before it can be of value. The problem with calcium is that it is capable of forming insoluble compounds with other foods. When this happens it cannot enter into solution with the digestive juices to pass through the intestinal wall. The insoluble complex passes out of the body in the feces. The foods which appear to promote calcium absorption most successfully are proteins and milk sugar (lactose). It is for this reason that milk and cheese are two of our best calcium foods.

Fat is also important in calcium absorption. It does not help calcium directly, but fat is vital for the absorption of vitamin D from the gut and this, in turn, helps in the absorption of calcium. At one time it was thought that phosphorus improved calcium absorption but this has been found to be incorrect. The calcium/ phosphorus ratio in the blood is controlled by the amount of phosphorus that is excreted or retained by the kidneys.

Some foods contain substances which hinder the absorption

of calcium. One of the paradoxes of nutrition is that brown bread and whole grains, which provide so many useful and important nutrients in our diet, also contain a substance called phytic acid which inhibits the absorption of calcium. It binds with the mineral forming an insoluble substance which cannot pass through the gut wall. This was understood after extensive work carried out in the 1930s by Professor R. A. McCance and Dr. Elsie Widdowson at Cambridge. One of their recommendations for fortifying bread during the war was that extra calcium should be added to the flour to offset this loss. This enrichment is still carried on in some countries, as well as in England. Later work showed that the properties of phytic acid vary considerably according to the type of flour used for baking. Wheat and rye contain an enzyme, phytase, which splits the phytic acid during the leavening process. Once this has happened the calcium-binding properties are lost and the calcium in the bread becomes "available" again as a nutrient. Oats contain very little phytase so they should not be thought of as a good source of calcium. However, oats in porridge are usually eaten with milk and this provides plenty of calcium. A cup of milk provides about a quarter of the daily requirement of calcium.

Oxalic acid is another substance that binds with calcium, making it insoluble. Tea and coffee have a high concentration of oxalic acid and some fruit and vegetables contain it (particularly rhubarb and spinach). There is no need to restrict these foods from your diet but they should not be thought of as a rich source of calcium.

Calcium balance

The balance between the calcium in the skeleton and that in the blood and soft tissues remains constant whether or not there is adequate calcium in the diet. If the diet is rich in calcium some of this excess will be stored in the bone, but there is a limit as to how much is needed and, when this optimum is reached, the rate of absorption from the gut will be slowed down. Some dietary calcium is lost in the feces and some in the urine. When this amount is equal to the amount that is eaten, the body is in calcium balance. In growing children calcium should be in positive balance with more laid down in the bones than is lost by excretion. In older people there may be a very small negative balance as some calcium is lost from bone after forty. This is a perfectly natural aging process and is not the same as osteomalacia, a condition where a great deal of mineral is lost from the bone. The regulation of this calcium balance is under the control of a hormone called parathormone, which is produced by the parathyroid glands in the neck. This works in conjunction with vitamin D in adjusting the absorption of calcium from the diet to meet the requirements of the body.

Another hormone called calcitonin was discovered recently. This takes calcium from the blood back into the bone when the concentration in the blood becomes too high. It also slows down absorption from the gut. This is a good example of the feedback system which operates in the body. The glands which produce the hormones are always in contact with the circulating blood. Changes are detected in the glands and the appropriate hormones are discharged into the blood to correct the change. This return to normality is referred to as the homeostasis. All organs within the body work toward maintaining this constant condition.

Phosphorus and calcium in the diet

Phosphorus is found in almost all the foods we eat. It is important in all living tissue, both for bone formation, enzyme systems, and for the production of energy. In the 1930s it was claimed by many "tonic" wines that their content of phosphates was beneficial to health. The claims have been discontinued as there was no evidence that any normal diet was likely to be deficient in phosphorus. If vitamin D and calcium are well supplied, phosphorus will be absorbed quite adequately from most diets.

36 · Sources and Requirements of Calcium

THERE HAS BEEN much debate about the body's calcium requirements. Growing children need more than adults. Experiments with human volunteers have shown that the body can stay in calcium balance on as little as 200 milligrams a day. It seems likely that the body adjusts its absorption rate according to the supply of calcium in the diet. With a low dietary intake, the absorption is high.

The best sources of calcium are milk and cheese. Milk is especially important in children's diets as it is thoroughly absorbed. Many foods contain small amounts of calcium but they need to be eaten in reasonable portions to make up the calcium requirements. These foods include nuts, green vegetables, oatmeal, fish, and lentils. Meat bones and fish bones are a good source of calcium but we are unlikely to eat a great deal of them. However, softened fish bones, such as we find in canned sardines and small fish, are often eaten and these are rich in calcium.

Some traditional cooking can provide an unexpected source of calcium. The Chinese have a popular dish of pickled spareribs. The bones are chopped and soaked in vinegar. This brings the calcium out of the bone, and a single helping will provide more than a day's supply of calcium.

Powdered skimmed milk is a useful addition to the diet. This provides all the benefits of fresh milk without the high-calorie fat content. Many adults find that they cannot drink 2 cups of milk a day without gaining weight. A pint of milk (2 cups) contains 370 calories. However, a pint of skimmed milk (which is reconstituted with plain water) contains only 180 calories. This provides most nutrients found in whole milk, including the rich calcium source. Powdered skimmed milk can be added to cooking either as a substitute for fresh milk or as an extra to improve the nutrient value of a dish. It is particularly useful when children refuse ordinary milk. They will take powdered milk in many foods without quibbling. Cakes, puddings, and custards can be enriched with dried milk and many soups, mashed potatoes, and sauces benefit from the addition of liquid skimmed milk. Powdered milk can also be used in homemade candy and ice cream. It is cheaper than fresh milk and will keep well in an airtight container.

Diets in most industrialized countries are unlikely to be deficient in calcium provided that some dairy products like milk and cheese are eaten. In the developing countries, the calcium in the diet will be influenced by availability of food and local diet. People living near the sea and lakes who eat fish are unlikely to be short of calcium but the poorer communities, living farther inland and subsisting mostly on fruits and vegetables, may have a relatively low intake. However, in tropical countries people are exposed to more sunshine and will therefore have a good supply of vitamin D in their bodies. This will help to utilize and absorb what little calcium there is in the diet. This principle applies in all parts of the world. Subminimal calcium diet is less likely to be harmful if vitamin D is available but without adequate vitamin D even a high calcium intake cannot be properly utilized.

The relationship of calcium, phosphorus, and vitamin D in maintaining the correct ratio of minerals in bone and blood is another example of the interdependence of nutrients in our diet. It is no good placing faith in one vitamin or one mineral. It is essential to understand how they all work together and plan a diet accordingly to get the best results.

37 · The Importance of Phosphorus

WE HAVE SEEN how vital calcium is for the proper growth of bones and teeth. Phosphorus is of similar importance. The adult body contains approximately 800 grams of phosphorus and about four-fifths of this is found in the skeleton. The remainder is found in the soft tissues and blood plasma. Phosphorus has many functions. It combines with fat to form phospholipids. These are the functional structures of all cell membranes and determine the transport of substances through the cell walls. Phosphorus is also an important element in the nucleus of the cell. It forms part of the nucleic acids, deoxyribonucleic acid and ribonucleic acid (DNA and RNA). It is also present in many enzyme systems and is important in the production and storage of energy in carbohydrate metabolism. This energy is released in muscular and nervous activity. Muscles use another phosphorus compound called creatine phosphate for part of their energy. Phosphates play an important role in the blood plasma where they help to maintain the correct acid/alkali balance.

Phosphorus and calcium parallels

In many ways the information gained from studying calcium also applies to phosphorus. It is essential for the formation of bones and teeth, and its absorption from the intestinal tract into the bloodstream is governed by factors which also affect calcium absorption. In a healthy individual the rate of absorption of phosphorus is equal to the rate of excretion from the kidneys and the amount of phosphorus and calcium in the blood remains at a fairly constant figure. Deposition of calcium and phosphorus in the bone tissues is determined by the concentration of these minerals at the bone surface. Bone cells called osteoblasts together with enzymes alter this concentration and cause the solution to crystallize and deposit the mineral salts within the bone. This concentration is critical and it is important that it should not be reached when the calcium and phosphorus are in solution in the blood plasma.

It is for this reason that when there is an increase in calcium levels more phosphorus is excreted from the kidneys. When calcium levels fall phosphorus is retained and the rate of excretion falls. This delicate balance is controlled by the parathyroid hormone, the amount of vitamin D in the body, and the absorption of calcium and phosphorus from the intestinal tract.

Phosphorus is found in many foods and it is difficult to think of any diet which would not supply all that we need. It is particularly abundant in the calcium-rich foods and for this reason it has been said, "Take care of the calcium and the phosphorus will take care of itself." The only occasion when a deficiency might occur would be in cases of kidney disease, or an oversecretion of parathormone (the hormone which raises the calcium level in the blood), or some disturbance in the metabolism of vitamin D. Phosphorus deficiencies have been reported among animals grazing on soils which have a very poor phosphorus content. Muscle weakness and bone deformities occur similar to those caused by a lack of calcium. Crops for humans grown on this type of soil would tend to have a low concentration of phosphorus but this would be offset by other foodstuffs in the diet. Richest sources are found in milk, eggs, meat, fish, nuts, cereals, and legumes.

38 · How Iodine Can Help Us

HAVE YOU EVER noticed how some people can eat large amounts of food without gaining weight while others gain easily although they seem to eat little? How some people are active and alert while others are sluggish and slow, both in movement and thought? How some appear never to feel the cold while others wear heavy clothes and always complain of cold hands and feet? How some people have thin hair and nails which break easily?

These differences are often due to the lack of one of the trace elements so important in our diet—iodine. Iodine is described as a trace element because the amount we store and use in our bodies is very small compared with minerals such as iron and calcium. We have 1.2 kilograms of calcium and 5 grams of iron in our bodies but only one-twentieth of a gram of iodine. It is tempting to think that the amount is so small that we need not bother about it. In fact, it is a very important twentieth of a gram.

The body's need for iodine

Iodine is needed by the thyroid glands, which are situated on both sides of the windpipe (the trachea). These glands use iodine to synthesize a chemical messenger, or hormone, known as thyroxine. This substance has a profound effect on our growth, our mental and physical development, and on maintenance of health throughout life. If the glands are to work efficiently there

221

must be a constant supply of iodine. It must be supplied in the diet day after day. The amount needed is very small; 150 micrograms are sufficient.

Partial lack of iodine

A partial lack of iodine causes goiter, which is an enlargement of the thyroid gland. Such an enlargement is an attempt by the body to compensate for the lack of iodine and to use what little there is more efficiently. The enlargement of the thyroid gland may not be evident in the early stages of iodine deficiency but if the shortage of this trace element persists over many years the gland will enlarge to a very noticeable swelling.

History of iodine deficiency

Goiter was described by Marco Polo in the 1300s as being common on the plains of Asia. It has especially afflicted people of mountainous regions where the soil lacks iodine. It is said that goiter was once so prevalent in parts of Switzerland that old men, holding grandchildren on their laps, would express the desire to live until the children's necks became enlarged! A full round neck was often considered a sign of beauty. On the other hand, the disease has been unknown in places where sea fish forms the principal item of food, as in Japan. Seaweed is also rich in iodine and this forms part of the diet of people living near the sea. Dried seaweed is a delicacy in many Japanese dishes.

The discovery that iodine was effective in the treatment of goiter was an indirect result of the Napoleonic Wars. The British blockade of the French coast cut off the import from South America of minerals used in making gunpowder. In an attempt to obtain these minerals from the ashes of seaweed iodine was found. The discovery of this mineral in seaweed led scientists to try iodine as a treatment for goiter, but early attempts proved unsuccessful. The iodine was administered in comparatively large doses and had toxic effects. When it was understood that it was needed only in small quantities, an experiment was carried out in 1917 in Akron, Ohio. Sodium iodide was given to about 2,000 schoolchildren. Goiter had been a common disease in that particular area. Within a year the incidence of goiter in the treated groups had dropped dramatically, whereas among another 2,000 not receiving the supplement more than 500 developed goiter.

Symptoms of iodine deficiency

We have seen that when iodine is insufficiently supplied, the thyroid gland enlarges in order to try to produce more thyroxin. Sometimes there is no visible enlargement but there is a definite iodine deficiency and too little thyroxin is produced. Many abnormalities can develop and these will have an adverse effect on health. It is important to recognize the symptoms. The thyroid is, in a sense, a pacemaker for the metabolic activities of the body. It can rev things up or slow them down. It can produce extra heat and activity in the body or it can put on the brakes and cause everything to slow down even to the point of becoming sluggish and lethargic. In the first example the person suffering from an overproduction of thyroxin will rush around, never sitting still, using up what appears to be boundless energy but all the while getting thinner and more and more high-strung. Underproduction of thyroxin produces the slow lethargic person with no energy for anything. He or she may appear lazy and sleepy while the whole system slows down—heartbeat and circulation, even gut movements. The results are poor circulation, poor elimination, and a tendency to become overweight.

Both these conditions seem to occur more frequently in women and are thought to be influenced by hormonal changes so may be more pronounced at puberty or at childbirth, but many of them can be corrected by adequate iodine in the diet. Sometimes therapeutic use of thryoxin extract is advised, but the aim in matters of this kind is always to get the body back to functioning on its own, so attention to diet is the best medicine. Occasionally it can happen that a tumor on the thyroid gland upsets its normal function and obviously no amount of iodine can put this right. But these are fairly rare cases and can usually be treated with surgery.

The taking of thyroxin

Apart from the conditions already mentioned for which a doctor may prescribe thyroxin, there are occasions when this preparation may be used inadvisedly. Some unethical advertisers or unorthodox practitioners may promote the use of pills and injections containing thyroxin as a remedy for reducing weight. The idea is that if it is possible to speed up the metabolism with this hormone the body will burn more sugar and produce more energy than it normally does. In this way excess fat will also be burned and weight loss will result. The theory is correct but the long-term results are far from satisfactory. First, the body may be speeded up much too quickly and exhaustion from overexcitability can result. This can often affect the heart and cause permanent damage. Second, even if results appear to be satisfactory and a weight loss is achieved, the preparation will have to be discontinued after a time because of side effects. The would-be slimmer reverts to her normal diet and life-style. This will produce an immediate return to the old weight and often beyond it. These preparations are also costly so at the end you have lost your money as well as your health.

Under normal conditions, the thyroid gland of a healthy person continually produces a certain quantity of thyroxin which circulates in the blood at all times. The healthy gland never produces too much of the hormone. When thyroxin is given in the form of tablets or by injection then there is no need for the gland to produce any more. Like an arm that is kept in a sling for too long, if this gland has no work to do it will lose its ability to carry on normal duties or functions. Remember, if you ever find it necessary to take thyroxin, it must be under the supervision of a doctor. Self-medication is dangerous.

Exophthalmic goiter

This condition occurs when the thyroid gland becomes overactive and produces too much of the hormone. The speeding up of the metabolic processes in the body increases the heart rate. Normal pulse rate for a healthy heart is 70 beats per minute. In exophthalmic goiter this rate can sometimes be nearly doubled. The patient loses weight, becomes nervous, and constantly feels too hot. The eyes often become protruding. The reason for this type of goiter is not always faulty diet; it can occur when hormones from the pituitary gland (the "master gland" of the body) tend to overstimulate the thyroid gland. Certain drugs are prescribed to control this condition but at all times medication should be backed up by a well-balanced diet. Many people believe that drugs are a form of magic and can cure an illness without any extra help. This is seldom the case. Your body needs all the help it can get if you are ill, and well-planned nutrition is one of the best aids to recovery.

Sources of iodine

Many foods lack iodine. The amount of iodine in foods varies enormously according to the iodine content of the soil and the water. The iodine content of vegetables and dairy products will depend directly on the content of iodine in the soil. Once the use of iodine in the prevention of goiter was understood many countries sought to introduce some means of adding iodine to the salt so that people would be able to add a small supplement to their diet without really thinking about it. Adding iodine to drinking water was partly successful in America in the thirties but the iodization of salt was the cheapest way to ensure that everyone had some iodine each day. Many people tend to buy uniodized salt as it is cheaper but the use of the iodized kind costs only a little bit more and is a safeguard against developing goiter and thyroid disease. It has been suggested that 100–150 micrograms of iodine a day is sufficient to prevent goiter. Even this small amount is unlikely to be provided by many "normal" diets. However, the addition of iodized salt to the diet would bring this up to the required amount. Iodine is particularly important in pregnancy and many vitamin supplements for pregnant women contain approximately 100 micrograms of iodine with the vitamins.

39 · Our Need for Other Minerals

THE ASHES LEFT when wood is completely burned are, in reality, the minerals once held in the cells of the tree. These minerals were necessary for its life processes. In the same way when foods are burned outside the body only ashes, or mineral matter, remain. In the body the same minerals are freed in digestion. Only the cellulose remains. When a food is analyzed for its mineral content, the chemist will first weigh the sample with great accuracy. He then places it in a porcelain dish in an oven where it can be heated to an extremely high temperature. After continued heating the food is completely burned to carbon dioxide and water, both of which escape into the air. Only white ash or minerals remain in the dish.

All natural, unrefined foods contain minerals. These minerals are necessary for the growth processes of the animal and vegetable life which we later use as food. When natural foods are burned, quantities of sodium, potassium, and chlorides are left as well as calcium, phosphorus, iron, and copper.

Sources of sodium, potassium, and chlorine

Potassium is widely found in muscle meats and vegetables. It is found in all living cells. Sodium is found in greater abundance in meat juices and the tissue fluids of plants and animals. Chlorine is a gas so it is found only in plant or animal tissues combined with another element. In this state it is described as a chloride.

Common table salt contains sodium and chlorine and is called sodium chloride.

Chloride ions are important in many functions in the body. They join with hydrogen to make up the hydrochloric acid which is secreted into the stomach to aid digestion. People who cannot make sufficient hydrochloric acid in their bodies suffer from achlorhydria (without hydrochloric acid). This can lead to many problems of malabsorption in the intestine and is often the first part of the problem in people who cannot absorb sufficient B_{12} from their diet to prevent anemia.

Most diets contain sufficient sodium, potassium, and chloride for their needs but in some areas of the world cattle may be short of sodium. It may be lacking in the soil and foliage. These animals are usually supplied with a block of sodium chloride, a salt lick, which is sufficient to supply the missing sodium.

The body's control of its minerals

Although our diet may vary daily in the amount of minerals it obtains, the quantities remaining in the body are quite constant. The kidneys either excrete the minerals not needed or retain those that the body needs.

One other important way in which the body controls its water content is through perspiration. Water leaves the surface of the body in all areas through minute pores in the skin. They are the openings of the ducts from the microscopic sweat glands. Sweat glands are distributed throughout the body. They are a basic heat regulator. As tiny amounts of watery sweat emerge from the duct onto the surface of the skin, the water evaporates, cooling the body's surface.

Some areas of the body have a great number of pores and we tend to sweat more profusely when we are exercising or working in a hot climate, or just excited or apprehensive about something. Sodium chloride is lost from the body in this way. Under normal circumstances, this works like the control system in the kidneys but in extremely hot weather we may lose too much salt and heat stroke can occur. This is usually characterized by nausea, giddiness, thirst, and extreme fatigue. Eating salt foods as well as drinking fluids helps restore the balance. Salt in water is often suggested as a remedy but remember that you must only take small amounts of salt in this way. *A quarter of a teaspoon* in a glass of water is plenty. More than this may cause vomiting and diarrhea in some people. Too much salt in the intestines will draw water from the blood and tissues into the gut. If you are working in a very hot climate and are worried about taking sufficient salt, it is best to have small amounts in food and drink throughout the day rather than taking it all at once. This can upset the balance and make matters worse.

Minerals, nerves, and muscles

The functioning of our nerves and muscles is dependent on minerals, particularly potassium and sodium. Potassium is most abundant inside the cells of the body and sodium is found outside, in the extracellular fluids. These minerals and other ions maintain an electrical "gradient," or voltage, across the cell membrane. Nerves depend on a change in this gradient to produce a current which can pass down the nerve fiber to the muscles. Proper functioning of muscles also depends on the right proportion of ions inside and outside their cells, especially potassium and calcium. A lack of calcium can cause death by stopping the heart muscles from working. Too much potassium can make the heart beat too fast.

Minerals as buffers

Many reactions occurring in the body can produce toxic and harmful substances. Strenuous exercise can cause a build-up of lactic acid in the muscles. Some foods may be very acid or alkaline. The minerals in the blood can neutralize these products by a process known as buffering. An example is the way hemoglobin in the blood changes its acidity according to whether it is carrying oxygen to the tissues or not. The change in acidity then controls the amount of carbon dioxide that can be transported back to the lungs. This constant flux between the negatively and positively charged ions in the body cells and fluids works to maintain the blood pH at the required value of 7.4. If you squeeze lemon juice into a glass of water the solution will become acid. This type of sudden change would not be tolerated in the bloodstream. It would be offset by the action of digestive juices in the gut, excretion of acid in the urine, and the removal of carbon dioxide in the lungs. All these processes are dependent on the availability of the minerals and their buffering effect.

Deficiency of sodium, potassium, and chloride

The body is very efficient at conserving minerals when they are in short supply. If the diet is short of one or more of them they will not be excreted in the urine but will be retained by the kidneys and so passed back into the circulation. Experiments with animals on low-sodium diets have shown that they lose their appetite and fail to grow. Potassium-deficient diets are difficult to prepare in experiments. Potassium is found in all plant and animal cells so constructing a potassium deficient diet is almost impossible. Particularly rich sources are molasses, nuts, and dried fruits. Chlorine-deficient diets prevent normal growth and produce a predisposition to infections in experimental animals. Such a shortage is unlikely in any normal diet.

Salt fallacies and the food faddist

The power of advertising is so great that many people, in the pursuit of health, are tempted to pay too much money for an ordinary product with a fancy name. Salt is just such a product.

Food faddists claim that vegetable salt, organic salt, or sea salt is far superior to common table salt. In fact this cannot be true. Salt is a crystal composed of sodium and chloride ions. Whether you extract it from seawater or cabbage leaves it is still going to be composed of sodium and chloride ions. Vegetable salt will probably be flavored and contain a few trace elements; sea salt may contain extra iodine and magnesium. It is often sold in large crystals; but the salt itself is the same familiar substance. If you like the flavor of the salt or the texture of the large crystals by all means choose the one you want, but do not be persuaded that there is a subtle difference in the sodium chloride you are buying.

Daily requirements

Salt is added to many foods today, and most of us add some when we are either cooking or eating a meal. It is unlikely that we shall have too little of it in normal conditions. On the contrary, our Western diet is commonly oversalted. The average American diet, with "average" use of the saltshaker, includes about 10 grams of salt daily. Most healthy adults can safely handle this amount. However, we have among us millions of people with actual or potential high blood pressure (hypertension). Most of these individuals have a very poor tolerance for salt, and their blood pressures on this average 10-gram salt diet may go from normal to high, from slightly high to dangerously high.

Many elderly people, with hearts somewhat weakened from the aging process, have difficulty in handling large amounts of salt. It causes them to retain more water in their bloodstream, forcing the heart to work harder, and in many cases, leads to "pump failure" or congestive heart failure, a condition often controllable simply by careful salt restriction.

Excess salt, as in extrasalty foods, is excreted from the body by the kidneys. The thirst we feel after eating salted peanuts or some salty fish or meat makes us replace the water that has been used by our bodies to excrete the surplus salt in the urine. Small babies do not have this ability to cope with excess salt and their foods should not be salted for the first few months of life. Some salt is added to baby foods but this is included more for the mother's taste buds than for the baby. If the mother thinks the food too bland she may add too much salt to the food.

40 · The Trace Elements

WE HAVE SEEN how some minerals, notably iron, calcium, and phosphorus, are needed in the body in small but measurable quantities. Other substances are equally important but are needed in much smaller quantities. One we have looked at is iodine. We need only about 150 micrograms of this a day—hardly an amount we could weigh on the kitchen scales even if we could buy it in its pure state.

Many other elements are important to the proper functioning of our bodies, but they occur in such small amounts that it is sometimes difficult to determine how much we need or even whether we need them in our diet regularly. Before the development of modern analytical instruments it was often difficult and time-consuming to analyze the elements in blood, bone, and tissues. One time-honored method was to record the colors, or spectra, of materials when heated to a certain temperature. Anyone at all familiar with school chemistry knows that sodium gives a yellow flame and copper a green color. Methods of analysis are more sophisticated now and most elements can be determined both quantitatively and qualitatively. The debate that remains is about how much we need of certain things, such as arsenic and lead, both of which are found in the body but are poisonous if taken in excess of a very small quantity. Tests, surveys, and long-term experiments are helping us establish the importance of certain trace elements which only a decade or two ago were banned as dangerous and unnecessary. Further research may help to establish the importance of many of the lesser-known elements. Some, like the following, have already been recognized as important in nutrition.

Magnesium

Magnesium is a mineral that is essential for life. It forms part of a substance called chlorophyll which is the green coloring matter in plants. It is therefore abundant in green leafy vegetables. Nuts, peas, and beans also contain generous amounts of magnesium. When animals are fed a diet that is low in magnesium they suffer from irritability, muscle weaknesses, and convulsions. It has been found that the role of magnesium in the body is similar to that of calcium. It forms part of the mineral of the bone and is also essential for the functioning of nerves and muscles, especially the heart. Although it is normally well supplied in the diet, certain conditions can cause a deficiency in the body. Alcoholics sometimes show a low level of magnesium in their blood. People suffering from kidney disease may fail to retain magnesium and much is lost in the urine. Other problems arise after operations on the intestines. This can upset the normal absorption of minerals; the magnesium, phosphorus, and calcium may not be well absorbed. Special treatments and injections may be necessary in this type of patient but for the normal person on a normal diet enough magnesium is supplied for the body's needs from a daily intake of fruit, vegetables, and cereals.

Magnesium is also associated with laxatives. Epsom salts (named after the famous spa waters in England) contain very large amounts of magnesium. This tends to draw water from the body into the intestinal tract and make the contents extremely fluid. This causes rapid transport through the small and large intestine, thus relieving constipation. This type of reaction would never occur from the small amount of the mineral we obtain from our food. Magnesium is also important as part of many of the enzyme systems. Without this element some of the metabolic processes cannot take place. Although it is only needed in a relatively small amount (200 milligrams a day), this is definitely an essential mineral.

Aluminum

Aluminum is found in the human body in small amounts but is not thought to be an essential trace element. Many people cook with aluminum pans and some take drugs and medicines which contain traces of aluminum. These low amounts may accumulate in the body. There is still no evidence that aluminum is either harmful or beneficial in these quantities.

Zinc

Zinc is an important mineral because it forms part of many enzyme systems in the body. It is vital for the metabolism of vitamin A, the transport of carbon dioxide to the lungs, the detoxification of alcohol in the liver, the synthesis of keratin in the skin and hair, formation of bone, and building of protein from amino acids. It is found in meats, cereals, peas, beans, lentils, and milk. Deficiencies are rare but diets that contain phytic acid tend to "bind" zinc and prevent its absorption through the gut wall in the same way that they can prevent the transport of calcium. Recent research has shown that zinc may play an important role in the control of diabetes, as much of it is located in the pancreas. In diabetes the concentration is much lower in this organ than in the nondiabetic person. Zinc has been found useful in promoting wound healing. The exact mechanism is not properly understood but it seems likely that it helps in the formation of collagen and other proteins for the new skin.

Cobalt

Cobalt is also an essential nutrient. The cobalt atom is the central structural unit of the vitamin B_{12}. It has been used to treat anemias, but this has proved unsatisfactory as very small amounts of cobalt produce toxic effects. It occurs naturally in buckwheat, figs, and many green vegetables. Normal daily intake is around 0.3 milligram and this same amount is found to be excreted each day in the urine.

Manganese

Manganese is another essential trace element for man. It is found in many foods, including cereals, legumes, and green vegetables. Tea is a particularly rich source. Some animals may suffer from a deficiency disease if they are feeding on pasture from a manganese-deficient soil. These animals, and experimental animals on a deficient diet, fail to reproduce. Their growth is stunted and they often show bone deformities. Humans are unlikely to suffer a deficiency. Manganese is extremely important in many enzyme systems in the body. It is also thought to be involved in the control of diabetes. Guinea pigs deprived of manganese as young animals develop diabetic symptoms and have an abnormal pancreas.

Chromium

Another essential mineral for humans is chromium, but it is required in such small amounts that a deficiency is unlikely to occur in most diets. It has been shown in animal experiments to play an important role in the activation of insulin and the subsequent uptake of glucose from the blood into the body cells. Recent research has been directed into investigating its use in connection with the treatment of diabetes. Some benefits have been reported in isolated cases but its true therapeutic value is hard to assess. The quantities of the mineral under consideration are so small that analysis becomes very difficult. Most people require only as little as 5 micrograms a day. It is difficult to find out exactly where this goes and what it does in the body.

Fluorine

Fluorine is found in teeth and bones and other tissues in the body. Most of the fluorine in the diet comes from fluoride in drinking water. Few foods contain much of this element except fish; tea is also a rich source. Fluorine tends to concentrate in the enamel of the teeth. A plentiful supply of fluorine during the growing period will ensure a strong enamel. Too much fluorine, however, can cause an excess to be deposited and mottling of the teeth with bands of dark and white enamel occurs. Surveys of areas which were supplied with drinking water containing no fluoride and areas with significant amounts of it were made in Grand Rapids, Michigan, and Newburgh, New York, in the 1950s. Children in the town where water contained fluoride had only half as many dental cavities as those in a nearby town where the water was fluoride free. Similar surveys proved that the correct amount of fluoride in drinking water could help to protect growing teeth from decay by forming stronger enamel. The decision to fluoridate public water supplies brought strong opposition here and in other countries. Reasons for the opposition were that fluorine can be toxic, can produce mottling of teeth, and might lead to other disturbances in the body. Also the enforcement benefits only the younger generation—it cannot improve bad teeth. Following the example of iodine which, added to table salt, can prevent goiter, it makes sense to help children develop healthy teeth by ensuring that they have the correct supplies of fluorine while their teeth are forming.

The benefits of fluoride in drinking water have prompted many companies to manufacture toothpaste and mouthwashes with additional fluorides. Theoretically this should not affect our total intake as we do not eat toothpaste but we do, involuntarily, ingest a small amount every time we clean our teeth, and children are notorious for swallowing a mouthwash instead of gargling with it. There is a very close margin between a beneficial dose and a toxic dose of fluorine and it would make better sense to accept the levels in drinking water as beneficial, and avoid additions from other things around us.

Unfortunately, fluorine has suffered the fate of many other minerals and vitamins. People believe that "if a little is good for you, more will be better." This is seldom true, nutritionally, and certainly not in the case of fluorine.

Arsenic and tin

Certain elements appear in plants and animals but do not seem to be essential for metabolic processes. In large doses arsenic can be toxic, but only when it is administered in the pure chemical state. In foods it is combined with other substances. Arsenic surplus to the body's needs is excreted in the feces. The same is true of tin. Substances that are excreted in this way are not absorbed into the bloodstream and so are unlikely to have any toxic effects.

Silver and nickel

Some minerals are found in the body in traces so small that it is very difficult to discover their role or whether they are essential in the diet. Many metals, such as tin, aluminum, silver, nickel, and silicon, are used in cooking pots, preserving cans, etc., but careful investigation has shown that the small amounts ingested are not toxic or harmful.

The question trace elements pose today is not so much "What do we need?" but rather "What are the things we need to avoid?" So many pesticides and fertilizers contaminate the food we eat, while industrial waste pollutes the air and water around us. Many of these chemicals are poisonous and it is important to monitor the environment to see that while we are worrying about our day-to-day diet we do not overlook the greater danger from external poisons.

41 · Vitamin Supplements: Do We Need Them?

IN THE LAST few chapters we have looked at all the vitamins and many of the minerals which we need in our diet. Normal daily intake varies from 1 to 2 grams of calcium to as little as a few micrograms of vitamin B_{12}, but these values do not represent a scale of importance. Each and every one of the nutrients is essential in the diet. The amount that is required for good health has been calculated after extensive surveys and tests on different communities throughout the world. The results of this work are summarized in a table of Recommended Daily Amounts (RDA), by the British Department of Health and Social Security (see *Appendix IV*).

Deficiency diseases occur when a vitamin is lacking from the diet or is available only in limited amounts. We have seen how some conditions continue to be a major problem in world health, particularly in Third World countries.

Vitamin A deficiencies can lead to xerophthalmia and blindness, and vitamin B deficiencies cause beriberi and pellagra. Initial treatment of these conditions is by administration of the missing vitamin, but continued prevention and eradication of the disease can be achieved only with nutrition education and a change in local agricultural policies. Vitamin supplements are too costly for many people to buy, and all the nutrients that are needed for health must come from the diet. This is a very important principle and one that we in the West tend to lose sight of. The list of recommended intakes is a practical table. It is not intended as a prescription or dosage chart. It shows us what we should be getting from our food in order to achieve optimum health.

Some nutrients are supplied easily by a normal diet. For instance, an orange contains a day's allowance of vitamin C, and many of us eat more than one piece of fruit in a day. We also have vegetables and salads with the main meals. In summer, with an abundance of fresh fruit and vegetables, we may take in as much as 200–300 milligrams of ascorbic acid without even realizing it. These foods contain many other useful nutrients and our general health will benefit accordingly. Unfortunately, some people believe that they can improve on this by taking vitamin pills. They imagine that a high intake of vitamin supplements will produce an even greater degree of health. To achieve this they spend money on vitamin pills and other health preparations. This is really not necessary. There are very few times of the year when we are short of fresh fruits and vegetables. We also have a constant supply of fish, meat, and dairy products and the shops are full of cereals and cereal products. All our dietary needs should come from these foods. If the diet is carefully planned there should be no trouble in aligning our actual daily intake with the desired daily intake shown in the tables.

There are circumstances when we do need help with supplements. Disease, infection, accidents, burns, and operations all put added demands on the body and can be helped with extra nutrients. Conditions such as pregnancy and breast-feeding also call for a higher intake of vitamins and minerals. These requirements are usually met by prescribed doses from the doctor or by intelligent use of vitamins purchased from the health shops or the chemist.

The word "vitamin" has been defined as a substance that the body needs but cannot make for itself in sufficient quantity. It has been shown that there are some vitamins which the body *can* make in small amounts. Niacin is an example. It is synthesized from an amino acid called tryptophan. It has also been suggested that some people are able to make a small amount of ascorbic acid. A healthy body on an adequate diet will have the correct balance of vitamins and minerals distributed among bone, blood, and tissues. A high intake of vitamin supplements will raise this level and create an unnatural condition. The body may come to depend on this new higher level rather than select what it needs from the foods we eat. We take aspirin if we have a headache but we do not take aspirin every day *in case* we have a headache. In the same way extra vitamins can certainly help special cases but, ideally, our requirements should come from the foods we eat, not from supplements.

Many people argue the case from the other side. They say that foods are so heavily adulterated with coloring and preservatives and so many nutrients are destroyed in processing that it is impossible to obtain what we need from the foods we eat. They insist that we should take every known kind of health supplement to make up for this loss. If you are living on nothing but processed foods and are not trying to balance your diet, then this may be true; but if you are following the principles laid down in this book you will be eating fresh and natural foods rich in the vitamins and minerals you need.

Many vitamin supplements on sale today are expensive. The process of extracting, distilling, or synthesizing them is costly. They must also contain some form of preservative and further expense will go on bottles, packaging, and advertising. If you buy any of the water-soluble vitamins (ascorbic acid and the B complex) and you take more than your body needs, any excess will be lost in the urine within a few hours. The body cannot store more than it requires. If your diet is rich in these vitamins, and you are taking supplements as well, then your money is wasted. The fat-soluble vitamins, A, D, E, and K will be retained in the body. A supplement of cod-liver oil in the winter can help to supply vitamin D when there is very little sunshine available to boost the body's natural store, but if you have been eating the right foods then you will have your own supply of these nutrients in the liver and seldom need to take any more.

A debate on the benefit of vitamin supplements often evokes extreme viewpoints. Some people believe in taking every known supplement as if we were living in a world where our food is totally worthless. At the other end of the scale is the immovable skeptic who will have nothing to do with "unnatural substances." The practical approach lies somewhere between these two schools. You should aim to manage without any supplements but take them if you need them. Everyone has a different life-style and you alone know what you eat and what factors may be missing from your diet. If you go to buy a vitamin supplement, ask yourself exactly why you need it and what it will do for you. Read the label on the bottle and check the contents of the tablets. These are usually expressed in milligrams or international units and/or micrograms. Compare this amount with your daily requirements and the amount you may be getting in your food. There is usually a variable dose which is suggested, for example, "one or two tablets, two or three times a day." It is your responsibility to decide what you want and don't be tempted to take more than you need. Vitamins are the fine balance to a diet, not the cornerstone. There is no short cut to good health and there is no substitute for sound nutrition.

HEALTH
FOR
THE
FAMILY

42 · Planning the Family's Health

THE KNOWLEDGE OF nutrition is of little value unless it is applied to your life and to the lives of those around you. The purpose of nutrition is to learn how to build the highest degree of health possible. Only through the constant application of nutritional findings can this be attained.

Early work on nutrition led to our understanding of essential vitamins, minerals, and amino acids in our diets. Laboratory animals were fed a diet that contained all the nutrients they needed except one. After some time, some form of deficiency disease showed. Addition of the missing element to the daily food usually effected a cure. To produce a deficiency disease deliberately in humans requires dedicated volunteers, but it has been done from time to time and has added immeasurably to our knowledge of nutrition. The difficulty of applying this knowledge is perhaps the most disheartening part of this type of work. It is a surprising fact that we are seldom ready to take advantage of all the research that has been done in the field of medicine and nutrition if it requires a little effort on our part. For instance, everyone knows that smoking may cause cancer, but thinks it will happen to other people. Year after year more money is spent on research to prove the dangers of smoking. At the same time more money is spent on increasing tobacco production and in advertising cigarettes. It is totally illogical. Nonsmokers may chide their smoking friends and point to the mistake they are making, but exactly the same thing is happening in the field of nutrition. We know which foods are good for us, which ones are not so good, and which are bad, but we do not follow the advice if it doesn't suit us. Every day we can do one of two things: we can build up our health—or we can undermine it. If you watch people eating in restaurants, cafeterias, or coffee shops you can see those who choose carefully in order to build their health and those who are eating their way to illness, overweight, and a shortened life span.

Your body requirements

Every person, regardless of age or degree of health, needs adequate amounts of liquids, vitamins, minerals, proteins, fats, and carbohydrates. Since certain foods are the best sources of various requirements, a summary of these foods will give you the basis of the day's dietary plan:

1. Half a pint (about ¼ liter) of whole milk or one pint (½ liter) of skimmed milk.
2. Wheat germ, brewer's yeast, blackstrap or raw cane molasses, whole-grain cereals, and whole-grain bread.
3. Some form of fish-liver oil if fish or liver is not a regular part of the diet.
4. Six ounces of orange or grapefruit juice or 8 ounces of tomato juice. At least one fresh salad a day and some vegetable eaten raw.
5. Use iodized salt both in cooking and on the table.
6. One serving of cheese.
7. One serving of meat, fowl, fish, eggs, or a meat substitute, such as baked beans or soya beans, whole-wheat spaghetti, noodles, or macaroni. Liver, heart, or other glandular meats should be served at least once a week. Some type of sea food or sea fish should be eaten once a week.
8. Three or more green or yellow vegetables and one serving of dark green leafy vegetables such as kale, beet greens, chard, collards, watercress, or turnip tops.
9. Three or more fruits besides the fruit juice. Colored fruits should be chosen in preference to colorless ones.
10. Vegetable oil for cooking and salad dressings.

Checking the body requirements

Now that we have the daily program outlined, let us analyze it in order to check the contents. It must stand the test; all body requirements must be met.

1. Vitamin A: fish-liver oil, colored fruits and vegetables, cheese, and egg yolk. Cream, butter, and liver.
2. Vitamin B complex: wheat germ, yeast, blackstrap molasses, whole-grain breads, and cereals.
3. Vitamin C: orange, grapefruit, and tomato juice; salads, raw vegetables, and fruits.
4. Vitamin D: fish-liver oil, herrings, pilchards, tunafish, mackerel, and sardines.
5. Vitamin E: wheat germ, green leafy vegetables, and vegetable oil.
6. Riboflavin: milk, cheese, egg, meat, and yeast extracts.
7. Pyridoxine: liver, vegetables, bran, and blackstrap molasses.
8. Niacin: whole-grain cereals, legumes, meat, and bran.
9. Vitamin K: green leafy vegetables and blackstrap molasses.
10. Calcium: milk and cheese, green leafy vegetables, nuts and legumes.
11. Phosphorus: milk, cheese, meat, fish, egg, whole-wheat cererals and legumes.
12. Iron: wheat germ, blackstrap molasses, egg yolk, red meats, cocoa, whole-grain cereals, and green vegetables.
13. Copper: egg yolk, blackstrap molasses, cocoa, liver, nuts, and bran.
14. Sodium, chlorine, and iodine: iodized salt.
15. Trace elements: many are found in blackstrap molasses, vegetables, and sea foods.
16. Unsaturated fatty acids: sunflower-seed oil, safflower-seed oil, soybean oil, and vegetable oils. Soft margarines made from these oils are also a good source.
17. Proteins: meat, fish, cheese, eggs, soya beans, and milk.
18. Carbohydrates: whole-grain cereals, whole-wheat bread, fruits, vegetables, honey, and molasses.

19. Fiber: fruit, vegetables, and whole-grain breads and cereals.
20. Liquids: milk, fruit juices, soups, and as much water as you like to drink.

This simplified method of checking is meant only to give a rough guideline. Requirements vary considerably according to age, sex, and occupation. As an example, the amount of milk taken each day will depend on the age and weight of the individual. Children need more milk than adults and, if they enjoy it, they should have a pint (½ liter) a day. Adults usually find that half a pint (¼ liter) is quite sufficient. Milk is a high-calorie food and too much can lead to overweight.

Basic daily menu

The following list will give some suggestions as to the best way to distribute the foods throughout the day.

BREAKFAST   6 ounces orange, grapefruit, or tomato juice
Piece of fruit
Wheat-germ cereal with milk
Egg, if desired
Whole-grain bread
Milk (for children), tea or coffee for adults

LUNCH   Egg (if not taken at breakfast), meat or cheese
1–3 vegetables, or a salad
Whole-grain bread and butter
Fruit
Glass of water, tea or coffee

3:30   Fruit juice, or a piece of fruit. Glass of milk for children as an alternative to fruit juice, or a cup of tea for adults

DINNER   Soup, if desired
           Meat, or meat substitute
           2 or 3 vegetables
           Salad
           Whole-grain bread and butter
           Fruit
           Cheese and nuts, if desired (and only if weight is
           not a problem)

AT BEDTIME   Herb tea, or milk with blackstrap molasses.

It must be stressed that this is only an outline to help you plan your meals. See Appendix I for menus and recipes for an average week. Numbers and ages in the family, as well as tastes, customs, and time available for preparing a meal will influence the eating pattern in all households. With these variations in mind we shall look at the various needs of the family. First, let us look at the different age groups. The model family is often depicted as two adults, Mr. and Mrs. Average, in their early thirties, with two or three school-age children. There are indeed many families like this but they don't stay that way very long and there are often variations within the household. Many have tiny babies and grandparents all under one roof. School children grow into teenagers and often there are twenty-year-olds still living at home. So the range of friends and family in need of your catering and good counsel could span from a newborn to age ninety.

The seven ages of man

The definition of the different ages of man is something which changes with each generation and never so much as in recent years with the advance of medicine, better nutrition, and hygiene, and a genuine attempt to help old people enjoy good health and useful occupations long after their retiring age. Jaques, in Shakespeare's *As You Like It*, speaks of the seven ages of man. He describes them as acts in a play: "One man in his time plays many parts,/His acts being seven ages: . . . the infant . . . the schoolboy . . . the lover . . . the soldier . . . the justice" then a lean old man, and finally a blind, toothless frail old man in his second childhood.

Some of these characters are less representative of society today than they were in Shakespeare's time, but it is not difficult to recognize the types. The lover is the moody teenager/twenty-year-old. The soldier with his "fire and energy" is in his twenties or early thirties, very much an action man, and could be an athlete, sportsman, policeman, or soldier. The justice "with fair round belly" describes, all too accurately, the middle-aged spread of the successful businessman in his forties or fifties, more affluent and less enthusiastic about exercise. The lean old man and the one in his dotage are still with us but much older now than in Shakespeare's time. The period between youth and middle age has also been expanded, particularly in the last few decades. Children reach physical and sexual maturity earlier and middle age has become a phrase used more for an attitude of mind than a sum of years. Most adult sportsmen have passed their best performance at thirty-five (with one or two exceptions such as cross-country runners, who peak at forty) but no one retiring from sport at thirty-five is likely to consider himself entering middle age. Some medical authorities place age into four simple categories: the child, the adolescent, the adult, and the aged. At a recent conference, the World Health Organization defined middle age as 46–60, elderly as 60–75, old as 75–85 and very old as over 85.

Different age groups can be defined, nutritionally speaking, by their dietary needs. The need for calories reaches a peak at eighteen years of age, continues until thirty-five, and then slowly declines. Body composition begins to change at this point and it has been noticed that there is a higher percentage of body protein to fat (protein 17 percent, fat 13 percent) in the young, whereas in the older person the reverse happens. These are the facts rather than the ideal, and if we want to continue good health through to middle age and beyond, then it is important that the diet should contain food which helps to maintain the protein balance.

The need for nutritional care makes sense when we look at the mortality statistics of the last few years. In America and Europe the highest proportion of deaths is due to heart and respiratory diseases, with intestinal disorders running a close second in England. Enteritis and other diarrheal diseases are fourth in the cause of death throughout the world. Many of these conditions are aggravated, if not induced, by overweight, and this means, quite simply, too much fat in the body which, in turn, means too much fat and sugar in the diet.

So part of our grand plan for the family must be to devise meals which build up the protein in the body and cut down on the fat. At the same time each and every member must be supplied with the right amount of energy for his or her own particular job and life-style.

The infant

Infants start out in life with a good supply of nutrients in their bodies since they store up the vitamins, minerals, fats, and proteins supplied to them from the mother before birth. For the first few months they are not, nutritionally speaking, very demanding, but they do like the food that was designed for them, namely, breast milk. There are many arguments for and against breast-feeding. Some of the arguments against it may be valid but more often they are rationalities or excuses that are nothing to do with the baby, and that is something rather different. Whenever possible babies should be breast-fed since breast milk exactly fits their requirements and in most cases supply and demand match perfectly. Many people stress the importance of the bond between mother and child that breast-feeding establishes and insist that this is the greatest benefit. Of course this union is good and important but in no way should it belittle the love a mother can give to her child when she is unable to feed it naturally. There are excellent milk formulas on the market today which can be used with confidence, but the instructions should be read carefully and the doctor or dietitian consulted if there are problems or the baby is not gaining weight. We all have likes and dislikes and the baby is no exception.

The first few weeks with a new baby, especially the first baby, can be full of surprises and difficulties and breast milk sometimes fails for a day or two. This is more common than many mothers realize. A supplementary bottle feed after a few minutes on the breast will satisfy the baby and keep your supply ticking over until you are more relaxed and rested or until your milk production has returned to normal. (Try to drink more water, fruit juices, and milk.) Then there is often the problem of whether to feed on demand or by the clock. No two babies are the same. Some sleep through the night without a murmur while others demand breakfast at 3:00 A.M. At birth babies' stomachs are very small with a capacity of 30–50 milliliters which is less than half a cup of liquid. This soon changes and by the time they are a year old the capacity is about a pint. Demand feeding may be necessary for the first few weeks but after this initial period some sort of routine is usually a good idea for all concerned. It is difficult to ignore crying babies, but provided they are not ill or losing weight they will soon learn that it is a waste of energy. The crying is more likely to upset you and the neighbors than harm the child.

One of the difficulties about breast-feeding today is that many mothers return to full-time jobs fairly soon after their baby is born, and they feel it is more sensible to get the child used to a bottle in the early weeks, but it is possible to compromise in a case like this. You can continue breast-feeds in the morning and last thing at night and leave bottle feeds for the day.

There are hidden benefits for the mother who can continue to breast-feed since extra body fat that is laid down during pregnancy is used up during the period of greatest milk production, usually around the fourth month of feeding. Between the fourth and sixth month weaning can be started with small supplements of new foods and tastes and the baby will require less breast milk. The final loss of mother's fat will occur during the last stages of weaning so that all that is left is one trim figure and one healthy thriving baby.

The high cost of some of the artificial feeds makes cow's milk an attractive and cheaper alternative for weaning. It can be used as food for the infant but is not usually recommended before six to eight months. Cow's milk contains more protein and calcium than human milk. (This is hardly surprising if you remember that it is designed as food for a growing calf with far more bone and muscle to build than a baby.) It also contains more of the electrolytes, sodium and potassium, which put a strain on the baby's kidneys. There is also less lactose (milk sugar) and less iron than are found in breast milk. To compensate for these differences it is best to add water to the cow's milk (one part water to two of milk is most usual for small babies) which will help to dilute the protein and electrolytes. The sugar can be made up by adding a very small amount of unrefined sugar, such as blackstrap molasses or dark brown sugar.

Human milk contains more vitamin A and C than cow's milk but neither are very good sources, and both are deficient in vitamin D. The newborn baby has a good supply of vitamin A and D in the liver and some iron stores. However, all of these will be used up in the first few months of life and need to be replenished. Orange juice and some form of cod-liver oil should be started as early as possible. Special preparations for this part of the diet and advice on dosage are usually available at child-care clinics. Iron supplements are not often recommended. The baby's own store and the small supply from milk and milk formulas are sufficient for the first few months of life, but as soon as weaning starts, iron-rich foods should become part of the diet. Egg yolk is a good source and also wheat germ and molasses. All these foods can be introduced into the diet in very small quantities.

One important factor to bear in mind when feeding small babies with cow's milk or formula feeds is that they may need extra liquid. Boiled water, cooled and flavored with a little fruit juice, but not sugar, can be given at any time. If the feeds have been too rich (for instance, if a formula feed has been made up with too much powder in the mixture), the baby will try to remove the extra electrolytes (sodium, potassium, etc.), by excreting more urine. This will draw more water from the body and the child will become dehydrated. Crying is sometimes put down to the child's being hungry so another rich feed is given which only aggravates the condition, whereas plain water was all that was needed. Extra feeds to "build-up baby" are harmful. Milk formulas are made to simulate mother's milk as closely as possible, but they must be reconstituted with the right amount of liquid for the child to receive the full benefit.

This is one of the biggest problems for health workers in the Third World countries where traditional breast-feeding has given way to artificial feeding because of the power and persuasion of advertising. Unfortunately, many mothers are illiterate and unable to read the instructions on the labels. They can neither sterilize the liquids and bottle nor can they afford to buy sufficient of the expensive formula. The result is that dilute mixtures in germ-laden bottles produce sick, malnourished children. The mortality rate among these babies is so high that a return to breast-feeding is imperative if there is to be an improvement in child health.

Weaning

Weaning can be started at four months, but if the baby is thriving on milk then six months is quite early enough. Cereals are the time-honored weaning foods for most babies, but fruit and vegetables are equally acceptable and provide a greater variety of nutrients. All foods should be pulped or sieved and only offered in small amounts. They may be rejected at first but if you make no fuss and reintroduce the food in a day or two's time, the baby may accept it quite happily. Meats can be introduced by the sixth month. These should be mashed and sieved like other foods at first until the child can manage very small pieces of solid food. At this age babies have only one or two teeth at best, so they cannot be expected to chew their food. Most babies enjoy cheese from quite an early age and cottage cheese is a good addition to their diet at six months. Refined sugar should be kept out of the diet for as long as possible. It can start a vicious circle because the child develops a sweet tooth. Babies do not crave sweet things if they are given good nutritious food.

The toddler

The toddler often gets less attention than is ideal. This can be due to many factors. Visits to the doctor or clinic may be less frequent and some mothers do not realize that it is important to continue with cod-liver oil, orange juice, and other supplements at this stage. It is also a time when a new baby in the family may make demands on the mother, leaving her with less chance of preparing nutritious meals for the toddler. This can lead to bad habits since it is only too easy to stop a child crying or nagging by giving him a sweet or biscuit. These tactics should be avoided at all costs. If snacks are needed small pieces of fresh fruit or some fresh fruit juice should be given. Mealtimes should be as regular and unhurried as possible and there should be salads and vegetables as a normal part of the midday meal.

This is a difficult time to stop children eating a lot of sweets since most of them go to nursery school, visit relatives, and make their own small friends. Inevitably sweets will become part of the pattern and it is useless to try to eradicate them totally from today's life-style for children. We all know that they cause harm when eaten in excess but they can be allowed in moderation without causing too much hysteria from the food reformists. What must be remembered is that they are high in calories and too much sweet stuff in a toddler's diet can be the beginning of overweight. The best time to let children have sweets is after a meal, then they will be well digested with the rest of the food.

Homemade sweets can be made quite easily and a child of three or four years often enjoys being part of such a ceremony. Honey, dried fruits, milk powder, molasses, nuts, and butter can be incorporated into simple fudge and toffee recipes. These provide nourishing foods and help to develop a taste for natural flavors rather than the many commercial products which contain artificial colors and flavorings. Candy or chocolate last thing at night should never be allowed. No child should go to bed with sugar stuck between his teeth. This is one area where you can and must be firm. If a child does eat something sweet just before bed then he must be taught to clean his teeth again.

A wider variety of foods can be introduced into the menu at this age. Every new food offers a strange taste which the child should learn to enjoy. In introducing any new food half a teaspoonful should be given at the beginning of the meal. No child, or adult, should be expected to eat large amounts of a strange food. As children grow up they become quite active, and nourishing between-meals snacks should be encouraged. Carbohydrate foods like bananas, dried fruits, and fresh fruits should be given. Whole-wheat bread, sandwiches, and homemade biscuits made with molasses and wheat germ are excellent snacks. They provide the energy the child needs, together with a good supply of vitamins and minerals.

The young teenager

From approximately thirteen years old the child experiences a rapid spurt of growth which causes the amounts of all his nutritional requirements to be greatly increased. At this time it is important to add extra calcium and protein to the diet. Cheese and milk are both good sources and should be part of the daily diet.

The need for vitamins of the B complex is increased, particularly in teenage boys who tend to eat more carbohydrate than girls. They should always be encouraged to eat unrefined cereals, grains, wheat germ, and natural sugars. Muesli (although sweet) is a useful food for teenagers, providing a good source of energy and extra vitamins. Vitamin D can be added to the diet in the winter. This should be taken as fish-liver capsules. It will help in the absorption of calcium and ensure the growth of strong bones. In planning a teenage girl's health, particular emphasis must be placed on supplying adequate iron. With the onset of puberty and menstruation there is a regular monthly loss of iron from the body. It is essential that this be replaced and body stores of this mineral replenished. This can only be achieved by eating an iron-rich diet. Blackstrap molasses is a good source and this can be added to milk drinks, yogurt, cookies, homemade cakes, and other recipes. Eggs, liver, and green leafy vegetables should also be a regular feature of the diet.

You can also add a vitamin C supplement to offset anemia. This can be given as extra oranges and citrus fruits or as a 50 milligram tablet when fresh fruit is in short supply. The acid of the vitamin C will help to make the iron in many foods easier to absorb in the small intestine. Iron in green vegetables and whole grains is ferric iron, Fe^{+++}, but you will remember that it is only as ferrous iron, Fe^{++}, that it will cross the gut barrier. Vitamin C helps bring about this change. This is why lemon juice and fruits in green salads are beneficial.

It is especially important that teenagers eat nutritious snacks. Fruits, whole-wheat cookies, and sandwiches provide a good source of energy. If the diet fulfills all nutritional requirements during these growing years, the problems of skin disorders, constipation, underweight, overweight, anemia, and tooth decay can be avoided and the teens need not be thought of as the difficult years.

The older teenager

Adolescents in their middle to late teens can swing between periods of extreme activity and energy to seemingly endless lethargy. Their eating habits often follow their moods and it is no use nagging them to eat or being shocked by the amount they eat. You must aim to supply the right sort of foods for them and trust their appetite and good sense to do the rest. This is a time when they become influenced by friends and start to eat away from home much more. If you have managed to instill a good pattern for eating habits then they will survive very well. If they are used to eating fruit for snacks and if they enjoy whole-wheat bread, milk, cheese, yogurt, green vegetables, meat, and fish then they are more likely to choose these nutritionally sound foods when they are away from home.

Adolescents will also begin to buy their own food. If they are at college or starting their first job they must learn how to choose their own diets and how to spend their money. Any guidance that you have given them in the past will be invaluable now. We are all surprisingly conservative about our food and tend to revert to the well-tried and familiar dishes even when we are in new surroundings.

Health of the adult

Adults are often the worst offenders when it comes to bad eating habits. There is a mistaken belief that when the body stops growing there is no great need to supply all the vitamins and minerals that children need. Not so. Earlier chapters have explained how the body is constantly renewing itself; even bone is not a static tissue. Cells are broken down and rebuilt throughout our lives. This gives a constant opportunity to renew and re-form good health. We all lead hectic and busy lives. Whether this involves bringing up a family, holding down an important job, training as an athlete, or studying, there is seldom as much time as we would like in each day. Unfortunately, the thought and preparation we put into our diet often gets less time than it deserves. You cannot expect to learn all you need to know about nutrition overnight, but do try to introduce the new ideas into your daily routine as you learn them.

If you are a recent convert to the idea of nutrition for health, then some cunning and a little psychology may be needed to help the rest of your family to good eating habits. The older ones will need just as much patience and tact as the baby when introduced to new ideas, tastes, and textures in meals. Don't rush it; just suggest they try whole-wheat or rye bread instead of white, and eat fresh fruit as a snack in the morning or afternoon. Try to see that the food you want them to eat is on the table or in the refrigerator. They will become familiar with it. They may eat it reluctantly to begin with but once they know how good it tastes they may choose it in preference to the less nutritious snacks next time. General improvement in health should also encourage them to follow your new ideas. In time you will find you have achieved a remarkable change in the diet and health of your family.

Health of older people

Helping old people with their meals is perhaps the most difficult problem for the nutritionist to tackle. They are often set in their ways and have fixed ideas that one thing is good for them and another bad, and they will probably refuse to accept a different theory. They often have problems with teeth and may have ill-fitting dentures or sore gums. Many suffer from fairly frequent stomach upsets, indigestion, etc. If you have old people staying with you and can afford a little extra time to prepare special soups and vegetables for them, this will help. Otherwise it may be necessary to try to add one or two things to their food without their knowing, such as a little wheat germ in porridge, or dried skimmed milk in soups. If they crave sweets try to make homemade fudge with butter and molasses. Try also to introduce as much roughage into the diet as possible. Constipation is often a complaint with elderly people. They tend to take laxatives instead of letting the intestines do the work. Whole cereals, vegetables, fresh fruit, and dried fruit can all alleviate the problem.

43 · Different Diets for Different People

WE HAVE LOOKED at all the age groups in a family but there are still a few people who do not fall into any category. These include pregnant women, vegetarians, athletes, dancers, and models; all perfectly healthy but needing something different, something extra from the food they eat.

Pregnancy

If you are pregnant, you do not need to eat for two. What you do need to do is eat well, for one! During the first few months of pregnancy you are supporting a very small being and it does not require quantities of food. It needs vitamins, minerals, and essential nutrients and it will take these from your blood supply, so your eating plan should be aimed at keeping your supplies stable rather than building some vast reserve.

It would be foolish to go short of vitamins and minerals at a time like this so you must concentrate on eating fresh fruit, vegetables, meat, fish, milk, cheese, and plenty of whole-grain cereals, brown bread, wheat germ, and blackstrap molasses. You will gain weight slowly at first. Ideally you should be only 8 pounds heavier than your normal weight by the end of the fifth month. After that you can expect a gradual increase of another 9 to 20 pounds for the last four months. Keep a careful check on weight gain. You should not put on more than this amount in a normal pregnancy and if you keep well within the limits then it is easier to regain your normal figure after the birth.

Vitamin and mineral supplements are sometimes prescribed during pregnancy. The usual ones include vitamin D for bones and teeth and vitamin B_{12}, folic acid and iron, to prevent anemia. All other vitamins and nutrients should be supplied by a sensible and well-balanced diet. Concentrate on getting your iron foods and, like the teenager, aim to eat them with extra citrus fruits or vitamin C. Extra protein can be added in small amounts during the last three months as this is the time the fetus will start to grow fast and build up body tissue. During the early months of pregnancy the body prepares for this by conserving more protein from food than normal. It appears that the body goes into a positive nitrogen balance (see page 73) and amino acids are retained in the amino-acid pool. This is nature's way of protecting both the baby and the mother. When protein is needed it is readily available for the fetus's sudden growth spurt and will not put an undue strain on the mother.

Babies are sometimes described as parasites, a term that could be said to hold some truth! In times of famine they suffer surprisingly few ill effects and are normally born healthy and only slightly underweight. They take all they need from the mother before the birth and it is she who will suffer, not the baby. However, if you eat wisely and well during pregnancy, you can do much to help the birth and your own health as well as ensuring a good supply of breast milk.

There are some other do's and don'ts which you should remember at this important time. Don't take any drugs during your pregnancy unless they have been prescribed by your physician. Many substances in the blood will cross the barrier at the placenta and enter the bloodstream of the fetus and, unfortunately, this barrier cannot protect the unborn child from some harmful substances. The thalidomide disaster which occurred a few years ago was a particularly tragic demonstration of this fact.

Another very strong prohibition is concerned with smoking. If you smoke then you must give it up for those vital nine months.

There are no ifs or buts about this. Just give it up. The smoke in the lungs produces a substance called carboxyhemoglobin in the blood and this cuts down the amount of hemoglobin available for transporting oxygen to the placenta. The air you breathe contains the oxygen your baby needs. If you smoke then you are cutting down this supply.

Ideally, also, alcohol should be cut out altogether, but the occasional glass of wine or beer is permitted if you really do feel you want it. Strong spirits, whisky, gin, etc., must be avoided. They contain a high percentage of alcohol that will put an extra strain on your liver and be of no help to the baby.

Strike a sensible attitude about rest and exercise. You need both. If you already have a family you probably get all the exercise you need so just concentrate on the rest, as and when you can get it but, if it is a first baby, try to take walks, swim, cycle, or do some gentle exercise that suits you each day. Fresh air and sunshine are also important. Think of all that vitamin D you can be storing up for your baby.

The vegetarian

Vegetarians were once rather a rare species, but with the contemporary mingling of cultures and religions, together with the scarcity and high price of meat, there is a strong swing in favor of this kind of eating. You may find that a single member of your family has decided to become vegetarian, or you may feel you want to try it yourself. Whatever the reason, remember that it is a very personal decision and not one to be either ridiculed or inflicted on others. It is perfectly simple to adjust any meal to suit all tastes so that everyone feels his or her particular needs are catered for.

The first question the new vegetarian needs to know is, "Where are the proteins?" And the answer is in cereals, vegetables, beans, milk, cheese, nuts, and even in fruits. There is little need for either a protein supplement or special, expensive foods from health stores. The golden rule for vegetarian meals is to eat as great a variety of foods as possible. They can be very small helpings of each but they should include all the different groups of foods. If you will refer to the section on proteins (page 71), you will find we cleared up the muddle about "first-class" and "second-class" protein. Vegetables were once labeled as second-class sources but this is only true if you fail to eat vegetables with other groups of foods such as cereals and beans and dairy products. There are different amino acids in the different groups, and if you mix these, you can make a perfect protein food. Wheat is short of lysine (one of the essential amino acids) but if you eat it with milk, the shortage is made good by the complementary food.

There are some vegetarians, known as vegans, who choose to avoid all animal products. These include milk, eggs, cheese, yogurt, butter, and cream as well as meat and fish. This decision cuts out a good source of protein, but it is still possible to provide adequate amounts if the beans, grains, and vegetables are well balanced at each meal. Some people call themselves vegetarians but continue to eat fish and white meat (i.e., chicken). It is difficult to rationalize this sort of diet on religious or compassionate grounds, but diet is a personal choice and if people wish to avoid what they describe as "blood" meats, their decision should be respected.

Being vegetarian in a meat-eating society can cause some social problems and this last type of semivegetarian diet may suit people who like to eat meat or fish at a dinner party or in a restaurant but remain strictly vegetarian when in their own home. There are other food restrictions and taboos which may seem odd, but remember that some of our own food choices appear strange to others. We eat cows, pigs, and sheep but not cats, dogs, and horses, and yet the cow is sacred to the Hindu and the pig is unclean to the Moslem. Similarly, horse meat is considered a perfectly acceptable food in France and cat meat and dog meat are served in many a Chinese meal. So be tolerant of others' habits and they will respect yours.

The athlete

The athlete is the highest calorie eater, but these calories must help build up protein in the body and not fat. If they take in more calories than they need, athletes have the advantage of usually burning them off without much trouble. It has been calculated that at least 2,000 calories are needed to run a marathon race and, since most runners train for long periods before this type of event, covering many miles, their daily intake could be over 4,000 calories a day and yet their bodies be lean and fit.

Some sports require more body weight than others. Skinny athletes are not caber tossers or weight lifters. Building up a body for sport evokes some surprising advice and theories but, if you find you have a budding Olympics champion in your home, apply common sense to the situation and do not be seduced away from nutritional logic. Milk is one of the best body builders with the right amount of energy and protein. Cheese and yogurt have similar properties. Whole grains, cereals, wheat germ, brewer's yeast, molasses, and all natural B vitamin foods are the best source of unrefined carbohydrate. The sportsman needs plenty of these nutrients for instant energy and to build up body tissues. There is a lot of protein in cereals and legumes as well as meat, fish, and eggs so there is no need to spend too much money on steak. There is a tradition that red meat builds strength. Steak is a good food but not the only one for the job, proved by the fact that some sportsmen are lifelong vegetarians. Athletes, particularly runners, can take more fat in their diet than most of us because they burn it up for energy, but it should be supplied as unsaturated fat whenever possible. This means using vegetable oils in cooking and having soft margarine on the table rather than butter for most occasions. Butter is a good food but it contains a high proportion of saturated fats so it should be kept for special dishes rather than used at every meal.

Recent research into diet and strenuous exercise has shown that a diet rich in carbohydrate for two days before a major event can help runners competing over a long distance. The carbohydrate, such as bread, rice, or spaghetti, helps to keep the stores of glycogen in the liver high so that these can supply the maximum instant energy needed during the race. This makes nutritional sense but the correct amount of extra carbohydrate that should be taken, both by the athlete and for the distance covered, is something that can be discovered only by the individual runner.

Vitamins are a much-debated subject in a diet for strength and energy. If the diet is right then there will be little need for supplements. The only difference will be in the amount of thiamine and other B vitamins. You will remember that the requirements for these are gauged on the amount of calories consumed, but normal food allowance tables do not cover the eventuality of anyone needing 5,000 calories per day! The B complex, however, takes part in many of the enzymic processes involved in carbohydrate metabolism, so a supplement here would be useful. Any excess will be excreted in the urine. Vitamin C is essential for building many of the body tissues, including tendons and ligaments. With plenty of fruit and vegetables in the diet the intake should be adequate but an additional 50–100 milligrams a day would ensure a topping up of supplies if necessary. Vitamin D is one vitamin the sportsman should not have to worry about. All the fresh air and sunshine on the skin should provide plenty for the needs of the body and the store in the liver.

Athletes should remember that they are likely to lose much more water through their lungs and skin than less active people and that with this water loss they will lose salt, particularly in hot climates. This can lead to exhaustion. The loss can be replaced by salt tablets, but a natural inclination to eat salty foods is often sufficient to restore the balance.

The dancer

Dancers and gymnasts are similar to athletes in many ways. Both groups need a lot of energy from their diet and yet must have strong muscles without extra fat. The main difference is that

Table 9.

Some "Empty" Calorie Foods and Alternatives

Calorie Values	Food with Less Useful Calories		Alternative Snack or Meal with Extra Nutrients (MORE NUTRITIOUS)	
100	Thick soup	White flour* (thickening)	Clear soup and a small egg salad	Vitamin C and protein
300	Meat pie	White flour* (pastry)	Two slices of lean meat, potato and a green vegetable	Vitamin B, C, and protein
300	Cheese sandwich with 2 slices of white bread	White flour* (bread)	Danish "open" sandwich made with 1 slice whole-wheat bread with extra cheese and salad	Vitamin B, C, and protein
150	Fruit yogurt	Sugar (sweetening)	Plain yogurt and 1 medium-sized apple	Vitamin C and minerals
140	Canned peaches	Sugar (syrup)	One peach, apple, and pear	Vitamin C and minerals
120	Small slice of sponge cake	Sugar and white flour*	Three oatmeal and molasses crisp cookies	Vitamin B and iron

*Flour contains protein and carbohydrate and should never be thought of as an "empty" calorie food, like sugar, but too much dancers and gymnasts cannot be indifferent to their size so the energy must be supplied in a form which will not result in extra weight. The sheer mechanics of their art require a trim body and the right combination of mass and movement. One of the first laws of physics that a school child learns is that Force is dependent on Mass and Acceleration ($F = ma$). If you apply this theory to someone flying through the air, then you can realize how important the correct mass is to ensure a safe landing. Many dancers know their bodies better than the rest of us and they know at what weight they perform best. They must keep their diet not only within the calories needed both for energy and weight, but the food they eat must also supply all the essential nutrients, vitamins, and minerals.

This means throwing out any empty calories. (*See Table 9.*) Every mouthful must earn its keep. Empty calories or junk foods need close scrutiny when energy is required. Active people can burn up far more sugar and flour than a sedentary worker, but it makes sense to supply that fuel with a few hidden extras. Whole-wheat flour and molasses provide a similar amount of protein and energy as white flour and white sugar but add extra iron and vitamins. The standby for energy and protein is again milk, cheese, and yogurt while all the other principles of a sound diet still apply, but the main difference between the dancer's and athlete's diet is in the total calorie intake and fat content. Little research has been done on diets for dancers but it seems reasonable to assume that they need at least 1,000 calories more than average requirements but rather less than athletes. Dancing uses up 300 calories an hour and most dancers practice for many hours during the day besides giving a performance in the evening.

The model

Fashion changes as frequently as the season but in recent years the ideal model's shape has been fairly constant, that is, very thin. Thin people can wear classic or bizarre clothes with equal chic and this is what the fashion designers want. So how do models achieve this envious size? First, they are young. Of all the so-called glamour jobs, modeling is perhaps one of the briefest and most demanding of careers. You must be young and beautiful. Being young does not guarantee an hourglass figure, of course. Some girls may go into modeling because they have a good figure but they must maintain and keep it if they are to be a success. Statistics on the average model girl's diet are not something likely to hit the scientific journals, but the life-style and general eating pattern of models observed would tend to suggest that most of them undereat or at least never eat the average calorie allowance for their age and height. To eat slightly less than the normal amount of food is not harmful if the food eaten provides the necessary vitamins and minerals. (Experiments have shown that rats fed this way live longer than a control group fed a higher calorie diet.) In order to pack the essential elements for good nutrition into smaller meals, enormous care must be taken to make every mouthful matter.

Actresses and models, unlike dancers and sportsmen, do not burn up energy in continuous exercise. Many of them are aware of the importance of exercise and attend dance classes or health clubs where they can keep fit and supple and also prevent any fat building up in the body. Professions such as these often have built-in anxiety factors that generate nervous excitement and increase the metabolic rate in the body, causing food to burn faster and the body to remain thin.

However, a thin body is not all that a model needs for her career. Her complexion must be flawless, her eyes bright, and her hair, nails, and skin all equally healthy-looking for the scrutiny of close-up photography. This is where the importance of nutritious food comes in and all the rules must be applied. Wheat germ, molasses, yeast, and whole-grain cereals will provide the B vitamins and help combat tiredness. Green vegetables and orange and red-colored fruits—oranges, apricots, and plums—together with liver and eggs, will supply the vitamin A necessary to combat tired eyes and to resist bacterial infections on skin surfaces. Citrus fruits of some kind should be eaten each day to give the vitamin C needed. A vitamin D supplement in the winter when a lot of time is taken up indoors and there is less chance to build up supplies with sunlight on the skin can help maintain the liver store. Alcohol, highly sweetened soft drinks, coffee, and tea should all be minimized or cut right out of the diet since many of these drinks contain stimulants which dilute the blood vessels. Mineral water or tap water should be drunk as alternatives when possible and fresh fruit juices are good for adding extra vitamins to the diet.

Most women find that they tend to put on weight just before menstruation. This can cause some discomfort and clothes can feel tight. For most of us this is a nuisance but for the model with a 22-inch waist and clothes to fit it, this is disastrous. Medical opinion favors cutting down on salt and fluids during the second half of the menstrual cycle to avoid this tension. The kidneys come under the influence of a different set of hormones during this latter part of the cycle and antidiuretic hormone (ADH) is released from the pituitary which encourages the kidney to reabsorb water. If there is less salt and water about at this time then this reabsorption, which is a perfectly natural procedure, will not bring such a bloated feeling.

Anorexia nervosa

While we are on the subject of staying thin, it is worth mentioning anorexia nervosa. Some mothers worry if their daughters lose weight too rapidly in their late teens, thinking they must be ill, but although anorexia nervosa (a refusal to eat) is a real and serious illness, it is, fortunately, fairly rare. It is usually linked with an emotional disturbance and most commonly seen in girls rather than boys. It is often a signal that a girl does not want to grow up. It has sometimes been described as the Peter Pan syndrome. At puberty girls start to menstruate and develop breasts and some girls feel that they are not ready for the changes in their relationship to the opposite sex, their work responsibilities, and the prospect of leaving home. One way they can show they are not ready to face reality is to become like a child again. By refusing food their bodies become smaller, normal menstruation stops and, at the same time, they become the center of attention in the home and can command time and energy from one or both of their parents. If this state continues untreated then the metabolic balance in the body is disturbed and learning to eat normally again is genuinely difficult.

This illness is unlikely to befall a healthy youngster keen to become a sylphlike model. The training and the job itself are very hard work and a would-be model with talent and looks is unlikely to have the time or inclination to become an anorectic patient.

44 · Family Health Problems

MANY PEOPLE put too much faith in medicines and pills. When they visit the doctor for ailments such as headaches, stomach-aches, or sore throats, they expect to come away with a prescription for a cure. They believe that this will solve the problem, but they seldom stop to think what caused the ailment in the first place.

Students who suffer from nerves, headaches, acne, or anemia expect to find relief by taking aspirin, vitamin pills, a tonic, or all three. They seldom look back over their eating habits for the last term and set those against their problems.

The achievement of full health through planned nutrition is a building process which requires a correct balance of vitamins, minerals, fats, carbohydrates, and protein in the diet. You can never hope to cure a particular illness by increasing the amount of one of these. The approach must be one of readjustment. The diet must be balanced with attention given to all the nutrients rather than an emphasis on one of them.

Let us suppose you suffer from excessive fatigue. You know that something is interfering with your energy production. Perhaps there is not enough hemoglobin to carry sufficient oxygen to the tissues to allow food to be burned normally; perhaps the heart is not working efficiently so that too little oxygen is reaching the tissues; perhaps you are short of carbohydrate so the glycogen stores have been used up and your blood sugar is too low; perhaps a lack of thiamine is causing incomplete oxidation of sugar; or an iodine deficiency has slowed down your metabolism, or lack of B vitamins is interfering with your production of energy. In short, your fatigue could be due to any or all of these things. In the same way, other minor ailments, such as susceptibility to infection, tooth decay, mild anemia, and many more, could be due to so many different factors. It is no good pinning your faith on one aspect of diet (though it is surprising how many people do). Every requirement is needed for the normal function of every cell in the body and all these nutrients must be adequately supplied.

Learn to enjoy your food

All that is required for building good health is available from food, but it can happen that a dislike of certain foods can upset the balance in a diet. Many children refuse to eat vegetables. A strong dislike of milk can cut out a good supply of protein and calcium in the diet. Many people refuse even to try a food, insisting they are allergic to it or that it may make them sick. Many of these beliefs date back to single incidents in childhood and are seldom relevant years later.

It is important to try to enjoy the taste of new foods (and some of the long-neglected old ones). You can undoubtedly remember the numerous foods you disliked the first time you tasted them but now enjoy. If any food can build health, set out to cultivate a taste for it. Expect to dislike it at first. Take only a small portion the first time you eat it but be prepared to try another small helping at the next opportunity. A little psychology, such as telling yourself how good the food is for you and how you are going to benefit from it, will help in the battle. You will be surprised at how soon you find you are actually enjoying the food and eating more and more of it.

Some foods are bitter or sour or have an unusual texture, but it is only because we are conditioned not to like them that we reject them. Many children like sucking lemons, and often enjoy yogurt and molasses the first time they taste them. We sometimes associate sourness with food going bad, and bitterness with medicine.

If we can forget these ideas we can reapproach some of the foods we should eat with a greater chance of success.

Packed lunches

Many people who take a packed lunch to work or school complain that it is monotonous. Those who have to pack it complain that they don't know what to put in it. The following foods are suggested:

1. Milk or a hot milk drink or cream soup in a Thermos.
2. Raw carrots; other vegetables such as celery, radishes, green pepper, cucumbers, tomatoes, kohlrabi, and raw turnips if desired.
3. A large cube of cheese or a carton of cottage cheese.
4. Dried apricots.
5. Fresh fruits.
6. A variety of dried fruits.
7. Nuts, especially peanuts.
8. Liverwurst or liver sausage.
9. Boiled egg.

The first four items should be included in every lunch each day. Those who wish to avoid bread, because of calories, may choose other foods listed and still have a pleasant lunch. Bread used in sandwiches should be 100 percent whole-wheat. Try black Russian bread for a change, or Swedish rye and pumpernickel. Lettuce or some green salad with mayonnaise and butter (if weight control is not a problem) should be added to the sandwiches. Fillings may be made of almost any food valuable to health, such as meats, fresh green peppers, liverwurst or liver sausage, chopped egg and celery, tuna fish, bacon, tomato, avocado, bananas, and peanut butter.

The aim is to build health and prevent disease, so there is no place in the lunchbox for cakes, pies, jellies, preserves, and sweet cookies. Homemade biscuits and small cakes which contain wheat germ, molasses, raisins, nuts, and skimmed milk are the best type of treat and are valuable in any lunch. Try to supply substitutes for sweets in the form of dried fruits and nuts.

School lunches vary enormously in quality from school to school. Some are good and imaginative, but, unfortunately, they often become a bone of contention among parents, children, and the school authorities. Vegetables are often overcooked or kept hot for too long so that there is a considerable loss of vitamin C in potatoes and other vegetables. Desserts usually contain a high percentage of carbohydrates and refined sugars and supply little more than a plateful of calories. It can be argued that lack of funds and trained staff aggravate the problem but a little thought and planning could produce a nutritious meal on the same budget.

Doctors are becoming aware of what this type of school meal can do to a child's health. Tooth decay, anemia, constant colds, and infection are all too frequent among school children. Many children leave home without breakfast and may not have a large meal with their family in the evening. The school lunch is their main meal of the day. It should therefore provide at least a third of the daily requirements in protein, vitamins, and minerals. The blame for inadequate nutrition should not be laid at the door of school meals alone. Many children have strong dislikes for certain foods. They also eat far too many sweet foods and snacks between meals and so have no appetite for the main meal.

Education in nutrition both at home and school should start at an early age. If children dislike school lunches or tend to eat too many snack foods then a lunchbox of the kind described can help them to develop a taste for the right kinds of food. It may cost as much as the school lunch but in terms of real profit from good health it is well worth the effort.

Minor health problems

Skin

Acne has long been the plague of the teenager. Many cases vanish as the child grows up, but the intervening years can bring a great deal of embarrassment and misery. With a positive approach to diet and skin cleanliness it is possible to avoid acne altogether. Major factors in any skin complaint often include lack of vitamin A, which is vital for the formation of epithelial layers of the skin and protection against infection. Vitamin C is important in the healing and building of connective tissues while B vitamins can help to improve circulation. Acne can often be improved with fresh air and exercise. Fresh fruits and vegetables should be used to satisfy the appetite rather than refined starchy foods, sugar, and sweets. Again it is a question of attending to all aspects of the diet rather than to one single factor. Doctors may prescribe lotions or a special soap to prevent the spread of infection, but it is the cause of the original attack which is the concern of the nutritionist. Until that is put right, the cure can only be temporary.

Preventing tooth decay

Many school children have serious dental decay before they are halfway through their school years. Much of the damage has been attributed to the constant eating of sugar and carbohydrate foods that are fermented in the mouth by bacteria. Acid is produced and this can dissolve the tooth enamel if it is in contact with it for a long time. In a healthy mouth any acid is neutralized by the saliva, but bacteria also form plaque, which adheres to the surface of the teeth. This allows a build-up of bacteria and any acid they produce is held close to the tooth enamel. This will soon produce cavities, so common in children who constantly eat sweets or candy.

Once the enamel barrier is broken, bacteria can invade the dentine of the tooth and produce decay. Time and again it has been shown by surveys that the greatest number of dental caries occurs in children who are allowed to eat sweets whenever they want them. When sweets are withdrawn and fresh fruit substituted for snacks there follows a low incidence of dental trouble. Education both at home and at school is important if children are to understand the dangers of damaging their teeth with sugary foods. They should also be taught to select the foods which contain the vitamins and minerals that build healthy teeth. Vitamin D and calcium together with ascorbic acid should be a regular part of their diet.

Eyestrain

Eyestrain from long hours of study increases your need for vitamin A. The daily consumption of apricots, carrots, and other colored fruits and vegetables, with a daily supplement of fish-liver oil or capsules, should provide for your needs in this respect. The B vitamins are important in all aspects of nervous and mental performance so these should be well supplied as an aid to clear thinking.

Students who have to study long hours do not often get a great deal of exercise. If they eat less than usual then they may be losing some vital nutrients, and if they eat too much they may put on weight. Some thought about diet is important at a time like this. Health should not be undermined by long hours of study. The student who disregards his health during study is less likely to perform well at examinations.

Dietary plan during infections

When you have a bad cold or another infectious disease you should stay at home. Many people say they can't afford the time but it is often better to take one or two days off work at the start of a cold than to struggle on and then have to take two weeks off later. Unless your physician has prescribed a special diet, the best remedy is to have plenty of fresh fruit juice to drink during the day. If you feel hungry, have light meals of meat, fish, fruit, or vegetables. Try to eat the vitamin-rich foods, particularly those that are rich in vitamins A and C.

Do not go out among people when you have a cold or any other infectious disease. It may seem of little importance to you, especially if you don't feel very ill, but some infections can cause a great deal of harm to old people. Your slight head cold could end up as bronchitis or pneumonia if it is passed on to someone who is prone to chest complaints.

Other problems

A doctor should be consulted about problems of a more serious nature. Many of the conditions mentioned here, such as mild anemia, fatigue, acne, etc., can usually be overcome by adherence to a good dietary routine provided that all the nutrients required are well absorbed. The important fact to bear in mind is that no one body requirement can solve your problem but that every need of the body must be met day after day, year in year out. This may sound too formidable a task but if you think of all the benefits in terms of food health then it is well worthwhile.

Your responsibility to others

We owe it both to ourselves and to others to be in the best of health at all times. This is the only way we can help other people as well as enjoy our work and leisure time every day. Obviously this is a very optimistic approach to the subject and it is unlikely that any of us, with the best will in the world, can achieve positive health for the rest of our lives without a bit of backsliding from time to time, but if you make health through nutrition a really positive goal then you have something to aim for each day.

Some of the best teaching is done by demonstration and example. If you can prove that good nutrition does build good health you may well persuade those around you to follow suit. No one would be foolhardy enough to lay the blame of all ill health at the door of faulty nutrition, but more and more research today is proving the importance of a healthy diet in avoiding many common ailments. If health can be achieved in this simple, enjoyable way, then we owe it to ourselves to follow it.

45 · Slightly Different Health Problems

THERE ARE SOME conditions which are slightly different from our last group of minor health problems. They usually require some medical attention—with diet playing a major part in the treatment. These illnesses include diabetes, obesity, hyperlipidemia or heart disease, gall bladder trouble, intestinal and celiac diseases.

We shall look at some of the terms used in these diet plans and see how they tie in with our understanding of nutrition. A little time spent clarifying the difficulties at the beginning of a new regime will often remove questions and speed up the benefits.

Diabetes

Diabetes is a strange disease. It can strike the young, old, fat, thin, phlegmatic, or nervous without any apparent cause, or much warning. It is sometimes described as the sugar disease and indeed it is a fault in glucose metabolism which causes all the problems. The disease starts in the pancreas. In a healthy person, this gland has a twofold function. First, it excretes digestive enzymes into the duodenum to aid in the digestion of amino acids, sugars, and fats. And second, it contains special cells which discharge the hormone insulin into the bloodstream to control the sugar level and aid in the absorption of glucose into the body tissues. These cells are found in an area of the pancreas called the islet of Langerhans. In the diabetic patient, these special beta-cells have ceased to work or can produce only a very small amount of the hormone.

If there is insufficient insulin in the body then sugar levels become too high in the blood after a meal. The glucose cannot be used by the tissues and will spill over into the urine. In healthy people excess sugar in the diet is met with increased production of insulin, glucose is taken up by muscle and fat cells, and the blood sugar soon resumes normal levels. However, in diabetes the lack of insulin means that even a small amount of sugar in the diet can cause problems. Fluid is lost from the body in removing the glucose from the blood via the urine, and this leaves the patient exhausted with the loss of energy and thirsty with the loss of fluid. Extreme tiredness and thirst are often the first signs that lead to the diagnosis of diabetes.

Fortunately, this problem can be corrected today as insulin can be supplied by injection, or drugs may be prescribed which can stimulate lazy beta cells and aid the absorption of glucose into the tissues. Children and teenagers developing diabetes are usually dependent on insulin injections to control their blood sugar, but older people of forty-plus develop a milder form, maturity-onset diabetes, which can often be alleviated with the use of oral drugs. Current medical theory is that juvenile diabetes, in which the pancreas totally ceases to manufacture insulin, may actually stem from a hereditary susceptibility of the beta-cells to certain viral infections. The infections can specifically destroy the cells which manufacture insulin, causing lifelong insulin dependence, that is, the need for insulin injections to prevent fatal acidosis and diabetic coma. Maturity-onset diabetes, on the other hand, is also hereditary, but is rarely associated with total loss of insulin. Almost every case is associated with some degree of obesity. Millions of individuals with a genetic potential for this form of diabetes could forestall or prevent its onset by holding close to "lean body weight" and practicing regular vigorous exercise.

In the section on carbohydrates (Chapter 8), we spoke of hidden sugar foods. These are the ones that the diabetic must watch for and limit in his diet. Most diet sheets list the carbohydrate value of common foods in grams, for example, a slice of bread weighing 20 grams will contain 10 grams of carbohydrate. The diabetic is allowed varying amounts of carbohydrate each day according to his dose of insulin or medication. This is usually between 150 and 200 grams per day but the correct amount is decided by the doctor.

It is important to distribute this allowance evenly between three main meals and three small snacks each day so that 30–40 grams of carbohydrate can be eaten in a main meal and 10–20 grams at a midmorning snack. The first approach to this new way of eating is to find out which foods are high in carbohydrate content and must be restricted, and which foods contain none, thus allowing them to be eaten in larger servings. One illuminating fact about the diabetic diet is its similarity to the sort of eating pattern we. are aiming for in this book. Empty calories are forbidden and the useful vitamins and mineral foods, such as green leafy vegetables, meat, fish, eggs, and cheese, are an important part of the diet.

If you find that you have to cater for a diabetic in the household, there is no need to make special meals, but if you do make desserts, cakes, and puddings, use only whole-wheat flour and artificial sweeteners. According to the amount of flour and fruit in the recipe, an average portion of cake or pie contains around 15–20 grams of carbohydrate. Servings of potatoes should be small while servings of green vegetables and salads should be large and substantial. Soups and gravies that use flour for thickening are not wise foods for a diabetic regime, but salads with dressings of oil and vinegar, clear soups, meat extracts, yogurt, herbs, nuts, and seeds can all be incorporated into sauces and flavorings as an accompaniment to the meal.

It is sensible to get a list of the carbohydrate values of foods and then weigh a few portions in your own home, for example, a spoonful of potato, a slice of bread, or an oatmeal cookie. In this way you can check to see if your idea of an average serving is the same as that on the list. Protein foods such as meats, eggs, cheese, and fish are virtually free of carbohydrate and should become an important part of the diet. If there is no weight problem, a little extra fat in the diet can often help make meals more satisfying.

Cereals contain approximately 20 grams of carbohydrate an ounce. Try to eat whole-wheat bread rather than white as this will provide extra fiber, vitamins, and minerals. Soya flour is a useful addition to home baking as it has only half the carbohydrate value of plain flour.

Sometimes theories are put forward that a certain mineral or vitamin is beneficial to a diabetic. There is not sufficient evidence to show that this is true except in isolated cases. Research is showing, however, that the roughage and fiber from unrefined foods help to control the rate that glucose is absorbed from the intestines, thus making for a slower absorption and allowing the body more time to cope with sugar in the bloodstream after a meal. This suggests that raw fruit and vegetables should become a regular feature of the diet.

In the U.S.A. diabetic "exchanges" recommend definite amounts of fat and protein as well as carbohydrate, thus encouraging the patient to select a balanced diet. In the U.K. the exchange system is based on the value of 10 grams of carbohydrate, thus allowing the exchange of, say, a piece of bread for a serving of potatoes or an apple for an ice cream. *(See Table 10 and note on page 291)*. These methods work well provided they are properly understood and there is a serious intention of making the system work. The conscientious diabetic can enjoy a truly healthy diet; in fact, it is a diet which could be followed to good advantage by all of us.

Obesity

To be told you are obese often seems an insult even though there is no hard and fast definition of the word. Being 10 percent overweight (i.e., weighing 155 pounds instead of 140 pounds) is "obese" by some standards but most people would view 30 or 40 pounds as nearer to the danger level. Whatever the limit, overweight is a bad thing. No one dies of being overweight but many people die of the conditions it produces. Heart, liver, kidneys, pancreas, circulation, limbs, joints, eyesight, and hearing are all states and conditions which can be adversely affected. So how do you go about losing weight?

Table 10.

Diabetic Exchange of 10 Grams of Carbohydrate Foods

Food	ounces	grams	carbohydrate
Apple	4	112	10
Grapes	2	56	10
Orange	4	112	10
Nuts	8	224	10
Carrots	8	224	10
Boiled rice	1	28	10
Canned peas	2	56	10
Potatoes	2	56	10
Bread	⅔	18	10
Breakfast cereal	½	14	10
Biscuits	½	14	10
Milk	⅓ pint	157 ml	10
Yogurt	6	168	10
Ice Cream	2	56	10

First, get on the scales and record your weight and then measure waist, chest, and hips. Write the measurements down and then make a list of everything you eat each day for a week. Check this against a calorie counter or food tables and find out how many calories you are eating. If it is well over 2,000 calories a day you are eating too much. Take another look at the list and find out where the danger areas are. Do you eat too much fat or sugar, or do you just eat too much too often? Decide whether you are prepared for a slow gentle attack on the problem or whether you want sudden drastic action. Consuming 1,500 calories a day produces a gradual weight loss in most people, whereas 1,000 calories a day shows a more dramatic drop.

Now list the things you know you must eat for your health's sake: the vegetables, meat, fish, fruit, and whole grains. Find out how many calories they will total in a normal day. If the total is too high then you must go back over the plan and make the meals a bit smaller. Make another chart to record your weight. Put the pounds on one side of the page and days of the month along the bottom. Arm yourself with some colored stars and put the first one where your weight and the date coincide. Pencil in the weight you would like to be and then see how long you take to get there. Don't weigh yourself too often. Every other day is quite often enough, or make it once a week if you prefer, but don't cheat and do try to wear roughly the same clothes (or none!) and weigh yourself at the same time of the day. (See Figure 6.)

A well-balanced slimming diet is good both for weight loss and for health. It should contain all the vitamins, minerals, and protein of a normal diet with a cutback in fat and carbohydrate. If you have only a few pounds to lose then wheat germ is the best food to supply your B vitamins. If reducing must be done more seriously, powdered brewer's yeast stirred into water or juice offers fewer calories and more vitamins. Frequent, small meals are absolutely essential. Skimmed milk, tomato juice, raw carrots, celery, or small amounts of fresh fruits should be eaten midmorning and midafternoon. Only lean meats should be used. Cottage cheese is much lower in calories than other cheeses. Eggs can be prepared in any way except fried. Fat should be kept to an absolute minimum. Most diets suggest as little as ½–1 ounce per day. This constitutes a one-inch cube of butter or just over a tablespoon of oil, 100 calories.

Perhaps the easiest of all ways to slim is to become a raw-food faddist. Raw foods are digested less completely because of their high cellulose content. They have a harder texture and stay in the stomach longer. They prevent hunger pangs better than cooked foods. It is almost impossible to eat sufficient celery, radishes, greens, onions, tomatoes, raw carrots, turnips, and similar vege-

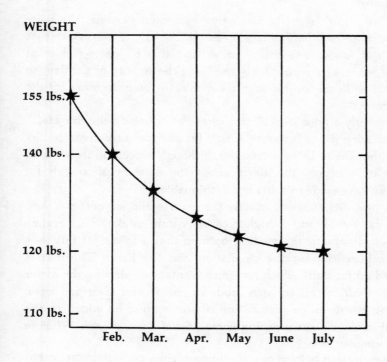

Figure 6

Weight Loss on 1,500 Calories

WEIGHT

tables to gain weight. They are the best slimming foods you can have. Check with the list in Chapter 8 to see that you are choosing the low-carbohydrate ones, e.g., 3, 5, and 10 percent vegetables.

Fruits do contain more sugar than vegetables and should be limited to about 100–200 calories per day. This would mean having two oranges and an apple, or one banana and one pear. The amount of fruit in your diet is also governed by how much weight you want to lose and how quickly. It would be a mistake to cut it out altogether as most fruits provide a good addition of natural sugar to the diet.

Soft drinks and carbonated sodas are dangerous on a diet. Most of them contribute more than 100 calories per glass. Some of the popular brands make calorie-free drinks and these can be used in the diet, but they do not contribute any useful nutrients or vitamins.

If you don't want to work out your own personal slimming plan, there are many different ones in books and magazines that you can follow. Most of them explain that to lose weight you must eat less than your body needs for the activity of the day, so that it will draw on fat supplies within the body to make up the energy.

Recently a great deal of work has been done on the role of fat in reducing diets. Formerly a high fat and low carbohydrate diet was thought to be beneficial but, although successful in terms of weight reduction, the alarm about the dangers of a high fat intake have made this diet less fashionable.

A new diet suggests exactly the reverse and advocates a very low fat intake and a higher carbohydrate intake. This regime falls in line with the medical opinion that a lower fat intake is more beneficial for the circulation and the heart. The diet is based on fat units which has the advantage of alerting the dieter to the hidden fats in such foods as cheese and meat and eggs. These are nutritious foods but all foods must be added to the total in the weight-watching game. *(See also note on page 291 about slimming diet units.)*

Exercise can help in any slimming regime provided you do not work up such an appetite that you eat too much at the next meal. Exercise is good for you and should be a regular part of everyone's life.

Special diets

There are times when you may be told to follow a diet for your health. There are certain conditions which need both medication and dietary control. These are most often concerned with heart and circulatory problems, gall bladder and liver complaints, and malfunctioning of the adrenal glands.

Diagnosis of various diseases includes physical tests, i.e., heart-beat, blood pressure and weight, and chemical tests which are used to analyze blood and urine samples. From these tests doctors can pinpoint the cause of the trouble. Too much fat and cholesterol in the blood often means that there is too much fat and cholesterol in the diet and the obvious way to correct this is to alter the diet. Sometimes the kidneys fail to regulate the salt content of the body. Too much salt in the body can cause fluid retention and an increase in blood volume and extra work for the heart. Cutting back on salty foods can help alleviate this type of problem. The liver and gall bladder secrete bile to help in the digestion of fats in the intestines. If they are diseased in any way they may need a rest while they recover and the obvious way to help this is to cut back the amount of fat in your meals. Attention to the diet is often as important as the medication in prescribing for these conditions. Most diet sheets are rather short and to the point with a list of do's and don'ts. It is often easier to stick to a diet if we can understand the reasoning behind the rules.

Low-salt diets

These diets usually fall into two categories according to the severity of the complaint. There are low-salt diets and salt-free diets. Low salt means that you should cook and eat without salt. No salt in the kitchen and no salt on the table. Foods which normally contain salt such as bread, butter, cakes, cheese, meat, and fish are allowed in small quantities. Salt-free diets are stricter. Everything must be avoided that has salt in it. You must say no to bacon, ham, canned fish and meats and salt butter, bread, cookies. Read the labels carefully on any cans or packets of processed and preserved foods that you intend to have with your meal. They may contain more salt that you realize. Also remember that its chemical name is sodium chloride. Salt-free diets are hard to follow and are usually prescribed for a short time only. Healthy kidneys can keep a salt balance in the body whether you eat a few grains or a tablespoon of salt in the course of one day, so if something has gone wrong with this regulatory control then it makes sense to lighten the load during the recovery period. Aldosterone, a hormone secreted by the adrenal glands, influences the amount of salt excreted or retained by the body. Some medical drugs are aimed at correcting its secretion and this, in turn, helps the kidneys back to normal functioning.

Low-fat diets

Low-fat diets are usually aimed at reducing the fat and cholesterol content of the blood. They go under the title of diets for hyperlipidemia, which means too much fat in the blood, or they may be prescribed to alleviate liver and gall bladder complaints.

You will probably be given a diet sheet which suggests different meals with a minimum fat content for each day. This can seem dull at first so try to introduce new tastes and dressings in place of the mayonnaises and sauces you are no longer allowed. There are plenty of low-fat foods on the market today. Many are designed for dieters but provided they do not contain fats and oil they will be fine for you. Buy a book on low-cholesterol cooking. Many people follow this type of diet today out of choice rather than for medical reasons. Avoid the meats which contain a lot of cholesterol. These are "organ meats" and include the liver, pancreas (sweetbreads), and kidneys. These are not for you. Go for white fish, chicken, and lean meats but don't have large helpings. All meat contains fat. You can eat plenty of fruits and vegetables so go to town on these.

Recent research into the best diet for lowering the blood cholesterol has favored high-fiber foods. These lower blood cholesterol both in animals and humans, so this is another good reason for stepping up the fruit and vegetables and sticking to whole-wheat bread and whole-grain products. These are your best sources of natural fiber.

The association of a high level of cholesterol in the blood and heart disease is under constant review. Medical research has shown that the fatty deposits in the arteries which narrow the passage for normal blood flow are formed from blood lipids including cholesterol. Current research has also shown us that the cholesterol we measure in the blood is not one substance, but an aggregate of several types of cholesterol, each with very different characteristics. With relation to coronary heart disease, there is a "bad" cholesterol, called LDL (low density lipoprotein) and a "good" cholesterol, called HDL (high density lipoprotein). It is now thought that LDL is "bad" because it causes changes in the lining of coronary and cerebral arteries, making them more susceptible to atherosclerosis, a dangerous form of narrowing. Excessive LDL levels may often be prevented by avoiding large amounts of animal fats, such as beef, pork, and dairy products rich in butter fat. It is now believed that HDL is "good" because large amounts of it in the blood may actually help prevent the development of atherosclerosis.

Cholesterol is a natural product of the body. It is synthesized in the liver and used to make bile acids, so we need a small amount. Cutting back fat in the diet from a high figure (45 percent of total energy) to a lower figure (about 30 percent) makes sense when viewed against statistics of the last thirty years that link the increase of heart disease with the increase in fat and sugar consumption. There are a number of specialist diets which are more in the domain of the dietitian than a health book, but a brief understanding of these can help if you have to entertain someone who is following such a regime.

Gluten-free diets

Gluten-free diets are for people who have an allergy to one of the proteins found in all-wheat products. This protein is called gluten, found in the grains wheat, rye, oats, and barley, and may cause inflammation of the mucosal wall of the small intestine so that the normal digestion and absorption that is carried on there is upset. This allergy has only recently been properly understood and it has been the cause of many cases of celiac disease. However, the protein can be removed from flour and many products are made today with gluten-free flour. These are more expensive than ordinary bread, cakes, etc., but can provide a wider choice of food for the celiac sufferer. If you have a friend visiting who follows this type of diet, then buy a bag of gluten-free flour and use it in soups, stews, and general cooking. It will help your guest and do no harm to the rest of the family.

Other products such as gluten-free breakfast cereals and cookies can be purchased from most health stores. Some individuals who suffer from multiple sclerosis (MS) have reported improved conditions after following a gluten-free diet. Large-scale tests have not been made to verify this, but it seems that the gluten-free food may help the general health of the intestinal walls and villi and thus allow greater absorption of trace elements and other vital nutrients into the bloodstream. It is the availability of these nutrients which is most likely to improve the condition of MS rather than the property of the flour.

Fad diets, fasting, etc.

New diets are as constant as the flowers in spring and few of them last as long. There are crash diets, cleansing diets, 10-day wonder diets, fasts, and minifasts. Be wary of these. They are usually unbalanced and do nothing except upset your finely tuned metabolic rate. Some diets concentrate on a single food such as rice or bananas and can be both boring and dangerous. Fasting also has its advocates. The dedicated ones will tell you that they are giving their stomach a rest or cleansing the system. The stomach was not designed to rest (our heart and lungs do not stop to rest so why should the stomach need to?) and as for cleansing the system, if you eat the right food your body will do its own spring-cleaning without any extra help. If, however, you have some stomach upset and cannot face food, then obviously there is little pleasure in trying to eat anything, but you should drink plenty of water and take fresh fruit juices or milk if you feel like it until your appetite returns. Be guided by how you feel. Many people do not "tune in" to the demands of their body either in health or disease. Unfortunately, we are too easily influenced by mealtimes, friends, and family. You are in charge of your body. Look after it.

NOTE: Some slimming diets are based on carbohydrate units. These units represent 5 grams of carbohydrate and should not be confused with the diabetic carbohydrate "portion" or "exchange" mentioned on pages 282–3, which is 10 grams of carbohydrate. A small slice of bread containing 10 grams of carbohydrate would count as 2 carbohydrate units in a slimming diet but as one carbohydrate "portion" in a diabetic diet.

46 · Preparing Food
to Retain Maximum Value

THE HOME-COOKING methods used today are largely those which have been handed down from generation to generation and date back to the time when the science of nutrition was unknown. As a result it is probably true that in the majority of homes about half the money spent on food is wasted. The nutrients in many foods are either destroyed or thrown away before the food reaches the table. If health is to be built from the food we grow and buy, scientific methods must be used in the handling and preparation.

Effect of room temperature

Many vitamins are destroyed by oxidation. This is a chemical combination between the oxygen in the air and the food we eat and it is accelerated by heat: more vitamins are destroyed at room temperature than when the food is refrigerated. Some oxidations occur in the presence of oxygen and an enzyme. Ascorbic acid is destroyed when exposed to an enzyme found in plant tissues.

Enzyme reactions can be slowed down by cooling and freezing and the enzymes themselves are destroyed on boiling. In order to save the vitamin C content it is necessary to store foods in cool conditions and to keep them in airtight containers. The skins of apples, oranges, and potatoes and so on certainly protect the food from the air, but some of the vitamin is lost after a long period of storage. Leafy vegetables left wilting and uncovered at room temperature will soon lose more than half their vitamin C content. All fresh foods should be carefully covered to minimize contact with air. When frozen foods are taken from the refrigerator and allowed to thaw, the destruction of vitamins is rapidly resumed. For this reason, no food should be allowed to stand for a long time in the kitchen before cooking and salads should be prepared immediately before serving.

Effect of soaking

Any nutrient that dissolves in water will quickly pass from the food to the water during soaking and cooking. Sugar, vitamins B and C, and some minerals dissolve readily in water. Much of the natural sugar in fruits and vegetables will be lost if they are left soaking or are boiled for too long. Quickly cooked vegetables, prepared in minimal amounts of water, baked or fried, taste much sweeter than the conventional boiled type served with many meals.

Foods should be washed quickly but thoroughly. They should never be soaked unless they are predried, such as lentils and soya beans. If foods are peeled before they are needed they should be placed in a plastic container and stored in the refrigerator away from the light. If salad vegetables need to be crisped, they can be sprinkled with water and kept in a plastic bag in the refrigerator for half an hour but on no account should they be left soaking in a bowl of water.

Beware of recipes which recommend soaking. These are often traditional methods of cooking and many come from a time when meat or fish was highly salted as a form of preservation. Soaking was then necessary to remove the salt. Fresh meats should not be soaked, as most of us know. The goodness of meat juices in the cooking liquid can be used in soups and gravies. The amount of water used in soaking foods such as dried fruits, lentils, and beans should only be as much as the food will absorb—with a little extra for cooking. This is usually about three-quarters of the volume of the food itself. The quantity of vitamins, minerals, and sugars lost by soaking depends on the time of soaking and the amount of the food exposed to the water.

Effect of peeling, slicing, grating, and chopping

All these processes can cause a great loss in food value. When foods are chopped into small pieces, a far larger area is exposed to the air and to the water. This means that more nutrients can be destroyed by oxidation and dissolved into the water. If the food has been well chilled before preparation, less damage is done, as oxidation and enzyme action will be slowed down. If the food is chopped and prepared quickly and either cooked or eaten immediately then losses will be kept to a minimum. Peeling should be avoided whenever possible. Many minerals and vitamins are concentrated in the tissues close to the skin and these will be completely wasted when fruit and vegetables are peeled, and the peelings discarded. Fruits and vegetables that can be baked or boiled in their skins contain more goodness and flavor than those that are peeled and then boiled.

Effect of cooking

The losses during cooking are largely due to three causes: continued enzyme action, the destruction of vitamins by heat, and the passing of nutrients into the cooking water. To destroy the enzymes quickly foods should be put straight into boiling water or placed in a hot oven. Your method of heating food will determine whether the ascorbic acid is retained or not. For example, if cabbage is placed straight into boiling water and cooked for five to ten minutes, only about 25 percent of the vitamin is lost. If it is put into cold or lukewarm water and then brought to the boil, 75 percent of the ascorbic acid will be lost. This high loss, due to bad cooking methods, can make an enormous difference to the amount of vitamin in the diet. Green vegetables are normally a good source of vitamins but bad cooking can leave them with almost no nutritional value.

Carotene and vitamin A are not so badly affected by cooking as the water-soluble vitamins. They are relatively stable in temperatures up to 212°F. (boiling point) but they are destroyed by higher temperatures that may be reached if they are cooked in oil.

Some vitamins are stable in acid but not alkaline solutions. When baking soda is added to the water to preserve the green color in vegetables it produces an alkaline solution. This may make the vegetables look more attractive on the table but unfortunately it will destroy the ascorbic acid and many of the B vitamins as well.

By far the greatest loss occurs by cooking foods in water and then discarding the liquid. The extent of this loss can be as much as 20–40 percent of thiamine and 30–40 percent of vitamin C from peas boiled for only five minutes. Many vegetables are cooked for longer than this and the losses will increase as the cooking time increases. It is obvious that the best method of cooking is not only one in which the food is cooked in the shortest possible time but also one which requires the least amount of water.

There is no objection to boiling, as long as the food is heated as rapidly as possible and all the cooking liquid is used. Many people feel that if only a little cooking water is left it is not worth saving. Actually the less liquid that is left, the richer it is in nutrients.

Effect of overcooking

Overcooking is a habit that is so destructive to health that it must be avoided at all costs. Long heating means that more nutrients are lost. Foods which have been chopped and crushed before cooking will make this loss even greater. The cell walls of the plant and animal tissues are broken down and even more nutrients can escape into the cooking water. Bad cooking ruins the flavor of good foods and it is also a waste in terms of money and health. People tend to dislike the taste of badly cooked vegetables to the point where they will give up eating them altogether.

Effect of salting

As a rule, salt should be added to foods after cooking rather than during the cooking. Many foods, including meat and beans, become tougher and less palatable if they are cooked in salt. Green vegetables and potatoes benefit from the addition of salt but if a lot is added to the cooking water the vegetable stock is too salty to use in other dishes. Salt added to soups, gravies, and other foods just before serving is generally quite sufficient for most tastes.

Effect of soda

Soda, as we have seen, causes rapid destruction of ascorbic acid. It should not be used in the preparation of vegetables. It is also harmful to many of the B vitamins in baking procedures. Baking powder should be used in very small amounts to minimize this loss and, whenever possible, yeast should be used as a rising agent for breakfast breads, doughnuts, and rolls.

Rules for saving food value

The rules for retaining the maximum amount of nutritive value may be summarized as follows:

1. Purchase only the amount of fresh food that you need or that can be kept in the refrigerator.
2. Wash all foods quickly.
3. Avoid peeling wherever possible.

4. Slice, grate, chop, and crush foods when they are thoroughly chilled. Prepare just before serving or cooking.
5. If foods must be prepared in advance, cover them from air and store in the refrigerator.
6. To freshen salads, sprinkle with water and keep in a plastic bag.
7. Soak no food unless it is dried (lentils, beans, etc.), and then use only the amount of water that it will absorb.
8. Reheat canned foods in their own juice.
9. Never add baking soda to vegetables.
10. Baking yeast is preferable to baking powder.
11. If foods are to be boiled, put them into water which is already boiling.
12. Use the shortest cooking methods and heat foods rapidly.
13. Start cooking frozen vegetables before they have thawed.
14. Serve frozen fruits immediately after thawing if they are to be eaten without cooking.
15. Never overcook.
16. Do not throw away liquid in which foods have been cooked. Keep in a covered jar in the refrigerator and use for gravies, sauces, and soups.

The intelligent person has two standards for the foods he or she chooses. First, they must build health and, second, they must taste delicious. Scientific methods of handling, preparing, and cooking foods bring out and preserve their natural flavors.

47 · Food Processing and Food Labeling

ANY DISCUSSION about shopping, cooking, or catering for the family is bound to include some reference to the use or abuse of canned, preserved, and convenience foods. Before we condemn them all out of hand in our campaign for the new healthy eating, let us take a closer look at their supposed evils and decide if the arguments are valid.

In every kitchen cupboard there are some preserved foods. These include coffee, tea, salt, sugar, herbs, preserves, rice, flour, raisins, and other stores that have been subjected to some process to keep them free from bacteria and spoilage. Foods can be dried, pickled, canned, frozen, packaged, freeze-dried, powdered, liquidized, dehydrated; the methods are many. But what does preserving do to the food in terms of essential nutrients, and how important, nutritionally, are these items in our diet?

We can answer the first question by seeing how the fat, carbohydrate, and protein content of foods survive. Pure fat, which we buy, includes oils, butter, lard, and margarine, but fats are also found in canned fish and meat and many other foods. Fats deteriorate on exposure to air and high temperatures due to oxidation, so similar slight changes will occur both in the preparation of meat for canning and in the preparation of fresh meat for the table. The deterioration of fats found in processed food is unlikely to be much greater than those that will occur in fresh foods.

Preservatives are used in cooking oils to prevent oxidation. The byproducts of oxidation affect the taste, color, and vitamin content of fats. If this deterioration can be avoided by the addition of harmless preservatives there seems little reason to condemn the procedure. Proteins are found in meat, cereals, legumes, and dairy products. How are their qualities affected by preservation and processing? Heating or freezing seldom alters the nutritional content of protein although it may alter the structure of the molecule. However, since protein is composed of amino acid units, provided these are unchanged the biological value of the protein will not decrease. Some processing actually enhances their value. For example, beans normally require a long cooking time in the home whereas canned beans need only a few minutes' heating and are much easier to digest. Vitamins will be lost in the juice that the product has been canned in but if this does not contain too much salt it can be added to soups or sauces, to good effect.

If we look at the method by which many vegetables such as spinach, peas, carrots, mushrooms, and string beans are canned and frozen they compare favorably with home cooking and may sometimes even surpass it! Canneries are situated near to the fields and crops in many instances and the produce is picked and canned within the day. Cooking or blanching, that is, subjecting the food to high temperatures for a short time, takes place only an hour or two after picking, whereas shop vegetables may not be prepared and eaten until two or three days later. The blanching of vegetables also helps to inactivate the enzymes which destroy the vitamins in pickled vegetables. An analysis of frozen vegetables against home-cooked "fresh" vegetables can often show a higher percentage of vitamin C in the frozen produce. Carbohydrates are seldom destroyed during heating and processing. Heating can help to break down some carbohydrates to simple sugars, thus assisting in their digestion and absorption.

In any meals that we plan we will want to provide a good balance of proteins, fats, and carbohydrates together with the vitamins and minerals that are needed each day. If processed and preserved food forms part of the meal, then it should contain, as nearly as possible, the essential nutrients you would expect from fresh produce. Meat is a good source of protein and provides a useful amount of iron in the diet. Canned meat retains all its protein but loses some iron when not packed in its own juice or gravy. Dairy products, such as cheese and butter, are not subjected to rigorous processing and therefore retain most of their nutrient value with only a slight loss of vitamin A and thiamine.

Milk is always pasteurized before it is sold to the public. This process involves heating the milk to a temperature that will kill any undesirable bacteria and also destroy any enzymes which alter the flavor of the milk. There will be a slight loss of vitamins, particularly thiamine and vitamin C, but the benefits outweigh the losses. Milk is an excellent food and contains a valuable source of calcium and protein in the diet. Some food faddists advocate unpasteurized milk as a super health food. If you live on a farm, and know that the cows are clean and healthy, unpasteurized milk will give you a fraction more protein and vitamins, but most of us do not live on farms and unpasteurized milk would be in no fit state to drink by the time it reached the towns. Dried milks are also a good source of additional protein and calcium in any diet, but skimmed milks have had their fat content removed and are not suitable for babies or invalids relying on the total food value of milk.

Rice, wheat, oats, and barley can be stored for long periods without nutritional loss provided they are kept dry. Plain flour keeps better than whole-wheat flour because the germ of the wheat has been removed. This part of the grain contains a high percentage of fat and, if it is not extracted in the milling, it is liable to go rancid and "spoil" the flour. A bag of white flour will keep longer in your store cupboard but you should aim to use the whole-wheat flour for your everyday baking. Many minerals and vitamins are lost from the whole grain in the milling processes though these are often replaced. Most bread is enriched with added thiamine, niacin, and calcium and iron.

In trying to assess the food value of processed foods it is often more pertinent to consider the additives rather than the losses. Many canned fruits contain a great deal of sugar, much more than would be found in fresh fruit. Canned vegetables contain extra salt, sugar, and coloring, as well as preservatives. Many meats are canned with added cereals, salt, and sugar. You should always look carefully at the labels on canned and packaged foods. The laws governing food labeling vary from country to country, but in the United States and England recent legislation has insisted that ingredients should be listed in order of quantity rather than attractiveness. For example, a food cannot be considered a useful source of meat if the first three ingredients on the list are flour, fat, and water. This type of information is useful, but it can bring some problems both to the manufacturer and the purchaser. Products such as bouillon cubes and meat extracts, for example, come in such small packages that there is no room for all the contents to be printed. Added to this is the fact that many of the items are listed in terms and units that are unfamiliar to the housewife. However, any attempt to safeguard our food is to be recommended and it is up to us to become familiar with the wording and presentation of processed foods so that we can evaluate their place in our diet.

There is often some confusion about the term "food enrichment" and "food fortification." Food enrichment is the term used when certain foods have been brought up to a specific nutritional value. This means that vitamins and minerals have been added to replace the ones that were lost, for example, vitamin C is added to canned orange juice, B vitamins are added to processed cereals, and vitamins A and D are added to margarine to make it the nutritional equivalent of butter. Food fortification means that the food contains more nutrients and vitamins than those found in the original item. Baby foods and cereal preparations are often fortified with iron, calcium, and B vitamins. Another group which falls into this category are some of the preparations sold in health-food shops and chemists. Health stores contain many excellent foods such as grains, nuts, herbs, honey, molasses, etc., but they are subject to the demands of fashion and must supply some popular brands of slimming foods, nighttime beverages, health tonics, and other nine-day wonders. A closer look at the labels on these packets will show you that though they may be fortified with a wide variety of vitamins and minerals they contain only a minuscule quantity of these supplements, and certainly no more than you would obtain in a well-planned diet. Since the product is often expensive, think carefully before you buy it. It is often more profitable, in nutritional terms, to spend your money on the nuts, honey, and grains at the other end of the store.

Many canned and processed foods contain coloring to restore the loss sustained in blanching and cooking. This is almost obligatory by public demand since people expect their peas to be green and their raspberries to be red. Most coloring matter has been subjected to rigorous toxicity tests before use by the food industry, but laws do vary from country to country and some imported foods contain coloring, flavoring, and preservatives which are, theoretically, "illegal." There is a curious mixture of lethargy and neurosis on the subject of food additives. Some form of universal legislation, though difficult, would be one way of adjusting the balance and ensuring common standards of food safety throughout the world.

48 · Buying Health on a Limited Budget

Health related to knowledge not income

THOUGH YOU MAY have the money to buy the food you like, this does not always ensure an adequate and healthy diet, as studies have shown. They have also shown that, after nutritional instruction, from ten to twenty times more nutritionally sound foods are bought with the same money. Even though a person may not have enough money to buy the particular food suggested in the basic dietary plan, other foods offering the same nutrients may be substituted and a well-balanced menu maintained. The trained, adaptable person can purchase a diet far superior to that obtained by an untrained person on an unlimited budget.

Substitutions due to limited income

Substitutions are often difficult and may require the development of new tastes and ideas, but they are by no means impossible. For example, if citrus fruits are too expensive, ascorbic acid must be obtained from other fruits and vegetables. If the budget, the season, or the locality makes fresh fruit unobtainable, raw cabbage and raw carrots should be eaten. These can be made into a vitamin-rich salad and will supply many of the same nutrients found in oranges and apples.

Powdered skimmed milk can be used to provide a good source of calcium in families where fresh milk may take up too much of the budget. Calcium can also be obtained from such vegetables as kale, mustard, greens, and turnip tops. Other valuable sources are dishes such as pickled pigs' feet or spareribs, where the bones are soaked in vinegar, dissolving the calcium. A careful study of the food tables at the end of the book will help to show how each important nutrient can be supplied at a cost to fit every pocket. Everyday foods can be just as nutritious as luxury ones.

Dietary improvements without increased cost

Small improvements in buying, meal planning, and preparation of foods lead to tremendous increases in supplying nutritional requirements without any increase in cost. For example, if a medium-sized potato is peeled in the usual manner, and the peel thrown away, about 20 percent of that potato is lost. If potatoes are eaten nearly every day for a year the amount of potato with all its vitamins and minerals that would be wasted by a family of four would be over 100 pounds.

Obviously a family on a limited budget should learn to enjoy raw unpeeled fruits and vegetables as often as possible. The peel of a baked potato is delicious. Potatoes should be boiled in their skins before mashing. They can also be sliced with skins on for frying and putting in casseroles. If you computed the amount of waste in one year of peeling carrots, parsnips, turnips, apples, pears, and other fruits and vegetables, the losses of nutrients, vitamins, and minerals would astound you.

Apart from waste, many products of high nutrient value cost the same or even less than those of a low value. The fashion for health foods has put up the price of whole-grain breads and brown rice but foods such as wheat germ and black molasses are still reasonably priced. Vitamin-rich yellow and green vegetables cost no more than the white varieties. There are many other ways of improving a diet without increasing the cost. And for many people the aim of building health within the family can become an exciting challenge rather than a daily chore.

Budgeting for health

Many guidelines have been suggested on how to divide up the family's food budget. Before the sharp increase in the price of meat and dairy products, it was suggested that the budget should be shared equally among five groups of foods. These were set out as:

one-fifth for milk, cheese, and butter or margarine
one-fifth for meat, fish, and eggs
one-fifth for bread, cererals, and grains
one-fifth for fruits and vegetables
one-fifth for dried legumes and other items

Today it is unlikely that the appetites or budgets of many families would be satisfied by this sort of division. Most of the money is spent on cereals, fruit, vegetables, eggs and cheese. The amount spent on meat varies according to the income of the family but meatless meals are quite common in affluent societies today. The untrained housewife seldom buys food for health reasons. She is more likely to be tempted by taste, price, and advertising. Unfortunately, the real price of poorly chosen food is paid later with ill health and dentists' and doctors' bills. By looking at these groups of foods in turn we can see how important they are in terms of food values and subsequent health.

Milk, cheese, and butter or margarine

If skimmed milk is used as the sole source of milk more butter or margarine should be used in the diet to ensure adequate supplies of vitamins A and D. Margarine is cheaper than butter but is fortified with vitamins and contains the same calories. Cheese is a good food and is relatively cheap compared with other protein foods such as fish and meat. It also provides a good source of calcium.

Meat, fish, and eggs

Fish and eggs are usually the best buy from the economic point of view but any money spent on meat should be allocated wisely. Chops and roasts are very expensive and not necessarily the most nutritious cuts. Liver, kidneys, brain, heart, and sweetbreads contain far more vitamins and nutrients and are usually a lot cheaper than muscle meats. Cheaper types of liver can be fried or stewed with vegetables. They can be eaten hot or sliced and made into liverwurst or pâté to have cold with salads. Kidneys can be fried or used in a stew or steak and kidney pie. Heart is delicious stuffed with sage or vegetable dressing. Brains can be cooked and served with scrambled eggs or browned with onions and served with a tomato sauce.

All these meats make delicious meat loaves. Brain and liver should be passed through a mincing machine after cooking in stock or milk and the juice should be added to the loaf. Meats impart a special flavor to all meals. If the budget is very limited then cheaper protein foods can be added to complement the meat. The following suggestions are made:

1. Meat, fish, or fowl prepared with noodles
2. Meat with beans as in chili con carne, pork and beans
3. Bacon and soya beans
4. Meat with brown rice
5. Meat and rice patties
6. Peppers stuffed with meat
7. Meat rolled in cabbage leaves and cooked in tomato sauce
8. Meat balls with spaghetti
9. Meat loaves with soybean flour, chopped vegetables, parsnips, turnips, etc.
10. Ham hocks and split peas

The ingenious cook can improvise many other dishes to save money and also contribute more nutritive value than meat alone.

Fish should always be part of the menu when possible. Cheaper types may have more bone or an unfamiliar flavor but they are just as nutritious as the very expensive Dover sole.

Eggs are an excellent food. They can be used as the center of a meal or can be incorporated into side dishes to give extra flavor and protein.

Bread, cereals, and grains

More grains and cereals are eaten when a family menu is limited by income. In some parts of the world cereals form as much as 70 percent of the diet. Cereals contain a good amount of protein as well as vitamins and minerals so that, if whole-wheat grains are eaten, a high percentage of cereal in the diet is not such a bad thing, but it is important to buy unrefined grains and flours. Brown rice, whole-wheat flour, noodles, and spaghetti are a good addition to any meal. Wheat germ should be eaten every day. Homemade bread is a bonus for any family. When baking bread (it is little extra work to make some rolls, biscuits, etc.), powdered milk, molasses, and wheat germ can be added to the mixture to make it especially nutritious. It is surprising how quickly this type of food is accepted in most families.

Fruits and vegetables

Some housewives fail to realize the importance of fruits and vegetables and they spend only a small part of the budget on them. Lack of these items in any diet is one of the major steps toward illness and disease. Remember to buy in season. There are times in the year when some fruits are too expensive for the average household. However, when in season, they can be bought plentifully and cheaply. Prices in shops should be watched carefully. Seasons for some fruits like strawberries are short so you should be ready to change the menu as the prices change.

Dried legumes

This group comprises the lentils, beans, dried peas, and others. They should be soaked before cooking. Soya beans are an excellent source of protein and should be added to recipes whenever possible. The choice of green and yellow fruit or vegetables and the addition of soya beans to meals will help provide all the vitamin A and protein needed.

Miscellaneous items

Anyone who is new to shopping for a family may fall into the trap of spending money on items that contain little or no food value. Sweets, pastries, soft drinks, pickles, syrups, and refined sugars are always tempting to the untrained eye but in fact are more harmful than useful on any budget. Before any money is spent the shopper should ask, "Can this food build health?" When the answer is no the money should be spent on some other worthwhile food. Some of the money for miscellaneous items should go on iodized salt, blackstrap molasses, vegetable oils, and foods not covered in the other sections. Treats should be nuts, dried fruits, sunflower and sesame seeds, and extra portions of fresh fruit.

Avoiding waste

Buying health means not only wise spending of the family allowance on food but also economical use of the food itself. Parts of vegetables that are normally thrown away, such as stalks, outer leaves of cabbages, peelings of carrots and root vegetables, can all be used to make delicious vegetable stock. Meat bones can be added for flavor and nutriment. Soups can be made from this type of stock by adding tomatoes, noodles, herbs, or meat.

Buying in quantity

When foods keep well and storage space is available, they should be bought in large quantities. This is always the cheapest way to buy. If money and space are in short supply it is often possible to share bulk purchases with a friend so that you both benefit.

Not a matter of money

Gardening for health can be fun but it is also hard work. Cultivating new tastes and ideas about food also demands certain strength of character. Shopping for the best prices can be tiring and time-consuming. Yet all these things are worthwhile when weighed against the choice between illness and good health. An adequate diet is not just a matter of money. It is a matter of planning, intelligence, and hard work. But the effort is not wasted. Good health is worth striving for.

49 · Vitality Through Planned Nutrition

THE ACHIEVEMENT of vitality and health is not an end in itself. It is merely a passport to clear thinking, judgment, and energy. It gives you freedom to become aware of your gifts and talents and to use them to the best of your ability. Health is a bonus. When you feel good life is good, but when you are ill your energy is diverted by pain or worry and life becomes a constant battle against fatigue.

Relationship of adequate nutrition to mental health

Many studies have shown that a close correlation exists between adequate nutrition and mental health. This can range from the inattentive school child to the adult who may suffer from depression and apathy. Surveys among schoolchildren show a marked difference in performance between those who have had an adequate lunch and those who have had little or none. This difference has been illustrated both in industrialized and Third World countries. Many children are labeled lazy or stupid who have the potential to be good students. The trouble can often be traced to poor health due to faulty nutrition.

Relationship of adequate nutrition to moral health

People may question the idea that nutrition and moral character are interrelated and yet, if we consider the matter logically, it is quite justified. People with a strong moral character are those who show a concern and responsibility for those around them. If you are worrying about your own aches and pains it is unlikely that there will be much energy left over for anybody else. If you can build up all the attributes of good health you will have energy to spare and will want to help others as well as enjoy your own life.

Studies have been made on the behavior of isolated communities living on their own natural, unrefined diet. The types of crime and outbursts so prevalent in our society today are almost nonexistent among these primitive peoples. Their energy goes toward maintaining and improving their own small society. Fighting or vandalism is not a natural mode of behavior. Fighting between nations will always bring its own kind of violence, but to find this same violence within a single society is a sign of sickness. *Mens sana in corpore sano* (a healthy mind in a healthy body) is a principle we seem to have lost sight of today. A healthy mind is born of more than simple nutrition, but a healthy body relies on much of what we have covered in this book.

Recognizing health

The average person often fails to recognize full health. He considers himself well when in reality this is far from the truth. The person who is unaware of the indications that his health is below par will take no steps to correct them. As a result minor abnormalities and ailments may lead to more serious illnesses.

These subtle deviations from health should receive our immediate attention.

It is no doubt true to say that every ill person has been well at some stage of his life. Had he recognized the deviations from health and corrected them when they arose then more serious illness might have been prevented in the majority of cases.

There are simple signs that we can watch for each day. These include weight, digestion, and elimination. Weight should be constant, digestion untroubled, and elimination regular. These sound simple but they are important factors in the pursuit of health. If you take regular exercise, such as swimming, cycling, or running, you will notice if you are unfit. A distance will seem long and tiring where previously it was enjoyably short. Checks on diet, sleep, and weight may be required. If your skin looks dry or your complexion is far from perfect, count up your vitamins. You could be short of vitamin A or C or both. Problems with teeth and bones must be dealt with on a long-term plan. You cannot alter bone deformation or bad teeth but you can prevent them from getting worse. Remember the importance of vitamin D and calcium in your diet. Do not make the mistake of neglecting them because your body has stopped growing.

A good supply of vitamins in all the foods you eat will help immeasurably with muscle tone and posture. Good posture inevitably leads to the proper use of your body whether you are sitting, standing, or walking. Tension, tiredness, and bad posture can lead to bone and joint deformities, bad circulation, headaches, and many other problems. If you sit and stand badly your body will get used to this habit; it will become "normal" and be even harder to correct.

The years to come

Most people are preoccupied with age. The young wish they were older and the old want to turn the clock back. No one can quite define the moment of change, the perfect age; for some people the best is yet to come. Whether you look old at forty or young at eighty is largely up to you. If you are prepared to work toward good health you can stay young beyond your years and the future can be full of promise at any age. Interests and opportunities can change at any time in life but to make good use of them we need to be ready for them. Unfortunately, illness is often given as a reason for missed opportunities.

Even the best-laid plans for nutrition and good health can go wrong without a little forethought. There are always a few problems ahead and it is worth taking an honest look at some of these. As you grow older it becomes increasingly difficult to maintain your health without some personal discipline. Each year you will be likely to take less exercise. This may be due to your work, life-style, or family commitments. Whatever the cause, if you cannot find time to take regular exercise you must guard against overweight. This will mean that you must cut down on the amount of calories you eat each day.

Most women consume 2,000–2,200 calories and men 2,700–3,000 calories each day. Women should try to cut back to 1,500 and men to 1,800 calories if weight is gained. There is no need to go short of vitamins and minerals on this lower intake of calories. If you eat plenty of vegetables, meat, and fish and cut back on the fats and refined carbohydrate foods you can enjoy a good nutritious diet and keep your weight from creeping up year after year.

This type of diet is a good exercise in following the basic principles of nutrition. To maintain an adequate intake of all the food you need while cutting back on calories means that all the empty calories, such as refined sugars and flours, can have no part in the diet. Every mouthful of food should be important and nutritious. Some people who have no need to slim follow this type of diet for a week or two every few months simply to benefit from the feeling of renewed energy that it gives them.

Nutrition has grown from obscurity to become a science in its own right during the last fifty years. It is important that we use this knowledge wisely. It is a science that we must apply. Many innovations of this century make life easier and more comfortable for us. Transport, entertainment, and technology make few demands on us. They do the work. Nutrition can give us health but it does make one important demand. We must use this new knowledge to choose and eat the right foods and to reject the wrong ones. Is this so very difficult? Absolutely not. Surely in the next few decades we can lift the mediocre health of many nations to one where real health, not sickness, is the order of the day.

You may ask, how can you help in this master plan? It is you, the individual, who is important. If you think of the people you admire, both in past history and in the present day, it is their own individual influence on the people around them that changed history and ideas. We cannot all claim a place in history in the way that famous men and women through the ages have done, but we can claim a part in the development of the nation's health. We can be among the first to show that nutrition really works. It is this demonstration and example which matters. There is no need to shout it from the rooftops, just get on and do it. Sooner or later people will notice. They will begin to wonder why you get fewer colds in the winter and have more energy to accomplish worthwhile projects. One day they will come and ask you how you do it. Tell them!

Following any religion, philosophy, or discipline is always hard work. After the first flush of enthusiasm has worn off it is hard to remember why you joined the group in the first place. The same thing will happen with nutrition. There is a constant temptation to break the rules and change them to our liking. Nobody can claim to eat perfectly day after day but at least we can try to do so. It is better to set the sights too high than too low. Nutrition is an enormous challenge to all of us. The basic raw materials for good health are all around us. It is up to us to use them.

Appendixes

I

One Week's Menus with a Selection of Recipes
from *Let's Cook It Right*

II

Weights and Measures

III

Food Tables

IV

Recommended Daily Amounts

One Week's Menus with a Selection of Recipes from *Let's Cook It Right*

These menus include the recommended daily quota of glucose and other natural sugars (Chapter 8), fats (Chapter 9), protein (Chapters 10–11), vitamin A (Chapters 15–18), thiamine (Chapter 19), riboflavin (Chapter 20), niacin (Chapter 21), B complex vitamins (Chapters 22–23), vitamin C (Chapters 24–26), vitamin D (Chapters 27–30), vitamins E and K (Chapter 31), calcium (Chapters 35–36), and phosphorus, iron, iodine, and other trace elements (Chapters 35–40).

In these recipes some measurements are given in "cups": for equivalents in milliliters and fluid ounces, see Appendix II on page 335.

AVERAGE ADULT

Breakfast	Lunch	Snacks	Dinner
6 oz. orange juice	Broiled Shrimp	Glass of	Half cantaloupe
Bacon and	Tomato and	skim	Quick Swiss
Scrambled	cucumber salad	milk	Steak
Eggs	Gingerbread with	Raisins	Celery sticks
Toast	whipped cream	Walnuts	Five-Minute
Beverage	Beverage		Lemon Custard
			Beverage

Bacon: Place several bacon strips on cake rack over pie pan, broil or place in slow oven to cook.

Eggs: Brush pan with vegetable oil, heat to moderate temperature. Break directly into pan 4 to 6 eggs. Stir in thoroughly ¼ to ½ cup evaporated milk, ⅛ teaspoon ground peppercorns, 1 teaspoon salt. Cook over extremely low heat 10 to 12 minutes, stirring two or three times. Keep pan covered as much as possible. Serve with crisp bacon.

Broiled Shrimp: Shell whole shrimps, leaving tails on. Dust with whole-wheat flour and paprika; set on oiled baking sheet and broil under low heat 4 or 5 minutes without turning. Serve with melted margarine or butter to which is added 1 minced clove garlic and finely chopped parsley.

Gingerbread: Combine and stir well:

⅓ cup vegetable oil	⅓ cup sugar
½ cup wheat germ	¾ cup sour milk, buttermilk,
1 egg	or yogurt
⅔ cup dark molasses	

Sift into moist ingredients:

1 cup sifted whole-wheat pastry flour	¼ cup powdered milk
	2 teaspoons ginger
3 teaspoons double-acting baking powder	1 teaspoon cinnamon
	½ teaspoon salt

Combine ingredients with no more than 20 strokes. Grease ring mold or 8-inch square loaf pan and dust with flour. Pour batter into pan and bake in moderate oven at 350°F. for 45 minutes; be careful not to overbake. Test with cake tester before taking out of oven. Serve warm with whipped cream.

Quick Swiss Steak: Pound 1½-inch thick Swiss steak thoroughly, dredge with flour, sauté with 3 tablespoons vegetable oil, cook slowly to an internal temperature 140 to 165°F., or about 30 minutes. Meanwhile, steam together in another utensil 1 or 2 each quartered onions, unpeeled potatoes, carrots, turnips. When vegetables are almost tender, add 1 cup fresh or frozen peas.

When steak is done, put on serving platter, keep warm, and prepare brown or tomato gravy.

Heat to boiling 1½ cups meat broth. Meanwhile stir together ½ cup cold milk and 4 tablespoons whole-wheat flour. Remove broth from heat, add thickening slowly. When well blended, add 1 teaspoon salt (if desired), ¼ teaspoon crushed white or black peppercorns, ½ teaspoon minced fresh or pinch dried herbs.

Simmer 10 minutes. (For tomato gravy, use tomato juice or canned tomatoes instead of milk. Add basil, oregano, chili powder or Worcestershire sauce.)

Five-Minute Lemon Custard: Combine in saucepan ½ cup sugar, ½ cup powdered milk, ⅛ teaspoon salt. Add and beat till smooth ½ cup fresh milk, 2 whole eggs or 4 egg yolks. Stir in after beating 1¼ cups fresh or reconstituted milk. Fasten thermometer to side of saucepan, and heat, stirring constantly until temperature reaches 180°F., or about 4 minutes. Remove from heat and cool at room temperature before chilling. When custard has chilled, add ¼ cup lemon juice and 1 teaspoon grated lemon rind.

OFFICE WORKER

Breakfast	Lunch	Snacks	Dinner
8 oz. tomato juice	Baked Liver	apple	Cheese Soufflé
Shredded Wheat	Boiled potato	sliced	Carrot and
with sliced	Coleslaw	carrots,	Apple Salad
banana	Fruit Gelatin	celery,	Orange Sherbet
Skim milk	Beverage	green	Beverage
Beverage		pepper	

Baked Liver: Cut 6 or 8 small pockets in sides of 1 or 2 pounds unsliced baby beef, lamb, or veal liver. Place in each slit 1 inch piece of bacon and bits of 1 minced clove garlic. Place in flat baking dish and put over top ¼ cup French dressing or 1 cup sour cream. Sprinkle with paprika. Insert meat thermometer in center of thickest portion; bake in moderate oven at 350°F. for 30 minutes or until internal temperature is 150 to 160°F.

Coleslaw: Shred very thin, then cut into 2-inch strips ½ head of green cabbage. Add and stir well: ⅔ cup yogurt or ⅓ cup each yogurt and sour cream, 2 or 3 tablespoons vinegar, 1 table-spoon sugar and ½ teaspoon salt. Garnish with paprika. Serve immediately or chill 1 hour or longer.

Fruit Gelatin: Heat to boiling 1½ cups pineapple, apple, or grapefruit juice. Dissolve in ¼ cup cold water and add 1 package or tablespoon unflavored gelatin. Stir well and chill until gelatin starts to congeal. Add ½ cup canned cherries, cut in half, ½ cup fresh seedless grapes, 1 cup sliced peaches, ¼ cup walnuts or pecans. Sweeten to taste, stir, pour into ring mold, and chill until firm. Unmold and serve with center filled with whipped evaporated milk flavored with vanilla.

Cheese Soufflé: Heat to simmering 1 cup whole milk. Meanwhile beat together or blend in liquefier and add to the hot milk:

½ cup cold milk	1½ teaspoons salt
¼ to ½ cup powdered milk	⅛ teaspoon freshly ground
3 tablespoons whole-wheat	white peppercorns
flour	

Simmer 5 minutes, stirring constantly; remove from heat, cool slightly; add and stir well:

4 egg yolks	2 or 3 tablespoons finely
¼ teaspoon dried basil	chopped parsley
1 to 2 cups diced American	1 or 2 teaspoons Worcester-
cheese	shire sauce

Beat stiffly and fold in:

4 egg whites

Pour into greased casserole and place in a slow preheated oven at 300°F. Set an upright oven thermometer on same level with soufflé and check temperature carefully; bake 45 to 50 minutes. If it cannot be served immediately, turn off heat, open oven door a moment to cool, then let casserole remain in closed oven.

Carrot and Apple Salad: Wash and shred 3 or 4 small chilled unpeeled carrots. Add: 1 diced unpeeled red apple, 6 or 8 sliced stuffed olives, ⅛ teaspoon celery seeds (optional), ½ teaspoon each salt and sugar, 2 or 3 tablespoons mayonnaise. Stir well and serve over a bed of watercress.

Orange Sherbet: Soak for 5 minutes in saucepan 2 teaspoons gelatin in ½ cup water. Heat until gelatin is dissolved, cool and add 1½ cups fresh or diluted frozen orange juice. Freeze slowly to soft mush, then beat until stiff 1 cup evaporated milk. Add and beat until velvety the grated rind of 1 orange and 2 table-spoons lemon juice. Sweeten to taste. Return to freezer com-partment and freeze to firm texture.

THE OVERWEIGHT

Breakfast	Lunch	Snacks	Dinner
Raspberry Yogurt	Summer Squash	Celery and	Chicken with
Blueberry Muffin	with Cheese	carrot	Rice
Beverage	"Baked" Apple	sticks	Green salad
	Beverage	Wheat crackers	Fruit Snow
			Beverage

Raspberry Yogurt: Shake, beat, or blend in liquefier until smooth 1 cup chilled juice from canned or frozen raspberries, ⅓ cup powdered milk. Add and beat slightly 1 cup yogurt. Pour into glasses and serve.

Blueberry Muffins: Sift into mixing bowl:

½ cup sifted whole-wheat flour

½ teaspoon salt

1½ teaspoons double-acting baking powder

⅛ cup powdered milk

Add and stir only enough to moisten:

½ cup wheat germ

½ cup sweet or sour milk, buttermilk, or yogurt

1 egg

⅙ cup sugar

1 tablespoon vegetable oil

½ cup fresh blueberries

Fill paper baking cups or well-greased muffin tins two-thirds full. Bake at 400°F. for 15 to 20 minutes, or until brown. Makes 6 muffins.

Summer Squash with Cheese: Slice or cut into 1-inch pieces 6 to 8 chilled unpeeled summer squash.

Sauté squash in 2 tablespoons partially hardened margarine or vegetable oil with 1 minced clove garlic, 1 chopped onion, pinch of savory or basil and crushed black peppercorns. Stir well, cover pot, heat quickly, then simmer 10 minutes. Remove from heat and add: 1 teaspoon salt and ½ cup diced American cheese. Stir well and put into serving dish.

In the utensil used for squash, heat quickly ¾ cup canned or diced fresh tomatoes, ¼ teaspoon salt, ½ teaspoon sugar. Pour tomatoes over squash.

"Baked" Apple: Wash quickly, dry, and core 4 or more large chilled apples. Remove peel from upper fourth of apples; put peeled side down into ½ cup boiling water in saucepan. Heat through quickly; reduce heat and simmer until almost tender when pierced with a toothpick, or about 10 minutes. Turn apples peeled side up and sprinkle with cinnamon, nutmeg, or grated lemon rind and ¼ cup sugar. Brown in oven or under broiler and serve with top milk, sour cream, or yogurt.

Chicken with Rice: Select a stewing chicken or disjointed pieces, put in utensil with 4 cups vegetable-cooking water, 2 tablespoons white vinegar, 2 teaspoons salt. Simmer 2½ to 3 hours or until nearly tender; if vinegar can be smelled, remove lid during last half-hour of cooking. Skim off fat.

Fifteen minutes before serving, add 2 cups cooked brown rice or 1 cup uncooked converted rice, ¾ cup diced carrots. Five minutes before serving, add 1 cup fresh or frozen peas.

Fruit Snow: Prepare in liquefier and heat to boiling 1 cup fruit purée (apple, apricot, plum, prune or peach). Meanwhile beat until stiff 2 egg whites. Fold egg whites into hot fruit, add sugar and lemon juice to taste. Cool slowly, then pour into serving dishes and chill.

SENIOR CITIZEN

Breakfast	Lunch	Snacks	Dinner
6 oz. orange juice	Beef broth	Soy Nuts	Apple, Carrot, and
Quick Egg Omelet	Melba toast	Carrot	Orange Salad
Wheat-Germ Muffin	Fruit Salad	sticks	Pan-Broiled Pork
Beverage	Bowl with	Wheat	Chops
	Cottage	crackers	Steamed Cabbage
	Cheese		Vanilla Junket
	Beverage		Beverage

Quick Egg Omelet: Beat until smooth ½ cup fresh milk, ¼ cup powdered milk. Add and beat slightly 4 to 6 eggs, 1½ teaspoons salt, ¼ teaspoon freshly ground black peppercorns. Pour into heated omelet pan brushed with vegetable oil, cover and heat slowly 6 to 10 minutes. Loosen edges with spatula and fold toward center, letting uncooked egg run to sides of pan. Again cover pan and heat slowly 5 to 8 minutes. Fold edges toward center and sprinkle with 2 to 4 tablespoons chopped parsley.

Wheat-Germ Muffins: Sift into mixing bowl:

½ cup sifted whole-wheat pastry flour	1½ teaspoons double-acting baking powder
½ teaspoon salt	⅛ cup powdered milk

Add and stir only enough to moisten:

½ cup wheat germ	⅛ cup honey or
½ cup sweet or sour milk, buttermilk, or yogurt	dark molasses
1 egg	1 tablespoon vegetable oil
	¼ cup raisins (optional)

Fill paper baking cups or well-greased muffin tins two-thirds full. Bake at 400°F. for 15 to 20 minutes, or until brown. Makes 6 muffins.

Fruit Salad Bowl: Line a salad bowl with leaves of 1 head romaine lettuce. Arrange in alternate layers 2 cups fresh or canned pineapple, 2 cups grapefruit sections, 1 red apple cut into thin wedges, 1 cup seeded or seedless grapes, 2 sliced oranges. Add scoop of cottage cheese, garnish with cherries.

Soya Nuts: Soak in ice tray for 2 hours or longer 1 cup soya beans and 1 cup water. Freeze for 2 hours or preferably overnight. Drop into ½ cup hot water. Simmer for 30 minutes; taste and cook longer if soya beans are not as tender as salted peanuts; remove lid of utensil and let water evaporate. Cool beans. Heat ¼ cup vegetable oil. Add beans and cook quickly to a delicate brown, or about 1 or 2 minutes; remove from heat at once, sprinkle with 1 teaspoon salt.

Apple, Carrot, and Orange Salad: Quarter, core, and dice 2 unpeeled red apples. Add 1 or 2 shredded carrots, ½ cup diced orange sections, 2 tablespoons mayonnaise, dash salt. Stir, put over bed of watercress on salad plates. Sprinkle with coconut and paprika.

Pan-Broiled Pork Chops: Choose pork chops 1 to 1½ inches thick; allow 30 to 35 minutes for cooking 1-inch chops; 40 to 45 for 1½-inch chops.

Trim fat, leaving ⅛ inch. Carefully pierce hole for thermometer, holding punch parallel to the surface of the meat and driving it into the center of the thickest portion. Insert thermometer. Sprinkle chops generously on both sides with paprika.

Put chops on extremely hot pan or grill; sear 2 or 3 minutes on each side; immediately turn off heat or move untensil until cooled; then continue cooking over extremely low heat. Do not salt the meat or cover the grill.

In 15 or 20 minutes turn the chops; drain off any rendered fat; continue to keep heat low. Take reading of meat thermometer frequently. Take up when the reading is 165 or 170°F. Sprinkle chops with freshly ground white peppercorns.

Heat on hot grill: ½ cup vegetable-cooking water, 1 tablespoon chopped chives and pinch each of savory and sage. Pour sauce over meat.

Steamed Cabbage: Dry well after washing and shred fine ½ head chilled cabbage. Put in saucepan. Add 2 tablespoons boiling water. Cover pot, heat rapidly, and reduce temperature. Simmer 8 minutes. Season with ½ teaspoon each salt and sugar.

Vanilla Junket: Blend in liquefier or combine and beat or shake until smooth:

1 cup fresh milk	1 teaspoon vanilla
⅔ cup powdered milk	pinch salt
¼ cup white or brown sugar	

Add and heat until lukewarm or 110°F. 1 cup fresh or reconstituted milk.

Meanwhile dissolve 1 rennet, or junket, tablet in 1 tablespoon water; add dissolved tablet to warm milk, stir no longer than 10 seconds, and pour immediately into sherbet glasses; do not move glasses until junket is firmly set, or about 10 minutes. Chill.

THE SPORTS MAN/WOMAN

Breakfast	Lunch	Snacks	Dinner
Grapefruit half	Navy-Bean Soup	Yogurt with	Meat Loaf
Poached egg on	Liverwurst on	fruit	Baked Tomatoes
whole-wheat	crackers	Peanuts	Creamed corn
toast	Molasses Drop		Rice Pudding
Beverage	Cookies		Beverage
	Beverage		

Navy-Bean Soup: Use bone and skin left from baked ham or purchase a ham hock. If cooked ham is used, trim off edible meat scraps and save. Pour over bones and skin 2 quarts water and bring to boiling.

Wash quickly, drain, and add without soaking 2 cups white navy beans. Cover pot, lower heat, and simmer 2 hours; add ¼ to ½ teaspoon crushed black peppercorns, ½ cup soy flour shaken with 1 cup water, 1 crushed bay leaf, ⅛ teaspoon marjoram, savory, and/or basil, 1 or 2 chopped onions, 1 small cayenne pepper or chili pepper, pierced with toothpick.

Simmer 20 minutes longer, or until beans are tender. Mash about half the beans, taste for salt and add more if needed.

Discard bones, skin, pepper. Add ham scraps if any and garnish with chives. Serve with garlic croutons.

Molasses Drop Cookies: Cream together:

½ cup partially hardened margarine, natural lard, or butter

⅓ cup sugar

Add:

1 egg
½ cup wheat germ

½ cup dark molasses
¼ cup evaporated or fresh milk

Sift in:

1 cup whole-wheat pastry flour
2 teaspoons double-acting baking powder
½ cup powdered milk

½ teaspoon salt
½ teaspoon each cinnamon, ginger, and nutmeg

Stir only enough to mix well, or about 25 strokes; drop from a teaspoon onto baking sheet covered with foil or well-greased heavy paper. Bake in moderate oven at 350°F. for 12 to 15 minutes. Remove from paper or foil after cooling, or freeze and remove later.

Meat Loaf: Crumble 2 slices whole-wheat bread into ½ cup fresh milk. When moist, add and mix well:

1 egg	½ pound pork sausage
1 or 2 shredded onions	1½ teaspoons salt
1 minced clove garlic	2 tablespoons chopped
¼ cup wheat germ	parsley
1½ pounds lean ground beef	¼ teaspoon each basil and
	freshly ground pepper-
	corns

Mix thoroughly, preferably with fingertips; mold into a loaf in a shallow baking dish or pack into a greased loaf pan. Sprinkle generously with paprika; bake in a moderate oven at 350°F. about 1 hour, or until temperature in center is 185°F.; insert thermometer when loaf is nearly done.

Baked Tomatoes: Cut in half and place in low heat-resistant serving dish:

2 or 3 large tomatoes

Mix together and pat over tomatoes: ¼ cup each fine chopped parsley and onions or olives, ⅓ cup wheat germ, ¼ teaspoon basil, 3 tablespoons mayonnaise. Sprinkle with paprika and bake in moderate oven at 350°F. for 8 to 10 minutes.

Rice Pudding: Combine and beat until smooth:

½ cup sugar stirred with	½ cup fresh milk
½ cup powdered milk	2 whole eggs or 4 yolks
¼ teaspoon salt	½ teaspoon vanilla

Add and stir well:

2 cups fresh or	2 cups cooked brown rice
reconstituted milk	or converted rice

Pour into greased baking dish; sprinkle with nutmeg. Bake in a slow oven at 325°F. for 30 minutes, or until temperature in center of pudding, taken with a meat thermometer, is 175°F. Stir once or twice during baking.

THE TEENAGER

Breakfast	Lunch	Snacks	Dinner
8 oz. apple juice	Pizza	Popcorn	Broiled Shad
8 oz. whole milk	Fruit Compote	Chocolate-	Baked Carrots
plus 2½ table-	Beverage	coated	and Apples
spoons powdered		peanuts	Oven "French
skim milk		Fruities	Fries"
Pancakes with			Walnut Torte
maple syrup			Beverage

Pancakes: Sift into mixing bowl 1 cup stone-ground whole-wheat pastry flour, ½ cup powdered milk, 1 teaspoon salt, 2 teaspoons baking powder.

Add 1½ cups sweet or sour milk, buttermilk, or yogurt, 2 eggs, 2 tablespoons vegetable oil, ½ cup fresh wheat germ.

Stir with no more than 50 strokes. Drop from tablespoon onto moderately hot griddle, cook slowly, turn and brown other side. Makes 10 to 12 pancakes.

Pizza: Mix thoroughly without heating:

1½ pounds lean ground meat	½ teaspoon each basil,
2 cups tomato purée	oregano, and freshly
or 2 cans tomato sauce	ground black peppercorns
1 shredded onion	1½ teaspoons salt

Set sauce aside. Combine and let stand 5 minutes:

1 cup warm water	1 teaspoon honey (optional)
1 tablespoon, package, or	1 tablespoon vegetable oil
cake bakers' yeast	1 teaspoon salt

Add without sifting: 2 cups high-protein stone-ground whole-wheat flour. Beat dough until smooth and elastic. Add ½ cup more flour, or enough to make a stiff dough; turn onto a floured canvas or bread board and knead until smooth.

If two large pizzas are to be made, cut dough in half; set one aside and make the other into a ball. Roll into a round sheet and transfer to a greased 13-inch pizza pan, pull and stretch dough gently to fit, turning up edges ⅛ inch. Sprinkle seasoned meat over dough, spreading it well to margins. Bake in a preheated oven at 450°F. for 15 minutes, being sure to put pizza to be served immediately on lower rack. The bottom of the crust must be crisp. Remove from oven and sprinkle over top:

½ to 1 cup shredded Cheddar cheese	1 to 2 tablespoons grated Parmesan or Romano cheese

Return pizza to be served immediately to oven until cheese melts. Serve piping hot.

Fruit Compote: Combine pineapple cubes or slices, fresh or canned peach halves, fresh or frozen raspberries.

Fruities: Put through the meat grinder, using medium knife, and measure after grinding:

1 cup dates	½ cup walnuts or pecans
½ cup graham-cracker crumbs	

Add and stir well:

3 tablespoons orange or pineapple juice	¼ cup powdered milk
	8 chopped marshmallows

Press firmly on waxed paper or buttered pan to thickness of ¾ inch; cut into squares or mold into balls or rolls. Chill. After chilling, roll in ground nuts, powdered sugar, coconut, or graham-cracker crumbs.

Broiled Shad with Herbs: Select steaks or fillets not more than 1½ inches thick; unless the steaks are to be rolled in crumbs, do not remove skin. Leave small fish whole. Carefully punch a hole for the meat thermometer in thickest part of the flesh, not touching bone. Brush with vegetable oil. Sprinkle surfaces with minced fresh dill or tarragon or crushed anise or dill seeds.

If using gas heat, set broiler pan on top ledge so that fish is about 1 inch from heat; keep the flames very small. If using electricity, set about 5 inches from heating unit. Leave broiler door open.

Use pancake turner and turn fish after 8 to 10 minutes, or when half the thickness has become opaque. Read the thermometer frequently and take up the fish as soon as 145 to 150°F. is reached. Allow 15 minutes for cooking fish 1 inch thick, 18 minutes if 1½ inches thick.

Garnish with chopped parsley. Serve with herb butter seasoned with fresh dill, tarragon, and chives.

Baked Carrots and Apples: Slice in alternate layers into a heat-resistant casserole:

4 or 5 chilled unpeeled carrots, cut into quarters lengthwise	1 to 3 unpeeled apples, quartered and sliced

Top with bits of partially hardened margarine or butter; sprinkle with:

1 teaspoon salt	3 tablespoons hot water
1 teaspoon grated lemon rind	

Cover casserole, steam 5 to 10 minutes, then bake in hot oven at 400°F. for 15 to 20 minutes, or until tender; or cook until tender over direct heat.

Oven "French Fries": Cut into ⅓-inch sticks 3 or 4 chilled unpeeled potatoes. Toss in salad bowl with 1 or 2 tablespoons vegetable oil.

Place on oiled baking sheet and put in hot oven at 450°F. until brown, or about 8 minutes; lower heat and cook until potatoes are tender; sprinkle with ½ teaspoon salt.

Walnut Torte: Line bottoms of two 8-inch layer-cake pans with heavy paper; brush paper with soft partially hardened margarine or butter. Stir together thoroughly:

1 cup sugar	2 cups ground walnuts
3 egg yolks	¾ cup wheat germ

Beat stiff and fold 6 egg whites into ingredients. Pour batter into pans, spread evenly to edges, and bake in slow oven at 325°F. for 30 minutes. Turn out of pans and remove paper immediately. Prepare filling by mixing thoroughly:

⅓ cup sugar   ⅓ cup powdered milk

Add and stir well:

3 egg yolks   ½ cup top milk or cream

Cook slowly over direct heat until thick, stirring constantly; do not let boil. Remove from heat and add 1 cup ground walnuts. Spread between layers of torte.

THE VEGETARIAN

Breakfast	*Lunch*	*Snacks*	*Dinner*
Grapefruit half	Egg salad with	Nuts	Shell Macaroni
Cream of Wheat	watercress and	Raisins	with Cheese
with skim milk	bean sprouts	Apricots	Stewed Tomatoes
Nut Bread	Whole-wheat	Chestnuts	Green Celery
Beverage	bread		with Leaves
	Strawberry		Fruit Cup
	Sponge		Beverage
	Beverage		

Nut Bread: Sift into mixing bowl:

1½ cups whole-wheat pastry flour	2 teaspoons double-acting baking powder
⅓ cup powdered milk	
1 teaspoon salt	

Add and mix until covered with flour 1 cup broken walnuts, pecans, or other nuts. Add:

1¼ cups sweet or sour milk, buttermilk, or yogurt	⅓ cup honey or dark molasses
3 tablespoons vegetable oil	½ cup wheat germ

Stir with no more than 40 strokes. Line bottom of loaf pan with heavy paper and grease well; pour batter into pan, forcing it into corners; make identation lengthwise through center. Bake at 350°F. for 45 minutes.

Strawberry Sponge: Combine and stir well:

1 cup boiling water   1 package strawberry gelatin

Cool by adding ¾ cup cold water. Chill until gelatin starts to congeal. Meanwhile beat until stiff ½ cup chilled evaporated milk. Add and beat slightly 2 tablespoons lemon juice and ¼ cup powdered milk. Fold whipped milk into gelatin with 1 cup sliced and sweetened fresh or frozen strawberries. Pour into mold and chill until set.

Shell Macaroni with Cheese: Bring to boiling in heat-resistant casserole 2 cups vegetable-cooking water. Add slowly to constantly boiling water 1 teaspoon salt and 2 cups shell macaroni. Cover casserole; if water starts to boil over add ½ teaspoon butter or margarine. Lower heat and simmer 10 minutes or until almost tender. Stir, evaporate off most of remaining moisture and remove from heat.

Add 1½ cups fresh or reconstituted milk, ⅔ cup instant powdered milk, 1 cup cubed Cheddar cheese. Stir until mixed. Sprinkle top with wheat germ, Parmesan cheese (optional) and paprika. Brown in moderate oven at 300°F. for 15 minutes.

Stewed Tomatoes: Use 2 cups or 3 to 5 peeled and diced fresh tomatoes; cook fresh tomatoes until tender, or about 10 minutes; bring canned ones to boil. Add:

1 tablespoon sugar
½ teaspoon salt
Crushed black peppercorns

1 tablespoon partially
hardened margarine
or butter

Crumble or cube 2 slices of stale whole-wheat bread and put into serving bowl. Pour boiling tomatoes over bread.

Green Celery with Leaves: Use outer green celery stalks and leaves; dice stalks into ¾-inch pieces and shred leaves. Add approximately:

2 cups diced stalks to ½ cup simmering milk

Stir well to cover all surfaces with milk protein. Cover utensil, heat quickly, and simmer 8 to 10 minutes. Add shredded celery leaves. Stir well and cook 2 minutes longer. Season with ½ teaspoon salt, dash of cayenne. Garnish with strips of canned pimento.

Fruit Cup: Cut into fourths 6 or 8 fresh or canned apricots. Add:

1 or 2 diced oranges
1 sliced banana or
  2 sliced peaches

½ cup strawberries or other
  fresh or canned berries

Sweeten to taste, mix well, and set in refrigerator; serve in sherbet glasses.

Weights and Measures

WEIGHTS (Avoirdupois)

icrogram (μg)

illigram (mg) = 1,000 μg 1 ounce (oz) = 28.35 g

ram (g) = 1,000 mg = 0.0353 oz 4 ounces = ¼ lb = 113.4 g

grams = 100,000 mg = 3.5 oz 1 pound (lb) = 16 oz = 0.4536 kg

ilogram (kg) = 1,000 g = 2.2046 lb

PACITY **CAPACITY**

illiliter (ml)

ter (li) = 1,000 ml 1 pint (pt) = 474 ml

liters = 2,500 ml 1 quart (qt) = 2 pints = 958 ml

ters = 5,000 ml 1 gallon (gal) = 8 pints = 3.785 liters

roximate values **Approximate values**

cup measure **for teaspoon and tablespoon**
measures

up = 30 ml = 1.0 fl. oz

up = 60 ml = 2.1 fl. oz ⅛ teaspoon = 0.6 ml

up = 80 ml = 2.8 fl. oz ¼ teaspoon = 1.2 ml

up = 125 ml = 4.4 fl. oz ½ teaspoon = 2.5 ml

p = 250 ml = 8.8 fl. oz 1 teaspoon = 5 ml

½ tablespoon = 7.5 ml

1 tablespoon = 15 ml

APPENDIX III

Food Tables

KEY TO FOOD TABLES

Tr   means that a trace of the nutrient is present
0   means no trace present
—   means no data available.

HOW TO USE THESE TABLES

Many tables of calories and food values refer to an average portion. There is really no such thing and people's ideas of average vary as much as their waistlines and their appetite. With a little simple arithmetic you can use these tables to calculate exactly what *you* eat. First get to know the weights of familiar foods. A slice of bread is approximately 30 grams (1 oz), an egg 60 grams (2 oz) and a small apple 100 grams (3½ oz). Most portions of meat and fish are between 100 grams and 200 grams (3½ oz and 7 oz).

Weigh the amount of food you normally eat. Look it up in the food tables (these give values for a 100 gram portion). Multiply this by the weight of your food (in grams), and divide by 100. The following examples show how it is done.

Calculating calories in a rasher of bacon

Bacon: 100 grams = 416 calories (as per tables)
Your portion (2 oz): 60 grams = 416 × 60 = 24960
Divide the answer by 100 = 249 calories

Calculating the iron in a portion of baked beans

Baked Beans: 100 grams = 1.4 milligrams
Your portion (5 oz): 150 grams = 1.4 × 150 = 210
Divide the answer by 100 = 2.1 milligrams

Calculate the amount of thiamin in one fresh apricot

Apricots: 100 grams = 0.04 milligrams (as per tables)
Your portion (1½ oz): 45 grams = 0.04 × 45 = 1.8
Divide the answer by 100 = 0.018 milligrams

Rough calculations of weights
100 grams = slightly less than ¼ lb
500 grams = slightly more than 1 lb

Rough calculations for weights of liquids and very small quantities of solids
100 grams of milk = 100 ml = 3.5 fl. oz
500 grams of milk = 500 ml = slightly less than 1 pint

Small dry measures may be calculated in the same way
1 teaspoon of sugar = 5 ml = 5 grams
1 tablespoon of sugar = 15 ml = 15 grams
(This type of approximation becomes inaccurate with larger quantities.)

Conversion of kilocalories to megajoules
1000 kcal = 4.2 MJ

$$1200 \text{ kcal} = \frac{1200 \times 4.2}{1000} = 5.04 \text{ MJ}$$

$$1500 \text{ kcal} = \frac{1500 \times 4.2}{1000} = 6.30 \text{ MJ}$$

Description of Food (100 g)	Energy Calories Kcals	Protein g	Fat g	'Sug Car hydr g
Almonds, shelled	598	18.6	54.2	4
Apples, raw	56	0.2	0.3	13
Apple pie	180	2.0	7.6	27
Apple sauce, sweetened	91	0.2	0.1	23
Apricots, canned	106	0.5	Tr	27
Apricots, dried	182	4.8	Tr	43
Apricots, fresh	51	1.0	0.2	12
Artichokes, Jerusalem (boiled)	18	1.6	Tr	3
Asparagus, cooked	18	3.4	Tr	1
Avocado	223	4.2	22.2	1
Bacon, grilled	416	24.9	35.1	0
Banana	79	1.1	0.3	19
Barley, pearl (boiled)	120	2.7	0.6	27
Beans, baked	64	5.1	0.5	10
Beans, broad, cooked	48	4.1	0.6	7
Beans, butter, cooked	95	7.1	0.3	17
Beans, string green	19	1.9	0.2	2
Beef, roast	192	27.6	9.1	0
Beef sausage, grilled	265	13.0	17.3	15
Beet greens, boiled	18	1.7	0.2	3
Beetroot, boiled	44	1.8	Tr	9
Bilberries, raw	56	0.6	Tr	14
Biscuits, plain digestive	471	9.8	20.5	66
Blackberries, raw	29	1.3	Tr	6
Blueberries, raw	62	0.7	0.5	15
Bologna sausage	277	13.3	22.8	3
Brains, boiled	152	12.7	11.2	0
Bran, wheat flakes	206	14.1	5.5	26
Bread, rye	243	9.1	1.1	52
Bread, white roll	233	7.8	1.7	49
Bread, wholewheat	216	8.8	2.7	41
Broccoli, cooked	18	3.1	Tr	1
Brussels sprouts, boiled	26	4.0	Tr	2
Buckwheat	355	11.7	2.4	72
Butter	740	0.4	82.0	T
Buttermilk	36	3.6	0.1	5
Cabbage, chinese (raw)	14	1.2	0.1	3
Cabbage, green (boiled)	7	1.1	Tr	0
Cabbage, white	15	1.7	Tr	2
Cake, Devil's Food (chocolate)	369	4.5	16.4	55
Cake, sponge	464	6.4	26.5	53
CANDIES AND SWEETS:				
Boiled sweets	327	Tr	Tr	87
Chocolate, milk	529	8.4	30.3	59
Chocolate, plain	525	4.7	29.2	64
Gum drops	172	1.0	0	44
Mars Bar	441	5.3	18.9	66
Marshmallows	319	2.0	Tr	80
Mints	392	0.5	0.7	102

Vitamin A Retinol Equivalents µg	B Vitamins Thiamin mg	Riboflavin mg	Niacin mg	Vitamin C Ascorbic Acid mg	Minerals Calcium mg	Iron mg
0	0.24	0.92	3.5	Tr	234	4.7
5	0.03	0.02	0.1	7	6	0.3
30	0.05	0.02	0.5	2	48	0.6
5	0.02	0.01	Tr	1	4	0.3
166	0.02	0.01	0.3	2	12	0.7
600	Tr	0.20	3.0	Tr	67	4.1
250	0.04	0.05	0.6	7	17	0.4
Tr	0.10	Tr	—	2	30	0.4
83	0.10	0.08	0.8	20	26	0.9
16	0.10	0.10	1.0	15	15	1.5
Tr	0.41	0.16	4.4	0	12	1.5
33	0.40	0.07	0.6	10	7	0.4
0	Tr	Tr	0.9	0	3	0.7
0	0.07	0.05	0.5	Tr	45	1.4
42	0.10	0.04	3.0	15	21	1.0
Tr	—	—	—	0	19	1.7
66	0.04	0.07	0.8	5	22	0.6
Tr	0.07	0.30	6.0	0	10	2.1
Tr	Tr	0.14	5.4	0	73	1.7
825	0.07	0.15	0.3	15	99	1.9
Tr	0.02	0.04	0.1	5	30	0.4
20	0.02	0.02	0.4	22	10	0.7
0	0.13	0.08	1.5	0	110	2.0
16.6	0.03	0.04	0.4	20	63	0.9
33	0.03	0.06	0.5	14	15	1.0
—	—	—	—	—	—	—
Tr	0.08	0.19	2.2	17	16	2.3
0	0.89	0.36	29.6	0	110	12.9
9	9.17	0.08	0.16	0	75	1.6
0	0.18	0.03	1.4	0	100	1.7
0	0.26	0.66	3.9	0	23	2.5
400	0.06	0.20	0.6	34	76	1.0
66	0.06	0.10	0.4	40	32	0.7
0	0.60	—	4.4	0	114	3.1
830	Tr	Tr	Tr	Tr	15	0.1
Tr	0.04	0.18	0.1	1	121	Tr
50	0.05	0.04	0.6	25	43	0.6
80	0.03	0.03	0.2	25	30	0.5
50	0.03	0.03	0.2	20	38	0.4
50	0.02	0.10	0.2	Tr	70	1.0
300	Tr	0.12	0.6	0	140	1.4
0	0	0	0	0	5	0.4
6.6	0.10	0.23	0.2	0	220	1.6
6.6	0.07	0.08	0.4	0	38	2.4
0	0	0	0	0	360	4.2
6	0.05	0.20	0.3	0	160	1.1
0	0	0	Tr	Tr	18	1.6
0	0	0	0	0	7	0.2

Description of Food (100 g)	Energy Calories Kcals	Protein g	Fat g	'Sug Carl hydr g
Pastilles	253	5.2	0	61
Toffees	430	2.1	17.2	71
Carrots, boiled	19	0.6	Tr	4
Carrots, raw	23	0.7	Tr	5
Cashew nuts	561	17.2	45.7	29
Cauliflower, boiled	9	1.6	Tr	0
Celery, boiled	5	0.6	Tr	0
Celery, raw	8	0.9	Tr	1
Chard, boiled	18	1.8	0.2	3
Cheese, American	370	23.2	30.0	1
Cheese, Cheddar	406	26.0	33.5	T
Cheese, cottage	96	13.6	4.0	1
Cheese, cream	439	3.1	47.4	T
Cheese, Swiss	355	26.4	26.9	1
Cheesecake	421	4.2	34.9	24
Cherries, canned	74	0.8	0.2	18
Cherries, raw	47	0.6	Tr	11
Chestnuts	170	2.0	2.7	36
Chicken, roast	148	24.8	5.4	0
Chocolate malted milk, powder	378	9.8	3.8	81
Chocolate milk shake	85	3.4	3.4	11
Chocolate pudding	125	3.0	2.5	24
Clams, meat only	82	14.0	1.9	1
Coca-cola	39	Tr	0	10
Cocoa, powder	312	18.5	21.7	11
Coconuts, desiccated	604	5.6	62.0	6
Cod, grilled	95	20.8	1.3	0
Cod-liver oil	899	Tr	99.9	0
Coffee, powder	100	14.6	0	11
Collards, boiled	33	6.4	10.6	76
Corn on the cob, canned	76	2.9	0.5	16
Corn on the cob, whole	123	4.1	2.3	22
Corn oil	899	Tr	99.9	0
Corned beef	217	26.9	12.1	0
Cornflakes, fortified	368	8.6	1.6	85
Cornmeal, enriched and degerminated	364	7.9	1.2	78
Cottonseed oil	899	Tr	99.9	0
Crab (without shell)	127	20.1	15.2	0
Crackers, cream	440	9.5	16.3	68
Crackers, Graham	384	8.4	9.4	73
Cranberries	15	0.4	Tr	3
Cranberry sauce	146	0.1	0.2	37
Cream, single	212	2.4	21.4	3
Cream, double	447	1.5	48.2	2
Cream, canned	230	2.6	23.3	2
Crispbread (Ryvita)	321	9.4	2.1	70
Cucumber	10	0.6	0.1	1
Currants, dried	243	1.7	Tr	63
Custard, made with milk	118	3.8	4.4	16

| Vitamin A | B Vitamins | | | Vitamin C | Minerals | |
| Retinol equivalents | Thiamin | Riboflavin | Niacin | Ascorbic Acid | Calcium | Iron |
µg	mg	mg	mg	mg	mg	mg
0	0	0	0	0	40	1.4
0	0	0	0	0	95	1.5
2000	0.05	0.04	0.4	4	37	0.4
2000	0.06	0.05	0.6	6	48	0.6
33	0.43	0.25	1.8	—	38	3.8
5	0.06	0.06	0.4	20	18	0.4
Tr	0.02	0.02	0.2	5	52	0.4
Tr	0.03	0.03	0.3	7	52	0.6
900	0.04	0.11	0.4	16	73	1.8
200	0.02	0.41	Tr	0	97	0.9
340	0.04	0.50	0.10	0	800	0.4
33	0.02	0.19	0.08	0	60	0.1
420	0.02	0.14	0.08	0	980	0.2
190	0.10	0.40	0.1	0	925	0.9
298	0.05	0.10	0.3	2	67	0.7
15	0.03	0.06	0.2	3	15	0.3
20	0.05	0.07	0.3	5	16	0.3
0	0.20	0.22	0.2	Tr	46	0.9
Tr	0.08	0.19	8.2	0	9	0.8
—	1.76	—	—	—	36	2.6
30	0.03	0.16	0.1	1	111	0.2
43	0.03	0.15	0.1	Tr	144	0.5
—	—	—	—	—	—	—
0	0	0	0	0	4	Tr
7	—	—	—	0	130	10.5
0	0.06	0.04	0.6	0	22	3.6
Tr	0.08	0.06	1.9	Tr	10	0.4
18000	0	0	0	0	Tr	Tr
0	0	0.10	22.0	0	160	4.4
10	0.04	0.06	0.7	0	51	0.8
35	0.05	0.08	1.2	5	3	0.6
40	0.20	0.08	1.7	9	4	0.9
Tr	Tr	Tr	Tr	Tr	Tr	Tr
Tr	Tr	0.23	2.5	0	14	2.9
0	1.80	1.60	21.0	0	3	0.6
36	0.06	0.04	0.5	0	1	0.4
Tr	0	0	0	0	0	Tr
Tr	0.10	0.15	2.5	Tr	29	Tr
0	0.13	0.08	1.5	0	110	1.3
0	0.04	0.21	1.5	0	40	1.5
3	0.03	0.02	0.1	12	15	1.7
7	0.01	0.01	Tr	2	6	1.1
220	0.03	0.12	0.07	1.2	79	0.2
496	0.02	0.08	0.04	0.8	50	0.2
208	0.01	0.10	0.06	Tr	80	0.3
0	0.28	0.14	1.1	0	50	3.7
Tr	0.04	0.04	0.2	8	23	0.3
5	0.03	0.08	0.5	0	95	1.8
43	0.06	0.21	0.1	Tr	140	0.1

Description of Food	Energy Calories	Protein	Fat	Carbo-hydrate
(100 g)	Kcals	g	g	g
Dandelion greens, boiled	33	2.0	0.6	6.
Dates	248	2.0	Tr	63.
Doughnuts	349	6.0	15.8	48.
Eggs, boiled	147	12.3	10.9	Tr
Egg white	36	9.0	Tr	Tr
Egg yolk	339	16.1	30.5	Tr
Egg plant, raw	14	0.7	Tr	3.
Endive, raw	11	1.8	Tr	1.
Escarol (chicory)	9	0.8	Tr	1.
Farina (enriched), cooked	42	1.3	0.1	8.
Figs, dried	213	3.6	Tr	52.
Figs, fresh	41	1.3	Tr	9.
Flour, buckwheat	333	11.7	2.5	72.
Flour, rye	327	16.3	2.6	68.
Flour, soya	421	36.7	20.3	30.
Flour, wheat (enriched)	337	11.3	1.2	74.
Flour, wheat (refined)	337	11.3	1.2	74.
Flour, wholewheat	318	13.2	2.0	65.
Fruit cake	354	5.1	12.9	57.
Frankfurters	274	9.5	25.0	3.
Gelatin	338	84.4	Tr	0
Ginger ale	31	0	0	8
Goose, roast	319	29.3	22.4	0
Gooseberries, raw	37	0.6	Tr	9.
Gooseberries, stewed with sugar	50	0.9	Tr	12.
Grapefruit, fresh	22	0.6	Tr	5.
Grapefruit juice, canned	40	0.5	0.1	9.
Grapefruit segments, canned	60	0.5	Tr	15.
Grapes	61	0.6	Tr	15.
Grape juice	66	0.2	Tr	16.
Guavas, canned	60	0.4	Tr	15.
Haddock, steamed	98	22.8	0.8	0
Haricot beans	93	6.6	0.5	16.
Ham, canned	120	18.4	5.1	0
Heart, beef	119	17.1	5.6	0
Herring, grilled	199	20.4	13.0	0
Ice-cream, dairy	167	3.7	6.6	24.
Jams	261	0.6	0	69.
Jellies, made with water	59	1.4	0	14.
Jellies, made with milk	86	2.8	1.6	16.
Kale	39	4.5	0.7	6.
Ketchup	98	2.1	Tr	24.
Kidneys, lamb's, fried	155	24.6	6.3	0
Kippers, baked	205	25.5	11.4	0
Kohl rabi, boiled	24	1.7	0.1	5.

Vitamin A	B Vitamins			Vitamin C	Minerals	
Retinol equivalents	Thiamin	Riboflavin	Niacin	Ascorbic Acid	Calcium	Iron
µg	mg	mg	mg	mg	mg	mg
1000	0.13	0.16	—	18	140	1.8
8.3	0.07	0.04	2.0	0	68	1.6
0	—	—	—	0	70	1.9
140	0.08	0.45	0.07	0	52	2.0
0	0	0.43	0.09	0	5	0.1
400	0.30	0.54	0.02	0	130	6.1
Tr	0.05	0.03	0.8	5	10	0.4
333	0.06	0.10	0.4	12	44	2.8
Tr	0.05	0.05	0.5	4	18	0.7
0	0.04	0.03	0.4	0	4	0.3
8.3	0.10	0.08	1.7	0	280	4.2
83.3	0.06	0.05	0.4	2	34	0.4
0	0.58	0.15	2.9	0	33	2.8
0	0.61	0.22	2.7	0	54	4.5
33	0.85	0.31	2.1	0	199	8.4
0	0.31	0.03	2.0	0	140	2.2
0	0.10	0.03	0.7	0	15	1.5
0	0.46	0.08	5.6	0	35	4.0
—	0.08	0.07	0.6	0	60	1.7
Tr	0.08	0.12	1.5	0	34	1.5
0	Tr	Tr	Tr	0	—	—
0	0	0	0	0	—	—
—	—	—	—	—	10	4.6
30	0.04	0.03	0.3	40	19	0.6
26	0.02	0.20	0.1	28	22	0.2
Tr	0.05	0.02	0.2	40	17	0.3
3	0.04	0.02	0.2	37	9	0.2
Tr	0.04	0.01	0.2	30	17	0.7
Tr	0.04	0.02	0.3	4	4	0.3
—	0.04	0.01	0.2	2	11	0.3
16	0.04	0.03	0.9	180	8	0.5
Tr	0.08	0.13	5.1	Tr	55	0.7
Tr	0.45	0.13	2.5	0	66	2.5
Tr	0.52	0.25	3.9	0	9	1.2
Tr	0.48	0.90	6.9	7	7	3.6
49	Tr	0.18	4.0	Tr	33	1.0
14	0.04	0.18	0.1	0	140	0.2
Tr	Tr	Tr	Tr	Tr	24	1.5
0	0	0	0	0	7	0.4
14	0.01	0.02	0.07	Tr	59	0.4
1000	0.10	0.18	2.1	186	187	1.6
Tr	—	—	—	0	25	1.2
160	0.56	2.30	9.6	9	13	12.0
49	Tr	0.18	4.0	Tr	65	1.4
7	0.06	0.03	0.2	43	33	0.3

Description of Food (100 g)	Energy Calories Kcals	Protein g	Fat g	'Suga Carb hydra g
Lamb chop, grilled	277	18.3	22.6	0
Lamb quarters (greens), boiled	32	3.2	0.7	5.(
Lard	891	Tr	99.0	0
Leeks, boiled	24	1.8	Tr	4.(
Lemon juice	7	0.3	Tr	1.(
Lentils, boiled	99	7.6	0.5	17.(
Lettuce	12	1.6	0.4	1.:
Lime juice, sweetened, concentrated	479	0.1	0	29.:
Liver, calf (fried)	254	26.9	13.2	7.:
Liver, chicken	194	20.7	10.9	3.(
Lobster, weighed with shell	42	7.9	1.2	0
Lobster, canned, meat only	119	22.1	3.4	0
Loganberries, raw	17	1.1	Tr	3.(
Macaroni, boiled	117	4.3	0.6	25.:
Malted milk (Horlicks) powder	396	13.8	7.5	72.(
Mandarins, canned	56	0.6	Tr	14.:
Margarine	730	0.1	81.0	0.:
Marmalade	261	0.1	0	69.(
Mayonnaise	718	1.8	78.9	0.:
Melon, canteloupe	24	0.6	Tr	5.:
Melon, honeydew	21	0.4	Tr	5.(
Milk, condensed, sweetened	322	8.3	9.0	55.(
Milk, dried skim, powder	355	36.4	1.3	52.(
Milk, fresh	65	3.3	3.8	4.:
Milk, goat's	71	3.3	4.5	4.(
Molasses, light	257	1.2	0	67.:
Molasses, Blackstrap	213	—	—	55.(
Muffins, bran	261	7.7	9.8	43.1
Muffins, wheatgerm	294	7.8	10.1	42.:
Mushrooms, raw	13	1.8	0.6	0
Mustard greens, boiled	23	22.2	0.4	4.(
Muesli	368	12.9	7.5	66.:
Oatmeal, raw	401	12.4	8.7	72.(
Oatcakes	441	10.0	18.3	63.(
Okra, raw	17	2.0	Tr	2.:
Olives, green	116	1.41	12.7	1.:
Olives, ripe, black	184	1.2	20.1	3.:
Olive oil	884	0	100.0	0
Onions, dry, flaked	350	8.7	1.3	82.1
Onions, fresh, boiled	13	0.6	Tr	2.:
Oranges, without skin	35	0.8	Tr	8.(
Orange juice, canned and sweetened	52	0.7	0.2	12.:
Orange juice, fresh	38	0.6	Tr	9.(
Oysters, weighed without shell	51	10.8	0.9	Tr
Parsley	21	5.2	Tr	Tr
Parsnips, boiled	56	1.3	Tr	13.(
Peached, canned	87	0.4	Tr	22.(
Peaches, dried	212	3.4	Tr	53.(

itamin A	B Vitamins			Vitamin C	Minerals	
Retinol uivalents	Thiamin	Riboflavin	Niacin	Ascorbic Acid	Calcium	Iron
µg	mg	mg	mg	mg	mg	mg
Tr	0.09	0.16	4.0	0	7	1.5
1000	0.10	0.26	0.9	37	258	0.7
Tr	Tr	Tr	Tr	0	1	0.1
6.5	0.07	0.03	0.4	15	61	2.0
Tr	0.02	0.01	0.1	50	8	0.1
3	0.11	0.04	0.4	1.2	13	2.4
166	0.07	0.08	0.3	15	23	0.9
Tr	Tr	Tr	Tr	Tr	9	0.3
4600	0.21	3.10	12.4	18	15	7.5
1100	0.37	1.70	10.5	13	15	9.1
Tr	0.03	0.02	0.5	Tr	22	0.3
Tr	0.08	0.05	1.5	Tr	62	0.9
13	0.02	0.03	0.4	35	35	1.4
0	0.01	0.01	0.3	0	8	0.5
465	0.84	1.06	11.2	0	230	1.8
8	0.07	0.02	0.2	14	18	0.4
900	Tr	Tr	Tr	0	4	0.3
8.2	Tr	Tr	Tr	10	35	0.6
80	0.06	0.11	Tr	0	16	0.7
300	0.05	0.03	0.5	25	19	0.8
16	0.05	0.02	0.5	25	14	0.7
100	0.08	0.48	2.0	2	280	0.2
38.2	0.04	0.19	0.08	15	1190	0.4
Tr	0.42	1.60	1.2	6	120	0.05
40	0.04	0.15	0.19	1.5	130	0.04
0	Tr	Tr	Tr	0	500	9.2
—	0.06	0.20	—	—	684	16.1
Tr	0.14	0.24	4.0	Tr	142	3.7
Tr	0.04	0.14	0.4	Tr	104	0.6
0	0.10	0.40	4.0	3	3	1.0
1000	0.08	0.14	0.6	48	138	1.8
0	0.33	0.27	2.7	Tr	200	4.6
0	0.50	0.10	1.0	2.8	55	4.1
0	0.32	0.09	0.7	0	54	4.5
13	0.10	0.10	1.0	25	70	1.0
1000	—	—	—	—	61	1.6
20	Tr	Tr	—	—	106	1.7
0	0	0	0	0	0	0
Tr	0.25	0.18	1.4	35	166	2.9
0	0.02	0.04	0.1	6	24	0.3
8.5	0.10	0.03	0.2	50	41	0.3
6.5	0.07	0.02	0.3	40	10	0.4
8.5	0.08	0.02	0.2	50	12	0.3
75	0.10	0.20	1.5	Tr	190	6.0
1160	0.15	0.30	1.0	150	330	8.0
Tr	0.07	0.06	0.7	10	36	0.5
30	0.01	0.02	0.6	4	4	0.4
300	Tr	0.19	5.3	Tr	36	6.8

Description of Food (100 g)	Energy Calories Kcals	Protein g	Fat g	'Suga Carb hydra g
Peaches, fresh	37	0.6	Tr	9.
Peanuts, fresh	570	24.3	49.0	8.
Peanut butter	623	22.6	53.7	13.
Pears, fresh	41	0.3	Tr	10.
Pears, canned	61	0.2	0.2	15.
Peas, canned	47	4.6	0.3	7.
Peas, fresh, boiled	52	5.0	0.4	7.
Pecans	687	9.2	71.2	14.
Peppers, green, raw	22	1.2	0.2	4.8
Persimmon, Japanese	77	0.7	0.4	19.
Pickles	134	0.6	0.3	34.
Pineapple, fresh	46	0.5	Tr	11.
Pineapple, canned	77	0.3	Tr	20.
Pineapple juice, canned	55	0.4	0.1	13.
Pizza	234	9.4	11.5	24.8
Plantain, boiled	122	1.0	0.1	31.1
Plums, fresh	38	0.6	Tr	9.
Plums, stewed with sugar	59	0.4	Tr	15.3
Pork chops	226	32.3	10.7	0
Pork sausages	318	13.3	24.6	11.5
Pork, roast	286	26.9	19.8	0
Porridge	44	1.4	0.9	8.
Potatoes, baked	105	2.6	0.1	25.
Potatoes, boiled	80	1.4	0.1	19.7
Potatoes, chips	253	3.8	10.9	37.3
Potatoes, roast	157	2.8	4.8	27.3
Potatoes, sweet, boiled, yellow	85	1.1	0.6	20.1
Prunes, stewed without sugar	82	1.3	Tr	20.4
Pumpkin, raw	15	0.6	Tr	3.4
Puffed wheat (sugar puffs)	348	5.9	0.8	84.5
Quiche lorraine	391	14.7	28.1	21.1
Rabbit, stewed	179	27.3	7.7	0
Radishes, raw	15	1.0	Tr	2.8
Raisins	246	1.1	Tr	64.4
Raspberries, canned	87	0.6	Tr	22.6
Raspberries, fresh	25	0.9	Tr	5.6
Red palm oil	900	0	100.0	0
Rhubarb, stewed with sugar	45	0.5	Tr	11.4
Rice, brown, boiled	119	2.5	0.6	25.5
Rice, white, boiled	123	2.2	0.3	29.6
Rutabagas, boiled	14	0.7	0.3	2.3
Salsify, boiled	18	1.9	Tr	2.8
Sardines, canned in oil	217	23.7	13.6	0
Sardines, fresh	160	19.2	8.6	0
Safflower-seed oil	899	Tr	99.9	0
Salmon	197	20.1	13.0	0
Sauerkraut	18	1.0	0.2	4.0
Scallops, steamed	105	23.8	1.4	Tr

Vitamin A	B Vitamins			Vitamin C	Minerals	
Retinol Equivalents	Thiamin	Riboflavin	Niacin	Ascorbic Acid	Calcium	Iron
µg	mg	mg	mg	mg	mg	mg
83	0.02	0.05	1.0	8	5	0.4
0	0.90	0.10	16.0	Tr	61	2.0
0	0.19	0.10	16.0	Tr	37	2.1
1.6	0.03	0.03	0.2	3	8	0.2
Tr	0.01	0.02	0.1	1	5	0.2
36	0.13	0.10	2.1	8	24	1.6
36	0.25	0.11	1.5	15	13	1.2
40	0.86	0.13	0.9	2	73	2.4
140	0.08	0.08	0.5	128	9	0.7
450	0.03	0.02	0.1	11	6	0.3
0	0.03	0.01	0.2	—	19	2.0
10	0.08	0.02	0.2	25	12	0.4
6.6	0.05	0.02	0.2	12	13	0.4
6.6	0.05	0.02	0.2	31	15	0.3
38	0.11	0.14	1.01	3	240	0.3
10	Tr	0.01	0.3	3	9	0.4
36	0.04	0.02	0.5	3	11	0.2
28	0.04	0.02	0.4	2	11	0.2
Tr	0.88	0.26	7.6	0	9	1.2
Tr	0.02	0.15	4.0	0	53	1.5
Tr	0.65	0.27	5.0	0	10	1.2
0	0.05	0.01	0.1	0	6	0.5
Tr	0.10	0.04	1.2	10	9	0.8
Tr	0.08	0.03	0.8	9	4	0.3
Tr	0.10	0.04	1.2	10	14	0.9
Tr	0.10	0.04	1.2	10	10	0.7
600	0.08	0.04	0.6	15	21	0.6
83	0.04	0.09	0.8	Tr	19	1.4
240	0.04	0.04	0.4	5	39	0.4
0	Tr	0.03	2.5	0	14	2.1
168	0.14	0.24	1.05	Tr	260	1.3
—	0.07	0.28	8.5	0	11	1.9
Tr	0.04	0.02	0.2	25	44	1.9
5	0.10	0.08	0.5	0	61	1.6
12	0.01	0.03	0.03	7	14	1.7
13	0.02	0.03	0.4	25	41	1.2
3000	0	0	0	0	0	0
8.5	Tr	0.03	0.3	7	84	0.3
0	0.09	0.02	1.4	0	12	0.5
0	0.10	0.01	0.3	0	1	0.2
0	0.03	0.04	0.4	17	55	0.4
0	0.03	—	—	4	48	0.6
Tr	0.04	0.36	8.2	Tr	550	2.9
—	—	—	—	—	33	1.8
Tr	Tr	Tr	Tr	Tr	Tr	—
50	0.04	0.11	7.0	Tr	29	0.8
16	0.03	0.04	0.2	14	36	0.5
Tr	—	—	—	Tr	120	3.0

Description of Food (100 g)	Energy Calories Kcals	Protein g	Fat g	'Suga Carbo hydra g
Shredded Wheat	324	10.6	3.0	67.
Shrimps, boiled	117	23.8	2.4	0
Soya beans, cooked	130	11.0	5.7	10.
Spaghetti, white, cooked	117	4.2	0.3	26.
Spaghetti, brown, cooked	148	5.0	0.5	30.
Spinach, cooked	30	5.1	0.5	1.
Squash, Hubbard, baked	50	1.8	0.4	11.
Squash, summer, boiled	14	0.9	0.1	3.
Steak, beef, fried	190	30.8	7.4	0
Strawberries, canned	81	0.4	Tr	21.
Strawberries, fresh	26	0.6	Tr	6.
Sugar, brown	394	0.5	0	104.
Sugar, white	394	Tr	0	105.
Sultanas	250	1.8	Tr	64.
Sunflower seeds	560	24.0	47.3	19.
Sunflower-seed oil	899	Tr	99.9	0
Sweets (see under 'Candy')				
Sweetbreads, fried	230	19.4	14.6	5.
Syrup, golden	298	0.3	0	79.
Syrup, maple	252	—	—	65
Tangerines, fresh	34	0.9	Tr	8.
Tapioca pudding	131	4.1	4.2	20.
Tea, infusion	Tr	0.1	Tr	Tr
Tomato ketchup	98	2.1	Tr	24.
Tomatoes, canned	12	1.1	Tr	2.
Tomatoes, fresh	14	0.9	Tr	2.8
Tomato juice	16	0.7	Tr	3.4
Tongue, lamb's	193	15.3	14.6	0
Turnips, cooked	14	0.7	0.3	2.3
Turnips, raw	20	0.8	0.3	3.8
Turnip tops, cooked	11	2.7	Tr	0.1
Tuna fish, canned in oil	289	22.8	22.0	0
Turkey, roast	140	28.8	2.7	0
Veal chops, fried	215	31.4	8.1	4.4
Walnuts, black	628	20.5	59.3	14.8
Walnuts, English	525	10.6	51.5	5.0
Watercress	14	2.9	Tr	0.7
Wheatgerm (Bemax)	347	26.5	8.1	44.7
Yams	119	1.6	0.1	29.8
Yeast, baker's fresh	86	12.0	0.4	11.0
Yeast, brewer's	283	38.8	1.0	38.4
Yoghurt, natural, unsweetened	52	5.0	1.0	6.2
Yoghurt, fruit and sweetened	95	4.8	1.0	17.9

itamin A	B Vitamins			Vitamin C	Minerals	
Retinol uivalents	Thiamin	Riboflavin	Niacin	Ascorbic Acid	Calcium	Iron
µg	mg	mg	mg	mg	mg	mg
0	0.27	0.05	4.5	0	38	4.2
Tr	0.03	0.03	3.0	Tr	320	1.8
10	0.21	0.09	0.6	0	73	2.7
0	0.01	0.01	0.3	0	7	0.4
0	0.02	0.02	0.4	0	11	0.5
1000	0.07	0.15	0.4	25	600	0.5
200	0.05	0.13	0.7	10	24	0.8
160	0.05	0.08	0.8	10	25	0.4
Tr	0.09	0.40	6.3	0	6	3.4
Tr	0.01	0.02	0.3	21	14	0.9
5	0.02	0.03	0.4	60	22	0.7
0	Tr	Tr	Tr	0	53	0.9
0	0	0	0	0	2	0
5	0.10	0.08	0.5	0	52	1.8
15	1.98	0.23	5.4	—	120	7.1
Tr	Tr	Tr	Tr	0	Tr	Tr
Tr	0.03	0.24	2.1	18	34	1.8
0	Tr	Tr	Tr	0	26	1.5
—	—	—	—	0	104	1.2
16.6	0.07	0.02	0.2	30	42	0.3
33	0.04	0.14	0.1	Tr	130	0.1
0	Tr	0.01	0.1	0	Tr	Tr
0	—	—	—	—	25	1.2
83	0.06	0.03	0.7	18	9	0.9
100	0.06	0.04	0.7	20	13	0.4
83	0.06	0.03	0.7	20	10	0.5
Tr	0.17	0.49	4.9	7	6	2.2
0	0.03	0.04	0.4	17	59	0.4
0	0.04	0.05	0.6	25	59	0.4
1000	0.06	0.20	0.50	40	98	3.1
Tr	0.04	0.11	12.9	Tr	7	1.1
Tr	0.07	0.21	8.5	0	9	0.9
Tr	—	—	—	0	10	1.6
25	0.22	0.11	0.7	—	Tr	6.0
2	0.30	0.13	1.0	Tr	61	2.4
500	0.10	0.10	0.6	60	220	1.6
0	1.45	0.61	5.8	0	17	10.0
2	0.05	0.01	0.5	2.0	9	0.3
Tr	0.71	1.65	11.2	Tr	13	4.9
Tr	15.61	4.28	37.9	Tr	2.0	17.3
9	0.05	0.26	0.12	0.4	180	0.1
9	0.05	0.23	0.11	1.8	160	0.2

Recommended daily amounts of food energy and some nutrients for population groups in the United Kingdom

Age range[a] years	Occupational category	Energy[b] MJ	Energy[b] Kcal	Protein[c] g	Thiamin mg	Ribofl. mg
Boys						
under 1		—	—	—	0.3	0.4
1		5.0	1200	30	0.5	0.6
2		5.75	1400	35	0.6	0.7
3–4		6.5	1560	39	0.6	0.8
5–6		7.25	1740	43	0.7	0.9
7–8		8.25	1980	49	0.8	1.0
9–11		9.5	2280	57	0.9	1.2
12–14		11.0	2640	66	1.1	1.4
15–17		12.0	2880	72	1.2	1.7
Girls						
under 1		—	—	—	0.3	0.4
1		4.5	1100	27	0.4	0.6
2		5.5	1300	32	0.5	0.7
3–4		6.25	1500	37	0.6	0.8
5–6		7.0	1680	42	0.7	0.9
7–8		8.0	1900	47	0.8	1.0
9–11		8.5	2050	51	0.8	1.2
12–14		9.0	2150	53	0.9	1.4
15–17		9.0	2150	53	0.9	1.7
Men						
18–34	Sedentary	10.5	2510	63	1.0	1.6
	Moderately active	12.0	2900	72	1.2	1.6
	Very active	14.0	3350	84	1.3	1.6
35–64	Sedentary	10.0	2400	60	1.0	1.6
	Moderately active	11.5	2750	69	1.1	1.6
	Very active	14.0	3350	84	1.3	1.6
65–74 ⎫	Assuming a	10.0	2400	60	1.0	1.6
75+ ⎭	sedentary life	9.0	2150	54	0.9	1.6
Women						
18–54	Most occupations	9.0	2150	54	0.9	1.3
	Very active	10.5	2500	62	1.0	1.3
55–74 ⎫	Assuming a	8.0	1900	47	0.8	1.3
75+ ⎭	sedentary life	7.0	1680	42	0.7	1.3
Pregnancy		10.0	2400	60	1.0	1.6
Lactation		11.5	2750	69	1.1	1.8

Notes:
a   Since the recommendations are average amounts, the figures for each age range represent the amounts recomme
   at the middle of the range. Within each age range, younger children will need less, and older children more, tha
   amount recommended.
b   Megajoules (10^6 joules). Calculated from the relation 1 kilocalorie = 4.184 kilojoules, that is to say, 1 megajou
   240 kilocalories.
c   Recommended amounts have been calculated as 10 percent of the recommendations for energy.
d   1 nicotinic acid equivalent = 1 mg available nicotinic acid or 60 mg tryptophan.
e   No information is available about requirements of children for folate. Graded amounts are recommended betwee
   figure shown for infants under 1 year, which is based upon the average folate content of mature human milk, an
   300 µg daily which is suggested for adults.

otinic acid uivalents mg[d]	Total folate[c] μg	Ascorbic acid mg	Vitamin A retinol equivalents μg[f]	Vitamin D[g] cholecalciferol μg	Calcium mg	Iron mg
5	50	20	450	7.5	600	6
7	100	20	300	10	600	7
8	100	20	300	10	600	7
9	100	20	300	10	600	8
10	200	20	300	[g]	600	10
11	200	20	400	[g]	600	10
14	200	25	575	[g]	700	12
16	300	25	725	[g]	700	12
19	300	30	750	[g]	600	12
5	50	20	450	7.5	600	6
7	100	20	300	10	600	7
8	100	20	300	10	600	7
9	100	20	300	10	600	8
10	200	20	300	[g]	600	10
11	200	20	400	[g]	600	10
14	300	25	575	[g]	700	12[i]
16	300	25	725	[g]	700	12[i]
19	300	30	750	[g]	600	12[i]
18	300	30	750	[g]	500	10
18	300	30	750	[g]	500	10
18	300	30	750	[g]	500	10
18	300	30	750	[g]	500	10
18	300	30	750	[g]	500	10
18	300	30	750	[g]	500	10
18	300	30	750	[g]	500	10
18	300	30	750	[g]	500	10
15	300	30	750	[g]	500	12[i]
15	300	30	750	—	500	12[i]
15	300	30	750	[g]	500	10
15	300	30	750	[g]	500	10
18	500	60	750	10	1200[h]	13
21	400	60	1200	10	1200	15

1 retinol equivalent = 1 μg retinol or 6 μg β-carotene or 12 μg other biologically active carotenoids.
No dietary sources may be necessary for children and adults who are sufficiently exposed to sunlight, but during the winter children and adolescents should receive 10 μg (400 iu) daily by supplementation. Adults with inadequate exposure to sunlight, for example those who are housebound, may also need a supplement of 10 μg daily.
For the third trimester only.
This intake may not be sufficient for 10 percent of girls and women with large menstrual losses.

rce: DHSS, *Report on Health and Social Subjects 15.*

351

APPENDIX IV – USA

Food and Nutrition Board, National Academy of Science National Research Council Recommended Daily Dietary Allowances,[a] Revised 1979

Designed for the maintenance of good nutrition of practically all healthy people in the USA

	Age	Weight		Height		Protein	Vita-min A	Vita-min D	Vita-min E mg α	Vita-min C	Th m
	years	kg	lbs	cm	in	g	µg RE[b]	µg[c]	TE[d]	mg	m
Infants	0.0–0.5	6	13	60	24	kg×2.2	420	10	3	35	0
	0.5–1.0	9	20	71	28	kg×2.0	400	10	4	35	0.
Children	1–3	13	29	90	35	23	400	10	5	45	0
	4–6	20	44	112	44	30	500	10	6	45	0
	7–10	28	62	132	52	34	700	10	7	45	1.
Males	11–14	45	99	157	62	45	1000	10	8	50	1.
	15–18	66	145	176	69	56	1000	10	10	60	1.
	19–22	70	154	177	70	56	1000	7.5	10	60	1.
	23–50	70	154	178	70	56	1000	5	10	60	1.
	51+	70	154	178	70	56	1000	5	10	60	1.
Females	11–14	46	101	157	62	46	800	10	8	50	1.
	15–18	55	120	163	64	46	800	10	8	60	1.
	19–22	55	120	163	64	44	800	7.5	8	60	1.
	23–50	55	120	163	64	44	800	5	8	60	1.
	51+	55	120	163	64	44	800	5	8	60	1.
Pregnant						+30	+200	+5	+2	+20	+0.
Lactating						+20	+400	+4	+3	+40	+0.

Notes:

a The allowances are intended to provide for individual variations among most normal persons as they live in the U States under usual environmental stresses. Diets should be based on a variety of common foods in order to pr other nutrients for which human requirements have been less well defined.

b Retinol equivalents. 1 Retinol equivalent = 1 µg retinol or 6 µg βcarotene.

c As cholecalciferol. 10 µg cholecalciferol = 400 IU vitamin D.

d α tocopherol equivalents. 1 mg d-α-tocopherol = 1 α TE.

e 1 NE (niacin equivalent) is equal to 1 mg of niacin or 60 mg of dietary tryptophan.

f The folacin allowances refer to dietary sources as determined by Lactobacillus casei assay after treatment with enz ("conjugases") to make polyglutamyl forms of the vitamin available to the test organism.

g The RDA for vitamin B12 in infants is based on average concentration of the vitamin in human milk. The allow after weaning are based on energy intake (as recommended by the American Academy of Pediatrics) and consider of other factors such as intestinal absorption.

h The increased requirement during pregnancy cannot be met by the iron content of habitual American diets nor t existing iron stores of many women; therefore the use of 30–60 mg of supplemental iron is recommended. Iron during lactation are not substantially different from those of non-pregnant women, but continued supplementati the mother for 2–3 months after parturition is advisable in order to replenish stores depleted by pregnancy.

Reproduced from: *Recommended Dietary Allowances*, Ninth Edition (1979, in press), with the permission of the Na Academy of Sciences, Washington, DC.

ribo-avin	Niacin	Vita-min B6	Folacin[f]	Vita-min B12	Cal-cium	Phos-phorus	Mag-nesium	Iron	Zinc	Iodine
mg	mg NE[e]	mg	µg	µg	mg	mg	mg	mg	mg	µg
0.4	6	0.3	30	0.5[g]	360	240	50	10	3	40
0.6	8	0.6	45	1.5	540	360	70	15	5	50
0.8	9	0.9	100	2.0	800	800	150	15	10	70
1.0	11	1.3	200	2.5	800	800	200	10	10	90
1.4	16	1.6	300	3.0	800	800	250	10	10	120
1.6	18	1.8	400	3.0	1200	1200	350	18	15	150
1.7	18	2.0	400	3.0	1200	1200	400	18	15	150
1.7	19	2.2	400	3.0	800	800	350	10	15	150
1.6	18	2.2	400	3.0	800	800	350	10	15	150
1.4	16	2.2	400	3.0	800	800	350	10	15	150
1.3	15	1.8	400	3.0	1200	1200	300	18	15	150
1.3	14	2.0	400	3.0	1200	1200	300	18	15	150
1.3	14	2.0	400	3.0	800	800	300	18	15	150
1.2	13	2.0	400	3.0	800	800	300	18	15	150
1.2	13	2.0	400	3.0	800	800	300	10	15	150
0.3	+2	+0.6	+400	+1.0	+400	+400	+150	[h]	+5	+25
0.5	+5	+0.5	+100	+1.0	+400	+400	+150	[h]	+10	+50

353

Bibliography

Good general reading on physiology and nutrition

Attenborough, D., *Life on Earth* (Collins, 1979)

Ballentine, R., *Diet and Nutrition* (Himalayan International Institute, 1978)

Bender, A. E., *Nutrition and Dietetics* (Leonard Hill, London, 1974)

Eyton, E., and Miller, D., *Dieting Revolution* (*Slimming Magazine* Publication, 1979)

Fisher, P., and Bender, A. E., *The Value of Food* (OUP, 2nd edn, 1975)

Green, J. H., *An Introduction to Human Physiology* (OUP, 4th edn, 1976)

Lewis, P., and Rubenstein, D., *The Human Body* (Hamlyn, 1970)

Miller, J., *The Body in Question* (Cape, 1978)

National Childbirth Trust, *Growing up with Good Food* (Unwin Paperbacks, 1982)

Pyke, M., *Nutrition* (Teach Yourself Books, 1961)

Ratcliff, J. D., *The Body and How it Works* (Reader's Digest, 1976)

Rattray Taylor, G., *The Science of Life* (Panther, 1976)

Stanway, A., *Taking the Rough with the Smooth* (Pan, 1976)

Wessells, N. K., *Readings from Scientific American: Vertebrate Structures and Functions* (W. H. Freeman, 1974)

More detailed reading

Bell, G. H., Emslie-Smith, D., and Patterson, C. R., *Textbook of Physiology and Biochemistry* (Churchill, Livingstone, 1976)

Bender, A. E., *Food Processing and Nutrition* (Academic Press, 1978)

Bourne, G. H., *Functional Histology* (Churchill, 2nd edn, 1960)

Clydesdale, F., *Food Science and Nutrition* (Prentice Hall, 1979)

Davenport, H. W., *A Digest of Digestion* (Year Book Medical Publishers, 2nd edn, 1978)

Davidson, S., Passmore, R., Brock, J. F., and Truswell, A. S., *Human Nutrition and Dietetics* (Churchill, Livingstone, 6th edn, 1975)

Dickerson, W. T., and Lee, H. A., *Nutrition in the Clinical Management of Disease* (Edward Arnold, 1978)

Falkner, F., and Tanner, J. M., *Human Growth*, vol. 2, *Postnatal Growth* (Plenum Press, 1978)

Ganong, W. F. *Review of Medical Physiology* (Lang Medical Publications, Los Altos, Cal., 1975)

Goldspink, G., *Differentiation and Growth of Cells in Vertebrate Tissues* (Chapman & Hall, 1974)

Goss, J. R., *The Physiology of Growth* (Academic Press, 1978)

Grove, A. J., and Newell, G. E., *Animal Biology* (University Tutorial Press, 1962)

Harrison, G. A., Weiner, J. S., Tanner, J. M. and Barnicot, N. A., *Human Biology* (OUP, 2nd edn, 1977)

Ministry of Agriculture, Fisheries and Food, *Food Quality and Safety: A Century of Progress* (HMSO, 1978)

Myers, H. M., *Fluorides and Dental Fluorosis. Monographs in Oral Science* (S. Karger, 1978)

Newth, D. R., *Animal Growth and Development. Studies in Biology No. 24* (Edward Arnold, 1970)

Orten, J. M., and Neuhaus, O. W., *Human Biochemistry* (The C. V. Mosby Co., St Louis, 9th edn, 1975)

Petrides, P. (translated by D. H. Williamson), *Diabetes Mellitus: Theory and Management* (Urban & Schwarzenberg, 1978)

Selkurt, E. E., *Physiology* (Little, Brown and Co., Boston, 4th edn, 1976)

Sinclair, D., *Human Growth after Birth* (OUP, 3rd edn, 1978)

Taylor, T. G., *The Importance of Vitamins to Human Health* (MTP Press, 1979)

Useful Reference Books

Davidson, S., and Macleod, J., *The Principles and Practice of Medicine* (Churchill, Livingstone, 10th edn, 1973)

Department of Health and Social Security, *Recommended Intakes of Nutrients for the United Kingdom* (HMSO, 1979)

Paul, A. A., and Southgate, D. A. T., *The Composition of Foods* (HMSO, 4th edn, 1978)

Watt, B. K., and Merrill, A. L., *Handbook of the Nutritional Contents of Foods* (New York, Dover Publications, 1963)

Wingate, P., *The Penguin Medical Encyclopaedia* (Penguin, 1972)

Reference Books for Anatomy

Bevan, J., *A Pictorial Handbook of Anatomy and Physiology* (Mitchell Beasley, 1978)

Burdon, I. M., and MacDonald, S., *Faber's Anatomical Atlas* (Faber & Faber, 4th edn, 1970)

Freeman, W. H., and Bracegirdle, B., *An Atlas of Histology* (Heinemann Educational Books, 2nd edn, 1968)

Gray, H., *Gray's Anatomy* (Longman, 35th edn, 1975)

Pansky, B., and House, E. L., *Review of Gross Anatomy* (Macmillan, 2nd edn, 1971)

Reith, E. J., Briedenbach, B., and Lorenc, M., *Text Book of Anatomy and Physiology* (McGraw Hill, 2nd edn, 1978)

Index

Abdomen, 20; in relation to the Heimlich maneuver, 31

Abdominal cavity, 33

Absorption, of calcium, 214, 215, 216, 217, 219, 220, 234, of food, 44, 45, 46, 89, 91, 170, 209, 214, 289, 290; of glucose, 279, 280, 282, of simple sugars, 48, of Vitamin A, 122–23, of Vitamin D, 178, 214, of Vitamin K, 182, of zinc, 235; is dependent on enzymes, 71; faulty, 147; from kidneys, 196; rate of iron, 210

Acetoacetic acid, 92

Acetone, 92

Acetyl coenzyme A, 91

Achlorhydria, 40, 228

Acid, balance in body, 22, 230; in enzymes, 29, in foods, 52, 229, in mouth, 275, in stomach secretions, 18, 25; niacin occurs as, 135; vitamins in, 295; see also Citric; Folic; Lactic; Linoleic; Malic; Pantothenic; Pyruvate; Pyruvic

Acidosis, 92; to prevent, 280

Acne, fat as a cause of, 5; improvement of, 275, 277; teenager and, 275

Active transport, 19

ADH, 196, 269

Adipose tissue, glucose stored in, 54, 61, 69, 102; of animals, 171; Vitamin D stored in, 178

Adolescents, eating habits of, 257–58

ADP, 81

Adrenal glands, aldosterone secreted from, 288; ascorbic acid from, 155; malfunctioning of, 286

Adrenaline, 100, 101

Adults, eating habits of, 258–59

Affector nerves, 21

Africa, diseases in, 115, 135

Age, and protein requirements, 78

Age, old, 249, 277, 313; effect of Vitamin E on, 181; good health in, 259; loss of calcium in, 216; salt and, 231; Vitamin C requirements, 162, 163

Air, 187, 192, 202, 262, 275; and lungs, 189, 190, 194

Air passages, 116, 192

Albumin, 68; maintaining osmotic pressure, 98

Alcohol, 98, 154, 269; detoxified by enzymes, 96, 235; and pregnancy, 262

Alcoholics, "fatty liver" disease and, 98; low level of

ing of liver, 42; essential part of diet, 5, 6, 57, 66, 246, 271; excess, 88, 224, 251, 267, 287, 313; exercise and, 102; functions of, 62; glucose is changed into, 54; glycerol is, 52, 54, 61; heat is produced by, 47, 82, 90; low-fat diet, 288–89; oxidation of, 59, 61, 90–91, 125, 142, 200; phosphorus and, 219; rancid, 59, 61, 125; relation of to other body requirements, 64; in relation to Vitamin A, 119, 123; replenishes food supply, 91; saturated, 58–59; sources of, 57–58, 144, 246, 286, 298; storage of, 61, 62, 69, 89, 102, 120; unsaturated, 58–59; weight of body, 88, 250; women have larger proportion of, 85–86

Fat droplets, 28

Fatigue, 114, 213, 277, 280; anemia and, 206–07, 210; causes of, 271–72; due to, insufficient Vitamin A, 119; loss of salt, 229; Vitamin D deficiency, 174; lactic acid causes, 129; in relation to frequency of meals, 93–94; thiamine deficiency as a cause for, 130, 131

Fat-soluble vitamins, fats needed for absorption of, 122; stored in body, 120, 175, 178, 181, 241; Vitamin, A, 62, 128, 178, 241; D, 62, 128, 169, 175, 178, 241; E, 62, 180, 181, 241; K, 62, 182, 241

Fatty acids, 62, 63, 90–91, 96, 187; end products in digestion, 28; fats are made of, 58–59, 61, 90

Fatty liver, 98

Feces, 12; arsenic excreted in, 238; calcium excreted in, 170, 214, 215–16; constipation and, 45; fat in, 63; iron in, 210; nitrogen in, 69, 78; vitamins lost in, 123

Ferric, 209, 257

Ferritin, 208

Fever, 77, 147

Fiber, 145, 146, 282

Fibrin, 182, 213

Fibrinogen, 98, 182

Figs, 342–43; carbohydrates in, 53; cobalt in, 236

Fish, 121, 190, 231, 240, 258, 260, 263, 277, 281, 284, 305, 306, 313, 342–43; B_{12} and folate in, 141; bone as a source of calcium, 217, 218; fats in, 298; fluorine in, 237; niacin in, 137; percent of water found in, 199; phosphorus in, 220; protein in, 36, 66, 74, 76, 79, 264; salt in, 287, 293; Vitamin D in, 177, 179

Fish-liver oil, 120, 171, 177, 179; Vitamin, A in, 107, 276; D, 256

Fish oil, loses potency in sun, 126; Vitamin, A in, 125; D, 64, 170

Flavonoids, 159

Flavoproteins, 133

Flour, 133, 144–45, 148, 215, 267, 298, 300, 313; gluten-free, 290; percent of water found in, 199; soy, 282; whole-wheat, 147, 267, 281, 300, 307, protein in, 79, 267

Fluoride, 237

Fluorine, 237, 238

Folic acid, 140, 142, 143; sources of, 141; used to prevent pernicious anemia, 141

Food, 3–4, 42, 88, 125, 189, 205, 263, 281, 308; absorption of,